César Mala

Life, Labours, and Writings ᴗ __. ᴍalan

minister of the gospel in the Church of Geneva, Doctor of Divinity, and Pastor of

l'Église du Témoignage

César Malan

Life, Labours, and Writings of Caesar Malan
minister of the gospel in the Church of Geneva, Doctor of Divinity, and Pastor of l'Église du Témoignage

ISBN/EAN: 9783337888497

Printed in Europe, USA, Canada, Australia, Japan

Cover: Foto ©Lupo / pixelio.de

More available books at **www.hansebooks.com**

THE

LIFE, LABOURS, AND WRITINGS

OF

CÆSAR MALAN,

MINISTER OF THE GOSPEL IN THE CHURCH OF GENEVA, DOCTOR OF
DIVINITY, AND PASTOR OF "L'ÉGLISE DU TÉMOIGNAGE."

BY

ONE OF HIS SONS.

(Fac-simile of the habitual Seal of Malan, drawn and engraved by himself
in the beginning of the Revival.)

LONDON:

JAMES NISBET & CO., 21 BERNERS STREET.

1869.

CONTENTS.

BOOK III.

MALAN'S PRIVATE AND DOMESTIC LIFE—HIS CLOSING RELATIONS TO THE CHURCH—THE EVENING OF HIS LIFE, AND HIS DEATH.

INTRODUCTION.

IMMEDIATELY after my father's death, I received numerous requests to undertake the task of writing his biography. It appeared to me at the time that such a task might easily have been entrusted to abler hands, and a stricter impartiality at the same time have been secured.

Though four years have elapsed since that event, still, with the exception of a few articles in French and English newspapers, and a short notice by the Rev. John Augustine Bost,* no record has been furnished of my father's career. Under these circumstances, I have yielded to the appeals of those friends who seemed to think that, in some respects, I possessed special qualifications for recording his history.

This they argued from their knowledge of the fact that I was most intimately associated with my father from the very nature of my own studies, and enjoyed the privilege

---

* Published in 1865. I eagerly seize this occasion of thanking my old friend, in my name, and in the name of all my family, not only for the pages referred to above, so full of friendly feeling, but also for all his kindness to my father in the last years of his life. Amongst the obituary articles in periodicals, the pages in the *Record* (8th June 1864), written by a friend of my father of long standing, are especially worthy of note.

A

of living near him, especially towards the close of his life, to a greater extent than any of my brothers.

On the other hand, thankfully admitting that I owe what religious light I may be at present enjoying to his teaching instrumentally, and more especially to his example, I must at the same time add that I was never a member of the community which acknowledged him as pastor, and that, from a very early period, I gave to the faith we shared in common, a dogmatic expression different from his.

This, however, proved no hindrance to the intimacy which I enjoyed with him, or to the confidence with which he favoured me, while in his living piety and fervent faith I ever sought and found the fire which warmed my soul.

Though the struggle which reflected such imperishable renown on his earlier days happened at a period beyond my recollection, I can distinctly recall the events which immediately followed. But my closest remembrances gather round his declining years, the long-protracted evening of his honourable life. Reduced by his isolation to a chilling obscurity, he persevered as undauntedly as ever in the activity which had always characterised him, and secured by his testimony, faithful to the last, and by the unvarying harmony between his principles and his life, a position of peculiar prominence in the religious world, in the midst of which he was placed.

It will be difficult—I feel it strongly—to reach and retain that elevation of spirit from which alone a faith like his—so simple, natural, candid, and fervent—can be fairly appreciated. Still, I will endeavour to distinguish, with such clearness as I may be able to employ, between that faith or living principle communicated to his will by divine agency and the semi-human or Christian expression which he gave to it in dogma. To me the living faith of his heart appeared not only as a special grace beautifying his life, but as a heaven-lit beacon at the entrance of mine, destined, I am well assured, to guide me to the end of my days. Its dogmatical expression, in common with any other of his peculiar characteristics, I shall regard in the following pages, as submitted to that particular kind of appreciation which may be looked for in a son; nor shall I, I trust, transgress in any subsequent criticism the limits which filial reverence would naturally impose.

A still greater difficulty, however, remains to be noticed. For one, educated as I was, under his immediate influence, and trained in the midst of the circumstances which isolated his family and himself, it will, I feel, be no easy task to maintain a strictly unbiassed judgment in reviewing his career.

Not that I have any expectation of satisfying all the different sections of our religious world; my only aim in this respect will be to avoid as far as possible all injury to just susceptibilities. To this end I shall endeavour, in imitation of him whose life I am recording, to maintain a spirit of brotherly love towards men I cannot wish to please, and to cherish a sincere respect for those whose opinions I cannot adopt. If I fail at times to suppress the personal element, if individual feelings prove too strong, my readers will have to judge from the facts submitted to them whether they justify the language employed.

Though born in the midst of the First Revival, I never witnessed under my father's roof the prejudice and narrowness of view with which the friends of that religious movement are so frequently credited. After an early visit to foreign countries, I commenced my studies in Germany, continued them at Lausanne under Vinet, and concluded them in the Theological School of the Evangelical Society of Geneva, at the time when E. Scheren was on the list of its professors. At a later period, I received many valued marks of esteem from our National Church. Dissociated at present from any particular communion, my aim is to occupy a position amongst those believers who desire not so much to serve any particular section of the Church as to serve God Himself in any organised form with which His Providence may for a time connect them.

Independent as is this position, which I felt it my duty to describe, I cannot but realise the difficulty of avoiding, on the one hand, indications of the partiality which no son could help experiencing for such a father, and, on the other, the undue influence of those emotions which will assert themselves whenever I recall his struggles and sufferings.

Had Geneva continued to be what it was when these sufferings were undergone, my feelings in reference to them would have sufficed to deter me from my present undertaking. But the religious animus of 1817 is now extinct, and while the incidents of that period deserve to be recorded, the fact that the dominion of the clergy, in some of its severer manifestations, has succumbed to the logic of progress will never fail to be regarded with satisfaction.

To sceptics on all "religious questions," it will suffice to say that, without dwelling on the interest which will ever attach to Malan's life in the eyes of those who shared the sentiments he so boldly asserted, his history will not be without its worth, even in the judgment of the indifferent, as being the career of a man persecuted and set aside for daring to remind the Church and nation of those traditions which alone have been the source of their past glory.

As a man of faith he realised in his own experience the promise uttered once on our earth by Him for Whose cause he suffered. A true representative of a sincere profession, and of the rights of individual convictions, he lived long enough to see the ecclesiastical body which had discarded him stripped of the privileges they had abused,—long enough also, to hail, along with all the friends of Christian liberty and an unshackled gospel, a return of new life to the ancient Church of his fathers, always dear to him,— long enough, to bear public testimony before strangers that all this had come to pass.

In undertaking to write his life, I believe that I am not only following my strongest inclination as a son, and a fellow-believer, but that I am even rendering a service to my country. Were I to seek to revive buried animosities, I know well that among the multitudes who would condemn me, he himself would be foremost. The death of strife is sufficiently lingering without unprincipled efforts to protract its agony. At the same time, in any historical retrospect, sufficient must be recalled to indicate the teaching of Him Whose sole glory all events, past, present, or future, must combine to promote.

But, indeed, it may be asked, what could there be in the history of the period to which we shall have to refer, which could at all rekindle strife in modern times? The days in which we live are characterised by a thoughtful—sometimes even by a painful and anxious expectation: hence they call for peace and reunion. The dangers that surround us are no longer those arising from the disturbance of religious parties; they spring rather from the silence of faith and the suppression of conviction. If only for this reason, it would be our duty to trace out the history of one who largely contributed to the inaugurating of the liberties in which we glory; for none of us can turn them to a good account who has not studied their origin.

The subject of this memoir was one of those whose motives will never be universally understood. Such persons as would content themselves with discovering, in the religious life of heroes like Augustin, Whitfield, or Havelock, a mere innate energy combined with an honesty of purpose and consistency deserving all esteem, will find nothing to attract them in these pages. They might notice for a moment the active faith of the central figure, but their attention would soon be wearied, probably their sympathies and prejudices outraged.

If I write not exclusively for men "full of the Holy Ghost and of faith," I would at least have those only for my readers, who, recognising that faith as the highest gift of heaven, desire ardently to partake of it.

The sources from which I have derived my information are documents, either in type or manuscript, of the existence of many of which I had been profoundly ignorant. In our private intercourse, my father never touched on any fact which tended to throw discredit on any single individual. So scrupulous was he in this respect that it was only on the occasion of my preparing a translation of Baron de Goltz's work in 1862, that he consented to put into my hands certain printed matter necessary for verifying the quotations of the German work.*

To my reiterated request that he would undertake his own biography, he invariably replied, that as it had pleased God to make him a man of strife (Jer. xv. 10,) he had been too much involved in personal debates to feel qualified for such a task. The few MS. notes of his, which I found after his death, contained only such proper names as had been already and frequently brought before the public.

For the first period of his life, more especially for his struggle with the Venerable Assembly of Geneva, I found, after an attentive perusal of the original documents themselves, no safer authority than the book which I have just mentioned. Some few works, not quoted in its pages, I shall refer to in the course of the narrative. To this may be added the following list of materials :—

1. Numerous letters, from 1816–63 : copies of his correspondence with different persons.

2. Notes and memoranda in his own handwriting, of various events in his life.

3. Numerous manuscripts ; *e.g.,* sermons, catechisms, from the first year of his ministry ; tracts ; essays on special points of divinity ; with more than a thousand unpublished hymns.

Of course I could not undertake to make a thorough examination of all these papers ; while the letters of a man

---

* " Genève religieuse, au xixme Siecle ; ou tableau des faits qui, depuis 1815, ont accompagné dans cette ville, le développement de l'individualisme ecclesiastique du Reveil, mis en regard de l'ancien système theocratique de l'eglise de Calvin, par le Baron H. de Goltz, chapelain de l'ambassade de Prusse à Rome, traduit de l'Allemand, sous les yeux de l'auteur. Par C. Malan, fils. Genève et Bâle. Georg. 1862 ; i. vol de 600 pages."

in the position he occupied could only be used with the strictest discretion. At the same time I may confidently state that the study of this accumulated evidence of activity produced a most vivid impression on my mind, and I notice it here to draw general attention to the fact that his meditation on, search into, and study and proclamation of the word, with the endless labours of his pen, closed only with his earnest and devoted life.

It is my pleasing duty to express my acknowledgments to the Venerable Assembly of the Church of Geneva for the readiness with which they forwarded my investigations by giving me access to the minutes of their Sessions; I may add too that, having submitted the following to my venerable mother, she confirmed the accuracy of the statements of facts they present.

It is further my duty to acknowledge the readiness with which the company of the pastors of Geneva granted me, in the prosecution of my researches, free access to the diary of their sittings, and the courtesy with which their secretary, the Rev. Siordet, put himself at my disposal for that purpose.

To such of my father's friends as may peruse the following chapters, I would address one special request : that should they note any inaccuracy, or recall, as they read, any facts of interest or importance which have escaped my notice, they would kindly communicate with me on the subject.

C. MALAN.

GENEVA, 1868.

CÆSAR MALAN, D.D.:

HIS LIFE AND WRITINGS.

BOOK I.

1787–1830.

CHAPTER I.

CHILDHOOD AND EARLY YEARS.

Deep, strong, and still,—an earnest stream
Flows darkly through a tangled glen,
By rocks and caves that give again
The awe of its mysterious dream.

THE religious awakening in the Reformed Churches of
France, of which the generation now passing away has
been the witness, whether regarded as one of the many
phases of the great social revolution which has characterised our age, or whether hailed as the dawn of a new era
in the free manifestation of individual faith, must still
remain, on either assumption, an accredited historical fact,
whose significance and value none may question. Nor
must it be forgotten, at the same time, that Geneva was
the cradle of its birth, and that the subject of these memoirs
has already, and justly, been called its hero.

He it was who dealt those decisive blows to that clerical dominion which, in the Churches to which we refer, had become so widespread at the commencement of the present century, eclipsing and absorbing the individual faith to which these very Churches owed, not merely their historical renown, but their very existence. He it was who, comprehending little at the outset of the vastness of the movement he was inaugurating, and by the simple force of inward principle, urging him to bow to what he deemed the most sacred obligation, was employed by God to destroy the false prestige of the clergy to whose body he himself belonged, by quitting a Church to whose ministry he had but recently been ordained ;—the Church of his native land—the Church in the van of the French reformed denomination—the Church, moreover, be it remembered, whose glorious traditions never ceased to be uppermost in his heart. For the second time, after an interval of 300 years, the tidings spread that a preacher had sprung up in Geneva, against whom the clergy of that city had raised the same cry which had been elicited from the Romish priests of 1532, at the proclamation made by G. Farel (the friend and precursor of Calvin) of salvation by grace.

In short, in that Protestant Rome, where the profession of faith had been so brilliant and so positive, there had sprung up in its place by slow degrees a system in itself vague and indefinite, and in declared hostility to every tendency in the direction of frank and outspoken opinions.* Hence, as a natural result, the more evident

* Merle D'Aubigné.—History of the Reformation in Europe, in the time of Calvin, iii. 274 (in French) ; see also, for a parallel of the revival of the 16th and of the 19th century in Geneva, the *Procès du Methodisme*, published by Malan in 1835.

the decay of spiritual life in the majority of professed
believers, the greater was the importance attached by the
public judgment, as well to that external moral propriety,
the guarantee for the maintenance of which rested generally with the influence of an esteemed and deserving
clergy, as to the institutions and observances of public
worship, with the direction of which that clergy had
hitherto been wholly and exclusively entrusted. Things
had reached such a condition that, if we except a few
isolated independent cases, not only was the customary
reading of the Scriptures neglected, not only was scriptural
teaching superseded by the fiat that "nothing in the
Bible was to be believed but what might be known apart
from it;" but even the Redeemer Himself was ignored in
those attributes and truths respecting Him most essential
to spiritual life. Meanwhile the religious sentiment of
the people would have been stifled, and the public sense of
propriety violated, had there been any falling off in the
traditional respect which the "Vénérable Compagnie des
Pasteurs" had hitherto enjoyed, or any questioning for
a moment the rights and prerogatives with which the
memory of old times and customs had invested them !*

Undoubtedly it must be admitted that the Genevese
Pastorate saw nothing in the revival of their rights which
approached in character a distinct usurpation. From the
period of the restoration of the republic in 1815 all
respectable citizens had agreed in regarding the " Com-

---

* " *La Vénérable Compagnie des Pasteurs* " is the official title (such as
the " convocation " in the Church of England) of the head body of the
clergy of the Genevese Church. There is now the *Consistoire* (the Presby-
tery), and the *V. Comp.* (the clerical body). This title is left untrans-
lated.—*Note by Translator.*

pagnie " not only as men whose morality was so unimpeachable that even their enemies could not but respect them; but, as representing a body which, for sixteen years of irreligious ascendency, at times violent and aggressive, had comprehended thoroughly the evils which had been let loose upon Geneva by the odious domination of a foreign rule; while they had preserved, in the integrity of its old tradition, the worship of their forefathers as well as the religious observances and institutions of the past. Therefore, in the eyes of a Genevese of that epoch to assail the reverence with which the heads of the Church were surrounded, would have been to touch the sacred palladium of his country.

And yet it was at such a period as this that a young minister appeared on the stage—hitherto the esteemed of his ecclesiastical superiors, the favourite of the people— now, however, prepared to start an opposition as undisguised as it was unexpected.

An opposition, however, by no means, as far as he was concerned, the fruit of preconsidered views or deliberate plans. His was no design to attack institutions which he revered; the cry he raised proceeded from no presumptuous innovator, from no unscrupulous demagogue. He assailed no one. At the commencement of his career, he reflected no censure on the religious customs and observances around him; his only desire was to fulfil with a clear conscience the ministry which had been committed to him, by preaching out of the abundance of his heart the faith received from his forefathers. His was no aim in any sense to play a particular part; he sought but to follow the leadings of duty, under a sense of obligation which he found it impossible to ignore. His very faith in God, asserting its mighty presence in his soul, compelled him, willingly or unwillingly, to trample under foot all the traditions of his childhood, to silence every instinct of his gentle disposition, to look on calmly at the rending one by one of the dearest and most cherished ties, and that too while he felt that the course he was taking would prejudice the interests of his children, inasmuch as it involved the entire desertion, for his own part, at the moment of its attainment, of the goal which it had been his earliest dream to reach.

Herein, indeed, lies the historical—let us rather say, the deeply tragical—aspect of the career we are about to chronicle. What man of feeling could fail to be touched by the spectacle of one, but a youth, unaided by reputation, influence, position, or rank, standing alone, with no external resources to sustain him, yet compelled, in all the weakness of his isolation, to aim direct blows at that which he had hitherto regarded with the deepest veneration—the authority of the fathers of his people, their moral and spiritual guides. A spectacle, too, the more striking when it is remembered that this young man belonged to a city conspicuous for the blind devotedness of her sons; while he himself gave evidence, to the last hour of his life, that the love of his country was deeply engraven in his heart.

Who, again, it may be urged, claiming kindred with our common humanity, more especially esteeming the eternal interests of the soul as transcending all else in importance, but would be struck at the sight of this same youth confronting authority in high places, and even a majority of his fellow-citizens, while he arrayed against him those very men whose esteem and affection he had hitherto enjoyed. And that, too, with no faltering heart nor failing courage; upheld alone by the presence of a simple, living faith, firm in his endurance as "seeing Him who is invisible;" and neither self-sufficiently nor yet hesitatingly, but with right onward step, advancing in a path beset by difficulties and, not unfrequently, by sufferings of every kind!

Henri Abraham Cæsar Malan was born at Geneva on the 7th July 1787. He belonged to a family still numerous in the Piedmontese valleys of the Waldenses, where it at first took root in the commune of St Jean. A portion of it, migrating to France, settled at Merindol in Dauphiny, where traces of them still exist, and where they would seem, from various collateral proofs, to have attained rank in the state. What is most deserving of record, however, is the fact that many of his name, both in Piedmont and France, have been conspicuous in the rolls of heroic confessors, as sealing with their life their attachment to liberty, conscience, and the truth of the gospel. My father, as appears in several of his writings, looked upon it as a real title of nobility to belong to this small race of Waldensian confessors, and to have in his family the glorious blood of martyrs. Sprung thus from an ancient stock of primitive Christians, the Malans of Merindol scrupled not, after the revocation of the Edict of Nantes, to sacrifice everything for their faith. While some sought in the wilds of Africa, at the Cape of Good Hope, the religious freedom which had been wrenched from them in their native land, one of them, Pierre Malan, the head of the family, and great-grandfather of the subject of this memoir, fled from Merindol in 1714, after the martyrdom of his sister, and reached Geneva in

1722 in a state of utter destitution. He entered as sergeant in the garrison of the city, and married a French exile, being in due course admitted among the inhabitants or "natifs." *

The resolve to accord to "natifs" in Geneva the right of burghers, was due to the influence of the great French Revolution. In the troublous times that inaugurated that memorable convulsion, my grandfather, though a natif, was the only one in his family enrolled among the "negatifs" or partizans of the government. My father used to relate, among the earliest memories of his childhood, the circumstance of his being girded with a miniature sword in token of his new dignity as a burgess of Geneva.

My grandfather, Jacques Imbert Malan, had succeeded, as College Master of the fourth class, his father-in-law, M. Prestreau, whose Greek and Latin Grammars had long served the pupils as manuals. He was univerally respected in the city to which he belonged. On one occasion, during the period of French rule, when it was open to him to succeed to considerable property, of which his grandfather had been deprived in the days of religious persecution, he declined to take the necessary steps, on discovering, after certain preliminary inquiries, that were he to claim possession, he would reduce several families to poverty. Moreover, when the Préfet, fully entering into his motives, pressed him nevertheless to consider the interests of his two sons, his reply was that he was fully convinced that the principles he meant to instil into them were such as,

* The "natifs" in the old Republic of Geneva, before the French dominion, were *not* citizens or burghers; they had no rights but such as might be *granted* them. They could not vote laws, taxes, &c. The English word "*native*" has an entirely different meaning.—*Note by Translator.*

when they reached man's estate, would make them the first to approve of the course he was pursuing. Conspicuous thus for his benevolence, as well as for the liveliness and refinement of his mind, he was unable at first, with the traditions of the eighteenth century strong within him, to enter into the motives which influenced his son to renounce a career, the brilliant promise of which had already more than satisfied his fatherly ambition. It was not till later that he learned to attach more submission to the dictates of living faith and personal piety. During the earlier years of his younger son, his influence only tended to throw him back upon the council and teaching of his pious mother. Without, indeed, earning the reputation of a scorner, my grandfather had succumbed in no small measure to the influence of Voltaire, whose works, with those of Rousseau, and the Encyclopædia of Diderot, occupied the place of honour on his library shelves.

To him all spiritual enthusiasm was, to say the least, suspicious; and while his thorough amiability of disposition rendered him incapable of individual sarcasm, he greeted religious topics with the smile of superior intellect, and encountered every utterance of fervent piety with the passionless rigour of what he called his common sense. Yet, with all this, he not only loved his son, but respected him as well. At this very moment I have at my side a letter in which the old man summons all the resources of chastened satire and honest indignation to censure the unjustifiable attacks with which the head of the Genevese clergy had visited Cæsar Malan.

His wife, who died in 1848, had been brought up at Clavelière, an old estate purchased by her father, about twenty-one miles from Geneva, on the lower ridge of the Jorat, and still traceable near the farm which at present occupies its site. Her earlier years had been spent in one of the best schools in Neufchatel.

The Prestreaus, like the Malans, were a family of refugees, and her father's history, full of romantic and dramatic incidents, never failed to appeal to my youthful imagination as I listened to my grandmother's account of it. They originally belonged to Nimes, where they moved in the upper circles of society. On their emigration from France, and consequent enrichment, they sought the most sequestered rural retirement, where they maintained the strictest observance of the traditional Huguenot worship. Thus it happened, that, not long after their settlement in Geneva, they furnished a pastor to the village of Vandœuvres in the person of one of their connections, the Marquis de Fougereux, one of the " desert preachers " as they were called. He it was who baptized my grandmother, who was his niece. He it was, too—so my father believed — who built the little house at Vandœuvres, which my grandfather subsequently purchased, and where my father passed the ten concluding years of his life.

My grandmother, whose influence, as will afterwards appear, was the means of planting in her son's mind the earliest seeds of divine truth, was singularly attractive in appearance and manners. With angelic sweetness of disposition, she combined a piety as simple as it was sincere. Deaf from a comparatively early period, her sight never good, she endeavoured, with admirable fortitude, to sustain herself under these infirmities by the assiduous discharge of family duties, and by daily select reading. To this she

B

owed a richly furnished mind, and a versatility of conversational power which gave a special charm to her society. My father was her favourite son, conducting himself towards her with the tenderest love, and the most unbounded attention and respect. At the close of her life he came and settled by her at Vandœuvres, never leaving her side except on the Sunday, to preach at Geneva, when he arranged that my mother or one of my sisters should supply his place.

After my grandfather's death, my grandmother, with her elder son, who lived abroad, continued to the last the object of my father's most anxious solicitude and tenderest affection. I have discovered in his desk many a letter which had passed between them, many a proof of their mutual attachment. Labled and locked up in his secret drawers, they gave evidence of belonging to his most treasured private relics. Amongst them were to be found a child's first efforts at writing: notes, all but illegible from age; scattered fragments revealing the clinging ardour of a mother's love.

My father's childhood was spent with his parents in a house in the Rue Verdaine, communicating by a passage with the library. Though never in absolute destitution, they were often in great straits, and especially at the time of which I am now writing; their circumstances, indeed, being so straitened as to make it necessary for them to dispense even with a maid-servant. Yet theirs was a happy home notwithstanding, whose brightness my grandmother loved to recall in the closing years of her life, as she related to me incident after incident in my father's early history; as, for example, how one day, to save his brother a scolding, he took his medicine ; how, another time, he was seen to give a beggar in the street the bread which had been furnished him for his breakfast on his going to school.   Let me recall one other occurrence in her own words, as serving to illustrate the circumstances and influences among which he grew up to manhood.

" It was during a severe winter, and in days when our circumstances were far from affluent, when your father was about seven years old, that I made him a present one day of a pair of warm woollen gloves. A morning or two afterwards, on his return from school, I noticed that he wasn't wearing them, and, by dint of questioning, elicited the explanation that he had given them to a poor boy with chilblained hands. ' You see, mamma,' he said, ' I can put my hands into my coat sleeves—his coat was not warm like mine.' "

My grandmother commended her boy for what he had done, telling him, however, at the same time, that he must not expect another pair, "though," she added, as she told me the story, " I often suffered that winter at the sight of his poor little frost-bitten hands.   Still, independent of the cost to me of replacing the gloves, which I could ill afford, it was of paramount importance that he should learn from experience that those only can have the privilege and pleasure of giving who give at the cost of personal sacrifice."

From his earliest childhood my father became remarkable for the precocity of his character and mind. Thus, his mother often told us how he had read to her the story of Gethsemane, as he sat on a little footstool at her feet, when he was only three years and a half old. My brothers and I, too, well remember another characteristic incident, often quoted by our grandfather as a stimulus to us to emulate our father's example when he was our age.

I may be permitted to recount the circumstance as related by an elder sister, who, in common with myself, had often heard it from our grandparents. When he was within a month of his fourth year, our father received the reading prize at college. It was on the occasion of the prize day, when medals and other rewards were distributed, and the pupils were advanced to higher forms. The four syndics,* their maces in their hands, preceded by their ushers, and followed by the magistracy, clergy, professors, and agents, walked in procession through the streets, at the head of the school, to the sound of church bells and military music, on their way to the cathedral. It was in 1792. The small Cæsar, in his child's dress, took his place, the only one in that attire and of that age, in the solemn cortège. His father had carefully instructed him on the subject of the three bows which he was to make, as he advanced, when his name was called, to the seat of the chief syndic who was to give the prize. He had also taken special pains to explain to him how, on retiring, after receiving his prize, he was to repeat his triple reverence *without turning his back*.

The critical moment arrived—the diminutive prizeman was summoned; he advanced—trembled an instant at the roar of applause with which he was greeted—collected himself, however, the next moment—accomplished his bows, and received his reward. As he withdrew, engrossed

* The syndic, or chief magistrate, answering to the consuls of the old Roman Republic.

though he was with his prize, he carefully remembered his father's orders, "You are to make three more bows on retiring." Forgetful of the rest of his instructions, however, he duly and reverently did homage with his back to the high officials, who could not refrain from smiling in concert with the tumultuous laughter of the assembly. Then, as ever through his after life, he was intent on obedience, though perhaps slightly oblivious of etiquette.

His education had been conducted from first to last at the Collegiate Institution, established by the great Reformer, and which, at the time of which I write, continued to be in much the same condition in which Calvin had left it. There it was that contemporary scholars contracted those lasting friendships which made Protestant Geneva less a city than a family and household. There it was that young men from their earliest days were trained to order, industry, obedience ; above all, to a faith in absolute equality in the presence of a common duty,—virtues which for so long a time have been the source of power and glory to the little republic.

There it was that, in the providence of God, he who was to exercise such a decisive influence in his native town was made to participate in these ancient institutions, that so, from the economies of the past, he might learn wisdom for the guidance of the future. There it was that he was taught to imbibe a deep and instinctive love for his country. There, too, that he first drew around him those personal attachments by which he was afterwards surrounded, and that esteem which, as soon as the voice of prejudice had subsided, was entertained towards him even by those who had not hesitated to place their passions at the service of the opposition.

Not that, while due place in the formation of his character is given to these outer influences, the inner and more sacred sway of his home life must be forgotten. His frequent visits at La Clavelière left remembrances which he loved to recall. Under that roof it was that he acquired that distinction of manner and constant self-respect which were so conspicuous in his mother, and which became to him eventually a kind of second nature.

In all the intimate intercourse to which my father admitted me, among all his constant manifestations of ease and unrestraint, never once did I know him to forget himself, or suffer his unreserve to degenerate into the slightest approach to laxity. Even on his deathbed, his exquisite politeness and thoughtfulness showed itself in the case of the servant who waited upon him.

His mechanical tastes, too, which clung to him to the end of his life, and served as a pleasant recreation through many years, were originally communicated to him by his maternal grandfather, and so readily taken up, that he became a speedy adept in their prosecution. One thing more, in connection with the formation and development of his tastes during his stay at La Clavelière, may be mentioned here. In this mountain home, and in the continual presence of the grandest natural scenery, he became an ardent lover of nature, and acquired a taste for sketching and painting, together with that inward passion for the beautiful, which is so apparent in his prose and poetical effusions.

To sum up my reminiscences of these his early years, let

me quote from some memoranda in his own handwriting, written in 1859 :—

" When I was seventeen years old, and during my prosecution of classical studies, I spent a year at Marseilles in a house of business. At that time I thought of being a merchant, principally to help my parents. But God kept me for a nobler destiny.

" It happened thus. The pastor of Marseilles requiring leave of absence, the committee of his church applied to me to read a sermon from the pulpit every Sunday. This I did, I think, for about two months, and to this incident I trace my first aspiration after the ministry. My father cordially approving of my wishes, I returned to Geneva, and was admitted by the academy professors into their philosophy class. They received me back into the first place, the position I had formerly occupied, and thus I lost nothing by my year's absence at Marseilles. It is true that while I was away, I had regularly kept up my classical studies, rising generally at four A.M., and even at three, that I might be able to work at them before going to business. In addition to this, after the labours of the desk were over for the day, I had a few pupils to whom I gave two or three lessons in history and general literature."

As a young man, my father became remarkable for the exemplary regularity of his life, and for his active and ungrudging benevolence. Many proofs are at hand that he exhibited from the very first in a high degree those sterling qualities which shone out so brilliantly in his after career. He was known as a " saint." It was said, (and the tradition was confirmed to me by one friend still alive, who assured me that he knew it as a fact, and was prepared to prove it,) that once, during an unusually bitter winter, he went, unknown to his parents, night after night, to a wood-yard to purchase bundles of fagots, which he carried off and distributed himself to sundry poor families. Testimony, too, abounds as to his courage and presence of mind. How he stopped, for instance, one day, two horses which had run away, no one being at hand to help him. Also as to the depth of his sympathy with distress, how with earnest solicitude he watched over some wounded Austrian soldiers. But let me recur to his memoranda :—

"During my four years' study of theology, and especially during the two last, I frequently preached, sometimes in the rural parishes of Geneva, sometimes in the neighbouring countries. At that time, I was utterly ignorant of gospel grace, and though my character as a young man was upright, even to severity, no thought had ever entered my mind of any other way of salvation than that of my own work and deservings.

"From the very first, and through my mother's teaching, I had learned to believe in the divinity of the Son of God, and I remember that, at the age of fourteen, I maintained this verity against some of my fellow-students in the college room ; yet the belief was as dead within me, and during my four years' study, not a syllable reached me from the lips of my instructors calculated to call it into life. Moreover, the theses which I wrote under the direction of the professor of sacred oratory, went no further than to treat of human wisdom and morality ; yet, with this only as the testimony of my conscience, I thought myself, and was thought by others, very religious ; my morals were unimpeachable, and my general conversation reputed devout."

What my father says here about his theological studies, recalls to my mind what he afterwards wrote in 1835. "Were I to go back to my recollections of academical life and its theological teaching," he remarks in his "Procès du Methodisme," (p. 18,) "I should fail to find a single instance in which instruction was given me on the divinity of our Saviour, man's fallen nature, or the doctrine of justification by faith. I think," he adds, "my contemporaries retain the same impression as myself."

This explains the testimony of Robert Haldane, who had had considerable intercourse with those "contemporaries" of whom my father speaks. "If they had been brought up in the schools of Socrates and Plato," he exclaims indignantly to one of their professors, "they could not have been more totally ignorant of the saving truths of the gospel. Their studies seem to have been entirely devoid of all scriptural teaching whatsoever."

"We learnt," adds one of them, (Rev. A. Bost, sen.,) "nothing beyond the dogmas of natural religion. The New Testament was not considered necessary as a text-book of study for the ministry;" a statement which confirms what my father has said to me over and over again, that so far from having been engaged in the study of the New Testament, in the ordinary course of his theological training, he never even read it through till long after he had left the academy.

Not that it is to be inferred from all this, that his tutors had failed utterly to set before him the sacredness of the Scriptures. As will appear by and by, the Church of Geneva herself had never yet given birth to an avowed and direct assailant of their authority. It was from a

man who, until then, had occupied a leading position in
the opposite camp, that such an attack eventually proceeded, in the lifetime of the present generation. But
there is a worse treatment of the Bible than this, and of
that she had been guilty. To attack it openly was only
to throw it on the defensive, to challenge a scrutiny of the
proofs on which its authority rested, to evoke all the
ancient ardour with which that authority was upheld.
Never *thus* did the Church of Geneva treat the Bible, to
no such prominence did she expose it, *she only ignored it,
she only passed it over in silence.* Investing it with an
exaggerated awe, her very reverence, amounting to superstition, held it back from general use. Whilst admitting
with the unhappy Rousseau, to the very fullest extent,
"the majesty of Scripture," she would have deemed it as
nothing short of exaggeration to take its authority as the
only rule of faith and aim of life. Mere assertion all this,
the proof of which remains to be established in the following pages.

In 1809, my father, being tutor at the time to a banker's
sons in the city, was appointed, after a brilliant examination,
master of the fifth form at the college. In this post, which
he occupied for nine years, he drew around him, in a
marked manner, the approval and the eulogiums of his
superiors. Full of enthusiasm in his new work, he was
among the first to introduce into Geneva the Bell and
Lancaster system of teaching. In order to make himself
acquainted with the method, he visited the school under the
management of Pestalozzi, at that time, at Yverdon. Nor
did he confine himself to the use of that schoolmaster's
text-books; he adopted also his method of logic and analysis

as falling in peculiarly with the bent of his own mind. His renown was not long in spreading beyond his native city, and he speedily attracted the notice of foreign professors, especially in the north of Europe, who travelled to Geneva for the express purpose of visiting his class.

It was for the use of this class, that he issued, in 1812, his maiden work, a "Selection from the Fables of Phædrus," with notes; and in 1818, the first part of an original Latin Poem, which contained the earliest dawnings of gospel faith. It is noteworthy that though ·this poem was introduced to the students with the approbation of the academy, it was afterwards ranked by those very men amongst the counts in the long indictment against him.

He was a prime favourite with his pupils. I have often heard men now advanced in life speak with deep emotion of the time when they were under his tuition, giving proof that no after acrimony of controversial dispute could efface his image from their hearts. "No one ever knew as he did," said De Goltz, "the magic art of enchaining attention by a spell incapable of resistance, while he led captive the hearts and intellects of those whom he taught." It was so with him to the very last. Even in his old age he was to the young men who knew him the object of tenderest and closest attachment—the repository of most sacred confidences.

In October 1810 he was ordained to the ministry, at the age of twenty-three. The ceremony took place in the church of Geneva—M. Picot, dean of the clerical body, presiding. The oath which he took on this occasion was to the following effect :—

"You swear before God, and on the Sacred Scriptures

open before you, to preach in its simplicity the gospel of our Lord Jesus Christ: to recognise as the only infallible rule of faith and conduct, the Word of God, as contained in the sacred books of the Old and New Testament: to abstain from all spirit of sectarianism: to shun every thing from which schism might arise, or which might tend to disturb the union of the Church: to hold inviolably secret all confessions made to you in the disburdening of individual consciences, except such as tend in the direction of high treason: and to exert yourself to the utmost for the edification of the Church of God, by living 'in the midst of the world,' in temperance, justice, and piety, and by devoting yourself to the zealous fulfilment of all the duties of your sacred calling."

This oath clearly bound the candidate by the authority of the Bible alone. From the year 1806 the catechism had given way to the apostles' creed, and that again had disappeared in its turn, so as to leave Scripture standing by itself. This must be remembered distinctly in order to harmonise the course my father afterwards followed with the terms of his ordination vows.

In the following year he married the younger daughter of M. Schönenberger of Glaris—a merchant long established at Geneva, where he lived in the small hamlet of Valavran. After having borne him twelve children, of whom eleven are now alive, and joined him in celebrating the thirtieth anniversary of their marriage, my mother closed his eyes. They lost, as I have just stated, only one of their number— my brother Jocelyn, who died in 1846.

But to return to the period immediately following his ordination and marriage.

The year was 1812; the epoch memorable as witnessing the birth of a religious movement in Geneva. Assemblies were frequent among certain theological students, of whom M. Empeytaz, attracted by this proceeding alone the displeasure of the Venerable Assembly. Although my father did not participate at first in these meetings, it was he, nevertheless, who was to play a decisive part of uncompromising testimony and action. To trace his career, however, at this point, will be my task in the next chapter.

CHAPTER II.

> On! on! till, in a bolder sweep,
>   By fewer flowers, and darker caves,
>   It rolls along its recent waves,
> And hurls them downward to the deep.

THE events which we are now going to describe have formed the subject-matter of several publications, both in Geneva and abroad, and have also been frequently described in other ways. More particular reference might be made to the work of M. de Goltz, already quoted, in which they are discussed with equal fairness and minuteness. Whilst reserving to myself the right to quote this authority for some details bearing upon my subject, I shall take care, at the same time, to travel the ground he has occupied in his reference to my father's life, with the aid of contemporary documents, of which the following are the most important:—

1. W. A. Schichedantz, Ph.D., and Licentiate in Theology at Berlin: The Geneva Church in the Nineteenth Century, first published (in German) in the "Archives of Modern Ecclesiastical History of Staudlin and Tjchirner," 1821.

2. Dr J. Pye Smith: A Vindication of the Citizens of Geneva, and other persons, who have been instrumental in the Revival of Scriptural Religion in that city. London, 1825.

3. The Reviewer Reviewed, by Heresiæ Mastix, (T. Fry, Rector of Emberton), 1821: A Reply to an English Religious Review which accused M. Malan of "sectarianism."

4. The True History (French) of the Momiers of Geneva, followed by a notice of the Momiers of Canton de Vaud. By an Eye-witness. Geneva, 1824.

5. Precis (French) of the Theological Debates which have for some years agitated Geneva. By T. J. Chenevière, Pastor and Professor of Theology, 1824.

6. Letter to M. Cheneviere in reply to his "Precis." By R. Haldane, 1824. Published in French and in English.

7. Religious Geneva in March 1819. By A. Bost, Minister of the Gospel.

8. A Defence of the Christians of Geneva who have constituted themselves into an Independent Church. By A. Bost. Paris, Lyons, and Geneva, 1825.

9. Prosecution of Bost (on account of the above-mentioned work), and his acquittal by two tribunals, 1826.

And, lastly, my father's own publications:—

10. Papers referring to his Deprivation of the College Mastership, 1819.

11. The Conventicle of Rolle, 1821.

12. Evangelical Testimony, by a Minister of God. (Papers referring to his compulsory secession from the National Church), 1823.

13. Le Procès du Methodisme in Geneva, 1835.

"So remarkable, and of such value, were Malan's talents and qualifications, that his future prominence became an assured thing. In appearance he was dignified and prepossessing; he was a poet and musician; had a good voice; painted skilfully; exhibited, in short, a genius as diversified as it was powerful. He had a rich and fruitful imagination; his thoughts were logical and impressive; his eloquence was fascinating; his temperament ardent and impassioned. Impelled by the nervous vigour of his thoughts, he pursued, with indefatigable exertion, a definite object—that object, under the influence of gospel grace, the salvation of souls."

Such is the graphic and truthful picture of my father, drawn by the pen of the historian of the Revival in Geneva. His concluding words bring us naturally to consider the change which he underwent in his own religious convictions. And here it ought to be premised that this change, though thorough, was by no means so apparent to others in any external reform, as it might have been, had his moral character been less unimpeachable. His was no renewal, furnishing such an outward contrast to the past it had subverted as to arrest the attention of the most heedless observer. If my father's case proved no exception to the rule that the experimental knowledge of salvation must be followed by a new life, this new life of his was not inaugurated by one of those tragical struggles of the soul which any observer may detect; nor yet did it erect itself on the ruins, we will not say of irregular morals, but even of worldly habits. Rather it was a quiet transition from a moral, and, in a limited sense, a devout life, to a life genuinely spiritual, and, in the gospel sense of the term, renewed. Further, this new principle in him did not start into being by concentrating a hitherto wavering mind, or by supplying, under divine grace, a force and symmetry of character as yet wanting. On the contrary, the message of the gospel found in him one to whom religion was no novelty, while morality was a sternest law ; a man whose candid and ingenuous spirit, and resolute following of right, had secured for him general esteem. This explains how the gospel always presented itself to him as the proclamation of a salvation wrought for him, and without him, rather than as the means God had put into his hands to dissipate doubts by which he had never been distracted, and to alleviate anxieties by which he had never been afflicted. So far from tending to detract from the grandeur of the work of conversion, what has been urged in reference to his peculiar case rather illustrates its absolute necessity. It was indispensable that God should appear as coming Himself, with His word of grace, to a soul that, in consequence of the very virtues with which it was adorned, could not possibly, if left to itself, have ever felt its need of salvation.

We have already traced to its source my father's acceptance of the central doctrine of the gospel. But it was not till long after his childhood had received its lesson, not till long after his young manhood had been consecrated to the sacred office, that what had hitherto been with him an accepted dogma became matter of heartfelt experience. For five or six years his preaching was in decided opposition to gospel truth. A stranger at that time to the religious movement which was beginning to assert itself around him, the Bible was to him an all but sealed book. Happening to be travelling, on one occasion, during this period, and having nothing to occupy him, he tried to read a chapter or two as a species of distraction. But he

C

found the style so old-fashioned, he declares, and the language so common-place, that he put the book aside, and betook himself to a volume of literature.

It may not be uninteresting to quote here his own words in reference to his conversion, addressed, in an explanatory paper in the year 1830, to some brother pastors, a paper to which we shall have occasion to recur by and by. It may be as well to abridge it in some places, and to supplement it in others by notes from a MS. of his in my possession.

"At the time of my ordination at Geneva I was in utter ignorance of the truth as it is in Jesus. In this darkness I lingered till 1814, at which time I first apprehended the truth that our Lord Jesus Christ is God. I had had some indefinite idea of the importance of this truth from the commencement of my ministry, after a series of conversations with a pastor of the Canton de Vaud, but it was not till the time above specified that I actually received it. Under the teaching of God's Holy Spirit, I owe this development of my faith to hearing the divine word from the lips of various Christians, among whom I may mention, in particular, M.M. Demellayer, Galland, Coulin, Gaussen, and Paul Henry of Berlin; and, above all, M. Moulin."

In his "Germain le Bucheron" my father furnishes a few details in reference to his eventful discussions with the Vaudois pastor, whose name never reached me. "I stopped at his village," he writes, "and preached for him. As we were leaving the church he said to me, with a grave and mournful expression, 'It appears to me, sir, that you have not yet learnt that, in order to convert others, you

must first be converted yourself. Your sermon was not a
Christian discourse, and I sincerely hope my people didn't
understand it.' Blessed salutary words ! From them
and from all that this faithful servant of Christ added to
them, I began to understand what a *Christian* means—
what it really is to be a Christian."

But to return to his explanatory letter. " From that
time I began," he writes, " to discern the doctrine of grace
and justification by faith without the works of the law.
Galland often spoke of it, and I found that, in the
expositions I made in the week-day services, I gradually
arrived at the truth that man is justified by faith alone.
This was in the year 1815. At the close of that year I
began to teach this doctrine to my pupils at the college,
and it was then that I first encountered the admonitions
and reproaches of those of my superiors who did not
relish the truth I was professing."

Whilst my father's mind was thus being gradually
enlightened under the influence of a few of the clergy of
Geneva, the majority of that body had already manifested a decided opposition to these scriptural opinions,
and had supplied unmistakable evidence of their hostility
to Malan himself. As a matter of fact, a revival had
already commenced some years back, and at the suggestion
of one of those very pastors, whose names we have given
above, a society of young men had been formed in 1810,
associated to some extent with a small Moravian community, the commencement of which dated back to the
visit of Count Zinzendorf to Geneva in 1740. This little
body numbered at that time some six or seven hundred
members, including on its roll the names of some even of

the magistrates of the republic. In 1810, however, the only fruit left of the personal exertions of Zinzendorf was an old lady who died eight years afterwards at the advanced age of ninety-four, and who, up to the time of her death, was the centre of a small circle of five or six persons. This little flock, hearing of the progress of a reviving work in other countries, joined in prayer for an extension of the blessed influence to their own. These prayers so regularly, so perseveringly, offered, kindled in the first instance that great spiritual awakening which burst out so gloriously not long afterwards. The first answer came in an inwrought impulse in the hearts of some of those who prayed to address themselves to the work about which they had been praying. Two of them, students in theology, whose names were Guers and Empeytaz, endeavoured (in the year 1813) to set up a small Sunday-school. The latter of them, after the visit of the famous Baroness de Kreudener to Geneva, acted so unhesitatingly on the subject of individual exertion in things spiritual as to provoke the authorities, in opposition, to append to the ordination oath the words by which the candidates were held to pledge themselves " to abstain from every species of sectarianism, and to avoid whatever might tend in the direction of schism, or threaten the unity of the Church." Eventually, at the period of which we are now speaking, this same student, who had just been refused orders in the National Church, published at Paris his work entitled " Considerations on the Divinity of Jesus Christ, addressed to the Students of Theology in the Church of Geneva."

This publication was not without its influence, according to my father, on those to whom it was addressed. Many of them joined with a few young ministers in preaching their new faith regularly in the rural parishes, or occasionally in the city. In addition to this they held religious meetings here and there, and their influence soon became felt among their fellow-students, and even in some families of the city.

Meanwhile my father, absorbed in his educational work, with which indeed he combined an occasional ministry in Geneva and the country round, avoided taking any part in all that was going on. Beyond the sensation caused by the publication of Empeytaz, little indeed was generally known of the revival movement at this time. It was not till long after he had detached himself, step by step, from the Church to which he had originally belonged, that he encountered these young men whom we have specified above. At all events his subsequent activity could scarcely be traced, as far as its origin was concerned, to any influence exercised upon him by the revival movement—a movement which had been before him in the field, and whose work he was now to undertake. According to his invariable rule he took an independent part in all that followed. With the independence of his character he suffered what all independent natures must suffer, and hence it is but fair to allow him that kind of honour which such natures may fairly claim.

Looking over a volume of sermons which he published in 1838, I find the fullest testimony to the change which occurred at this time in his spiritual life.

" I have stated, on some occasions, that my conversion to the Lord Jesus might, with propriety, be compared to a mother rousing an infant with a kiss—a simile answering exactly to my experience in recalling it. Nor can I look back to that blessed epoch in my life without magnifying His tender loving-kindness Who spared me the doubts, terrors, and perplexities through which so many souls have passed ere they tasted 'joy and peace in believing.'

"For many years of my ministry I was a stranger, experimentally, to the doctrines of grace: teaching the merits of human righteousness, flattering human excellence, and holding forth a heaven of glory as the certain reward of human effort; no thought even of that divine righteousness 'which is unto all and upon all them that believe,' ever crossed my mind, and consequently no suspicion that I was opposing it. Mine was the uttermost repose of ignorance, the most entire freedom from all misgiving as to the truth of my creed. I spoke as I felt, as, indeed, I had been taught, with all the warmth and animation of youth. My teaching was of a God and Saviour alike unknown; setting forth, as a substitute for the witness of the Spirit, the cold morality of reason and the deceits of an unbelieving heart."

In proof of his assertions, my father adds an analysis of a sermon preached by him in 1813 (Phil. iii. 13, 14), and which had been written under the special superintendence of one of his professors.

In it is set forth the innocence of human nature, and a sinner's justification by his own merits and efforts. It concludes as follows : "As you contemplate the excellences you have already attained, and see opening before you the path to new achievements, you will taste a secret, ineffable joy. The consciousness of progress will fill your hearts

with sweetest hope; and thus, in adding day by day to
your previous merits, a hoard of gold tried in the fire, the
purchase-money of immortality, you will anticipate with
heavenly delight the arrival of that happy hour wherein
you shall be called to render back to the Creator the souls
which you have embellished with accumulated virtues(!)"

He refers also to another sermon preached by him in the
following year, in which he laboured to prove that religion
was the only firm foundation of national virtue—a sermon
which he says had been suggested to him by the indignation which he had felt at hearing another discourse, setting
forth "man's natural dignity as the true basis of popular
virtue and prosperity;" and handling the subject precisely
after the fashion of a heathen philosopher, ascribing all
power and glory to human reason and human will.

"Much general excitement resulted from this controversy. A multitude filled the church at the time my
sermon was preached, and listened with enthusiasm to my
flattering appeal to the national sentiment, while I talked
about 'religion' and 'the God of our fathers,' and electri-
fied my congregation after a fashion by fine words about
the love of our country, and how our national piety was the
only sure guardian of its glory."

Let us pause here a few moments, that we may apprehend the more clearly the starting-point in my father's
new life. At first the prominent sentiment is one of surprise at the contrast between teaching such as we have
quoted above, and that of which he was afterwards the
foremost champion. And yet the attentive observer would
feel that this by no means exhausted the whole matter.
If the Holy Spirit, by a divine and mysterious action,

implants in the unconscious centre of the human will and personality, a new and heavenly principle, He never, in a direct and violent manner, changes that which remains— the essential and distinctive feature of the individuality itself, which appears in its conscious activity.

Hence the unparalleled interest of noticing the choice of the instrumentalities by which God is pleased to carry out His purposes,—the peculiar motives which lead Him in His wisdom to summon one man in particular, in preference to all others, to the execution of some particular work, He having already prepared him for it.

Under the influence of these considerations, there are two things which will strike us at once in connection with the extracts quoted above. In the first place, we find at this point in Malan's life a religious profession, with a public confession of His faith in God, long before that special moment in which his soul was converted to the gospel of grace. For Malan's faith, God was the living God of conscience, considerably in advance of that time when He became enthroned in his heart as a God of sovereign love and free forgiving mercy.

Our second remark points to the authority, and therefore to the dogmatical form which already characterised his religious convictions. The preacher of gospel grace has often been charged with this reproach. And yet it was observable in his teaching long before he apprehended the truth of a free salvation. Every item in his religious faith was in his eyes from the very first—even before his conversion—a truth of God, to be declared and enjoined as such. This is evident in the few words quoted above from his sermon on human merit. After having laid down the

principle, that the heart and soul of man might be infinitely
ennobled by virtuous efforts, "Think not," he adds, "that
this is any mere human teaching, to be accepted or rejected
at your pleasure; it is the very word of God, and you cannot discard it blamelessly." How often, in after years, he
employed the self-same words in enforcing doctrine to
which this was diametrically opposed! Hence he was one
of those men who take, not the mere indistinct authority
only, but even the very voice of conscience, as coming to
them direct from God. Already before his conversion to
the gospel, Malan appears to us as a man whose solemnity
in the treatment of religious truth was so startling, that he
conjured up in the mind of those who heard him the image
of a Hebrew seer; a man who, without offending his
hearers, might have spoken of "the God before Whom I
stand." This extreme reverence, which thus displayed
itself long before he stood forth as a witness for the gospel,
was in him a prominent characteristic. Ere yet the eternal
Jehovah was to him a Father, Whose love was shed abroad
in his heart, he beheld in Him the true and living God,
the God in Whose awful presence his conscience ever
uttered her voice.

And so this belief in the living God, to be feared, and
loved, and trusted, became in him the starting-point in a
marked manner, the very foundation, indeed, of his whole
religious life. Nor was it strange that it should be so,
when we look at the simplicity and decision of his spiritual
progress. In short, if it be true that Christ leads us to the
Father, it is God, as God, Who leads us to the Saviour.

In proof of what has now been said, I might advance
many an incident in his life. I will content myself, how-

ever, with quoting a single circumstance, which happened
at the precise period of which we are now treating:—

It was towards the close of 1814 that my mother nearly
succumbed to an attack of that terrible typhoid epidemic
which followed the allied armies in their progress through
the country; and often and often has my father described
to us these terrible days. For many weeks he never left
her chamber, while she, lying in utter unconsciousness, had
long been given over by the physicians. One of them,
however, in going away, suggested the use of wine, so that
no possible remedy might be neglected. "Never shall I
forget that moment," said my father. "I took the cellar
key, and went to fetch some. As I reached the foot of the
stairs with it in my hand, I fell on my knees and prayed
God to have mercy on me, and on you all. In my moment
of extremity I felt as though two mighty hands were raising me, and setting me on my feet. I ascended the stair-
case full of a strange elation; the crisis had passed, and
your mother was saved, but I doubt not God Himself had
vouchsafed me succour from on high?"

Those who knew him best know how thoroughly free he
was from any tinge of superstition; that is to say, from
anything that tended in the direction of trust in the mysterious or unknown. Yet, at the same time, he equally
repudiated that practical infidelity which denies to the
Almighty the right of exercising a direct control over individual occurrences in human life. I may add that I have
quoted this incident, not so much with the view of calling
up a mere bygone recollection, of which numbers might
readily have been communicated by any of his family.
I have placed it on record to show that even before his

conversion, as he himself describes it, God was always to him a living God; that, so far from referring the history of his life to second and proximate causes, he was in the habit of ascribing it to the sole Supreme Cause Who ordained them all.

This fundamental thought in my father's spiritual life, explaining, as it does, that absolute independence of character and conduct, and more especially of teaching which distinguished him, must ever be regarded as the prominent feature of his inner history. His was one of those great natures to which absolute truth is a sheer necessity, and which draw towards it from every point, as towards an atmosphere essential to their very life. Before the eyes of such there stands out but one stupendous fact—a fact eclipsing every other, namely, the infinite and ever-present reality, the constantly actual truth, the ever-efficacious and essentially free will of the living God.

And if I put this stress on the living theism which, in my father's case, preceded a not less living Christianity, it is because, as it seems to me, truth such as this demands clearest and most emphatic notice at the time when believers are compelled, by the open negation of the supernatural in historical facts, to summon even greater decision to the maintenance of their faith in its eternal reality, such as they derived it from their personal experience of the living God.

With my father, the fear of the Lord in fullest operation was the secret of all his activity. Hence flowed that early decision and lucidity of word and action which purged him from all taint of hesitation, which suffered no doubt to cross his mind, which, in a word, made him a man whose walk was stamped with simplicity, independence, and acknowledged superiority.

Such a man was eminently needed in Geneva, at the time of which we are writing, to recall in its pulpits the lively and definite preaching of evangelical truth, among a clergy who knew nothing of the doctrines of grace, and in the midst of a population who had lost even the remembrance of them. Later, the same city needed such a man again, to keep up, in the midst of the disputings of dissenters who constantly felt themselves in danger of putting too much stress upon Church questions, (with all the noisy personal debates which such questions are apt to raise up), the simple living testimony of those same gospel doctrines as of the one thing really needful.

As has been already remarked, it was in the year 1816 that my father attained to the faith of salvation by grace, a year termed by himself " the year of deliverance." At its commencement he contracted an intimacy with two pious foreigners, M. de Sach from Berlin, as well as with M. Wendt, the worthy Lutheran pastor in Geneva. " One evening," he writes, " we had a Bible reading in Ch. de Sach's apartment. The subject was the 5th of Romans. I was greatly impressed by the whole of it, particularly by the 10th verse, ' For in that He died, He died unto sin once ; but in that He liveth, He liveth unto God.' " At the same period in his life the incident occurred which is stated in his preface to his " Témoignage de Dieu." " One afternoon, while I was reading the New Testament at my desk, while my pupils were preparing their next lesson, I I turned to the 2d chapter of Ephesians. When I came to the words, ' By grace are ye saved through faith, and that not of yourselves, it is the gift of God,' the passage seemed to shine out before my eyes. I was so deeply moved by it that I was compelled to leave the room and take a turn in the courtyard, where I walked up and down exclaiming with intensest feeling, ' I am saved! I am saved!'"

The significance of all this is obvious. My father's lively recollection of it, after an interval of so many years, shows that it was indeed the starting-point in his spiritual experience. The Word of God effected it with its emphatic declaration that God makes us a free gift of eternal life through faith alone.

It was not till afterwards that he began to read, as I learn from his own memoranda, "L'Abrogé des Doctrines," by B. Pictet, and "La Confession de Foi de Pays Bas." It was not till a still subsequent period in the autumn of 1816, that he met casually for the first time at a hotel the venerable R. Haldane. Some months afterwards, in the spring of 1817, he was constantly with him. To that man of God he owed his first lucid and definite apprehension of salvation by grace alone. "From that time," he says himself in the paper to which reference has already been made, "I was in the faith, though I had not the assurance of salvation. That blessing I experienced while Mr Haldane, whom I love as a father, instructed me in the way of the Lord more perfectly. This was at the commencement of the year 1817, a period at which I made the acquaintance also of Dr Mason, and of the Rev. M. Bruen of New York, with whom I read and meditated over the Word of God."

The following passage, referring to the visit then made

to Geneva by these two men, occurs in a letter of Rev. M. Bruen, dated March, 16, 1816, quoted in Dr Mason's Memoirs, page 454.*

".... It gives me great pleasure to find that .... especially among the young ministers and the students, there is a strong inclination towards the truth. .... They are anxious to seize every opportunity of instruction." After having mentioned R. Haldane's visit, he also speaks of student meetings which took place at Dr Mason's lodgings : "It could not fail to strike me as very remarkable that we should have arrived here just at this time, when the line is become marked; and it is evident that Dr Mason's character and instructions will not be without effect." "Yes, my dear and venerable friend," writes my father himself to Dr Mason some time later, "nothing is more certain than that your remembrance and that of Bruen have guided me in critical moments." (Ibid. p. 458.) We shall see presently to what sort of influence my father alluded in these words.

A detailed account occurs in his "Conventicule de Rolle" of his interviews with R. Haldane.

More than forty years afterwards the remembrance of these interviews was still vivid. Here are some passages from a letter he wrote in 1859 to the nephew of R. Haldane, who had sent him the memoir of his uncle and his father. (Memoir of R. and J. Haldane.) "I cannot refrain, my dear Alexander, from speaking to you of your father and of your uncle. I have just perused their biography, and I humble myself deeply before the sight of their

---

* Memoir of John M. Mason, D.D., &c. By Jacob van Vechten. New York: Carter, 1856, 1 vol.

activity. How poor seems the work of present workmen in the Church of the Lord Jesus, when we compare it with the works and the offerings of a Robert and of a James Haldane! I am literally astounded at the sight of such labours, and I cannot say how much I regret not having been aware that these men had been put into such circumstances by the Lord Jesus, when I had the happiness and the great privilege of knowing them. But how could I have been aware of it? Was it even possible to discern such workmen of God in these humble, modest, and, as one may say, humble instruments of His grace? How I delight in recalling them to my mind's eye, going over, as much as I am able, both their teachings and their counsels, seeing in both of them that light of the Bible, to which alone they bowed.

"As for myself, dear friend, endeavouring as I do, until my end, to proclaim that same voice, I feel more and more every day how much I need that the Lord should put in me the same spirit, the same fervour, the same self-abnegation which he implanted in your worthy and kind father, in your beloved and so justly-honoured uncle! May God strengthen all who understand what their work has been! How I long to hear you speaking to me once more of both these *examples*. I dare not say of these *masters*, as they would say with myself, poor unworthy that I am, we have only one *Master*," &c.

That truly apostolic Christian was the means of imparting, not only to him, but also to his friend Gaussen, that joyous and lively assurance of salvation which stamped from that time his Christian course. At the time that he recorded all this, that change had only just occurred. But here is his after testimony on the subject, written in 1824, to a Scotch friend :—

" It pleased the Lord, about this period, to enlighten and convert my soul, and to dispose me to listen to the pious instruction of an Apollos from your country, who taught me from the Scriptures *the value of the pearl of great price, of the treasure hid in the field.* I was made rich, and, from that blessed hour, I viewed the world and heaven, time and eternity, man and his God, under quite a different aspect. A total reformation seemed to have taken place in my moral and intellectual being. The Bible taught me that the duration of this world bears no proportion to eternity ; and that that man only appeared to me to be, in truth, alive, whose life is *hid with Christ in God;* out of Christ everything seemed to me to be dead ; and therefore I relinquished several of the common branches of education, which I deemed unconnected with true life, with the existence of the soul in that kingdom which the gospel had taught me to know and love as my everlasting habitation." — (Letter on the Principles of Christian Education, addressed to J. Campbell, of Carbrook, by Dr Malan. Edinburgh, 1826, page 35, *seq.*)

This may serve to show us how, from its very beginning, the change which happened in my father's convictions and views, was to himself, at the same time, an absolute and irrevocable relinquishing of his past life and pursuits. The new birth was for him no mere resuscitation of the proper human nature of the soul, but, in the fullest sense of the term, a new creation ; a fact entirely and absolutely new. He apprehended Christ and His work not as the mere con-summation of all work of God, subjective or objective,

but as an unprecedented fact in the history of humanity;
as a fact whose unlooked-for occurrence eclipsed in his
eyes all the incidents in the long detail of preparation
that had inaugurated it. Challenged to a struggle with
traditions, deriving no little strength from their age and
respectability, to a struggle in which he was to stand
alone, and through which he was to be upheld by his
reliance on a personal Saviour, it was only to be expected
that his faith should assume a proportionate abrupt-
ness of assertion. Naturally he clung to it, (not as others
might,) as the highest exercise of the human soul, such
as God at first conceived it. He regarded faith in the
special aspect which it ever presents to man fallen
from his celestial origin, as directly miraculous in its
character. But this peculiarity of his renewed life,
which, if it had merely shown itself in his teaching or in
his bearing towards others, would have deservedly procured him the reproach of intolerant and fanatical bigotry,
displayed itself, above all, in the sacrifices to which,
under its influence, he was impelled. From the very
outset his personal piety was strictly practical, and free
from any taint of indecision or guilty compromise. Hence,
no sooner had he received from the divine word the
impressions he has described, than he not only set to
work at once to destroy all his previous manuscripts,
but also a large collection of classic authors which he had
carefully amassed, and which had been up to that time his
choicest possession. Of course he did this on the impulse
of the moment, inasmuch as he put copies of the very
same classics afterwards into the hands of his sons, though
he never resumed the reading of them himself, seeing

D

the Word of God only in the Bible, restricting the service of God to the preaching of that Word. Doubtless there may have been something in such a mode of action calculated to shock those who were apt to get discouraged at the sight of a decision they could not imitate, together with those who, although fully agreeing with him in their faith in the reality of God's kingdom, did not, nevertheless, limit that kingdom to the mere invisible world. Yet these even showed themselves eager to rekindle their faith at the fire of his ; nor could they, whenever they approached him, fail to admire that simplicity and consistency which imparted to his belief a real character of greatness.

It was impossible for such a man to remain long without rendering public testimony to the truth which was possessing his soul.

It was on the 15th March 1817, that it pleased God to enable Malan to uprear once more in Geneva, the soiled standard of her ancient faith, and to proclaim openly from Calvin's pulpit that gospel whose blessed echoes had so long ceased to be heard in her national churches.

Even before his intercourse with Haldane he had preached in a country church (on Christmas Day, 1816, and January 19, 1817,) a sermon on "justification by faith alone." It was not, however, till after that intercourse that he preached it again in the city, on the 5th and 6th of March at the Easter Festival.

That sermon was a national event, and became a date in the religious history of Geneva. "The preacher's burning utterances," says Haldane, "fell like a thunderclap on those who heard him," all which is best described in his own words :—

"I preached," he writes, "in a large church which was too small, however, for the congregation which thronged to it. The time was evening, and the solemnity of the twilight gloom added its impression to the appeal which I pressed home to the consciences of the unbelieving and self-righteous among my hearers. I was listened to at first in the most profound silence: a silence resulting, however, from surprise and displeasure. Signs of dissatisfaction were speedily apparent as I went on to demonstrate the falsehood of human righteousness, and to exalt the righteousness of God which is by faith in Jesus Christ. There arose murmurs of discontent, and movements of ill-concealed impatience, and when I pointed with my hand to the wall at the right of the pulpit, exclaiming, 'If at this moment the mysterious hand, which in Babylon of old—in the midst of an idolatrous revel—wrote in silence on the wall the death doom of a dissolute king; if that hand were to appear now and trace upon these stones the history of the months, and days, and hours of your life from the time when you first dedicated it to God; if these mysterious characters shone forth in betrayal of your deeds and thoughts, wrought and conceived when no eye but that of the Holy One was upon you;—tell me which of you would dare to confront the writing? Does not the bare thought of such a thing make you tremble? and is not the involuntary desire to banish such a possibility from your minds none other than the voice of conscience reproaching you with similar indignities, with similar consciousness of guilt?' At this moment several of my hearers turned unconsciously towards the wall at which I had been pointing, others

shrugged their shoulders, while the greater number manifested an impatience which broke loose from all restraint
when, addressing myself a moment afterwards to the
sinner who hoped to earn salvation by his own deservings, I exclaimed, 'Seek then to know, O transgressor,
what it is that keeps thee from Christ! Inquire without,
inquire within : leave no means untried to ascertain the
hindrance. As I ask the momentous question, I wait for
your reply. Search through the whole of your inner life
and its history : what can you discover—of what are you
possessed fit to offer to your God ? Your body is defiled,
your heart is earthly, your soul stained with sin. What
have you then to bring forth ? Answer before God Whose
presence fills this house! What—what can you offer as
the price of your soul ?

"'Poor sinner! God asks thee for gold, for gold weighed
in the balance of the sanctuary, and you have nothing but
dross, and a righteousness, as saith the prophet, which is
but filthy rags. What, then, is the issue of all controversies with God ? What but the utter confusion of the
flesh, the utter destruction of claims to human merit, and
the hopelessness of those efforts¦ by which you sought to
save your souls ?

"'And what is to become of you if you have no other
ground of confidence ? Say, proud man, where will be
your refuge on the judgment-day if you yourself are your
own advocate with the Father, your own propitiation for
your numberless sins ?

"'It is an easy matter now to answer with apparent confidence, while the longsuffering of your God is sparing
you, "What, but my virtues, my righteousness, my in-

tegrity?" But it will not be always so; a few years more, and what then? Oh, follow me to the throne of the Holy God; come into the presence of Him Who tries the very hearts and reins, Who hath purer eyes than to behold iniquity. Stand there with all your works, your virtues, your pride, your presumption. See the heavens passing away with a great noise, and the elements melting with fervent heat! See this Christ Whom thou hast rejected, on the throne of judgment: no longer meek and lowly, but clothed with glory and girded about with power, ready to execute justice, and to destroy the despisers of His gospel. See His elect gathered from the four winds; His angels veiling their faces; His saints casting their crowns at the feet of Him Who *was* dead, but Who is alive for evermore! See heaven united in praising His loving-kindness, whilst the rebellious wail because of Him, and smite their hands upon their breasts. See yet again Satan the accuser standing in the presence of your Judge. Now come forward, step forth into the midst. Fear not. What! don't you know that you are righteous, that you are upright, that you are pure, that you are honest. Haven't you said as much a thousand times over? Why then this deadly pallor? Why this confusion of face, this horrible dread carrying away your very soul? You—all of you—sinners without Christ—how comes it that the mere conjecture of such things, the mere word of a fellow-sinner describing them, fills you with unutterable dismay. . . .'"

At these words, a movement as of derision ran through the congregation; and when the preacher left the pulpit he strode through the crowd like a soldier drummed out by his comrades, or a criminal marching to execution.

In the present day, those who would have resented the preacher's words, who would have cowered with dismay under the terrible irony that accompanied them, or shrunk from the pointed application which his apocalyptical imagery conveyed, would have contented themselves simply with avoiding his ministry for the future; and that because men are at length beginning to learn that most elementary, though most sacred of truths, that religion is a personal concern. At the time, however, of which I am writing, the prevalent idea, not in Geneva only, but throughout the Continent generally, was that of a national religion, a religion whose institutions were to be submitted to in such sort as not to aggress on the individual conscience. Under such circumstances, the religious public felt justified in looking for deferential consideration from the organ of their so-called religious system, or, in other words, from each of their preachers. Meanwhile, when national Churches have reached the climax of extinguishing the sense of duty and obligation in the individual members of their Churches, their days are numbered; and secession, with all that the word implies, is the inevitable result of so false a position, a truth which, even in the present day, we do well to remember.

But to return to the events of the 8th March 1817, and to the sermon of that day, a sermon characterised by De Goltz as an eloquent, powerful, and singularly lucid exposition of gospel truth.

His own parents, says Haldane's biographer, deserted him. His wife even was extremely distressed. Each look she gave him seemed to reproach him with the destruction of the dreams of the past—the shipwreck of the bright hopes of the future. He returned home in his robes, followed by the scorn of the populace, and borne down by its weight. But as he crossed the threshold of his door, and was about to retire into his study, he caught sight of the dignified figure and benevolent face of Robert Haldane, who exclaimed, as he shook him warmly by the hand, "Thank God, the gospel has again been preached in Geneva;" and added, "You will be a martyr to the truth in this place," meaning "a witness."

"I shall never forget," says Haldane, "the signs of amazement and indignation which I beheld in the countenances of some of those who were present during that sermon." Of this the young minister himself had speedy proof in a visit, the next day, from the Pastor Chenevière, who came to implore him, in the name of the clerical body, "to change his doctrine on account of the mischief that might ensue from preaching that good works were not required as the procuring cause of salvation." "Such is my firm belief," he answered, and closed the controversy; and from that time all the city pulpits, and most of those in the country, were firmly shut against him.

But it required more than human power to close his lips. Burning with a holy zeal to proclaim to his fellow citizens the truths to which he owed his own spiritual life, he became all the more convinced, as he himself said, that the joy which filled his own soul would yet be communicated to the hearts of those who should hear him; and that they, too, delighting in the blessed tidings of salvation by faith in Jesus Christ, would accept it heartily, and repudiate the unscriptural figments of human righteousness.

And yet he had, by no means, contemplated at this time a secession from the National Church, as was evident from his refusing, in the month of July in that very year, sundry brilliant offers made to him on condition of his forming a congregation of his own, and becoming pastor of an independent body.* Still less were his religious requirements satisfied by those small meetings, which had been a subject of debate for two or three years. " I attended one of them," he said, " and was by no means pleased with the result. Too much sensation—too little truth. And those of my own family, who had spoken

---

* I quote once more, on this special point, the testimony of Mr Bruen, as I find it in a letter of his to Dr Mason, dated 7th Nov. 1817, touching the events of which he was a witness in Geneva (Memoirs of Dr Mason, p. 454.)

" While Malan suffered in this way, he was incessantly pressed to separate himself entirely from the Church, and to be at the head of a small number who had left the communion. Motives were presented to him in every shape, especially in that most likely to affect a man of such ardent feelings. . . . . I cannot but rejoice that Malan has not joined them. Although with his energy, eloquence, and piety, things would at present have borne a very different aspect, yet we must doubt whether, with so many pastors decidedly orthodox in the Church (there are five avowedly so), this measure of *dernier ressort* was necessary. If the question were, whether Malan should preach at all or not, it were easy to answer ; but this interdict may be temporary. Some think it will be so ; and the ground taken by its authors and defenders always goes on this supposition— and it does not extend beyond the limits of our Canton—so that Malan has within a few days been preaching at Bern and Neufchatel. To have joined in that separation would have been to shut himself from all connection with the Helvetic Churches, and from a large and promising field of usefulness. . . . . As to the Church of Geneva in particular, there is a great deal to be said for, as well as against, breaking communion with it. To be obliged to acknowledge the ministrations of Arian pastors, who hold and exercise rights most contradictory to Christian principles and liberty, is deeply distressing. . . . . If there had been here a man of Calvin's power to organise a separation of the precious from the vile, and shake off at once, with the heretics, those shackles which bind religion to the state ; if the orthodox could have been closely united or brought to this, it had been a glorious result," &c.

to me about them, I discouraged from being present at them; saying that I did not approve of the doctrine taught, or the hymns sung."

It was at this time that certain views of baptism, imparted from England, began to find favour in the Church of the "Bourg de Four."* By and by it will be seen that, at the moment when he was on the point of embracing them, he turned round and denounced them publicly.

And yet, notwithstanding all this, and that the divergence between Malan and the rest of the clergy was on a question strictly dogmatic, that body had come to a firm resolve to suffer none of their Churches to be infected with his teaching. And on the 3d May 1817 they issued, in their capacity as an ecclesiastical authority, the following "Regulation :"—

"The clergy of Geneva, in a spirit of humility, peace, and Christian love, convinced that the present circumstances of the Church committed to their care, call for measures of a wise and prudential character, determines—without attempting to prejudge the questions involved, and without seeking to trench on liberty of opinion—to exact of all candidates to the ministry, and of all ministers seeking to exercise their functions in the Church of Geneva, a pledge of which the following shall be the substance :—

"We bind ourselves, so long as we continue to reside and to preach in the Canton of Geneva, to abstain from dogmatising, either through an entire discourse or portion of it,—

* The name given to the congregation of dissenters which had just seceded to these meetings.

" 1. On the manner whereby the divine and human natures are united in the person of Jesus Christ;

" 2. On original sin;

" 3. On the mode of the operations of grace, or on the nature and degree of its efficacy;

" 4. On predestination.

" We bind ourselves also not to attack, in any public discourse, the opinions of any individual minister on these points.

" And, lastly, should we be led to speak on any of these subjects, to do so calmly, and avoiding expressions foreign to Holy Scripture, and confining ourselves as closely as possible to the language of the Bible."

Such was the tenor of the Regulation of the 3d May, which we may confidently style the beginning of the religious troubles of Protestantism in Geneva.

At first sight this step would appear to have been taken merely with a view of calming the excitement that was beginning to make itself apparent. On looking at it a little closer, however, more especially in the light of subsequent events, it will be clear that everything turned on the construction placed upon its language by the authorities, and the way in which they employed it. We are not a little surprised, after a closer examination, to notice that the doctrines which, according to its stipulations, are to be announced in the words of Scripture only, are spoken of in the same breath as " individual opinions," or as " views." Evidently those who had had a hand in drawing up this document confounded dogma and faith. Thanks to that confusion, they qualified themselves, as it should please them, either to force dogma to give way before what they would call the sacred rights of faith, or should the interests of the latter only be concerned, to represent the claim they urged as the inopportune affirmation of an effete dogmatism. Events soon proved for which of these two contingencies this Regulation had been framed.

At all events, none could assert that its main object was to prohibit the putting forth of theological subtleties from the pulpit. Such an idea never occurred to any one. Indeed, the scientific questions these points imply were not only new to the religious public of Geneva, but the clergy themselves on both sides were entirely wanting in that peculiar scientific lore which has a tendency to create in certain minds an enthusiasm for pure theological controversy. It was the fact of our Lord's divinity that was being disputed, and that alone.

As a melancholy result of that spirit of tergiversation and disingenuousness—that fettering of opinion and craft of policy which Rousseau had already satirised in his caustic fashion among the clergy of his own country in the preceding century—this Regulation was only quoted for the purpose of excluding from the pulpit, not the indiscreet proclamation of what would have been a mere theological dogmatism, but men of mark, of ability, and zeal, whose only aim it was to plant in the bosom of a "Christianised deism" the eternal verities of the gospel.

At first the Regulation was kept a secret. When it had been originally proposed to the ecclesiastical authorities in the Venerable Assembly, three of them refused their assent. As for Malan, being only a minister,* and not one of

---

* *i.e.*, a preacher without office. The *Compagnie* is the assembly of the pastors, viz., of the clergymen *in office.—Note by Translator.*

the " body," he only heard of it indirectly, and received at once an assurance from the majority of his brethren (he was the senior of the ministers and entitled to act in their name) that they would unite with him in at once protesting against it.

As soon as the issuing of the Regulation had reached the ears of M. Cellerier de Satigny—a man universally and most justly beloved and esteemed—he hastened to my father and implored him to abstain from any immediate protest. In a letter in reply, dated 20th May, my father says :—" You cannot think what anxiety your arguments have caused me. They have tended greatly to modify any expressions I might use on this question, but my main conviction remains unaltered. I have an unconquerable aversion to any temporising course, or to the appearance even of failing, by my silence, in my duty to God and the pure faith of the gospel. My brother," he added in conclusion, " is it not possible to make no mention of such an engagement ?"

Meanwhile, on the 22d of May, the day of the annual conference of ministers, my father, who had to be present on the occasion, was so deeply moved that my mother, (who, I may mention in passing, had for some time come to share in his views), being similarly affected, put a paper into his hands containing these words :—" This is a day wherein you should give glory to God ! Abide by your vows to Him, and fear nothing !"

The Regulation having been read and presented to the ministers for their acceptance, Malan, who had received the thanks of the meeting at its commencement for his teaching at the college, wanted to reply. He was refused permission, however, and that, too, in a very decided fashion. Eventually, he had to leave the assembly without being able to do more than declare that he would never submit to its requirements. As for those who had promised to join him in such a protest, they remained silent.

On that day week he addressed a letter to the Assembly, in which, while he expressly stated that he could not submit to their will in the matter of the Regulation, he at the same time gave them to understand that he was prepared to follow their guidance in everything appertaining to the management of the Church in non-spiritual things, and concluded by asking permission to preach on the 8th of June.

Whereupon the moderator replied that his protest was returned to him, that he could not be suffered to preach unless he complied with the Regulation, adding that the clerical body would regard a renewal of that request as a virtual submission. What followed I will record in my father's words :—

"From that time, every effort was made to convince me that this Regulation did not touch upon matters of conscience. Those who had prepared it, I was reminded, were the same friends, the same pastors, that I had known and honoured from my childhood. No one knows what distress it caused me to refuse compliance, or the anxiety with which I pondered every possible method of reconciling their wishes and my duty. On the other hand, I was then but an infant in the faith, a new convert, and almost staggered at my own apparent audacity in opposing the Venerable Assembly.

"Then it was that I looked away for a moment from my Bible and the will of my God to the concern of my friends. As a natural result, and by their advice, I consented to apply for permission to preach, assuring the Moderator that my sermon would in no way violate the stipulations of the Regulation."

The application was not granted, however, and Malan renewed it two months afterwards in a long letter to the Assembly, dated the 1st August. It ran as follows:—

"Remember, gentlemen, that I am more than thirty years old; remember how, during that time, I have diligently followed the course of study prescribed for the ministry; that I have received holy orders at your hands; that I have acquitted myself as a minister of Christ for more than six years, without reproach. Remember, too, that the ministry of the gospel has ever been my chosen work, and that I have ever held myself as belonging heart and soul to the Church, and especially to the Church of Geneva. Consider also, venerable brethren, that I have never preached any doctrine or advocated any opinion that was not strictly evangelical; and that, if I find it utterly impossible now to comply with your wishes in this matter of the Regulation, it is because I cannot be disloyal to those dictates of my conscience which you yourselves have taught me to respect and obey. I have been accused of wishing to secede from the Church; yet, God knows, the bare thought of secession is foreign to my soul. My reverend brethren, I am no sectarian; my only desire, the one wish of my heart, is to prove by faithful preaching of the gospel that I have not been unwisely entrusted with that sacred ministry which, by the grace of God, I have received at your hands."

He then goes on to say, in reference to an appeal addressed to him from abroad, and also to those offers to which reference has already been made, "Though I were besought to discharge by other means that ministry of which your adverse decision would seek to deprive me, I would pointedly refuse, until I had again had recourse, and had recourse in vain, to your charity—or, shall I say, to your justice.

" I implore you, therefore, by the peace which should reign in the Church of Christ, to suffer me to exercise my ministry without let or hindrance, and thus to put an end to the cavils and blasphemies of ignorant and wicked men."

On referring to certain expressions in this letter in the year 1823, my father did not scruple to censure them as smacking of a carnal sensibility, and to point out the hidden thirst for approbation lurking in them. It was not even read, however, in the Assembly, as the writer withdrew it at the instigation of the Moderator, and postponed all further action on the subject, while the dispute was pending between them, for more than a year.

Meanwhile, the movements of Dissent were by no means arrested in Geneva, and, to quote my father's testimony, "the blows which were aimed at the faithful, only served to strengthen the stakes of the reviving Church." The "Petite Eglise"* was set up, the Lord's Supper was administered in it, and the clergy began to take note of its

---

* "La petite Eglise" was the first name given to the dissenters of the Bourg de Four.

existence. Notwithstanding their undoubted influence, the magistracy gave reiterated proof of their determination to maintain religious liberty. As for my father, he gave himself up entirely to his college work, and carefully abstained from any act of adhesion to the new community. When, however, he found that, in consequence of the proceedings of the clerical body, no pulpit was accessible to him in Geneva, he began in June 1817 to preach at Ferney Voltaire, a village three miles from the city, on the French frontiers. Impelled, at the same time, by the constraining desire to spread abroad the knowledge of the faith he held so precious, he established a Sunday school in his college class-room, which numbered some two hundred and fifty young people. Five months had scarcely elapsed before the ecclesiastical authorities deprived him of the use of the class-room for that purpose, and the school was broken up for a year, till it was re-opened by my father in the year 1818 in his own house, which he had purchased in the Faubourg du Pré l'Evêque. The next move of the authorities was to recommend the pastors to do all in their power to keep the youth of their parishes from attending that school. In spite, however, of this opposition, my father soon had a hundred and twenty pupils—sixty boys and sixty girls, or upwards. It was for the use of these classes that he published, in 1818 and 1824, two little catechisms, with seventy-one questions and answers, under the title " The Little Christian Boy," and "The Little Christian Girl." These catechisms are models of simplicity, clearness, and systematic arrangement. They were soon afterwards translated into English.

In 1816, he had established an asylum for outcast girls,

which he maintained by means of funds collected by him in Geneva and abroad, and in the direction of which he exhibited, as might easily be proved by instances, the marvellous energy and charity of his spirit. Of these unhappy ones, rescued by Malan himself from the purlieus of the city, and even from a higher grade, some were so benefited under the discipline of their new home, and derived such advantage from the kindly and judicious administration to which they were subjected, that the majority of them were not only restored to society, but of these not a few became denizens of a better, a heavenly kingdom. In a certain English volume, I met once with an account of a visit which the author, in company with my father, made to two of these women. He speaks in the passage to which I refer of " that Israelite, indeed, to whom, notwithstanding the calumnies heaped upon him, so many anxious souls are looking amongst those who desire the regeneration of Geneva." As for the special work to which we have been referring, he says that Malan's ministry in this particular had been sufficiently blessed to give him abundant encouragement to persevere. After years of prayer, enteaty, and longing, he had seen some of them bowed down like Mary at the feet of Jesus. And then follow details in proof of these assertions.

In this asylum my father preached every Sunday After he had been dismissed from his collegiate post, it slipped out of his hands, and soon ceased to exist. Some years ago, one of the established clergy of Geneva founded it anew, and the fact of his having done so, as well as the way in which he did it, was a special gratification to my father at the close of his life.

E

It would appear from his notes, that in this same year, 1817, he devoted himself almost entirely to studying the New Testament, taking it with him wherever he went, that he might avail himself of every possible opportunity of reading it.

A letter written to my mother from Chamouni, where he was staying at the time with a Christian friend, will give the best idea of his state of mind at this period. After having described his sensations on visiting the "Mer de Glace," he goes on to say, "We have had most earnest Christian intercourse with with old Balmat, one of M. de Saussure's guides. How blessed a thing it is thus to consecrate all our enjoyments! How sweet to walk in communion with the Creator of all these glories, our personal Saviour, Who hath loved us with such unutterable love!" Then, in reference to some pious English people whom he had met, he adds, "What thanks, my dear one, are due to our gracious Father for giving me already so many Christian friends. Alas! He had to choose them for me amongst foreigners! My countrymen do not know what it is to live in Christ. I never enjoyed a trip like this before. It is true that it is the first time I ever travelled with a kindred spirit, with one whose soul cleaves to what I feel to be beyond everything in worth." Then, after a few lines of poetry in which he lifts up his soul in view of the magnificence around him, to "the hope of eternal life," he adds others on the subject of "heart-union," bearing upon the "Hotel de l'Union," which was then being built.

At Geneva, however, he felt very keenly his exclusion from the pulpit. Meanwhile, he was urged on all sides to submit to the Regulation, as bearing only on questions of

Church discipline, and not of faith. In the month of January 1818 more especially, he tells us that many of the clergy pressed him anew to follow the example of his brethren who had accepted it in a pacific spirit, with no other end in view than the maintenance of peace. Among these, the venerable Cellerier made every effort to convince my father of his own view that the obnoxious edict was purely a question of ecclesiastical rule.

"God only knows," he writes, "how sorely I was beset. I, a young minister, as yet so slightly grounded in the knowledge of the Word, and entreated so earnestly to yield to the demonstrations of zeal and attachment which poured in from every quarter." In a letter addressed to one who had been the most vehement in his representation, he goes into the whole question, and shows him how impossible he felt it, whatever might be the sacrifice, to prove unfaithful to his convictions. "I act according to my faith," he writes, "without judging or anathematising any one, but believing that it is the truth. My first concern as a minister of God should be to preach the truths in question."

M. Cellerier, however, in no way slackened his efforts, and endeavoured at the same time to induce the Assembly to put such an interpretation on the Regulation as to make it evident that it pertained exclusively to discipline. As soon as he thought he had succeeded in this endeavour, he paid a fresh visit to my father, adjuring him, in the name of the Saviour, and in the interests of Christian love, no longer to refuse his assent. Then he escorted him to the presence of a deputation of three pastors who had been commissioned to interpret to him the real meaning of the Regulation.

My father assured them that he had either misunderstood the document, or that it had been considerably modified, so much so that he had no further hesitation, after the explanations which had been afforded him, to declare that he saw nothing in the way of his assent.

It was under the influence of these feelings that he wrote to the Assembly on the 6th of May, close upon the time of the great religious festivals, a letter which breathes all the impulsive nature of his feelings. "I have sinned against your authority, venerable brethren," he says, " impelled by an unhappy narrow-mindedness, very different from the wisdom which cometh down from above. If you have wronged me in anything, the wrong has been so insignificant that I dare not recall it. Mine towards you has been so great that I may well desire that the past should be forgotten. I would fain assure you, brethren, in the presence of this happy change of feeling, that my future bearing shall be all that you could desire. My conduct shall be ruled by your authority, and if I cannot give my cordial approval to a Regulation which runs counter to my principles, I am prepared at all events to submit to it in the interests of peace. Yes, brethren, brotherly love is more precious than the triumph of opinions, however lawful. I have felt this keenly. I am ready to prove it."

My father was the first to acknowledge that, however much he might have felt all that this letter contained at the time he wrote it, it was nevertheless rather the gushing effusion of a young disciple, than the calm and judicious utterance of a minister of God. He did not hesitate to detect in it sentiment rather than true charity, and to affirm that he displayed in it a greater eagerness to please those in power, and to pacify their minds, than to guard the interests of the truth.

Meanwhile, this letter, in which we can only trace the impression of a somewhat impulsive record of generous and confiding feeling, was unsparingly quoted against him. It was taken as proof of a vacillating character, and even as a lapse from the honest maintenance of his principles. It was nothing more, however, as he acknowledged afterwards, than the product of a too hasty eagerness to yield to natural affections, which ought never to sway the judgment of a minister of God. Moreover, he always felt, in common with all his friends, that, thanks to his impetuosity, his confidence, as De Goltz assures us, had been taken unfair advantage of. At all events, those to whom he had written so unreservedly, soon gave him to understand that this was the case.

Meanwhile, in consequence of his letter, he was re-admitted at once to the pulpit of Geneva, nor did he hesitate to avail himself of the restored permission, preaching twice in the months of May and August.

The extraordinary sensation occasioned at the time by these two sermons, which to-day would pass unnoticed except for their strength, clearness, and eloquence of diction—the fact that men who meant to be in earnest pretended that they saw in them an attempt to introduce into the pulpit theological "subtleties"—all this shows how utterly the gospel message, however simply delivered, had become an unknown sound in Geneva.

And what is still more surprising is the displeasure which these same sermons created in the Assembly itself. "After their delivery," writes my father, "instead of that personal interest and kindly feeling which so many of the pastors had shown me, I experienced nothing but coldness, reproaches, and false accusations." One cannot help asking whether in this struggle the Assembly did not, after all, see a mere question of supremacy or competency. However that may be, a decree was issued forthwith, absolutely interdicting Malan from pulpit ministrations. A request to be heard in his own defence was denied him. Sentence was passed. They even refused to accept the offer he made them to take cognisance of his discourses before he preached them; and a decision was arrived at on the 9th of August, that no application from him would even be admitted for debate unless it were supported by nine members of the Assembly.

Nor did matters stop here. While Malan spared no efforts to induce them to reconsider their decision, the academical "Compagnie," a mere branch of the "Compagnie des Pasteurs," addressed him in significant terms in reference to his college teaching. On the 24th of August, a fortnight after the last prohibition had been issued, he was called upon to undergo a cross-examination in the presence of the rector and moderator. He remained firm throughout, and in the month of September had to write to them that his trust was in the Lord Jesus, Who would provide for him and his (he had six children at the time), if his means of livelihood were taken from him. This leads us to inquire as to what was the new kind of teaching that appeared so reprehensible to the authorities. We find it detailed by himself in the letter to Mr T. Campbell, quoted above. Here is what he says upon the subject:—

" When I was a *Christian* only in name, I was guided by the maxims of the world, and, like it, was in all things deceived. At that period I was a great admirer of pagan philosophy. The image of virtue, as enshrined by the men of this world, was the idol which I worshipped. Dignity, elevation of sentiment, sublimity of thought, energy, generosity, glory and honour, were my favourite expressions. The name of the Lord did not rest on my lips, and my heart was a stranger to the sanctifying influence of the Holy Spirit. That man appeared to me to have attained his highest destination, of whom it could be said, *He is the greatest, the wisest, and most virtuous of his countrymen.* I imagined that education had no other end than to form good citizens and great men; and it was my highest ambition to render my pupils more distinguished than those of any other school, and to hear them eulogised.

" What man, impressed with the fear of God, does not tremble at beholding those great manufactories of worldly education—those workshops of *reason* and *virtue*, where, for views and feelings, the intelligence is reduced to its own imaginings—where the heart, to the exclusion of the Creator, is merely directed to creatures and creation. Yet this was the plan on which I conducted my school. *Emulation*, that is to say, pride— unbounded pride—was the moving principle. Disgrace and punishment were the portion of the idle, praise and reward were bestowed on the diligent. And it was at this period, my dear friend, that I was most regarded as an intelligent and valuable master; that the friends of my scholars 'united with my superiors in commending the rare talents I displayed in my method with my scholars.

" It pleased God, about this time, to enlighten and convert my soul. The children now appeared to me in quite another character. Hitherto I had only regarded them as members of human society, as men not arrived at manhood. I henceforth considered them as immortal beings, and consequently as destined to be citizens of heaven, or heirs of wrath; and this solemn consideration produced a complete revolution in my principles of instruction.

" The innate rectitude of man, his equal bias to good and evil, the infallibility of his understanding in the pursuit and discovery of truth, his capability of attaining infinite perfection, his moral ability for everything noble and virtuous,—in a word, the maxims of the wise, reechoed and admired in every age and every school, were presented to my mind in their true colours. I learned from the Bible that God, Who knows what this wisdom is, has pronounced it *folly.*

" You may well conceive, my much respected friend, that this entire revolution in my sentiments must have produced as great a change in the education and management of my pupils. I thought it my duty to give them the truth just as God has revealed it to man by His Son. The *Holy Bible* was introduced into my school. Each child had a copy of his own; mine was always upon my table; and this blessed book of heavenly wisdom became our treasury, from which we daily drew forth true knowledge.

" What a change, in a short period, was thus effected in the economy of the school, by means of a few just principles inculcated in the minds of the children! I particularly impressed upon them the necessity of having their hearts and understandings renewed by the Spirit of God, before they could acquire any real wisdom or solid virtue, —that is to say, any holiness.

"So much friendly intercourse and uninterrupted confidence prevailed thereby between my scholars and myself, that we seemed rather to be friends and relations than master and pupils. I told them their faults, but I did not palliate my own, and I encouraged my young friends to admonish me with all confidence."

He then proceeds to illustrate the thorough respectful, and, at the same time, candid way in which his boys one day took him at his word. I quote it as he related it in 1842 to some friends in Holland.

"At that time I had the bad habit of saying, '*Mon Dieu, oui! mon Dieu, non!*' and my pupils imitated it. Accordingly, I said to them one day, 'Let us make a bargain; I'll take you up whenever you say that, and you'll take me up whenever I do.' It was agreed, and I kept strict watch over my words, from a desire certainly not to commit the fault, but from a desire also, I must confess, not to be pulled up by my lads. But one day, after I had been speaking impulsively to one of them, suddenly the whole school rose up and remained standing in silence. 'What is the matter, my boys?' I asked. Very, very respectfully the senior answered, 'You have just said, "Mon Dieu, oui," sir.'" My father thanked them, and, kneeling down with them, prayed to be forgiven, and delivered from that sin; and, "thank God," he adds, "from that day to this I have never, I believe, been guilty of the same offence."

But to return to his letter to Mr Campbell. He continues the subject of it by relating to his friend the struggles evinced by many of his pupils with the word of truth. "It assailed their pride," he says, "but it was seldom that the love of their God and Saviour failed where the terrors of the law proved entirely ineffectual; and to that love I constantly appealed. I often prayed with them, but I never judged or denounced them. As a rule, I asserted my authority as little as possible, that I might make the authority of God and His Word their great standard. My school was an evangelical theocracy."

Having thus unfolded thoroughly the new principles by which he was actuated, he proceeds to indicate the results which followed from putting them in practice. This was shown, he urges, in the startling difference between a boy brought up on a worldly system, with only the glory of the world to stimulate his ambitions in duty, and a Christian student comparing his present attainments with what his God and Saviour would have him to be. The latter estimate had growth not by a worldly standard, but by the perfect stature of the fulness that is in Christ, by which, though still a child, he must be tried.

So that it is not the emulation which the world employs and admires, that urges the pious disciple of Christ to press forward in the career of study and duty; it is the *good pleasure of his Lord.* He walks at liberty, he does more than strictly follow the narrow path of obedience, he goes before it, because he loves Him Whom he serves, and delights in His holy and blessed will.

"During the two or three years that I adopted this plan with my scholars, I universally found that a child whom the Lord has enlightened is as capable of comprehending the eternal truths of the word of life, as any science which can be communicated to him; and that the Word of God imparts an elevation, a dignity, an energy, which he cannot receive from any worldly motive."

He caused to be written up in large characters on the walls of his school those words of Holy Scripture: "To whomsoever much is given, of them shall much be required;" and it was by that text that he roused the boys to diligence. Moreover, he tells us that attention paid by each of the pupils to his own proper work, and kindliest conduct towards the weaker and younger, had entirely superseded the old spirit of envy and rivalry, while, at the same time, the less gifted among them ran no further risk of being discouraged. After having adduced several striking illustrations of this fact, he goes on to tell his correspondent how one day the whole class came to him in a body without his having been in the smallest degree made aware of their intention, and restored to him certain silver medals which he had made for them some time back as rewards of conspicuous merit, beseeching him to take them back and sell them for the benefit of a collection for a benevolent purpose.

I thought it best to give the above narrative in my father's own words, as not only placing the facts themselves before us, but also in the particular light in which he regarded them.

"All this time," so the letter resumes, "the book of God was not established noiselessly among the books of the world. Many voices were raised in protest against the 'innovation!'" Not indeed that it must be supposed that my father, carried away by his ardour, had introduced into the school a system of religious teaching not contemplated by statute. For such teaching was not merely part of the allotted work of each master, but my father was so far from exhibiting any rash zeal, that he had been the first to request the school authorities — the Compagnie Académique and his brother masters—to sanction the introduction of the present system, by which their teaching is intrusted to the specially appointed chaplain. What was objected to was not the fact of the religious instruction, but his "method" of imparting it. Now, apart from the Christian spirit and earnestness which breathed through it, and which they could scarcely have made the subject of an official censure, his "method" differed in no other respect from the plan he had previously followed, except in the fact that he had introduced the Bible into the class, though not until he had first obtained the consent of the principal.

He was not, however, left without occasional encouragement in his work. "Shortly after my conversion," he writes, "an aged and very worthy pastor, who visited the school from time to time, said to me once, on going away, 'How thankful I am to see you working here like a true missionary!'" Then having assured him that he never forgot his work in his private prayers, he adds, 'From that day I felt I could never come to my class without first saying to myself, Whatever you are in your work here, be a true missionary!'"

This circumstance shows him as already being what his entire after career proved him to be, not only a man of prayer, but also one who up to the very end was eminently a *missionary*. His true character appears also in the effect produced upon him by the opposition of which he found himself to be the object. "As for me," he continues, "I recognised in all this that the work was not of the world, and I strengthened myself in the Lord."

And much he needed that strength and that reliance. In spite of the continued success of his teaching, in spite of the increasing attachment felt towards him by his boys and their parents, the academical authorities,—after long discussion, in which, says a contemporary, (Schichedantz,) Malan exhibited the utmost moderation and frankness,—decided, without regard to the numberless representations made in his favour, to deprive him of the post he had occupied for nine years.

Setting aside mere idle pretexts, on which those who devised them did not venture to insist, the great reason which they alleged was that Malan had introduced the Bible into his class as a text-book, and that, though he declared in the most explicit terms not to have even had the thought of opposing the catechism in teaching his pupils, he would not bind himself to observe in his religious instruction the precise terms of that manual."

"This decree of the Compagnie Académique," writes M. Bost, a year afterwards, "required the sanction of the executive council of the republic. Malan handed in an appeal. He proved in that remarkable document (Schichedantz calls it a model of temperate and modest argument,) that 'for this rule to be binding it ought to be backed up either by some known law, or by some ecclesiastical decree in force, or by some established regulation, or else by some agreement previously entered into with himself, and binding on his conscience.' After having demonstrated that none of these supports existed, he replies as follows to the objection, that such was the good pleasure of his lawful superiors :—

"'But, Right Honourable Sirs, leaving out of the question for a moment the theological point which lies at the root of the matter, and restricting myself entirely to a matter of right and fact, apart from the consideration that there is a God above, before Whose supreme authority in His direction of my conduct in religious matters, all earthly rule must give way, and even while I admit that the school authorities on the inspection of studies have undoubted right to lay down at their pleasure this or that rule for imparting secular teaching—this argument by no means holds good with reference to spiritual instruction. Here they cease to possess arbitrary power; and even though I acknowledged their good pleasure as an authority exacting my conscientious submission, how am I to ascertain it in sufficiently precise terms to rule my system by its stipulations ?

"'Surely it will never be maintained that such an authority in a matter of supreme importance resides in the doubtful suggestions, the uncertain and often contradictory opinions, of the scattered individual members of a public body. I am well assured indeed, for they have said as much in my hearing, that some of them deny the divinity of our Lord Jesus Christ, and original sin; others, the efficacy of divine grace; and the greater number of them, a free salvation. These are points about which I have heard them disputing amongst themselves; so that, though they may constitute in themselves an authoritative corporation, yet forasmuch as they can adduce no definite precise authentic official declaration of united sentiment, ought I to seek to please one of them at the expense of the other; or renounce the collective convictions of my faith in favour of the vacillating theories of superiors, who rather allow men to guess at their opinions than receive them openly from their lips? Had they set before me some known confession of faith, setting forth such and such dogmas proved by them, and given to me as a guide for my teaching—my adhesion being obtained to its contents—and had I afterwards departed from it, I should most assuredly have been greatly to blame. But as that never was the case, is not the case now, but, on the contrary, the Venerable Assembly has expressly discarded all such confessions, have I not been, I respectfully submit, am I not, in the right, after the spirit of our glorious Reformation, in selecting for myself that confession which seemed to me to be the most scriptural — the confession of the Helvetian Churches, admitted and sworn to throughout our confederate Protestant cantons, and to which, in better days, Geneva herself had subscribed?

"'Moreover, is it not rather inconsistent on their part thus to renounce all positive confessions, and at the same time to cashier one of their masters who, in consequence of this very act of theirs, finds himself absolutely free to teach according to the faith, simply because his method of dealing with Holy Scripture does not happen to accord with the views of some of his superiors, who, nevertheless, have established no rule in the matter? Let the Compagnie state their mind clearly. Let them tell me authoritatively what they would have me teach, what are the dogmas they would repudiate, to what confession of faith they would tie me down. This they can do if they like; but so long as they think it expedient to maintain their present discreet silence on this point, they cannot righteously reproach me with ignorance of it.' He then concludes by representing that, 'to allow the decree of the Compagnie to stand upon no other authority but the mere will and pleasure of that body, would be to introduce arbitrary law, and set might and oppression over right and justice.' "

Passing on to the objection that his teaching was beyond the comprehension of his pupils, he recalls the attention of the magistrates whom he is addressing to the instruction they themselves had received in their childhood, and what prevailed, at the time he was speaking, in other Protestant countries. He communicates his own schoolroom experience, and pointing out the obvious difference between the case of those children of 'orthodox families,' and those whose parents showed themselves indifferent as far as the doctrine of the gospel was concerned, he appeals to them to decide whether the day had actually arrived in which those blessed and eternal verities could injure those whom they were intended to save.

In a letter to one of the clergy, published at the same time, my father speaks still more plainly :—

"I do assure you, were it only a question of my individual right, however certain I might be of the integrity of my motives, I would not hesitate a moment to acquiesce in their judgment. I would submit willingly to the charge of rashness, precipitation, and even culpability; and I would renounce utterly all attempts at self-defence, out of sole regard for their credit and reputation. If any steps I may have taken, any words of mine, my mode of argument, any collateral inferences of mine, have wounded in any way either propriety or charity, it has been by no intention of mine; and were this proved to me, I would hasten to repair my error. As touching this point, sir, I am ready to make all public allowance. For the form I gave to my protest, I alone am responsible; any defects in it, put to my account exclusively; hence it is for me alone to eliminate them. But as for the main question at issue, as for the principles and doctrine involved, it is not I alone who am concerned here; it is not for me to give way in anything, as though these were mere personal matters. 'It is required of stewards, that a man be found faithful.' And what am I in my capacity of a Christian master but a steward of the truth of God committed to my keeping?"

My father foresaw, however, that the steps he had taken would be productive of no good result. A letter which he addressed to the rector of the academy shows the spirit in which he contemplated this possibility.

"Let the venerable Campagnie Académique," he writes, "act as their wisdom and prudence dictate. Should they decide to deprive me of the post entrusted to me by another authority, and confirmed to me by themselves, I should hold their resolve to be the result of the sovereign and most gracious will of Him Who directs all the events of this world. Such a decree would deprive me of my only means of support for my family. I shall find myself without any apparent resources; but in perfect reliance, through divine grace, on my adorable Master, to Whose gracious keeping I commit all my affairs, I shall reverently and joyfully submit to all His wisdom may ordain."

F

Umbrage has been taken at the word "hero" applied to him by De Goltz. No one, however, reading these letters could help acknowledging that it was not without reason that the writer of them, in respect of the spirit that animated him, was compared to Luther at Worms. Of course there was at stake only the rejection of an unknown schoolmaster from a post of public instruction in a small city, but, at the same time, be it remembered, it is not the circumstances that invest it, which, in themselves, constitute the heroism of a believer's faith.

Fifteen days after, his appeal had been lodged with the council of state, on the 4th of November. That body confirmed the judgment of the Compagnie Académique, a decision which was at once intimated to my father on the 6th of the same month, without any, even the most ordinary, marks of courtesy and consideration, which, under the circumstances, might have been exhibited. He was told on the Friday evening that his class would be undertaken by his successor on the Monday morning. He took leave of his boys by dictating to them "Rules for the Guidance of a Young Christian," and withdrew to a house which he had just purchased from his father in the "Pré l'Evêque."

Feeling confident from the first that his appeal against the sentence of deprivation (most unjust as he always felt it to be) would certainly fail, while my mother herself, at this sorrowful crisis, failed to rise to his standard of unquestioning reliance, he never suffered himself to be cast down, but set to work at once to face the difficulties of the position to which he had been reduced.

Nor did He, in Whom he trusted, fail His faithful servant? Let the reader mark the testimony of a well-known and much-esteemed servant of God upon this point. "Malan's enemies did all in their power to plunge that good man, with his wife and numerous family, into the deepest penury, into absolute destitution. At this critical moment, a few friends, chiefly English and Würtemburgers, stepped forward, and, partly by a loan, and partly by a respectful present, in which the givers felt themselves the most obliged, saved this oppressed and faithful servant of Christ from sinking into the extremity of distress. From that time, M. Malan has laboured to support himself and his large family by taking pupils."

I have only just been made cognisant of this circumstance, but my father mentioned to me an incident of the same nature which occurred at the close of his tenure of his office, which I will proceed to relate.

When he was on the point of purchasing the house in the Pré l'Evêque, which he had previously rented from my grandfather, he suddenly found himself, by the fault of a third person, unable to pay the money on the prescribed day. Meanwhile, it was absolutely essential that his father should have it. After a night of deep anxiety and fervent prayer, he betook himself to his schoolroom on the morning of the day in question. While he was giving the usual lessons, and was engaged in secret prayer to God to show him a way of escape from his distress, he saw a stranger at the class-room door, who made him a sign to come out. The visitor proved to be an Englishman who happened to be passing through Geneva; and though he was not personally acquainted with my father, took the greatest interest in all that had befallen him. He then went on to tell him that he had heard of the embarrassment in which he was placed through no fault of his, and begged to be allowed to advance the necessary money. My father received it as though it had come from God Himself. He was soon enabled to repay it, and the kindly assistance laid the foundation of a lasting friendship.

This circumstance, in itself so purely ordinary, did not fail to produce a deep impression on my father's mind. Even in his old age he loved to recall it, as a proof of the tender care of his heavenly Father.

From that time his pupils, to whom Dr Pye Smith refers, and the proceeds of his literary works, proved his chief means of subsistence. As we shall yet have occasion to see, he never, except in the isolated instances we have just recorded, received any regular assistance of any kind whatever. At the commencement, especially, he had nearly fourteen boarders in his house, chiefly English. At first young men, afterwards young ladies.

Thenceforth the sole remaining link attaching him to his country was his position as minister of the gospel in the Church of Geneva, an office the functions of which he was forbidden to discharge, though its official status remained to him. Every one urged him to leave a place where, as a minister, his hands were tied. He himself was unable to decide upon taking the step. First, undoubtedly, because he was unwilling to withdraw in the presence of a measure, as he thought, illegal, and which must, he concluded, die a natural death in the course of time—of a decision which he was compelled to regard as proceeding from the direction of the National Church being for a while in the hands of a mere section which, looking merely at its heterodoxy, could not be uppermost long. This was not, however, the only motive which induced him to brave the opposition of the national clergy and the excesses of a mob, only too ready to insult a man marked out for their attacks by his clerical superiors. A higher, deeper feeling actuated his conduct : the simple, earnest desire to proclaim to his fellow-citizens that message of salvation which had brought such blessedness to himself ; to testify the faith of Christ in the midst of his own people, whom, the more thoroughly he believed them to be the victims of deadly error, the more ardently he loved ; while he longed with his whole soul to carry out his ordination vow in seeking to evangelise them.*

Having issued a publication entitled, " Documents relative to the Deposition of the minister Malan from his Mastership," he set himself to work to compass this great end. Remitting no effort, either by letter or by any other means,

---

* A letter written by my father to Dr Mason, dated Havre, April the 2d, 1819, shows us, in all their fervency, the sentiments which then animated him.—(*Memoirs of Dr Mason*, p. 507.) " My good and respected friend,—What events in Geneva since your departure ! How mightily does the Lord work ! What vigorous and sustained wrestling ! Heresy must tremble ! The idol has feet of clay ; we will strike them, and it will crumble, to the shame of those who have adored it. Already it has received a mortal blow. . . . There is a holy people at Geneva. We have only a little strength, but He has permitted us to confess His name, and to keep the word of His patience. . . . Oh, how excellent, how sweet, and dear to my heart is the reproach of Christ with which I have been covered ! What faithfulness, what tenderness in our kind Saviour ! I remember to have seen your tears flow in speaking of that best of masters. At that time I did not understand these sentiments as I do now. I had not yet learned in the happy school of tribulation, that *it is good to be afflicted.* Let us, dear doctor, go on boldly and sincerely. See ! life is so short, so little a thing ! It will soon be ended. We shall then see Christ. Yes, we ourselves shall see Him Whom we love and follow without seeing. Oh, what servant could be so unworthy, so obstinate, as to hesitate and calculate with himself ! No, no, my brother, we will not do it."

to induce the Compagnie to reconsider their steps—efforts which, however, were wholly unnoticed—he preached as often as he possibly could at Ferney, and was the first to earn the title Momier, applied to him in the month of October in that year, an epithet which has remained as a popular byword awarded to any one whose piety, or even moral strictness only, may have condemned, by painful contrast, surrounding laxity. In the month of September he commenced devotional meetings in his house, and there, too, he conducted his Sunday-school. Soon afterwards he was compelled to adjourn for want of room to a small house which he had had constructed in his garden.

His meetings were such as are now frequent in every part of Geneva. " Reading and meditation over the word," says Schichedantz, (to whose mind they recalled the " Collegia prétatis" of Spener,) " occupied the principal time of those assembled; a psalm was then sung, followed by an extempore prayer from some one of those present, or by one borrowed from the collections of Osterwald or Doddridge." " These little meetings," says my father, " differed in nothing from the ordinary devotion in numerous families." By degrees, for order's sake, he conducted them entirely himself. They were held frequently during the week, in the morning or evening; and on the Sunday at an hour in no way interfering with the time of public worship at the various churches. About one hundred and fifty people came in the evening, in the morning generally fifty.

As the population was greatly excited by the reports circulated with reference to these evening meetings, Malan published a little tract entitled " Come and See," in which he reasserted his attachment to the National Church. At this time he had in no way felt himself compelled to secede. He had not attached himself to "the little Church," and communicated regularly with his family in the public temples.

All this time he was receiving continual encouragement, not only from old friends, but from strangers also. Gaussen writes to him, in reference to his published "Documents," &c., "I bless God for the correspondence you have just issued. I think your doing so, right and serviceable—a religious duty, and an absolute necessity." Charles Rieu, also one of his fellow-students, wrote a letter to him full of ardour and piety. I only wish I could quote it entire. His triumphant death at the outset of his devoted ministry will never be forgotten by those who watched with fondest interest over the early days of this awakening. I must confine myself, however, to the concluding paragraph, which gives a clue to the kind of atmosphere in which Malan and his friends lived.

It was dated from Fredericia, January 29, 1819, and is addressed to Mr Malan, a faithful minister of Jesus Christ. Its contents glow with holy enthusiasm, and seem to be as it were lighted up with a realised view of heavenly glory.

"Vitam dat Christus! Such has been the thought in my mind a thousand times in recurring to you and your history, my dear excellent brother; compassionating from the bottom of my heart your troubles and anxieties, and blessing God for enabling you to stand firm by the cause of Christ. What a blessed thing it is, dear brother, to be enabled to do anything in the service of such a Master! To Him I render continual thanks for all that He has done in strengthening His servant to revive the pure teaching of His word in our Sion. What He has done in your case is evident: freeing you from a thousand entanglements of earth to employ you more thoroughly in His work. Courage, brother! let us fight the good fight! Tell me all about your work, my dear friend; what results have followed from your meetings; how your Sunday-school is prospering." After detailing the success which had attended on his adoption of "Haldane's plan"— the plan, that is, of using Scripture itself as a universal commentary, and making those present at Scripture-readings turn up the required passages—he goes on to speak of a new orthodox theological society, about which Gaussen had just been writing to him :—

"With the utmost heartiness I give you the hand of fellowship. In associations, where unity can only be maintained by dissimulating opinions, the word is inevitably silenced without any of its fruit being exhibited. . . . . You have done well in publishing your correspondence with the authorities. Truth must shine out eventually in all its glory. To declare war against sin and unbelief—to show the utmost tenderness, meanwhile, to sinners and unbelievers—this is our task. Let us seek to conquer our enemies rather by our example than by our words. Nor let us cease to join in earnest prayer for their conversion to God."

I would add here a few extracts from a letter addressed at that time to my father by the Rev. T. Fry, rector of Emberton, who had just taken up his defence in England, (in his Heresiæ Mastix) :—

"*October* 22, 1821.—I am deeply interested in what the

Lord is doing by you. It would be presumptuous in me to offer you advice in the perilous path you are treading. It will, however, strengthen and comfort your hands (for it would comfort an apostle) to know that very many are offering prayers in your behalf, that they sympathise in your sufferings, and are rejoicing in your faith, your zeal, and your love. There is proof that these prayers have been heard, for you breathe the mind of Christ, and we have read your letters with tears of thankfulness. I cannot form a just idea of your difficulties, and yet I can conceive you will find new trials await you, and it will be well you should be prepared to meet them. A Reformer is hated of Satan above all men. The world was for a time the great enemy of Calvin and Luther; but, as his malice ceased, the tares sprung up amongst the wheat, and so it will probably be with you. There will be things to grieve you amongst yourselves, and sorer trials than the opposition of ignorant men. I take it for granted you will be exercised in this way, and that you will find the words true, ' A man's foes are often those of his own household.' Every covenant mercy be yours! May you long live blessed and blessing, having many seals to your ministry, and many souls for your exceeding great reward!"

It was at that time, too, that my father received a letter from a British nobleman, the Earl of Roden, then a perfect stranger to him, but who became afterwards his intimate friend. " Day after day, brother, in family worship and in private prayer, I offer my humble but earnest intercession for you and your work." Five and twenty years afterwards my father delighted to record the joy and thanksgiving with which he had learnt that the children of God were being stirred up to pray for him. About the same time a German princess, the Duchess Henrietta of Würtemberg, who happened to be staying at Geneva with her daughters, attended his meetings regularly, her daughters accompanying her. These ladies, more than one of whom eventually shared a throne, retained a most lively recollection of my father's teaching. One of them, the Archduchess Mary, Palatine of Hungary, a lady quoted for the strength and superiority of her mind, in a letter to my father, dated 1843, speaks of "this Malan whose explanation of the 15th of John, given to us by him in June 1819, will never be forgotten by me." In another letter she thanks him again " for the ineffaceable words which she had heard from his lips at Geneva in 1819, and which still resounded in her soul." While their mother, who, at the close of her long life—a life full of blessing and delight to all who knew her—spoke of him to me as " her father in the faith," and entrusted to the man who had been ostracised by the Genevan clergy the religious instruction of two young princes of her family.

It was at the commencement of the year 1819, on his return from a trip to England, where he had been visiting an American who was anxious to send his sons to him, that he agreed, after much pressing on the part of those who had been in the habit of attending regularly on his ministrations, to allow himself to be regarded thenceforth as their pastor. This, of course, was a first step towards secession, though he was not aware of it, and his opponents were not slow in convincing him that they so regarded it. At the same time, however, he drew nearer in the spirit to M. Empeytaz. This appears not only from certain letters which passed between him and my mother, but also in the application itself, now about to be referred to; and also, a year later, in his "Declaration of Fidelity to the Church of Geneva," in which he publicly espoused the rights of the Church, called at that time "The Church of the Bourg de Four."

Meanwhile, seeing that the number of his hearers was steadily on the increase, he applied to the Council of State for permission to use one of the town churches. After having stated how, under the influence of the awakening which had been spreading for the last ten years, certain Christians had been compelled, for conscience sake, to separate from the National Church, "There are others," he added—"I speak of ourselves, right hon. sirs—who have felt it a duty to remain, and protest from within the bosom of the Church, against the errors from which she is suffering." He then goes on to mention the violent opposition of which they had been, and still were, the objects, and defends his brethren and himself from the charge of enthusiasm, fanaticism, or ambition. He recalls to the minds of those whom he is addressing the fact that their doctrines were such as their fathers professed, and were the same as those held by all the Reformed Churches. "Hence," he adds, "right hon. sirs, we Genevan Calvinists look upon ourselves as the persecuted, but not the less faithful, Genevan Church, despised by the world, but graciously owned of God." Then, in the name of their rights and privileges as citizens, he asks the authorities to restore them that of which they had been unjustly deprived—liberty to exercise their Christian faith, the faith of old time—to extend to those

who had remained true to that faith the benefits of the
glorious reformation enjoyed by their brethren, whether
Lutherans, German Calvinists, or Anglicans, by conceding
to them the use of a church in the city.

The appeal wound up as follows :—

"Fathers of our country! we ask no strange favour,
but an ancient right at your hands; we ask it reverently of
our natural protectors. We ask no mere temporal, no
needless boon—we seek the greatest blessing man can
desire, and we implore you to listen to our prayer. We
crave but free leave to worship publicly our common
Lord and Saviour. Not only as citizens and your servants,
but as the redeemed of Christ we address you, in His
name. Our prayer respects not merely the interests of
the moment. It is an eternal need that we ask you to
consider. We urge our request in the midst of no worldly
surroundings. We bear it and you to the throne of the
Son of man, and it is there, as ministers of God, that we
present you our petition."

The petition having been read in council on the 28th
Dec. 1819, it was ruled that there was no occasion for
deliberation.

My father now resolved to build a chapel in his garden.
He proceeded to do it in the year 1820, after having obtained the sanction of the magistrates, on the understanding "that he had no intention of disturbing the peace of
the state."

Thus he took up a definite position as an independent
minister. And here it will be as well to terminate all
reference to, or exposure of, his official relation with the
Established Church, though his actual secession did not

occur till 1823. Of this final rupture I will first give a concise history, and then express an individual opinion on the merits of the whole question.

At the time he built his chapel he looked upon it in no other light than as a house of prayer, where he might have liberty to preach the gospel to his fellow-citizens. This position of mere preacher, however, he was soon compelled to abandon. "In spite of the opposition which he had to encounter," says De Goltz, "his influence, and the number of those who attended his meetings, increased rapidly," till, by degrees, as we have seen, he allowed himself to be regarded as a pastor, though declining to administer the sacraments in his exceptional position. He had prepared some young people for the communion without the sanction of their respective ministers; he had encouraged certain Romanists who had been converted to the Protestant faith to attend the Lord's Supper, without requiring from them the abjuration of their former creed, in such cases strictly required by the Church of Geneva. That Church, indeed, having long lost sight of religious freedom, the essential characteristic of an evangelical ministry, and altogether confounding that ministry with the particular office of those appointed to exercise its functions within her pale, regarded such a course of proceeding not only as a breach of good order, but as a deliberate outrage on the rights and prerogatives of her clergy. It is notorious that the greater the vagueness of assumed rights, the greater the jealousy with which such rights are guarded.

As far as Malan was concerned, he was by no means conscious of having given occasion for their sentiments. Regarding his position simply from a spiritual point of view, he felt that his ministry was no charge for which he was accountable to those who had forbidden him all exercise of the pastoral calling, but a holy trust confided to him directly by God Himself. Its duties appeared to him to involve obligations which he was called upon to fulfil in virtue of an office, not indeed bestowed, but merely recognised by his ordination in the Church of Geneva.

Then it was that the Assembly, without heeding a distinction with which, as Protestant teachers, they ought to have been familiar, and confining themselves rigorously to their position of purely administrative authority, wound up their attacks by decreeing his " suspension " from his ecclesiastical functions—the consistory proposing to the Council of State, in April 1823, a resolution to that effect. That civil body, however, putting the interests of general good order above those of ecclesiastical rights, called upon the appellants to make every effort to bring about a peaceable arrangement of the whole controversy.

Meanwhile, the subject of their negotiations was occupied entirely with his pastoral and missionary work. Having had no communication with the higher powers for the last five or six years, he was, to quote his own words, " extremely surprised at the sudden summons to appear in his own behalf before the consistory."

He complied with that command, first in April, and subsequently in July, in the same year. At his examination, and afterwards by letter, he endeavoured to explain to the consistory that it was not till he had found that all his communications in connection with his exclusion from the national pulpit (addressed by him both to the clerical

authorities and also to the magistrates) were passed over
in silence, that he decided first on holding devotional
meetings in his house, and subsequently in a house of prayer
built in his garden, where he took God to witness he had
preached no doctrine contrary to those held by the Church
of Geneva from its earliest date. " I never was a sectary,"
he exclaimed, "God knows, as will be seen in that day
when the secrets of all hearts will be disclosed. I have
never been a schismatic; no schismatic ever sought, and
that repeatedly, to be heard, to be judged, to be criticised.
It has been mine to guard the faith, and the 'good thing'
of Scripture as it was committed to me. This much I have
sought to do, after the strength which God vouchsafed me.

"Beyond all doubt, sirs, in taking this course I have
suffered much. It has been with no little sorrow that I
have found myself at war with those whom I have been
accustomed to regard as fathers and brethren, among whom
it would have been an easier and pleasanter task to have
exercised my ministry quietly, than to enter upon a cruelly
isolated path of opposition, with the feeling that I was
drawing down upon myself their grave displeasure. Don't
suppose for a moment, sirs, that in all this six years' conflict I could forget, or have ever forgotten, that I have been
brought up in your midst, and that I have received from
you many and many a proof of love and esteem. I cherish
the consciousness of this in my inmost soul; and it is the
grateful emotion, begotten of this consciousness, which has
made it so hard a task to me to acquit myself of the higher
duty of fidelity to my Lord and Master, and in so doing to
appear as the opponent of your authority, incurring the
penalty of your decided disapproval."

Having read this defence, the consistory exacting simply a statement of his future intentions, to be explicitly delivered on certain heads submitted to him, touching the requirements of ecclesiastical discipline; and Malan declining to make any specific promise, except with the reservation, "According to the Lord;" this reservation was looked upon as a positive refusal, and sentence of absolute suspension was accordingly pronounced.

Once more he had to present himself to hear the judgment given, together with a confirmatory decree from the Council of State. This was to the effect, that in consequence of his numerous acts of insubordination, he was deprived of his ecclesiastical status in the canton of Geneva. As soon as the Moderator had concluded his address, my father rose, bowed to the assembly, and withdrew without uttering a single word. He was not to leave that hall, however, for the last time, without a signal proof of the loving-kindness of his God. In a letter written on the following day to a friend, he says :—

"My joy, since yesterday, has been very great. That day was the happiest in my life. I had wished to be enabled to bear witness for the truth, and my prayer was abundantly answered." Having detailed the events of that memorable episode in his life, he goes on to say, "As I was leaving the hall, and just as I reached the entrance, a pastor left his place and came up to me in the presence of the entire assembly. It was the worthy Gaussen. He seized me warmly by the hand, and detained me for a moment before them all. May God remember him, and deal graciously by him, in the hour of his need !"

Every one knows how that prayer was answered, when,

eight years afterwards, Gaussen himself was subjected to the same ordeal.

"Now I can truly say I have finished the work which was given me to do. God only knows His own purposes, and shows Himself glorious in His Church."

It may be as well to add the concluding paragraphs of his published account of the whole affair. It was issued in the year 1823 :—

"In November 1818 I was reported to the Council of State by the clerical body as contumacious and disorderly, and the magistrates consequently deposed me from my collegiate post.

"In July 1823 I was further accused on a similar charge, by the same, or nearly the same, men; and the secular powers deprived me of my ecclesiastical functions.

"The eternal God, Whom I fear, and Whom I worship in all sincerity of heart, is my witness, that in 1818 I was guilty of no act of insubordination, except it were that I could not conform to the opinions of those whose views of the gospel contradicted mine, and that I could not reply to their interrogations otherwise than as my conscience dictated in the presence of the Lord.

"As a minister of Jesus Christ, I can safely and solemnly say that in the day of His appearing *He* will not pronounce me 'contumacious.' And if man has thus stigmatised me, has condemned me on this pretext, his judgment will not accord with the judgment of my Lord and Master."

On the 14th of August my father addressed the following letter to the Council of State :—

"Illustrious and Right Honourable Sirs,—The Venerable

G

Consistory of the National Protestant Church has informed me of the decree of suspension which you have pronounced.

"My principles enjoin upon me submission to your authority, and the recognition of the least of your commands 'according to the Lord.' Hence in the delicate position in which I now find myself, and in order the better to exhibit the obedience which I owe you as a citizen, and to show myself at the same time a faithful servant of God, Who has entrusted me with the ministry of the gospel, I am compelled to follow a new course—a course which I had hoped I never should have been called upon to adopt, namely, to retire both in my ministerial and private capacity from the Protestant Church of our Canton as at present constituted.

"I have therefore to request, with all deference and civil obedience, that you will not regard me henceforth as bound by your authority in spiritual matters, nor as being any longer a member of the National Church.

"Most unwillingly do I abandon the Church of my fathers. I have declared, in a published document, my continued loyalty to the ancient Church of Geneva, whose tenets still live in our ecclesiastical formularies, and whose existence, as established and protected by our ancestors, has been protracted through two hundred years. But I dare not—the Word of God and my conscience alike forbidding it—acknowledge, for a moment, any command which interferes with the requirements laid upon me by the gospel of Christ to preach the word, and to exercise my ministry.

"So I have only to beg of you, sirs, to accord, both to

myself as a minister, and to those of my fellow-citizens who may elect to worship God as I would seek to worship Him, full right to exercise our religion, together with the same toleration, the same legal protection, which the Anglicans, Moravians, the Independents at the Bourg de Four, and the Jewish community, receive at your hands.

" May the God of heaven bless both our State and our rulers !—Your most obedient servant, for the sake of the Lord Jesus, CÆSAR MALAN, Minister of God."

This application (in which, in order to maintain his character as a minister, as well as the possibility of discharging the ministerial duties, my father was thus constrained to withdraw from the Church in which he was born) was not rejected by the Council of the State. His petition was granted by the authorities "so long as their doing so in no way interfered with public order."

But while the civil power, however unwilling it might be to arrest the persecution with which he had been hunted down, still showed itself ready to protect individual rights and privileges, the ecclesiastical rulers, on the other hand, did not hesitate to withhold all recognition of that pastoral capacity so fully admitted by the Council of State.

For no sooner had Malan's letter to the latter been communicated to the " Compagnie des Pasteurs " than, not contenting themselves with pronouncing him to be removed from the clergy list—the natural result, the object, indeed, of the step he had been compelled to take—they exceeded altogether their administrative power, so constantly alleged in the course of the dispute, with the view of ignoring the theological aspect of the question, and

assumed the character of official representatives of the
Catholic Church of Christ. By virtue of that usurped
authority they declared him, on the 18th of Sept. 1823, to
have "fallen from his ecclesiastical ministry," thus not
merely depriving him of his position in the Church of
Geneva—a position which he himself had abandoned, but
denying him all right or title to regard himself as a
minister of the gospel, a denial constantly asserted in a
practical form by ignoring his existence in that capacity.
In virtue of that decree my father was constantly refused
the acknowledgment of his ecclesiastical character at the
hands of the Genevese civil authorities, until the time
when, in consequence of a subsequent political revolution,
many years later, the influence of the clergy had ceased to
predominate in the official departments of government.

To this, however, my father could never submit. He
neither admitted its justice, nor failed to assert against it
his personal right, conveyed through his ordination, to his
office. This right he declared himself unable to forfeit,
the very constitution of the Church itself forbidding him
to do so, except by a voluntary act on his part, or a
regular legal proceeding furnished with sufficient evidence
to justify its course. Admitting that the ecclesiastical
rulers had full right to forbid his *exercising* his ministry,
he altogether denied that they had the power to deprive
him, by a mere arbitrary decree, of functions, in his eyes
not only sacred but absolutely indelible, and with which,
by his ordination in the Church of Geneva, he had been
virtually invested in the eyes of the whole evangelical
Church. From the moment that this last step was taken
against him (to him the most painful of all) he never

ceased to protest against its utter illegality, and to look for its retractation. In his eyes it was not merely unauthorised, but amounted to a personal libel, inasmuch as, according to the constitution of the Church which had dealt thus with him, such a sentence could only be passed on one convicted either of immorality or heresy; nor even then, except after a formal trial which, in spite of all his entreaties, had never been granted him.

If *Protestant* clergymen have thus the right of pronouncing administratively, not only upon the exercise, but upon the very existence of that *ministry* which their "ordination" can only recognise and declare, it certainly does not clearly appear what, on that particular point, may be the difference between the authority of the clergy, which is essentially *delegated*, and the *absolute* powers of the Romish *priests*. At all events the latter could only act thus in virtue of clearly established laws, and in cases most carefully and strictly defined.

It will appear by and by that, towards the close of his life, he had reason to believe that this decree would at length be rescinded, though, from circumstances that will be stated in their order, his expectations were never realised.

In writing thus, I ask myself whether I ought not to maintain pretentions, whose justice I also fully admit, or whether, taking a view of the question he never was able to take, I should estimate such a step at its true worth, and hold it to be utterly unimportant. Certainly when we see how God Himself has testified to the ministry of His servant, such a question cannot even be raised. At all events, the course pursued in the face of such a life as his could only compromise those who met his reiterated appeals with silent contempt, and those, too, who, after the turbulence of the excitement had subsided, failed still to take a right view of the merits of the question.

Of course, it might be urged that the Genevan Church could not continue to be held responsible for the deeds of fifty years back. Reserving to myself the right, when I come to that portion of my narrative, of defining the limits and extent within which that objection may be held valid, I confine myself at present to specifying the action of the civil powers in relation to the unwarrantable proceedings of the ecclesiastical authorities.

The better to do this, let me refer to a letter from my father to the first syndic magistrate, dated July 1824, in which he protests against the qualification given to him of *schoolmaster*, on the electors' rolls of that year, and, that protestation being left unnoticed, makes a further appeal to be at least exempted by authority from military service. In October 1825 he forwarded a fresh application to the same quarter for due recognition as a minister of the gospel, inclosing, at the same time, a report of the official acts by which the Secession Church of Scotland had incorporated him among their clergy.* The reply was a distinct refusal, to which was appended the declaration " that he wasn't even *tolerated*, that he was only *endured*." To which he rejoined that he asked for no favour, but simply to be dealt with constitutionally by the ecclesiastical laws.

Of course, it is not by this solitary occurrence that his

---

* His original intention, indeed, had been to unite with the Scotch (Presbyterian) Establishment, but it could not have been done without his having first passed through the prescribed four years of study in a Scotch college.

treatment at the hands of the civil power must be esti-
mated. Though, for a long period, the circumstance of
their ignoring his ecclesiastical status excluded him, as a
matter of course, from participation in the civil privileges
and duties of a country like ours, (for example, in elections, at which he had always been present from the time
when he was first entered as a minister on the qualification
roll), still, from the very outset, it must in justice be
admitted that their relations generally towards each other
were very satisfactory. As an instance of this, I may
mention that on one occasion, during some popular disturbance in 1825, he promptly complied with a request from
the lieutenant of police, who asked him as a favour to
suspend his evening meetings for a short time. Should
the reply of the first syndic, quoted above, appear somewhat offensive, it must be remembered that the Geneva of
that time was quite different from the Geneva of the present day. Although its magistrates, who were then taken
out of the real aristocracy of its population, were known
and quoted in neighbouring countries for the elevation of
their mind and their zeal for progress, the laws were still
those of the ancient republic, and by the letter of their
requirements, the mere charge of discussing doctrines constituted of itself a civil offence ; so that, if the magistrates
of that day did not press the statute to its utmost, it was
because, in the matter of toleration, they were in advance
of the ordinances of the State. It is notorious that, when
on their restoration to power by the popular vote in 1847,
those who had had the chief hand in bringing about their
reinstatement recast the old statutes, so as to give the
widest scope for liberty of opinion, they did but legalise a

state of things which the clear-sightedness of previous rulers had already virtually anticipated.

Yet, in spite of all this—owing to the strong union which existed between the secular and ecclesiastical authorities—the former, so far from interfering in Malan's case, sanctioned the proceedings against him, by giving a legal character to the acts of the clergy, and then perpetuating their consequences to my father and his family.

And thus it is easy for us, without following the litigation any further, to form a general opinion on the entire merits of the question.

In arriving at such a judgment, however, everything depends on the point of view from which the matter in dispute is regarded. In this case there are clearly but two ways of looking at it. Either we must estimate the entire history as illustrating a phase in what is commonly called "national religious life," and so come to treat it as a natural and necessary development of social life; or else, passing by this theory, we must see, apart from this, and far above it, a higher state, an *individual* religious life, resulting in the believer from a full apprehension of the special facts which are testified in the gospel.

Undoubtedly those who draw no distinction, such as immeasurably exists between the *holiness* to which the Christian is "called," and *human virtue*, cannot understand what Jesus Christ Himself taught about the necessity of a new birth, but as a metaphor, intended to illustrate more strikingly the old truth of a moral progress in itself natural and everywhere insisted on. Such men will always look upon Christianity as being nothing but

one of the natural phases of the natural development of
man on earth. For them, the name of Christian will
simply be a conventional designation of the inhabitants of
certain countries on the globe at a certain period of their
history. Such persons, of course, will only see, in the
events we have traced out, one of these "religious quarrels,"
of no importance in itself, incapable of making any general
impression, the history of which it would be unwise to
present to people happily ignorant of its very existence.

And yet, even from this point of view, my father's biographer has this to consider—whether he should raise the
question as to the justifiableness or unjustifiableness of the
proceedings from which Malan suffered, or whether, passing that matter by, he may content himself with drawing
the picture of an honoured and respected old age, in the
lustre of whose private virtues these earlier occurrences
might be regarded as eclipsed.

And on this point the true guide to a decision is to be
found in an answer to these two questions : First, Did the
academical and ecclesiastical rulers act within the limits of
their authority from the time of their deposition of Malan
from his collegiate post, or in the adoption of these hostile
measures, which compelled his withdrawal from the Establishment ? and, secondly, admitting that their proceedings
were justifiable, did they, in the conduct of them, exhibit
such skill and judgment as were necessary, even with regard to the external interests of the Church, so continually
alleged as their sole consideration ?

It would be going out of our way here to meet these
two questions with a formal reply. That has been fur-

nished elsewhere. Enough for us to express our conviction
that public opinion in Geneva will be on our side, when
we affirm, in view of the occurrences, that, as a matter
of fact, Malan was most unjustly treated by the clergy of
Geneva; and that the clergy themselves, looking merely at
the considerations which they put forward, exhibited a
singular want of tact and judgment.

As a *Protestant* clergy, there was nothing they should
more scrupulously have guarded against than the bare
suspicion that they were laying claim to absolute authority,
without check and without appeal in matters of doctrine.
To act otherwise was most effectually to endanger the
unity of the Church, by rousing up in independent minds
a violent reaction against their summary measures.

Moreover, apart from their official acts, couched, as a
matter of course, in official phraseology, their total ignorance of their real position was sufficiently proved not only
by the relentlessly aggressive character of this or that particular step, but by the numberless pamphlets issued at
the time by the representatives of their body—pamphlets,
whose angry and personal tone, degenerating at times into
vulgar insult, was utterly unworthy of the position of their
authors, and furnished a remarkable contrast to the quiet
dignity which characterised my father throughout, though
they succeeded, nevertheless, in exposing him to public
derision and contempt.

All which is so indisputably true, that the question is
forcibly suggested whether it was not, after all, their object
so to act, as to render a reconciliation simply impossible.

Whatever reply we may give to this conjecture, we may
content ourselves with observing that, meeting them on

their own ground, they appear to have been called upon to act in an entirely opposite manner. They should have conciliated to the Church—assuming their avowed interest in its welfare—those whom they drove from it. They should have endeavoured not merely to respect the position these men had already acquired, but, by gradually enlarging the sphere of their activity, they should have left it to an earnest duty-doing career to soften down any possible error of judgment or impetuous zeal incident to young and enthusiastic temperaments. Above all, affecting to trace in Malan violent ambition, it was, at the best, but mistaken policy to inflame it by a pedantic, irritating, and paltry opposition. They should, at all hazards, have enlisted on their side that deep attachment to their Church and country, which distinguished him through the whole struggle, and which, in spite of his sincerity and candour, involved him once in a false position.

In a word, we maintain that it should have been their first consideration to win over, in the interests of the cause they pretended to have at heart, a man in whose character they detected the operation of such powerful and serviceable influences.

So far from acting thus, they forced him, against his instincts, to live mixed up with the anti-ecclesiastical party, from which not only his very sympathies estranged him, but who openly stigmatised his hesitation and delays in clinging to the old institutions of his country, as a weakness or want of faithfulness.

In a word, they might have displayed tact, only they did not know how to do it. It was in their power to be moderate and judicious; they preferred to be violent. It is this that brings out, in its true light, their deplorable infatuation. They had no notion of the true character of that religious liberty of which they claimed to be the representatives; and hence, while they indulged in high-sounding talk about their position as the heads of the Reformed Church of Geneva, they ended by resembling those fanatical obscurantists to whom Rome owes all her faults. Following close upon the traces of the old enemies of Protestantism, they would have acted far more prudently had they chosen for repetition those epochs in the history of the past wherein their Church had had the wisdom to turn to her profit, and to secure in her service, such occasionally indiscreet enthusiasm as she might chance to observe in her children.

Admitting, therefore—what indeed is difficult to admit—that the Regulation of the 3d of May had not been directed against Malan personally—admitting that, so far from interfering by act and deed of theirs to enjoin silence with regard to dogmas openly avowed and formularised by that very Church of which they claimed the name and privileges, they had but put in force a regulation originally incorporated in her ecclesiastical provisions, still it certainly was the part of a Protestant authority—exulting, by the way, in its Protestant liberalism—to seek to soften down the wording of engagements so violently opposed to the faith of many of her members.

Instead of doing this, it was that authority which framed these very engagements, in order to drive out from amongst them, under pretence of insubordination, not such of their clergy as actually held that Regulation to be a virtual denial of the ancient faith, but the only one amongst

them who was bold and sincere enough to avow openly
what others thought as well as he.

That authority of the clergy in matters of doctrine—in
the name and by virtue of which the ministers of that
day drove Malan from the school-desk and from the
pulpit, and finally sought to deprive him of his ecclesiastical status—does not, and cannot exist in a Protestant
Church. In fact, a clergy worthy of such a designation
aims exclusively at *protesting*, like the Reformers of
the sixteenth century, in the name of the *faith of the
heart*, against the tyranny of such doctrines or such institutions as have no other title to our respect but their
merely traditional character.

And it may be safely added that what is true generally
holds good more particularly in the case of those who had
themselves departed so entirely from ancient forms. Not
to speak of the abstract rights of religious liberty—to pass
over which, in such a case, is, to say the least of it, singular, and judging the clergy of Geneva only by the standard
of their acts—it is evident that, from the time they entered
on the abolition of old forms, they had no other duty, as
far as matters of faith are concerned, than to be the impar-
tial representatives of the faith of the flock committed to
their care.

When we look at the present state of the Church of
Geneva, at the entire religious toleration which pervades
it, at the fact that the most advanced broad churchman, or
the most enthusiastic evangelical, may each find its pulpits
occupied to his individual taste, it is not easy to realise
that there was a time when such a censure as we have
just recorded could justly be passed on that Church.

Undoubtedly the times then were very different from the present epoch, and my father had to do battle with prejudices which are already in a visible decline.

At the time that he built his chapel in his garden, there had been no such open appearance in Geneva of a dissenting congregation. In all the Protestant countries on the Continent, the Church was invariably regarded as attached to the State; in Geneva, indeed, the latter had derived not only her lustre from the former, but her strength and security. Seceders, therefore, or sectaries, as they were sometimes called, were looked upon by the people as semirebels and insurgents, as promoters of disaffection, and disturbers of the national peace.

In such a case, it was clearly the duty of the heads of the Protestant Church, instead of conniving at, and even stimulating popular passions, to encounter, by all the means in their power, the prejudices of the multitude, due to their own neglect, and, by every possible effort, to enlighten public opinion.

If it be urged, therefore, that the narrow-mindedness of the lower orders, and their utter ignorance of the rights of liberty of thought, furnish the only clue to the attitude assumed by the old Genevan clergy, and consequently explain the proceedings which resulted from their view of the question, there is nothing in all this to free their measures from that stigma which will always attach to them in the opinion of every lover of justice and freedom.

But in order to form a due estimate of the whole case, there yet remains a position more exalted, less personal, less painful, therefore, and embracing more important interests. This is the position resulting from faith in those

eternal realities to which the gospel testifies; it is the
position assumed by him who believes in the presence of a
spiritual kingdom distinct from that earthly kingdom of
God to which our natural birth introduces us :—a kingdom
into which no one can penetrate but through the " new
birth," which we are told takes place in our souls through
the direct agency of the Holy Spirit.

Taking up this position—the only right one, to our
mind, from which to regard a spiritual topic—we see at
once that the clerical body of Geneva displayed not merely
want of tact and equity of dealing, but, as has been loudly
testified from every quarter, in their resistance to the
revival they were found fighting against God !

For most assuredly that which they opposed was none
other than the grace of the living God, Who speaks directly
to the human conscience. It was the cause of the freedom
of the soul—the cause of the gospel, as the supreme law
to the hearts of men. It was that holy and awful cause
which who will may freely advocate now in the pulpits of
Geneva. It was in its defence that Malan suffered ! And
hence we have no hesitation in affirming that those who
cherish it in their inmost souls will cherish, side by side
with it, the memory of Malan.

As for those who hold that there are some yet alive who
would fain bury in oblivion the record of his achievements,
can they give a satisfactory explanation of this want of
sympathy ? Is it to the defects of the man himself that
their indifference is to be ascribed ? We can hardly think
so ; his faults, whatever they may have been, found their
harshest critic in himself. " Oh, but the injury he has
done to clerical authority in Geneva," say some ; " He has

troubled us," say others. As for the authority of the clergy, Malan never assailed it; he never even thought of such a thing. If that authority has injured itself by its attacks upon the unconquerable faith of that man of God, there is no thinking man who would regret its condemnation, actually involved in that very fact. As regards this general indictment that my father had troubled his country, it can only be met in his own words, when in 1817 he begged his opponents to distinguish accurately between offence given and offence taken; not to refer, for additional illustration and reply, to a case more ancient still—the case of One Who found Himself a stumblingblock in his native town.

Malan's entire life, and, more particularly, his public struggle with the clerical body, rank among those facts of history which compel men either to shut their eyes altogether, or to submit candidly to the alternative compelling them to choose between the glory that cometh from man, and that which proceeds from God alone. No one can study such a narrative honestly without seeing himself forced, either to side with the prejudices of a world which, while it calls itself Christian, can still too often manage to deny the rights of the faith and the obligations it entails, or with those whose sincerity and decision has led them to prefer to the approval of men, what saints and martyrs have hailed for two thousand years, " The reproach of our Lord Jesus Christ."

CHAPTER III.

> "Who loved, who suffered countless ills,
> Who battled for the True, the Just."

ON the 19th March 1820, Malan commenced to build his chapel in the garden of the Pré l'Evêque.

At the first blows of the pick-axe, Felix Noeff, (who, at that time a soldier in the garrison, used to employ his leisure days in working for private families,) turned over in the soil a small piece of copper, which he carried to my father. It was a medal, with an effigy of a sower on one side, and the inscription "*Ejactura lucrum.*" As he looked at the device, my father could not help recalling the words of the Psalmist, in which an abundant harvest is promised to him "who goes forth weeping, bearing precious seed." He remembered, too, the coin which Franke had found when he was laying the foundation of his orphanage.

Indeed he had good need to look for the help of God upon his work. "When I began," he said, "I had only £10 to count upon, a subscription given me by a brother in Ireland. The day that the medal was found I received unexpectedly, through the post, £24, which the brethren

II

at Würtemberg had forwarded to help me "in rebuilding the walls of Jerusalem." This was, however, the only funds that he possessed for a long time, till, in the mouth of June, when, after my mother had tried in vain to persuade him to appropriate her property, he determined to sell his house for the benefit of the new chapel. As he was about to carry out his intention, however, he suddenly received abundant supplies from various quarters, addressed in each case to himself personally, and sent to aid him in his work.

Let me mention an incident which he related to me by way of showing "how effectually he was taught, in the whole affair, to rest on God alone." He was in the midst of his building operations, and had to pay the architect a particular sum on a given day, when he received three letters by the same post. He hastened to open two of them, in the address of which he detected the handwriting of some friends he had relied upon for help; but inside he found nothing but excuses, and even indirect censures of his undertaking. As he showed them to my mother, with the simple remark that He Who would not that we should make flesh our arm, would be sure to provide, she asked him to open the third. He did so, and found inside an order for £100, sent, with a few cheering words, by an entire stranger.

Such was the way in which the chapel, which took six months to build, was paid for within eight months of its commencement, so that, as he used to say, it might well have been called "Philadelphia." He styled it "La Chapelle du Temoignage," the Chapel of Testimony, partly as expressing his intention to deliver within it none other message than the testimony God had given of His Son, and partly because he wished it to be a standing testimony against the clergy of Geneva who had cast him out for the gospel's sake.

He placed under the corner-stone a leaden box containing a parchment, which I myself removed when the building was taken down in 1864. The document, written in his own hand, ran as follows :—

"In the name of the Father, the Son, and the Holy Ghost. O Eternal God! my God and Saviour! my heart is filled with joy for the mercy Thou hast bestowed on Thy servant in permitting him to build this church. I implore Thee to bless it with Thy sovereign grace, for the alone merits' sake of Thy well-beloved Son, Jesus Christ, my Redeemer, my Master.

"O Lord, according to Thy promise, let Thy Name be there! Amen.

"The Church of Geneva is desolate. The gospel is seldom heard in our midst. A deadly heresy is destroying souls. Christ is no longer worshipped as God eternal, manifest in the flesh, and His merits are likened to the merits of a creature.

"The Lord has raised up in our city, for some years, preachers of the truth, who have withdrawn from the National Church.

"God has had compassion upon me! I have been deprived of my collegiate appointment, and banished from the pulpit of my country because I was faithful to the ministry conferred upon me by man in 1820, and by the Lord in 1817.

"Without separating from the Church, I have now been preaching in this garden for a year and a half in a little chapel. Required for the accommodation of an increasing flock, this larger building will witness the glory of God, for He has erected it. It is my resolve to preach in it the gospel of Christ as embodied in the Confession of Faith of the Swiss Churches.

"Christians in Germany, (Stuttgardt, Leomberg, Metzingen,) in England, Scotland, Ireland, France, America, and Switzerland, have supplied the funds for its erection.

"This corner-stone, which I pray God to erect spiritually on the Great Corner-stone which the builders rejected, has been laid by me and my house to the glory of the most Holy Trinity.   "CÆSAR MALAN,

"Minister of the Church of Geneva.

"*Friday, 28th April,* 1820."

That same year, on the 7th October, my father, occupying the little temporary building for the last time, gave thanks to God, with the whole congregation, for all that His hand had done. The next day he inaugurated the new chapel.

A congregation of about eight hundred people was present at that solemnity, appointed for two P.M. There were gens d'armes stationed along the approach, and at the entrance, to prevent confusion. After the reading of the Confession of Faith and the Ten Commandments, chanting, and prayer, my father, taking for his text Solomon's words at the dedication of the temple, "The Lord our God be with us as He was with our fathers," (1 Kings viii. 57, 58), explained to his hearers that his one object was to supply a place in the midst of them, where they might hear, in its simplicity, the gospel of Christ, as received and declared by their fathers, to the words, faith, and deeds of whom he made a brief reference.

Thus began, in a manner independent of the traditional habits of the official Church, the work of public testimony, exacted by the circumstances in which he had been involved, with the irrevocable declaration of his resolve, all Church decrees notwithstanding, to exercise the office with which he had been solemnly entrusted.

His position at this time was that of an established minister, supported by an ever-increasing congregation, and desiring to remain steadfast in his allegiance to the doctrines of the Reformation. If, four years later, at the time of his coerced secession, he found himself with a settled flock around him, it must be remembered that he was as far as possible from anticipating this contingency when he signed himself at the foot of the document I have quoted, " Minister of the Church of Geneva," or when he opened his chapel in the October of the same year. Some time after that event, in January 1821, he published his declaration of fidelity to the National Church, in which he cast from him the reproach of having created a schism, which he said, when the terms of his ordination oath were remembered, amounted to nothing short of a charge of perjury.

That declaration contains some passages which, while they show the humility of my father's spirit, furnish also a very correct description of his relation to the Church. After stating that, at the close of eight years, in which his doctrine had been utterly opposed to the gospel of Christ, he was converted from a rationalist to a Christian, he continues as follows :—

"I experienced at my first awakening what Paul himself dreaded for the new converts. I fell into spiritual pride, and my speech, too, smacked often of a severity which Christian love condemns, and which I now abhor." And he adds, that it was probably to his vehemence and want of tact that the severity of the measures against him might be attributed.

"At that time," he goes on to say, "I went over to England, where I met several ministers of the various Churches. Their faith served to strengthen mine. Their writings and sermons showed me that we were bound to set forth the truth firmly but kindly, and their Christian charity made me feel how sadly I had been wanting in that virtue myself. Hence, on my return to Geneva, I tried to bring about a reconciliation with my superiors. My appeals, however, met with no response, and I was left in my deposed condition. However, I had learnt a fact most important to me, and of which I had previously been ignorant, that our Church of Geneva had held, from its earliest establishment, and in accordance with its unalterable character for more than two hundred years, the very same opinions which I professed myself. This discovery warranted my acting as a minister of that Church. Many a time the dread of innovating had held me back, but as soon as I understood that, by attaching myself to our ancient faith, I was most effectually upholding my ordination vows, I did not hesitate to adhere to my ministerial office, and to fulfil its obligations."

He then relates how he had been induced to build a "house of prayer," and exclaims, "I declare before God that my only aim has been to discharge my obligations in the presence of my fellow-citizens, by simply doing, to the utmost of my power, the work of an evangelical minister and guardian of the precious trust of the gospel of grace."

All his earlier publications prove that this was his one object, and show to what extent he regarded his involuntary secession, as an evil to which he was compelled to submit for conscience' sake, and in the interests of the truth, the integrity of which he deemed to be infinitely more important than any considerations arising from mere feeling, tradition, or regard for external unity.

Already, in 1818, in his little tract, entitled "Come and See," he had avowed his deliberate resolve never to separate willingly from what he called "our Church of Geneva." At the same time he affirmed (in contradistinction from the clergy at its head), that he desired to maintain with the seceders the same relations that he would wish to see subsisting between himself and any other Christians in Geneva, or in the whole world. "Whether they style themselves Protestants or Romanists, Greeks or Anglicans, Lutherans or Calvinists, Quakers or Moravians, what matters it to me! Whoever believes with all his heart in the merits of the Lord Jesus, is my brother, and as soon as I have recognised him as such, I testify it to him as much as it is in my power."

No one can help recognising in all this, that Christianity of the heart which should ever supersede all purely ecclesiastical questions, inasmuch as it takes precedence of all mere ecclesiastical life, and, being eternal itself, like the God Who implants it in the believing soul, is destined to survive the overthrow of denominations, and the wreck of

Churches. Should it appear, at a later period, that my father lost sight occasionally of that catholicity of spirit which the passage just quoted indicates, this never arose, as will be abundantly evident, from any sectarian bitterness, but simply from a perhaps too tenacious grasp of exclusively doctrinal views.

It began in sheer fidelity, a fidelity which had beheld the sacrifice of his most cherished natural inclinations. If it be alleged, with reference to the seceders who had gone before him, that they too had left the Church for the same reason, the statement must be amplified and extended in his case, inasmuch as his secession, so far from being voluntary, was the result of positive compulsion. He never ceased to declare, that had he been permitted to preach the doctrine of Christ's divinity, and of a free salvation as it was inscribed in their ancient formularies, he would never have quitted the Church.

When, after three years' service in the garden chapel, he was driven to that step, the very existence of his ministry being at stake, he was careful to have it understood that he withdrew only from the Establishment as then existing. And we have just seen that he never felt himself at liberty to preach the word, from the time of his exclusion from the national pulpits, till he discovered that the truths which he taught were the faith of the ancient Church, a Church loved by none more passionately than himself, as none held more emphatically than he did the doctrines of her founder. Over and over again did he assert that he had by no means withdrawn himself from the Church of his ancestors, but that, on the contrary, his sufferings had resulted from fidelity to her cause.

And not only was this his own view of the case, but it was also shared by such as regarded the whole matter simply in the light of historic truth as well as by those who partook of his faith.

Let it be added, that if he did thus rend the ties which attached him to the Establishment, he did so, not under the influence of particular opinions on Church matters properly so called, but simply and solely at the bidding of evangelical truth. Not as a pastor, not as the "incumbent of a church," but as a minister, or mere preacher, he commenced a vocation outside the walls of the national sanctuary in which he had been reared, and from which he found himself eventually expelled.

If I appear to dwell upon this point at some length, it is because there have been those who have thought that the "Church of Testimony" was an attempted revival of the old Theocratic Church of Calvin. This was so little the case, that as we have just heard it stated by himself, it was not till long after he had been refused the use of the pulpit, that he discovered what had in reality been the doctrine and institutions of the primitive Church of Geneva. If, therefore, in a certain measure, there be found, in the religious sentiments of my father, what can justly be called a *theocratical* tendency, it is not to that tendency that we are to trace his secession from the Church. Still less can it be urged with truth, that while his doctrine was akin to the doctrine of the great Reformer, it was that circumstance which impelled him to adopt it.

As we shall have occasion to see, he had not even read the writings of Calvin when he first affirmed his doctrine, which, at least until R. Haldane's visit, was solely the

confession of his feelings as a Christian. In general, it
must be allowed that my father's work was, on the whole,
or in its essential features, one of confession and testimony
of personal faith. We shall see how his *ecclesiastical work*,
far from having originated his secession, came to be added
at a much later period, in consequence of peculiar circumstances, to what he had always considered his peculiar mission, viz., the duty of "*witnessing for the truth in Geneva.*"
Even then, (in his Church work,) he did not think of
copying Calvin.

This confusion of the Church with the nation, resulting
in an intimate alliance between the civil and ecclesiastical
powers, and a consequent rigid system of Church discipline,
never found favour in his eyes. So far from regarding
himself as representing institutions which, in his judgment,
belonged to a different age, he never ceased to uphold the
idea of a historic development of the visible institutions
of the Church, in opposition to that of a permanent and
divinely revealed Church constitution, which was more or
less expressly professed around him.

Possessing to a high degree that historical and traditional
instinct which generally accompanies a powerful imagination and a heart prone to emotion, nothing ever appeared
to him so distasteful as to assume the character of an innovator. It certainly was not his ambition to be thus regarded, nor did he consider such a reputation as by any
means creditable. He was so far from aspiring to the distinction, that, in his requests to the magistrates, he based
his appeals on the rights he claimed as a member of the
old and only true Church of the country. He did not even
hesitate in his application to affirm that the clergy had

no right to the powers they exercised, simply because in an innovating spirit they had gradually and surreptitiously grafted new doctrines on the catechism and regulations of the ancient Church. Confident that he would himself be permitted to see the Church emerge from a state of virtual secession from itself, and return to the faith of its founders, or, in other words, to the pure gospel, he looked upon his rupture with the powers ecclesiastical, at first as merely temporary, and the position in which for a time it had placed him as simply provisional.

This is apparent not only from his "Declaration of Fidelity," &c., but from all his writings of that period. It especially shows itself in his "Conventicule de Rolle," which he published in November 1821. Through all its pages there breathes a spirit of holy confidence and joyous hope in the anticipation of this event—an event to be marked by a revival, "attended," he says, "by more Christian charity, possibly by more liberality of sentiment than even the Reformation itself displayed. The harvest is just beginning. We are on the threshold of glorious days. The Sun of Righteousness has arisen upon our beautiful Switzerland, and I trust that we are nearing a time of conspicuous triumph for the gospel in the world."

Who can fail to detect in these words the gracious kindness of our heavenly Father illuminating the path of his servants with the light of a future they are not destined to behold in the flesh. So it was with Moses; so, too, with prophets and apostles. So it was supremely with the Master Himself, Who inaugurated with the joyful days of Galilee a ministry which was soon to encounter the angry outcries of Jerusalem, and the bitter hatred of her Sanhedrim.

My father's sentiments, so devoid of any special ecclesiastical bias, show how it was that he and his were able to continue, up to the building of his chapel, in full communion with the National Church, and how, up to the year 1821, he invariably presented his children for baptism in that Church.

Even strangers perfectly understood that such was his position. As a proof of it, let me quote here a few extracts from letters addressed to him in 1821 and 1823, by the Rev. D. Bogue of Gosport, in reference to which my father writes to A. Haldane in 1826, on the occasion of the demise of the writer: "I was sincerely attached to him, and possess two of his letters, which will be useful not only to myself, but to my children after me." After telling him his impression on reading his *document*, and seeing how they had compelled him to withdraw from the Church of Geneva, he adds : "I bless God, Who has endowed you with such gifts for the edification of mankind, and instilled into your mind the pure principles of the Gospel of Christ, in a place where they have been too generally refuted. The Lord Jesus has, I trust, raised you up to be the instrument of an extensive reformation in Geneva and the neighbouring countries. The opposition you met with, though painful, was to be expected; and it is matter of great thankfulness to God that you were strengthened to stand up against it with so much firmness and success. I rejoiced greatly at the truly Christian spirit which you were enabled to manifest in your answers to your adversaries. There was nothing in them of the wrath of man which worketh not the righteousness of God, but, on the contrary, that meekness which cometh from above, and which could not fail to produce the most beneficial effects. If the clergy could not be moved, yet the people must have felt deeply your truly Christian defence of your principles and conduct. I was greatly pleased, too, that you did not recede from the mode of government and regulations of the Church of Geneva. It grieved me when I heard that some pious people had set up a new system of Church government, and blended adult baptism with the controversy, because it gave the adversaries of the truth a handle against them, and called away the minds of the people from the grand doctrinal controversy to subjects of a very inferior nature. But your continuance in the same principles of Church government with the clergy, prevented them from charging you with introducing a new ecclesiastical system, and kept the eyes of the public fixed on the grand subject of the controversy, namely, the fundamental doctrines of the gospel of Christ. You have only to persevere in following the same method, and your success is certain. Already I understand it has been considerable, and I have no doubt you will see greater things, and that there will be a gradual return from these dangerous opinions which have torn up the very foundations of real piety, to the pure truths of the gospel which Calvin and Beza, F. Turrettini and Pictet, maintained in ancient days. I have not a doubt, if you live many years, you will see these doctrines revived in all their former glory, and cordially received by the people." Speaking of the general revival of the faith which was then taking place in England and on the Continent: "Young ministers," he says, "have joyful days before them, and you may labour with a hope of seeing a rapid advancement of the kingdom of Christ. With such prospects before you, how important that you should be daily wrestling with God in prayer." "You must still expect," writes the same venerable friend in another letter two years later, "determined and bitter opposition, but in the end you will prevail, while Arians and Socinians will sink in the public estimation. They want the principles which give life and energy to a system, and, do what they will, they will experience a gradual decay. Be not discouraged, then, but assure yourself of victory and of the triumph of the Redeemer's cause."

We may see from these letters how my father had assumed towards the dissenters the same position of liberty and superiority in matters of ecclesiastical policy, which characterised his dealings with the Establishment. Thus, in July 1820, while he was building his chapel, he declined an offer from M. Empeytaz to join "The Little Church." The fact was, as we shall presently see in various ways, that though he was joined in faith with the men who presided over the meetings in that Church, their object materially differed from his. And this led him to set aside the proposal just referred to, with the explanation that he and they were scarcely pursuing the same path, and that the work to which he had been led to devote himself was by no means identical with theirs. Their separation from the Church arose simply from a desire to establish an independent religious communion. Without speaking of the Church question with those individual prejudices which it is so apt to call up, we may state that their great anxiety was

rather to create an intimate brotherly union than to secure
an accurate and well-defined system of dogmatic theology ;
in that respect, except as regards the great facts of salvation, they held no clear and precise opinions.

In my father's judgment, this was a capital error.
Whilst they reproached him with a tendency to dogmatic
isolation, his answer was, that he could not sympathise
with their religion of feeling.

Religious sentiment, what the Germans call *poetism*,
and what we may term mere *devotion*, inasmuch as this
appellation describes the more sensuous side of religious
life,—had few charms for him. It always appeared to
him as the evidence of a morbid, self-seeking tendency,
a weakness repugnant to the sobriety and manliness of
his character. His spiritual life, from the very first,
was marked by no idle study of his own personal feelings, but rather by an active, healthy, earnest obedience
to the will of Him Whose holy presence ever filled his
soul.

Not that it is to be inferred from all this, that he held
himself aloof from them, or that he estranged himself from
the various dissenting Churches which persecution had
called forth in the Canton de Vaud. Their members were
his brethren in the faith. More than that, he looked upon
them as "saints," as "elect," as "children of God," and as
such, regarded them with tenderest affection. "Not many
years ago," he said in 1821, "I should have been ashamed
to associate with them. Now their companionship is to
me a source of sweet delight." Nor did he confine himself
to cordial relations with the young ministers who were the
prime movers in the Vaudois revival, or the pastors of the

Bourg de Four, he endeavoured to render them solid service, by espousing their cause in public, and by sharing with them the supplies which he received for his work.

Among them all, M. Empeytaz was more especially his friend. In a note in his handwriting, dated 6th September 1821, he says, "The Lord has put it into my heart to give up my pulpit to-day, for the first time, to M. Empeytaz, who is to preach, please God, this evening. I look upon this as an important step in the right direction." Commenting next on the remarks that had been made about his presence in one of the temples of the National Church, at the communion, the Sunday before, he observes, "My doing so, as a proof of tolerance and Christian charity, increases the value of any service I may render to my seceding brethren."

A few days afterwards, my father, in concert with them, wrote a circular letter "to the faithful pastors in Geneva, and in the rest of Switzerland," inviting them to join him in the ordination of M. Empeytaz. It was to be signed by him as minister of Geneva. In it, though the arrangement proposed was not carried out, as the ordination did not take place at the time, he carefully stated with reference to the candidate, "that though he had been called upon to do battle with error, he had never judged or condemned erring ones. Asserting pointedly his utter aversion to schism, and to all separation from his brethren, he had only consented to preside over a gathering of some amongst them, for the sake of rendering open testimony of his attachment to the doctrines of the gospel. A declaration which his present conduct warrants, as he wishes to be ordained a minister in the Presbyterian Church of Geneva."

It is apparent at once, how far, even at the time that he was exhibiting such decision in his testimony, his ecclesiastical position was defined, and to what extent he kept up his relation to the Church in conjunction with his maintenance of purity of doctrine.

Gradually, however, circumstances led him to determine his position more accurately. In January 1821, just after publishing his "Declaration of Fidelity," he became convinced that it was his duty to introduce a system of discipline into what had hitherto been a mere assembly of hearers. This impression arose out of a conversation with an English dissenting minister. He hesitated, however, so long, that he began at last to accuse himself of unfaithfulness and apathy. "As I was lying awake one night," he writes, "I sat up on my bed, and solemnly pledged myself and my whole being to the service of Christ, beseeching Him to consecrate me thoroughly to Himself, and to tear asunder every bond that held me back from entire obedience. The next day, as I was walking and reading the Scriptures, I asked to be guided to a passage for my meditation, which would reveal His will concerning me. After I had closed the Bible, a thousand thoughts rushed into my mind; but one only reigned supreme, filling my soul with strength and repose: it was the conviction that I ought to exercise a godly supervision over the souls begotten again by the Word I had been permitted to preach —by establishing discipline amongst them. From that moment I experienced the most tranquil joy and greater freedom than ever in my delivery of the message. I felt an inward support, and a trust in the Lord Jesus all but new to me. This was the finger of God." He goes on to

I

say that in this enterprise he met with the sanction and encouragement of those around him.

In thus abandoning himself to the liveliness of his emotions, he little thought that he was taking the first step towards forming an Independent Church. The discipline here indicated had nothing to do with admission to the sacrament, which was not then given in his chapel. It was simply applied to constituting what had been hitherto a mere congregation of habitual hearers—a community of selected members. Nevertheless, three years afterwards, when the final links of attachment were sundered, he found himself—thanks to this first step—at the head of a separate and thoroughly constituted community. Up to that time he had confidently hoped to be permitted to assist in winning back the Church of his fathers to its original position, seeing in that a common meeting ground for all true evangelical Christians. This will serve to explain his peculiar position from 1821 to 1823.

What proves, moreover, our last statement, is the fact that the same persons who had been all encouragement, when, in 1821, he sought to honour the ancient laws of the Church with reference to the government of the faithful, opposed him openly in 1824, on the assumption that he was endeavouring to establish an independent body. One of those, in his most intimate confidence, in particular, used every effort at this crisis to make him abandon his decision by representing to him that the position of leader of a flock was ill-suited to his independence of character and of action—that in such a capacity he would be like an eagle in a cage, wounding himself and others—wasting his powers, and ending by destroying them.

Still he was not convinced. The establishment of an independent community appeared to him to be not only his duty, side by side with those which devolved upon him as a preacher: he viewed it as constituting in itself a permanent protest against the disorderly condition of the Church he had just quitted.

Now that the subject of Free Churches is a familiar one, not merely in religious circles, his hesitation in this matter may occasion surprise, more particularly when his natural clearness of judgment and decision of character are taken into consideration. But, as De Goltz has well observed, in reference to this and all kindred topics, and the light in which they presented themselves at the commencement of the revival, "All these cases showed that it was not theories that started facts, but facts that produced theories." These words of De Goltz I find underlined in my father's copy of his book.

Now, the "facts" in reference to the Church of Geneva at this time, were well known. From the middle of the last century the decay of independent belief in individuals had led to this result, that the Church, becoming more and more confounded with the nation, Protestant rights —tantamount then to the rights of a citizen of Geneva— superseded the duties of a Christian in the exact sense of the word. Hence it arose, that communions in Geneva degenerated into mere national solemnities, which no one could omit without casting suspicion on his patriotism and respectability. In accordance with this tradition, in the great annual fast-day sermons, in which our pastors are in the habit of speaking in a more pointed and special manner to their parishioners, infrequent attendance at the

Lord's table figured constantly in the list of the scandalous offences with which the population, considered as such, were charged. Participation in that solemn ordinance had come to be regarded without reference to the living faith in the heart of the communicant, but merely as a thing to be done; and that not only because it was proper and incumbent, but because the doing of it secured the favour of heaven. Impressions such as these were not wanting in other Protestant Churches; they were nowhere perhaps more apparent than in the Church of Geneva.

Such a state of things as this called loudly for a protest. How this protest was to be expressed became a question only to be decided by the circumstances which rendered it necessary. Theoretically, of course, there were two ways open; either to regard all discipline in reference to the Holy Communion as a matter to be left to the responsibility of the communicant himself, care being taken on the one hand to instruct him as to his duty, while all risk of placing him in a false position by the misapplication of rules and requirements was avoided; or, on the other hand, to entrust that discipline to the ministers themselves to exercise it in behalf of their flocks, by welcome or exclusion, as occasion should arise.

As a matter of fact, however, such an alternative as this, which even now might fail to be immediately obvious to many of the clergy, could scarcely have presented itself to Malan, brought up as he had been in a Church where the predominating influence of the clergy had resulted in depriving the religious life of the faithful of all unfettered individual action. From the moment, therefore, when he detected the abuses we have just pointed out, he fastened upon the question of discipline, not as one to be studied anxiously on its own merits, but as involving particular obligations incumbent upon him in his ecclesiastical capacity—obligations all the more urgent in his eyes, as he had daily proof of the evils resulting from their neglect.

Granted that these abuses constituted a *primâ facie* ground for maintaining as a principle the necessity for ecclesiastical discipline, the mere contemplation of them could never have sufficed as a practical guide, in respect of ways and means of remedy, to the founder of a model Church. Such an enterprise required an experience and a class of qualifications very different from his. To him the task was far from reducing itself to a mere servile repetition of what he might have imagined to be the constitution of the Apostolic Churches. Opposed to such a principle of imitation, as it is sometimes called, a principle which had made Puritans of some amongst his brethren, in the strict historical sense of the term, no sooner had he felt himself called upon to found a religious community, than he saw it to be his duty to frame its future constitution.

Meanwhile, he had no precedents to guide him to his task, and no other material to work upon, than his general conception of the Presbyterian Constitution. But this was not enough for all that he required. To fit him for his undertaking, he needed a thorough insight into the history of Genevan Protestantism; more than this, of the Christian Church itself, from which the Protestant Communion had sprung, in all the principles of its origin, and all the details of its protracted and laborious progress. Over against these indispensable qualifications, we must set his own alleged total ignorance on the subject, and the consideration that it had never been comprehended in any of his earlier studies.

But more even than this. To found a Church requires not only a definite and perspicuous creed, a decided and consistent character, Christian charity equally sincere and active, with a heart thoroughly renewed—all this my father had in a high degree—but, in addition to these qualifications, infinite capacity for management, a minute study of details, an ever-watchful caution, and, to crown all, consummate tact, the fruit of an intimate insight into men and character, impossible to a man in an isolated position, from sheer want of opportunity.

These qualifications, however, were neither natural to him, nor were his circumstances such as to admit of his acquiring them. Truth compels me to allow that not only was a pastor's work unsuited to him, but that it differed essentially, both in character and significance, from the duties he had been led to undertake. Called to be a witness, a confessor, and an apostle, we may say of him what the chief of the apostles scrupled not to say of himself, that "he was not sent to baptize, but to preach the gospel." If, as will appear, he proved himself a loved and revered pastor to his little flock, if his memory survives to this hour in the cherished affections of his people, it is not the less true that the task to which he was summoned was one of personal testimony, and that his chapel, which had been expressly and solely founded in view of such a work, was really to cease with his own labours.

The leading difference between the work of a pastor and a missionary lies in this, that while the latter is concerned only with eternal truths and absolute facts, the former is for ever being associated with up-springing interests, and hence is called upon to exhibit a capacity for devoting himself, without neglect of higher duties, to the thousand various contingencies which they involve. This was very far from his gift. Looking at everything from the most serious point of view, tracing each offence, not to its secondary or accidental source, but to those abstract principles which his spirit so rapidly divined, and the issues of which he so vividly apprehended, it was too probable that with him every act of heedlessness would be a crime, every unenlightened sentiment a heresy, every opposition to his personal influence a flat rebellion against his ministerial office.

Still, there is one characteristic of the pastoral office, as it exists in Geneva up to the present day, which may serve to throw light upon his compliance with the wishes of his congregation. I refer to that custom of a rotation of preachers in the town churches, which has so often arrested the attention of chance visitors.

In Geneva the pastors of the National Church preach, in due succession, in each of the city pulpits. Thus the town is in the position of one large parish, with several ministers. The result is that, though certainly the poor and the young are looked after to a greater extent than generally prevails, as far as the religious life in individuals is concerned, the system works indifferently. Those personal and sustained relations which should exist between a minister and the separate members of his flock are lost sight of, in the absence of that uniting influence which leads those who hear the same pastor, Sunday after Sunday, to regard themselves as parts of a special religious community.

Possibly it was owing to this that, in the country where each Church had its own pastor, dissent failed to gain ground. This, too, even more than the special circumstances which troubled it in 1830, may serve to explain how the Church of Testimony was arrested in its progressive career. It was at that time that the district in which it stood was formed by the Venerable Assembly into a separate parish, and furnished with a resident minister.

And yet, however correct these various conjectures may be, and however indisputable the fact that my father became a pastor, more from special circumstances than in consequence of what would have been a decided vocation to that particular office, it must, nevertheless, be acknowledged that although he fulfilled pastoral duties towards a congregation of some magnitude only for the space of six years, he discharged the obligations of his office, to the very end of his life, with the utmost perseverance and conscientiousness.

I have before me a private register from the year 1825 to November 1863, when he preached for the last time. It is entitled, "Transactions du Troupeau et de la Diaconie de l'Eglise." Here we find set down, his admissions of catechumens, the receptions or retirements, and sometimes even the expulsion of members, with a list of baptisms and marriages. It is written in his own hand, and, till 1830 especially, Sunday after Sunday. Up to that period it appeared like a record of the deliberations of a self-governing community, after which it resembled more the personal notes of the ruler of a Church. On the the first page, dated February 1825, we find the question to be answered by every candidate for admission: "Are you convinced, from the Word of God, that you ought to separate yourself unreservedly from the Church of the multitude; and are you really doing it?"

In spite of its smallness, this little community escaped those contracted views which too often prove the bane of isolated congregations. It is only right to say that, amongst all the dissenting communions around, it was pre-eminently conspicuous for the catholicity of its spirit.

Always at peace within itself, and, thanks to the clear teaching and elevated spirit of its pastor, enjoying a happy immunity from those intestine divisions with which other communities were visited, it displayed genuine spiritual life and practical consistency. Though composed of some amongst the poorest classes, the frequent collections for any special cause, or for general evangelical purposes, surpassed, in amount, the highest expectations of its pastor. Then, too, the destitute were carefully looked after. It supported schools, and made itself acquainted more or less directly with such occurrences among its individual members as called for peculiar sympathy or prayer. Thus it was, in the fullest sense of the term, a large spiritual family, thoroughly pervaded by mutual intimacy, —those who composed it living near one another, and meeting one another, Sunday after Sunday, in the quiet and pleasant garden, and in the chapel where he who ministered was at once their pastor and their friend.

Apropos of the above, we may say of this little community that, like other separate congregations which had arisen out of the first revival, it was essentially personal in its character; in other words, both in its origin and construction, it was the creation of an individual influence.

Not that we are to infer from this that it lacked independent life. Its pastor, not contented with urging it to separate action, insisted most emphatically on the general principle, that a Church is nothing more than a body of Christians fortuitously associated for mutual edification; so that the fact of being admitted into it does not make any one a Christian. This proposition was as distinctly opposed to the theory of the divine right of ministers, with which my father was credited, as to that of the divine institution of the Church visible, which had also been asserted around him.

Agreeably with this, he held excommunication to be nothing more than a matter of external discipline, and to be no exclusion from the spiritual body. Admission to the Lord's Supper, moreover, and admission to the Church, he kept carefully distinct. Hence he prevailed upon his people to resolve (in 1827) that young people should not become members of the Church but on their written application, and after they had been communicants a whole year. The fact is, that refusals of admission were determined by reasons in no way affecting Christian character. For example, in 1825 the Church decided not to receive a husband or a wife, whose partner in either case remained a member of another congregation; and, in 1826, any applicants whose affairs were in confusion or who had not paid their debts. Remissness in Sabbath observance was also a plea of exclusion. We may observe that this discipline was by no means due to the pastor alone; on the contrary, his influence was often exerted to moderate the extreme rigour which some of the brethren were disposed to exhibit (as for example, on the Sunday question).

To these details, we may add that the community nominated the deacons, who had to present a report, signed by the minister and themselves. It also voted the regulation of admission or exclusion; to it were addressed all letters from other Churches, or from private individuals. It sent out evangelists, and nominated a committee of home missions, and finally set apart for observance special fasts and festivals.

Such was the state of things from 1825 to 1830, as shown by the register to which I have referred. It is impossible to read its pages without deep interest, and a passing regret that so important a movement was on so small a scale; more particularly that the powerful originality, the incessant activity, and the talents of its leader were so often involuntarily exercised on insignificant trifles, or in repelling personal attacks, directed from without, against the character and authority of his ministry.

From such a regret, however, my father was altogether free. Though, more particularly towards the end of his life, his position became oppressive, as he keenly realised his isolation; though he felt by degrees that his congregation must necessarily dissolve at his death, he never shrank from his work. Now that he is gone, we to whom he ministered can see the wisdom of God in not suffering a Church which had originated under His divine blessing, out of the living faith of its pastor, to degenerate into a sectarian community, with nothing but the old name retained. We feel, how often, where the human element creeps in, it tends to expel the presence of that blessed Spirit, likened, in all His operations, to the wind " blowing as it lists."

But to return to the time when the little chapel was

still flourishing, and when its pastor, in the full maturity of his talents, took care to make it participate in all the work of his ministry. Whenever he set out on a mission tour he asked the prayers of his congregation, and on his return related to them anything that might interest or edify. He invited them to participate in the joys and sorrows of those amongst its numbers who wished him to do so, and was wont even, with his characteristic simplicity and kindliness, to announce any special occurrence in his own family leading him to ask for their intercessions. He asked them to be present at marriages or baptisms, or on the occasion of the admission of young members, who were always expected to make public profession of their faith, or at the ordination of ministers—a not uncommon solemnity in his chapel—at which various nonconforming pastors in Geneva, and often from other countries, were accustomed to assist.

Besides his own congregation, his chapel was visited by numerous strangers. More particularly, in the twelve years previous to the foundation of the *Oratoire*,[*] there was frequently a crowded attendance, and, as the greater part was generally English, after he had preached in French, he would resume his discourse in that language. In those days he was many a time followed as he left the pulpit, so that he was occupied in incessant ministry throughout the day, both public and private.

Occasionally ministers from abroad applied for his pulpit, and to such of them as could not express themselves fluently in French, he himself acted as interpreter. We

* The name of the chapel founded in 1830 by the Evangelical Society under Gaussen, Merle d'Aubigné, &c.—*Note by Translator.*

shall have occasion, by and by, to describe a communion Sunday in his congregation. Thus his life, and that of his Church, came into mutual contact in a thousand ways, and that by an influence as simply exercised as it was freely accepted; so that his ministry, especially up to 1830, would have been eminently peaceable but for the collisions with the seceding communion, whose formation had preceded that of his own congregation at a considerable interval. Surrounded by simple-minded people who owed to his ministrations all the spiritual light which they sought ever to increase at his hands, esteemed as everything to them, in not merely furnishing them with a place of worship, but with the very instruction and exhortation they desired, even with the very hymns in which they celebrated the praises of God, it would seem that he was destined to continue with them to the end, their beloved and revered pastor.

Never did a note of discord make itself heard within the community. His influence was too overwhelming, the veneration which hedged him in too profound, to admit of any opposition to his ministry arising from among his own people.*

---

* A word here respecting the pecuniary advantages which my father derived from his congregation, a matter about which much misrepresentation has taken place. At first such a question was not even entertained. A little before 1830, however, a friend of his, a Vaudois clergyman, happening to visit him, spoke to the members of the congregation and to my father himself of the necessity, on many accounts, of their presenting him with a salary. That visit decided the arrangement, which was kept up for about fifteen years. The sum, at first collected by the deacons, and afterwards deposited (as successive members desired to contribute) in a church box, labelled, "for the ministry of the chapel," amounted, on an average, to 500f. a year, or £20. These details were procured by the author from one of the surviving deacons of the Church, a man well known in the congregation, and who helped Malan in his ministry nearly from its commencement.

But outside it was different. The Church of the Bourg de Four, more especially, distinguished by religious individualism, and indisposed to bow to its own pastors, was not likely to bow to him. And hence it came to pass that in its occasional interchanges with Malan's congregation, it often seemed to forget that the pastor of that congregation was the very man whose courage and constancy had once received so much of their applause.

To Malan himself, however much he might desire it, a complete fusion with his brethren was simply impossible, partly from the indefiniteness of their views on the doctrines of grace, partly from certain Baptist tendencies which sprang up amongst them. To this must be added, on their side, all those discussions concerning the constitution and government of a religious community, which, inasmuch as they necessarily, especially in so reduced a sphere, involved personal questions, could not fail to mix up bitter dissensions with what ought to have merely given rise to a *distinction* between the two communities. At that fact of a distinction my father wished them to stop. Even when he found himself obliged to constitute a separate Church, its external regulation never appeared to him of primary importance ; nor did it involve in his eyes a question of dogma. From the very beginning he handled all such matters in the most liberal spirit, reserving the widest possible margin for difference of sentiment, and adaptation to the peculiar circumstances of each Church. While Establishment men and dissenters around him were wrangling about things essentially external ; while, especially, (at the time of which we are speaking, 1824–1825), the congregation of the Bourg de Four was confounding visible with spiritual unity, he did not hesitate to affirm what M. Bost repeated afterwards, that "invisible agreement amid visible disagreements was the constant law of the kingdom of God." High as were the views he held of the dignity of the pastoral office, he never could regard the Church external as directly and expressly constituted and ordained from above. Hence arose the difficulties which beset him in his relations with the Bourg de Four.

Admitting the inexpediency of setting down here the details of this quasi-collision, it will be desirable to glance at them sufficiently to show the special line my father took, and the spirit which animated his flock. The subjects which led to the disagreements were purely passing questions, such as cannot fail even now to present themselves to the consideration of the Churches in proportion as they diverge from the path of old traditions, while it is to be remarked that all modern ecclesiastical progress is invariably in that direction.

But, in order clearly to understand the point, it may be as well to refer to the position of the Church of the Bourg de Four at the time of which we are speaking.

Anxious, above everything, to cultivate intimate relations with their brethren in the faith, the members of this congregation were penetrated by a peculiar dread of isolation, or, as they termed it, sectarianism. This is evident from an "exposé," addressed by their pastors in October 1825, "to all the Churches of Christ."

After recalling the truth that there is "one fold and one shepherd," they went on to show how each minister was not the shepherd, but the mere servant of his flock. They then went on to say that each separate Church was but a portion of the fold of Jesus Christ. Each sheep, they argued, belonged to the general fold, and not to that particular portion of it where the shepherd might have placed him. This led to the obvious conclusion that no sheep could submit himself to one under shepherd exclusively; and that, on the other hand, all faithful shepherds should hold themselves, in a measure, responsible to give spiritual nurture to all sheep in the universal fold.

Under the influence of these opinions the Church of the Bourg de Four published a rule by which it declared that every believer, communicating in its chapel, was bound to submit himself to all that Scripture teaches in reference to the mutual relation between pastors and flocks; in other words, that every one who took the communion in that congregation was expected to bow to the pastoral authority of its special conductors.

On receiving this singular declaration, Malan's congregation responded by a letter the length of which compels me reluctantly to quote it only in part. Setting forth their high esteem for the pastors of the other Church, the members of the Pré l'Evêque express their regret that, by the declaration come to hand, they are virtually precluded from communicating henceforth, as they had frequently done, in the Bourg de Four, inasmuch as to do so, according to the terms of that declaration, would require them to withdraw themselves from the care of their own minister, to be presided over by one of the sister community.

"To show you," says the letter, "that we greatly regret the necessity to which your rule has reduced us, we prayerfully invite you, in the Name of the Lord, to come amongst us, and communicate with us as often as opportunity offers. We assure you that, by so receiving you, we should place no yoke on your necks; that it would be far from our thought that, by fraternising with us, you would come under our pastor's authority. So come, dear brethren, for we interpose no hindrance. Be present with us at the table of the same Lord. You prevent us from coming to you, but since the same difficulties do not present themselves in our case, rejoice our hearts by your presence."

In addition to this letter, my father wrote himself to the pastors of the sister congregations.

In this letter he enters into a full justification of the reply forwarded by his people. I need quote but one sentence, in which he censures the idea "that a national Church is the world, or that any one, in taking the communion in such a church, would, by that act alone, fail in his duty as a child of God." All this, however, he laid down in detail in an essay called "Unity in Diversity," which, though it was printed by him at the time, unhappily was never circulated.

Distinguishing at the outset between the inward and spiritual, and outward and visible Church, he declares that essential unity can co-exist with external diversity. He then goes on to obviate all confusion of ideas, to which such theories may have given rise: 1. As to the visible unity of the universal Church; 2. As to the mutual attitude of separate Churches; 3. As to the pastoral duties and authority.

On the first point he remarks: "As for the unity of the

K

Church, it appears to me that the Saviour's kingdom is not of this world; that is, is not visible. In a spiritual sense the Lord Jesus is the sole Shepherd of the flock. But as far as earthly and temporal circumstances are concerned, does He show Himself in that capacity? Even at the Millennium will He appear as a visible Shepherd? I do not think so. Hence He calls Himself Supreme Bishop and Pastor, implying that He has others under Him, whose flocks should submit themselves to an administration adapted to their peculiar wants and circumstances.

St Paul, dwelling upon this point in a letter to two temporal shepherds, recalls to their minds, not the great abstract principles of ecclesiastical discipline, but the particular instructions they had received from his own life. That over-ruling Providence, wonderful in counsel, and infinite in resource, settles for such and such souls the discipline best adapted to their condition: nor does He work otherwise in the general body, wherever represented and however characterised. Whilst the sheep feed in different pastures, and are nourished up unto God's kingdom and glory, the great fold is preparing above; that fold is the city of God, the new Jerusalem.

With regard to the second point, he found that this want of distinction between the temporal and spiritual element in the Church had the effect of preventing those he was addressing from arriving at a fair estimate of the mutual relation subsisting between visible communions, inasmuch as it led them to conclude that the pastors of any special congregation were pastors of the Church collectively, as soon as the whole Church was in spiritual communion with that single body. He then shows them how by such a theory they mix up general and strictly pastoral discipline.

"Of course," he adds, "it would be most desirable to see Churches united in discipline as well as faith, so long as they continued true to the gospel they professed. But such uniformity does not exist, and we must allow that the Chief Shepherd of the flock can give His own reasons of infinite wisdom for dispensing with it. Nor can we doubt that He approves of this external diversity, since He owns and prospers communions differing materially in mere externals. Yours is a proof of the truth of this. I know that it has been abundantly blessed; but then the same is true of others also."

"The greatest Church privilege," he resumes,—and the word is characteristic from his point of view,—"is the spiritual guidance which the pastoral office provides; all other benefits fall infinitely short of this,—to be under the discipline of the Lord Himself, to be taught, reproved, corrected, and instructed in righteousness by men of God, to whom He has entrusted this solemn charge." Then, as a proof that this statement in no way exhibited a sectarian spirit, he supposes that there would be in Geneva three or four other faithful Churches, national or independent, and professing the same faith as his own. A stranger passing through the city, and communicating in all of these, could scarcely be held to be a member of each. Otherwise, to which of them would he belong, in points wherein they differed from one another; as, for instance, baptism?

From this he passes on to the third point relating to the pastoral charge. "Of course, most honoured brethren, particular Churches are mere sections of the universal

Church, but, I think each flock should have its own shepherd, who should call in assistance, such as the Diaconate furnishes, chosen by the Church for its temporal government." Observing that each of the seven Churches of Asia received separate and special instructions, he argues the solemn responsibility laid on Christian ministers to guard the truth committed to them, of which they will have to give account.

He undertakes to demonstrate that as each individual soul has its own separate needs, the pastor could not exercise his office satisfactorily, in utter ignorance of these personal details. Touching the pastoral authority, he quotes the direction to a bishop to employ in the government of the Church of God that careful administration which he would exercise in his own household (1 Tim. iii. 4.) As each family has its Head, so should it be with every flock; and we may rest assured that He Who has been appointed over His own spiritual house—that is, the Son of God—will ever be found distributing to separate pastors such wisdom and prudence as shall tend, in their manifestation, to the honour and praise of God.

Thus, it will appear, that in the Church, the spiritual and the temporal, the duties of ministers and the office of pastors must never be confounded. Nor must we confine ourselves to seeing, on the one hand, only the invisible kingdom of the Lord Jesus, as established by His Spirit in the hearts of believers; or, on the other, a mere system of scientific evangelical lore; neglecting, meanwhile, "that personal and progressive application which bears upon the everyday life of the people of God."

He then glanced at the practical impossibility of subjecting one Church to the rule of many pastors. "From the autocrat who sways the destinies of an empire to the humble swain who has but a few goats to look after, all power proceeds from the only true absolute Source of Power, and Who, in the eternity of His resources, and the wisdom of His appliances, governs the whole creation, not only in a grandly comprehensive sense, but in respect of its minutest details. But it is clear that over this vast concourse of powers or inferior agencies there cannot be two supreme wills in exercise at one and the same time. Find me a kingdom, or a province, a society, or a household, with two absolute heads, and you would produce a mere human anomaly, and not a divine economy. And, even should you succeed, you would soon ascertain that, after all, there was but one positive Head, one will for every effect produced ; that the really higher cause was virtually acquiesced in by the others, or, in other words, existed alone.

"To say that any congregation not refusing to admit the governance of many pastors is a sect, is to affix that stigma to the congregations of those faithful and renowned Churches which God has planted in England, Scotland, Ireland, France, Switzerland, Germany, Holland, throughout America, in Asia and Africa; all which maintain and teach that a Church which has many flocks has as many pastors as flocks. So stands the case, for example, with the Presbyterian Church of Geneva, or with that of France." He concludes by examining one by one the Scripture passages quoted against him.

I thought it desirable to give this long extract, because Malan has been credited with extreme narrow-mindedness in reference to the entire dispute. For my own part, as I glance at the piety, moderation, and (once admit the idea of the Church common to both parties) the conclusiveness of his arguments, I cannot help recalling Noeff's letter on the same subject, and regretting once more that two men so well adapted for understanding each other, had been separated by the aversion Noeff entertained to my father's method of preaching election.

As we shall see, no alteration took place in my father's views of the question. If he appeared to waive them on certain occasions,—as, for example, when in 1827, as he was starting on a missionary journey, he recommended his flock to abstain from worshipping in the National Church,—the reasons he gave prove that it was not the constitution of the Establishment that he objected to, but its erroneous teaching. These principles explain the position he alone, of all the dissenting ministers, took with reference to the question of separation between Church and State, as well as his attitude towards the Free Church of Scotland, and also the Evangelical Church which was established in Geneva in 1849. On these different occasions, while entirely sympathising with his brethren, he invariably postponed to the right of private judgment and independence of individual members, the desire to identify a more visible conformity with that true and essential unity which the truth creates.

Referring only to the period antecedent to 1830, this disagreement on ecclesiastical points rendered it increasingly hopeless for him to attempt to come to a thorough union with his dissenting brethren round him.

Not only did he deeply regret that estrangement, but it also involved him in much misrepresentation. Yet, though he was known to lament this among his private friends, he was never heard to recriminate. It was not till after he died, that I met with documents which put the matter in its proper light. As I read them, they conjured up before me, with regard to the relation existing between my father and the leaders on the opposite side, the unhappy spectacle of an enthusiastic and generous man, a stranger to every species of dissimulation and suspicion, encountering minds too often unable to understand him, and hearts that could seldom rise to the level of his feelings. As far as he was concerned, he seems to me to have been too little able to place himself in the position of those whose judgments he too keenly resented. In his dealings with his "beloved brethren," as he continually calls them, he appeared never to have been able to unite with the harmlessness of the dove, which all recognised in his bearing, that wisdom of the serpent which the heavenly Master no less enjoins.

As has been already said, it would be better to avoid dwelling longer on debates in which both sides appeared to give to the questions at issue an exaggerated importance. Unquestionably, there were not wanting those who were ready to attribute to individual bias an opposition naturally arising from an essential divergence in first principles. On the one hand, it would have been well to have seen in the "brethren," not the spirit of this world, which had been so loudly repudiated, with its polished fashions and plausible forms, but of another, its superior even in this special respect; while, on the other hand, the truth might have been more constantly remembered, that this better world, instead of being promised to the faithful below, is part of that future which all are taught to expect. From the moment any one made a distinct profession, he was expected to exhibit in fullest development all the crowning graces of ideal Christianity. This was to forget that the Communion of Saints is a thing of faith, as well as of sight; and that Christ's kingdom is not, and cannot be, of this world.

Considerations like the above may serve to explain the spirit and attitude of the congregation in the Bourg de Four. Starting into life in 1817, eight years before the community in the Pré l'Evêque was established, my father's act in preferring a congregation of his own to union with them was openly attributed to a sectarian and schismatical spirit. This judgment they supported by a declaration of ecclesiastical principles, published in 1825. Although they freely withdrew it three years afterwards, they did not scruple to return the decided refusal which my father, (not as a Christian brother, but in his capacity as the conductor of a distinct congregation,) opposed to their desire of external unity, by attacks aimed not only at his public ministry, but even at his private character.

I have before me a lengthy memoir, in which, setting aside all private and personal questions, he reviews his public life from 1818, with the object of refuting these accusations. He brings before those to whom he is writing the numerous proofs he had given them from the very first, of his brotherly spirit, and explains at the same time the real character of the question on which they split. The address is quiet, dignified, and affectionate. I will confine myself to one extract, illustrative of what has been already said as to his views on the necessity for separate communions.

In connection with the opinion which had been put forth that one Church was sufficient for a town, he says, "It is by no means reasoning soundly in the interests of Church constitution and discipline to urge that we ought to reproduce a servile imitation of the Primitive Church, since, in laying down such a principle, we suffer ourselves to be led by the Church instead of by the Spirit of God. That Divine Teacher, Whose infinite wisdom adapts itself to all the phases of varying conditions, while He has given, in the letters to Timothy and Titus, endless directions for the ministers of God, can vouchsafe to us and our flocks like holy guidance, suggesting, directing, or deciding, both with reference to their peculiar and special wants, and to the greater advancement of the cause of the gospel, in the presence of various particular circumstances."

Elsewhere he makes earnest appeal to the fraternal spirit of those to whom he is writing, by reminding them that they had replied to the letter from his congregation, referred to above, with the utmost wisdom and charity; and recalling the circumstance that, in 1827 and 1828, the two bodies had frequently communicated together, and the pastors exchanged pulpits.

He regrets that divisions should have transpired between them, while the explanations which he adds show that his chief offences consisted in his using his academical title of doctor in theology, his wearing his bachelor's gown in the pulpit, or rather, as it was called, his preacher's robe, but, above all, the absolute independence which he claimed for himself and his special work.

The very fact that he was thus assailed, gave a prominence to himself and everything connected with him, which could not fail to be in a measure irksome to his flock.

Meanwhile his work continued to prosper. Not only, especially after 1827, did the attendance of strangers at his chapel become very considerable; but, in March 1830, the congregation was forced to take into consideration the expediency of erecting a second building elsewhere for its regular members, now too numerous to be accommodated in the Pré l'Evêque.

All this could not but revive either the susceptibilities or the scruples of the sister Church. Taken up with their ecclesiastical views, they saw, in an ordinary illustration of the law of progress, the advancing shade of arrogance, and premeditated priestly despotism. Especially at a time when, in the religious as well as in the political world, the very semblance of authority was apt to raise a cry, (French Revolution of 1830,) such an accusation needed only to be hinted at to find eager acceptance. We cannot wonder, therefore, at its having spread by degrees amongst the members of the congregation of the Pré l'Evêque, whose community had so long been characterised by the peace it enjoyed.

In May 1830, my father, perceiving signs of uneasiness in many members of his flock, appealed to them generally for a vote of confidence. True to himself, he grounded his application, not on the claims of his ministry, but the soundness of his teaching; taking care, at the same time, in his conscientious uprightness, to present them with a summary of it, most explicitly worded. Thus he transformed his Church into a theological council. The result might easily have been anticipated. Even those who were capable of following their pastor into the field of dogmatic theology, did not fail to detect, when they arrived there, matter for scruple. The majority denied his right to impose upon them officially the faith which they held spontaneously, and thus the most advanced and the most independent of his adherents withdrew from the Church. It lost about a third of its members, who went over forthwith to the Bourg de Four.

This secession has been occasionally represented as the consequence of the pride of success, which my father is said to have displayed. This was the opinion taken up by Dr Ostertag of Bâle, in the truthful and touching notice of Malan, which he published. He would have found in this dogmatism, which he so justly appreciated, a more satisfactory explanation of facts which he could only have apprehended but by report.

The truth is that my father, in his dealings with his church, had no choice but to exercise an influence heartily acknowledged; still further, that in the zealous and loving discharge of the duties which a trusting people had laid upon him, there was nothing to give rise either to pride or ambition in a man of his parts. On the contrary—and here my testimony merits acceptance—no one was less of a despot than he, if by despotism we understand, as we ought, not the absorbing influence exercised involuntarily by a superior mind, but that pedantic and restless tyranny which asserts itself by gratuitous assaults on the rights and feelings of those it seeks to rule.* To confine myself,

---

* To a person who consulted him on a point of ecclesiastical polity, he writes in 1828 :—" Why address yourself to any other but our gracious Lord, in order to know His will about these questions. Could I ever have that authority over your conscience which belongs only to God ?"

however, to the case before us. Nothing, so far as I can remember, (and of the incidents of May 1830 I have a most vivid recollection), or others whom I have questioned on the subject—nothing, more especially in the numerous documents before me referring to that time, gives the faintest colour to this imputation. On the contrary, everything that occurred, so far as he was concerned, tended to impress, and even edify, any unprejudiced person.

That he had throughout such faults as God alone can be judge of, he openly acknowledged to the brethren, but the very frankness with which he makes his confession deprives his critics of the right of laying others to his charge.

He writes thus (November 1830) in the "Memoir" already referred to, with reference to the recent incidents in his Church :—

"As for these troubles, I am prepared to give account to my Lord and Master of the souls committed to my charge, and He will have mercy on His servant. He knows whereof I am made; that I am a man prone to error, to every species of infirmity, to every possibility of falling, and His compassions are from everlasting to everlasting. I would fall into His hands, and not into the hands of man. Leave me, I beseech you, in my Saviour's arms, and if you think that I am neither happy nor peaceful there — pray the more that I may realise the blessedness of His perfect peace. I have erred, I have been led astray, with regard to my authority. I have used it to abuse it. I have wronged my flock, my brethren—those dear to me as my own children. The eternal God, in His mercy, has roused me from my delusion; He has anointed my eyes; He has taken me in hand and taught me, and the chastisement has been applied by His fatherly love. The Lord's name be praised! He has not let me go. He has come to my soul, and quickened it with new life. Had I regarded iniquity in my heart, He would not have heard me, but I know that He has not withdrawn His tender mercies from me. My humiliation is from Him, and He has enabled me to ask forgiveness of my brethren whom I have offended. I do so with all my heart and all my soul, and I will do so more pointedly still if for their satisfaction they require it." He adds, " that in all that had occurred no wrong had been done to those who had reproached him, towards whom he was conscious of no offence, either in thought or action."

This will show how he condemned himself at this time. It will show, too, his entire freedom from bitterness as he thought of occurrences which could not fail to remind him, though from a different point of view, of his own secession six years before from the National Church. Subsequently, many of the deserters came back, and in no single case did the separation prove a lasting one. Soon after this the Evangelical Society occupied the ground which had hitherto been monopolised by the two congregations which had represented the Revival movement in Geneva, and greatly diminished their importance.

From this period (1830), although my father's congregation continued for a considerable time to hold a marked place in the religious world in Geneva, it never witnessed a return of its former days. The secession, especially at the time of its occurrence, was a very painful blow to him. Still he did not suffer himself to despond. His pas-

toral duties being thus considerably reduced, he occupied
himself with writing and evangelising (the latter a task
for which he was eminently fitted).   The records of his
missionary efforts will now demand our attention.

Before quitting our present subject, however, there are.
two observations to be made—

And first, and chiefly; however deplorable some of
the circumstances just recorded may appear, it is but fair
to state that, even by those whose hostility was most
openly expressed, the claims of Christian consistency were
never utterly and finally disregarded.

Our second remark bears upon the explanation required
of doings so little to be expected from unaffectedly
religious men.   The truth of the matter is that, except on
isolated occasions, the relations between the two congregations were never cordial.   Both my personal recollections,
and an anxious study of the documents before me—giving
a detailed history of events before and after 1830—confirm me in the opinion that the cause of these difficulties
must be attributed to an essential discrepancy in the
lines which each one of these two communities was
respectively following.

Of this my father was distinctly conscious.   Ever ready
to yield to the impulses of a truly Christian feeling of
fraternity; prepared, too, to make advances himself;
anxious to prove the liveliness of his esteem by an entire
obliviousness of what had distressed him in the past, and
by those sacrifices of his own importance to which his
generous nature was so ready to urge him; he had to deal
with men who, from the very fact of their inability to give
a categorical account of the reasons of their estrangement,

were unhappily induced to seek them on personal grounds,
thus interposing always a personal element in what
ought to have been a purely abstract and independent
difference of opinion. Meanwhile, if we reflect a little on
the spirit which has disturbed the Church of the Bourg
de Four from its commencement—on the constant striv-
ings which it has made to realise an external religious
unity—on the utopian schemes which it has projected
from time to time—on the sensitive jealousy of its members with reference to their rights—on the extreme importance attached by them to questions of ecclesiastical
administration ; if we go on to recall the period at which,
after its augmentation through the secession from the
Pré l'Evêque, it was invaded by Darbyism—we shall
understand how, from the very beginning, its pastors have
had to deal with that same ambitious aggressive spirit,
that spirit of levelling—envious, and suspicious : which
ere long revealed itself in the political life of our little
country.

It will be evident that it was hopeless to expect that
one with Malan's temperament,—an ardent lover of
symmetry and good order, a poet by nature, with a
strong chivalrous leaning to old historical traditions and
associations, as well as to the worship of the past,—could
harmonise with men like these, except by an effort of
charity; or meet them on any other ground than that of
Christian brotherhood.

We may state with confidence that the primary source
of these lamentable occurrences is to be traced to this
opposition, invariably existing between "religious radical-
ism" and the conservative ecclesiastical spirit which leans

not a little on traditional guidance. Meanwhile, it must undoubtedly be admitted that the events themselves seriously thwarted my father's pastoral work, to which he was so entirely devoted, and occasioned no little suffering to himself.

And yet, this story told, the relations between the two Churches were by no means broken off. As a proof of this, in 1835 a collection was made in the Chapel of Testimony in aid of an institute connected with the other congregation, while, in 1839, the two bodies communicated together. Gradually, however, in consequence of the inroads of Darbyism, the oratory of the Evangelical Society became the only asylum of a ministry such as had always existed in Malan's congregation.

Later on we shall discover what prevented the remnant of that little Church from joining that union which, under the one title of " the Evangelical Church," came to reunite, in 1849, the various dissenting Presbyterians of Geneva.

I have thought it desirable to add to this chapter a few letters from my father's pastoral correspondence. Ever active as it was, it was one of the most conspicuous elements in his influence. My selection, however, will be limited to the following, which I deem characteristic, the greater part of which I have chosen from those written at the period just reviewed :—

I.—TO A CLERGYMAN INTERRUPTED IN HIS WORK BY A VISITATION OF SICKNESS.

" *March* 7, 1827.

"It is not along the easy path of health and unchecked obedience that the minister of Christ learns himself. In the midst of the noble task entrusted to him, and of the blessings of which he is the steward to so many souls, nothing is easier than for him to become remiss in self-knowledge. You are highly favoured, brother, in being withdrawn into the silence of Divine teaching, that you may learn for yourself that true self-renunciation brings with it the positive and living experience of the good pleasure and of the life of God. When would the minister of the Lord understand that the work entrusted to him is not his own, if not when he is withdrawn from activity and forced to inaction? The fisherman, sitting down to mend his nets, is no idler! The faithful and tender Master be present with you! May you rejoice that He has thus prepared you for nearer communion with Himself!"

II.—TO AN OLD FRIEND, REV. G—— N——.

"*March* 29, 1827.

"Life is very short, and to employ the least part of it in deprivation of communion with God, through doubt and unbelief, is to forget this. Each day solemnises me more; death seems to me so serious, and meeting with my God so near, that I abstain from forming any plans. The words, 'Haste Thee!' seem to be constantly repeated to me; and I feel, in short, 'how frail I am.' I am fain to weep, too, over my trifling spirit and feeble devotion to the glorious Master I profess to serve!

"Serve! Is the preaching of a gospel so sweet to proclaim—*serving* Jesus? The pulpit should be our resting-place. Our work lies in the whole conduct of the brief life allotted us; that conduct should be to us a beginning

L

of heaven. Let us realise, let us realise the gospel! We are not actors on a stage, but men in life, and on the threshold of the unseen world. Eternity, my friend, ... an awful word! What duration! Think of the amazement of a Christian first opening his eyes in heaven; while, as he takes in the reality of what he believed and heard, he receives into his whole soul the conception and the force of the word ' for ever.'

"Let us curtail our vanities. There are plenty of them in the ordinary life of Christians : long conversations, long calls, long meals, long nothings, long hypocrisy of sentiment, long talks about religion; while, on the one hand, the world with its fashion is passing away; and, on the other, Jesus stands at the door and knocks.

"As for religious intelligence, I know not what to say. ' One day at a time,' is my motto; I am ignorant of the art of conjecturing."

III.—TO A SOLDIER AT COURT.

" *May* 16, 1828.

"My DEAR SIR,—First let me say, that, as it appears to me, you make a great mistake in regarding your condition as a soldier as a hindrance to your conversion. The gospel of the grace of God is for all conditions; it is calculated to make a monarch successful in his difficult task, and a workman equally so, in his obscure and far easier life.

"In the condition in which you are now placed, and wherein your own will is in submission to that of your superiors, you have the very greatest facilities for learning obedience, and humbling that pride and self-complacency to which we are so prone. Your duty is, 'not to entangle yourself with the things of this life, that you may please those who have called you to be a soldier;' those, in short, whom God has placed over you, with an authority entrusted to them by Himself. The more attentive you are in the discharge of duty, even in the smallest details, the happier you will be, the freer from reproach. For God blesses order, and a well-regulated life, wherever it is to be found; and He has attached peace and temporal prosperity to the conscientious fulfilling of the requirements of our position. I invite you, then, to show yourself exemplary in your trust, and to neglect nothing, so that those over you may have a full and entire satisfaction in you.

"For example; should you omit any portion of your duty, even for the reading of the Word of God, you fail to observe that command which calls upon you to render to all their dues, and to the king the king's. Now, the sovereign you serve has a right to receive from you the service he enjoins. You are in no way permitted to divert or detract even a minute from his time, nor to relax in any way the devotion which your earthly ruler requires and expects. Your readings, therefore, must take place at another time than that demanded for your duties; nor must they ever interfere in the least degree with what you are engaged to do in behalf of the company in which you serve, and the honour of your superiors.

"Hence it follows, my friend, that your degradation may have arisen from some negligence of yours, rather than from any hostility on the part of the authorities to the principles you profess; and you may be wrong in attributing to the reproach of Christ a chastisement with which

God Himself has visited your unfaithfulness in your duty. Not that I can speak authoritatively on this head, ignorant as I am of the circumstances. I only say this, that before setting to the account of persecution against the Lord or His children any possible treatment at the hands of man, it would be well for us to examine whether we are ourselves responsible for it, and whether we are not receiving the due reward of our own imprudence."

IV.—TO A LADY, AGAINST THE ABUSE OF IMAGINATION AND DOGMATISM.

"*January* 18, 1832.

". . . . Observe well, whether the Lord Jesus, in His heavenly hidden life, is better known, is better served, by a doctrine. If it be so, if, in short, the soul exercised in these matters, is more humble, more withdrawn from fame and renown, more absorbed into, more intimate with heaven, not through speculation, but the power of spiritual life; if that soul be, in a word, more clothed with Christ, and not with religious science, then you may conclude that it lives in fact with Jesus. Now the first effect of that life will be, or I am mistaken, not external movement, even in truths the most generally received in the Churches, but inward meditation, and inward occupation with a blessed immortality. Here then, are my directions, dear sister; the Holy Spirit can, if He deems them right, make use of them for your good; and if I have not spoken according to the word, He can no less remove their impression, that your soul may not suffer from my counsel.

"You complain that you have little joy in communion with your Lord. Unquestionably the cause of this is to be found in ourselves: either in our want of honest watchfulness, or of thorough belief that God really loves us, or of attentive study of the full scope of His promises in His Word. Our hearts are dull, they would fain enjoy surrounding things; and, since our imagination lives too frequently in fictitious excitements and illusions, the solemn and holy reality of faith, of the love of an invisible God, enchains us but little, as being too severe for our nature. It is very necessary to learn this, and to combat it honestly, with habitual prayer, and a solemn vow before God to banish all imaginations and reveries, whencesoever they may arise, and to substitute for them meditation on Himself; for this sincerity is needed.

"If you love little, let your soul cheer itself with the bliss of being loved. Here, there is no room for doubt; for what a love is that which the Saviour feels!"

V.—TO HIS CHURCH, ON THE SPRINGS OF SANCTIFICATION IN THE SOUL.

"*June* 14, 1832.

"We journey together through the world, drawing daily nearer to death, and to that solemn moment when faith will be exchanged for sight, when we shall cease to learn, when there will be no more error, no more delusion, no more temptation, no more sin. God has caused us to know the mystery of His love towards us. It is for us to glorify Him with the adoration and humble trust of reconciled children, to whom their father has forgiven everything, and whom He is leading tenderly by the hand to the paternal home, where He will cause them to know all His love.

"Wherefore, dear friends in the Lord, learn well what

should be the issue of such assurance. Has God done these great things? has He smitten, has He sacrificed, His Only Begotten? Has He raised Him up again, only that His elect may be delivered from condemnation; and that, by believing this, they may rejoice together at freedom from the fear of hell? Rather, is it not that God has prepared and called unto Himself a peculiar people, that they may, first of all, declare His praises here, and that they may, hereafter dwell, for ever in heaven—living monuments of His grace and glory? We are raised from the dead, my brethren! Our soul participates in the first resurrection; the life that we now live in the flesh we live by faith in Jesus Who has loved us; and, for the issue, the aim, the accomplishment of that faith which is the image of God in us. In heaven it will be found true that it was not for our sakes that God chose us, but rather for Himself, to show forth His glory in us His creatures, the exceeding riches of His justice and goodness, and to manifest to the world and the powers of heaven the infinite wisdom and holiness of His Divine compassion. Hence we rob God of His right, we take from Him what belongs to Him, if we imagine that a chosen one belongs to himself, that he is at liberty to live according to his own will, and to content himself with merely ceasing to fear hell, and hoping for and expecting heaven.

"Meditate on these things, my dear flock, whom I am called to nourish in the truth, and for whom I shall have to give account to my Master. Think seriously, you who are in Christ, on that life in Christ which you ought to live. And how will you say, one day, that your life has been lived, according to the life of Christ, if Christ has not dwelt in the details, the constituents of that life; if your own desires, your own thoughts, your own wisdom, your own interests, your own glory, your own ease, have been the mainspring of your actions. If this has been the case from minute to minute, from hour to hour, without a thought of Christ or His word, without the influence of His Spirit, how will you be able even to *suppose* hereafter that you have *lived in Christ?*"

VI.—WRITTEN IN 1838, IN HIS OWN NAME AND IN THE NAME OF HIS CONGREGATION, TO CERTAIN SECEDING CHURCHES AT THAT TIME PASSING THROUGH A PERIOD OF PERSECUTION.*

"DEAR AND HONOURED BRETHREN IN JESUS CHRIST— our Life, our Strength, our Hope!

"We have experienced in your affliction, from the day we heard of it, the truth that we are one body in Christ, and, through His Spirit, members one of another. The trials that you have had to encounter, and which you are still enduring, in the upholding of your faith, are no strange thing to us, seeing that it has already been our privilege to receive unrighteous dealing from the world, with the weight of its scorn, for the name of the Lord Jesus. Moreover, even before your brotherly love had solicited us to humble ourselves with you, we had been led, of the Lord, to remember you before Him in the closest fellowship of prayer. It was needful for us to unite with you in His gracious presence, Who, if He visits and judges His own House,

* I am sorry I cannot give it all. It is dated October 29, and addressed "to the Dutch Churches, suffering for the truth's sake."

and tries the genuineness of our faith in Him, does it only out of the depth of His compassions, which lie at the root of all His dealings, and who is afflicted in all the affliction of His people.

" Undoubtedly, dear and honoured brethren, the path of renunciation, of sacrifice, and of persecution, which you have now for a long time been traversing, is hard to tread. To be oppressed, to be spoiled of our goods, imprisoned, driven from our home, esteemed as evil, denounced as accursed by stern laws, is severe discipline. But what soul is there, really taught by the Holy Spirit, that does not know that it is at such a time that the Holy Son of God vouchsafes His mighty consolation ?

" And even, beloved brethren, supposing that this were not the case, that the Lord were to wait for another season to comfort your hearts, it would never be for a long time that you would have to endure the trial of your faith. Were you in prosperity, your life would be what it always is, short, swift, soon over. Passing it in affliction, you pass it with the same Lord as then, and under the same conditions ; in other words, as strangers and foreigners, as pilgrims to the celestial country, to the Home whither Jesus has preceded you, and where He will receive you to His glorious repose.

" To Him, then, we would have each of you cling through this painful struggle. It is easy, beloved, when we are engaged in a fight—even in the good and holy fight of faith—and when we are called upon to contend earnestly for the sacred depository of truth, it is only too easy *then* to deceive ourselves, by taking the externals of belief for faith itself, the honour of the Church for truth, Church

principles for Jesus Himself. How many persons profess to follow the teaching of the Word, and yet, at a
time when they ought to be exhibiting a firm consistency,
become estranged from the heart of Jesus, and forget, even
outrage, the spirit of love, while they are displaying at the
same time the most devoted zeal, and submitting to the
most costly sacrifices! What an injury it is to the good
work of faith when the children of God commit the fatal
error of putting their Church in the place of the spouse of
Jesus; and fidelity to it, for that obedience which faith owes
to the King of Zion.

"Be on your guard, then, dear and honoured brethren,
and cherish, as your deepest and most abiding feeling, a
humble desire to follow Jesus, and to exalt Him, and not
yourselves, in your Churches.

"Alas, beloved brethren, it is because we ourselves at
Geneva, and others in other parts of Switzerland, have
sinned a sin still in this respect, that we speak thus.
Let the sword of persecution be in the hands of the world,
never of the brethren. Never let differences of views or
opinions in what does not appertain to Christ Himself,
separate the members of His Body. We have learnt that
this evil has reached you. Alas, if we, the children of
God, were more penetrated with a sense of the unspeakable
value of the Father's gift in His Son, earthly things would
cease to have any undue influence over us.

"Men of the world, and among them many children of
God, weak, and still under worldly influence, stand aloof
from you. They regard you as enemies of their Church,
and overbearing children. They despise you, they push you
from them, they visit you with ignominious treatment!

Well, be it so ! They will yet be compelled to admit, that if you are firm in your faith and in the public profession you are justified in making, you are not the less distinguished for the charity which unites you in Jesus, the King of your souls, for your compassion for your persecutors, as well as for your meek submission under their iniquitous proceedings, which affect not merely yourselves as Christians, but even the very Christ of God.

"May the Lord Jesus see us walking in the light of His countenance, apart from the darkness of this wicked world, on the narrow path where His footsteps may be traced. It matters little whether we are honoured, welcomed, approved, or upheld even, by our brethren; but it matters much whether we are holy and blameless, and whether the light of our faith, love, and patience, burns uninterruptedly before the eyes of our fellow-men, and whether thus, in Holland, Switzerland, or elsewhere, those who know the Lord and rejoice in the light of His countenance, show forth by their steadfast and holy conversation the glories of Him Who has loved them in Christ Jesus with an everlasting love."

CHAPTER IV.

> Mine be the reverend, listening love,
>   That waits all day on Thee,
> With the service of a watchful heart,
>   Which no one else can see.
> The faith that, in a hidden way
>   No other eye may know,
> Finds all its daily work prepared,
>   And loves to have it so.

IN the previous chapter, we traced out Malan's pastoral work as far as 1830. We will now retrace our steps for the purpose of taking a general view of his exertions during that period, besides his pastoral duties. As the narrative of his missionary efforts is to be reserved for the period when he was led to devote himself more especially to them, our present review will be chiefly directed to his literary labours.

As we have already seen, before his conversion he published only two class text-books of no great importance. When, however, he found himself debarred from preaching, he felt all the stirrings of that desire to propagate the truth, which is so universal in the hearts of living Christians. From that time, he sought means to reach by his pen those whom he was not suffered to address from the pulpit. Already in 1814, when what he himself calls the first dawnings of the truth were breaking in upon his soul, he had translated some English tracts, and shortly afterwards, he presented his pupils with " The Old Man of Ellacombe," a little book which M. Guers had just rendered in French, from the same language.

It was not till 1819 that he issued his three first tracts, which were almost immediately translated into English, German, and Italian. These were, " Germain the Woodcutter," " The Two Old Men," and " The Young Plaster Figure Vendors." From that time, up to 1830, new works issued from his pen; among which were some of the best he ever produced. To mention only a few : In 1821 appeared " The Poor Watchmaker of Geneva," and " La Valaisanne;" in 1823, " The Truly Catholic Protestant;" in 1825, " The Conversion of the Atheist;" in 1827, " The New Bartimaeus;" in 1829, " The Good Bargain."

These little publications made a sensation. In 1820, an old magistrate of Geneva, M. Rocca, said, in an " Address to the Genevese," in reference to the " Poor Watchmaker" and " La Valaisanne :" " These two works are masterpieces of feeling, and often of good sense as well. Every line, every word is inspired by the love of virtue and of honest toil. They show their author to be a hero in goodness, and the champion of the weak." As a proof of the state of feeling in Geneva at that time, we may mention that this same authority, a few weeks after, was obliged to publish " Eclaircissements" of his previous address. While he continues to recommend the perusal of the works he had praised, he protests against the idea that he himself was a visionary, a " Mômier," or a partisan of Malan, in respect of his religious views. His address, he says, had been

dictated simply by his indignation at the way in which
such a man had been publicly treated. It was but the expression of a warm feeling in favour of justice and fairness.

Particular notices of his productions I reserve for the
period of their issue. At present it may be as well to form
a general estimate of his powers as a religious writer.

Without referring to his sacred songs and school hymns,
which have been permanently accepted in our Churches
and families, it may be stated that his numerous prose
works abound with pleasant pages of truthful, fresh, and
animated writing. At the same time, he was scarcely so
eloquent with his pen as he was in the pulpit, or in
general conversation.

That force of conviction which was for ever arresting
his hearers with fresh energy, and at times all but over-
powering them with a strange vigour, showed itself in his
writings rather in his close method of reasoning, or in
the persistency with which he affirms and re-affirms the
thought he desires to express, than in that hidden power
of persuasion, which allures and enthrals a reader's attention. Thus, only to instance his tracts, which first gained
him notoriety; in many of them a prolonged elaboration,
combined with purely abstract reasoning, following close
upon some terse recital, betrays the preacher. The reader
is subdued, it is true, and lays down the book in silence.
But he is not unfrequently compelled to wonder why,
after all, he is not convinced.

The apostle of a faith, as clear as it is earnest, Malan's
writings bear emphatic testimony as to what his soul
believes, though, at the same time, he has a difficulty in
quitting his personal experience to investigate that of

others. Those who share his convictions will be urged on with him to embrace all the results to which they lead. Those who do not, however genuine his emotion may appear, will probably find it unintelligible. Hence, it will be understood that he has been charged with monotony, and, occasionally, in his attempted expositions of the faith, with a measure of prolixity; yet, for all that, he has succeeded in compelling men to read his writings. More than that, many of his pages will never fail to arrest and fascinate from the powerful ever-present sincerity of a conviction full of force, freshness, and vigour.*

His style is most successful in the conversational parts, in his narrative, and in the striking and pointed expressions which constantly fall from his pen. His writings abound in passages which merit perpetuity, if on this ground only, and of which a useful and attractive collection might easily be made.

He wrote often, and with great ease and despatch. His sermons and religious tracts procured him fame, which

---

* The following extract from a letter to a lady, written before 1819, will give an idea of his deep love of nature at this period of his life :—

"There are times and seasons when the soul appears to delight in sweet and mysterious longings. It seems as if it had lost half of its life, and had no interest left but for what could pine and complain along with itself. In such days, it likes to linger in the loneliness and profound silence of the country. The light wind which stirs the dried-up foliage of groves and hedges ; the mists slowly rising from the marshes or rivers, and gliding, in fantastic shapes, between the woods or the hills ; the smoke of the village settling down on the fields, through whose haze may be discerned the haystacks or roofs of stubble-covered cottages ; the distant, and, as it were, muffled tones of the bells, or the vanishing tints of the mountains already half covered with sleet and snow—all that external world still lovely in its decay, as it appears, when the Lord bids the sun to weaken the power of his rays—seizes, absorbs the soul, and awakens in us a kindred sympathy, an intimate and mysterious responsive note of stillness and sadness."

was not diminished by his essays as a controversialist, and his publications dictated by passing events. As to the first, we have already noticed them. His controversies will be referred to by and by. With regard to his tracts, their chief merit lies in a happy delineation of character and manners, and in the charming anecdotes on which they are based. Quick and accurate in his notice of passing things, he would not unfrequently return from a walk bringing with him, out of some occurrence he had noticed, or a chance conversation in the street, a word, a touch of character, a prompt reply, which he immediately noted down, quoting the results to us afterwards with the comment, "Here is a tract to write." Especially in his writings for children he abounds in these happy illustrations, secured at the moment they happened, sometimes in his own family circle. We may recognise here the painter's art of comprehending a scene at a glance, exemplified in that faculty of truthful and rapid apprehension no less required in accurate delineation of character.

With all his earnestness of thought, rather in consequence of that earnestness, of the thirst for truth and symmetry which inspired him, he had a quick perception of incongruities, and consequently a keen sense of the ridiculous. But not only was everything personal utterly repugnant to the habitual loftiness of his mind, but his thorough lovingness of spirit made it additionally impossible for him to use this faculty by way of sarcastic or jesting retaliation. It was only employed in furnishing a picturesque style of writing which deepened the impression of any word, trait, or gesture which he recorded.

In his pamphlets called forth by passing events, in

which he rapidly recorded his convictions occasioned by any occurrence demanding, as he thought, testimony to the faith in the presence of the multitude, he knew and practised the wisdom of a concise, grave, and conclusive style. If in this class of writing he failed to rival the incisive fervour of others of his brethren, he never forgot the dignity that declines, be the provocation what it may, to descend to open personalities, or even to veiled insinuations.

On reading several of his tracts over again, after many years, and with reference to the present publication, I could not but be vividly impressed with their power. Writings like Germain the Woodcutter, the opening portion of La Valaisanne, the beautiful story of the Converted Atheist, various passages in the Poor Clockmaker of Geneva, or in the Truly Catholic Protestant, not to mention others, deserve an extended circulation. Their simplicity and truth of feeling must for ever enrol them among the standard classical specimens of this department of sacred literature.

What especially distinguishes his earlier writings is that joyous hopeful trustfulness which we have already had occasion to notice in his " Conventicule de Rolle." Looking at the clerical opposition he had encountered, as a solitary instance of intolerance on the part of a particular association of teachers, he gives free vent to his benevolent and loving spirit towards the population itself (the mass of the people.) He declares that the evil seems to him to be already sensibly diminished. " Indeed," he adds, " an observing and judicious population cannot persevere in a course of unjust attacks. "Better natures insensibly recoil from them, and persuade the others. Passions calm down; groundless animosity becomes wearisome, and the best way of anticipating this happy climax is to persist in loving those who still feel it their duty to hold back, many of them on conscientious grounds, which, if it be a mistake, it is no disgrace to adhere to. I feel that we are on the eve of better days, and I rejoice at the prospect of regenerated Geneva."

And what he wrote he felt, as appears from his letters to my mother during his occasional absence from home. Subsequent experience of many years taught him, not indeed to relinquish hopes dictated to him by his trust in God, but to content himself with their slow and partial realisation.

His first works exhibit him rather in the light of a confessor than a teacher. We still find in them more a testimony given to the divine facts of salvation, than, as was the case afterwards, what seemed to aim at being an explanation of the reasons and motives of these facts. By and by, as the succeeding incidents in the struggle led him to examine more carefully into the grounds of his creed, a systematic analysis of them found a place in his writings. This new feature in their contents was displayed, for example, in "The Eldest Son," 1825; while, in 1826, he applied himself to a vindication of it in the tract entitled, "Add to Your Faith, Knowledge."

At the same time, as we shall see, when we come to touch upon his Roman controversy, he never suffered his dogmatic teaching to degenerate into bigotry, or what might have been deservedly termed the fanaticism of party spirit.

I may mention, further, among his tracts published

M

before 1830, "The Half-penny Well Employed; or, The Duty of Contributing to the Work of Foreign Missions;" "Home Missions," in which, in advance of his age, he pleads for those home efforts to which he was daily devoted; "The Dead Burying their Dead;" "The Heathen at our Door," delineating under various aspects the Geneva of that day; "Corn Gathered on the Highway;" and, "What God Keeps is Well Kept:" all narratives of incidents which had occurred under his eye, or conversations in which he had been engaged, together with "The Blind Bartimaeus," a familiar exposition of the way of salvation.

But his literary efforts did not stop here. At this time also he produced his "True Friend of the Young," besides many doctrinal works. Above all, not to mention occasional publications, the fruit of passing events, it was then that he produced his hymns, with appropriate tunes, and a versification of the first fifty Psalms.

Before speaking of his hymns, well known in the present day as "Songs of Zion," it may be remarked that it is difficult to form any idea of the literary activity thus displayed, and of the place it occupied in our happy home life. His tracts spread by thousands, his occasional pamphlets were read with avidity, his hymns were everywhere sung by Christian congregations, whether of the dissenting communities in Geneva, or especially abroad. Surrounded as he was by a numerous family, this period of his life was passed in overflowing health and energy. We, his children, were enlisted in the technical department of his work. Some of these numerous editions were folded under his own roof. He had devised and constructed a small machine which considerably abridged the work, and it was a high day for us when tutor and governess announced that books were to be thrown aside, and the eating-room was converted into a merry workshop.

Whilst we were busy at our toil, some one would read a fresh page or two, or relate how the new tract had been received here or there, or its contents would be discussed, my father all the while present, everywhere encouraging us in our work, the very soul of animation, good humour, and cheerfulness. Young friends and colporteurs came to fetch away the scarcely bound tracts, distributing them in every direction. My brothers and I helped him in making up large packages, to be forwarded to various quarters. Occasionally our task was suspended when strangers called, or when one of my sisters went into an adjoining room to play over some hymn which our father had just composed, and to which we were anxious to listen.

In this way my father was enabled, by his own exertions and the practice of strict economy, to defray the cost of publishing his numerous works. Afterwards, friends contributed for this special object. I have before me an account-book, from November 1843 to September 1863, on the first page of which I find the following inscription, in his handwriting :—

"*Tracts.*—I have been occupied with this work since 1819, and have spent a considerable sum out of my own pocket; but, since 1840, finding I was unable to bear the sole expenses any longer, I applied for assistance in various quarters. Having visited in England, in 1843, and received £50 to promote this undertaking, I have determined to keep an account both of money subscribed and tracts distributed."

A catalogue of his productions, as complete as I could make it, will show that their numbers increased the older he grew.* As his physical strength diminished, he sought solace in his pen ; and it is but fair to add, that the weakness of advancing age never betrayed itself in his pages. He left also numerous MSS. behind him, together with many hundred hymns ready for publication ; which brings me to make a few remarks on his attempts in the field of sacred poetry.

He inherited from his father a natural talent for versification. His young man's note-books are full of "essays in versification;" and he had an invariable partiality for expressing, in either French or Latin impromptu verses, some passing thought to which he wished to give special emphasis.

This gift, like every other, he enlisted in the service of the faith. Postponing further reference to his hymns, I would add that he issued, from time to time, sacred poems, graceful and musical in their flow, and containing many happily turned stanzas. In 1824, "The Blind Receives his Sight;" in 1826, "A Letter to our Young Poet," addressed to a relation of his, " Imbert Galloix," probably the best of its kind. One verse will be sufficient as a specimen :—

> Ah, look around . . . .
> See God's high gifts—His holy day,—
> In ribald laughter jeered away ;
> While His redeemed, by sufferings pressed,
> Learn that the world is not their rest.

In 1830 appeared his " Hymn on Peace," in which, in nearly nine hundred Alexandrines, he endeavours to set

* Added to the original work " La Vie de Malan," &c.—*Note by Translator.*

before an old fellow-student the grounds of the assurance
and repose which he had derived from the faith. In the
following passage, he treats of its nature and the foundation on which it rests :—

> " The undying germ of truth divine,
>   From heaven it comes, He makes it thine ;
>   While faith the treasured seed applies,
>   And makes a bliss that never dies.
>   Seek not her characters to read
>   In toil-worn phrase of borrowed creed ;
>   His most who best by rote can learn,
>   If once the sire's, the son's in turn—
>
>   .   .   .   .
>
>   So trustful youth, to kiss or blow
>   A strange indifference will show,
>   And, guided by a teacher's nod,
>   Bow down to Baal, or to God."

Another example may be quoted :—

> " Christians in name, but citizens of earth,
>   Of lifeless graces take the righteous worth.
>   Ye can't offend who every wrong excuse,
>   Dread honest speech, and to condemn refuse.
>   Who blend the Bible with the wild romance,
>   Or vary solemn prayers with games of chance ;
>   Who, by a secret strange, to heaven unknown,
>   License to sin relieve with grace t' atone ;
>   Homage to faith at idols' shrines afford,
>   And in the gilded play-house serve the Lord."

In 1846, he published " Virtue and Grace," with a preface, in which, in connection with principles of literature,
he shows how far he was under the influence of that essentially theocratic idea which expects to realise, in domestic
education and national life, the highest principles of the
gospel.

At this time, at the age of sixty, he addressed the following to a fellow-citizen, a well-known poet :—

" Hoar are our locks, our footsteps frail,
  With tottering gait, and limbs that fail.
  Through all our frame we hear the sigh ;
  ' Child of the dust, 'tis thine to die ! '

" How often, still, on yonder height,
  Shall we behold the blushing light ;
  Or there, when evening whispers peace,
  Wander in sweet forgetfulness.

" Ah, think, eternity is near,
  With thoughts of bliss, or thoughts of fear ;
  Be ours to choose, while erst we may,
  For endless life an endless day."

Thanks to the subject of these verses,—the characteristic defect of all didactic poetry betrays itself here in a special manner. In order thoroughly to appreciate its charms, and enter into its spirit, we ought first to be imbued with those particular impressions which its stately and somewhat elaborate numbers are designed to communicate. Hence, in spite of the occurrence, here and there, of pleasing passages, and notwithstanding all the care and toil which their author has bestowed on them, his poems of this class have never found readers. Unquestionably, his chastened style and graceful versification found better scope in lyrical than in didactic poems on his one favourite subject—living faith. And be it remembered that faith never takes us by surprise. Its morning entrance into the soul succeeds the night of struggle ; while the hearts that it has conquered it awakes from silence, and kindles into praise.

My father's reputation as a Christian poet will always rest upon his hymns. To this effect is the testimony in a well-known religious journal of the time, " Le Semeur," published in Paris (August 1837), given at the close of an article on Hymnology in France.

" Among ourselves, with the revival of faith has come the revival of its song; and that, too, after a silence of more than a hundred years. God has taught His servants to perpetuate the language of His praise, and has given them new hymns through the instrumentality of this truly Christian poet. M. Malan has re-awakened the lay. His hymns belong already to history, because they have interwoven themselves, and, while the revival lasts, will interweave themselves, with the joys and sorrows of the Church."

These words have been realised. These hymns are now being sung even in the National Church of Geneva. To this testimony it would be superfluous in me to add a word of my own in praise of those sacred lyrics which greeted me as an infant, and conveyed to me, in my early years, my first impressions of Christian truth. They have roused the warmest enthusiasm in Albert Knapp, the popular religious poet of Germany; and more than once I have heard German musicians, and those of other countries, expressing cordial admiration of the melodies attached to them. Nor can I help observing how painful it is to those who have become lovingly familiar with them, to hear them attributed to other authors, or, worse still, to find them abridged, and even spoilt, by unskilful corrections; to hear them sung at times to strange tunes, or even to airs not in the least recalling those to which they were originally set. I may be permitted, also, to add, with reluctance, that these observations apply to the restricted use made of them by the Established Churches of Geneva, Vaud, and Neufchatel, for their new psalters; though persons who have hailed with delight the arrival of better

days in their official return to hymns, the use of which was
dear to them from habit, will see undoubtedly in this new
move a hopeful augury for the future.

It was in 1823 that he published his first hymns,
though he made an attempt in that direction in 1821.
At first he merely intended them for the use of families,
as might be gathered from the title-page, "Sacred Songs
for Family Worship." The earliest edition contained only
thirty-five. To these, however, sixty more were soon
added in a second issue, with the music arranged for two
or three voices by one of his friends, M. Wolff Hanlock,
professor of music in Geneva.

In 1824 he sent out, also with tunes attached, the first
edition of a metrical version of the Psalms, reaching to
the 50th, under the title, "Songs of Zion," or "Bible
Psalms, Hymns, and Canticles." This publication, which
we shall have occasion to notice by and by, not meeting
with a favourable reception, he devoted himself entirely
to his hymns, of which he now issued a hundred under the
title of "Songs of Zion." The edition of 1828 comprised
two hundred already; that of 1832, two hundred and
thirty-four; that of 1836, three hundred; that total was
never exceeded. The last issue was in 1855.

These hymns were composed at particular periods in
his own history. After having laid aside his pen for a
considerable time, he would suddenly resume his poetical
efforts, as a rule when he was resting from some protracted
work. He wrote them thus on the spur of the moment;
not unfrequently when he was walking, or away on a
journey.

Appended to some of them, at the time they were jotted

down, are notes of the places or circumstances that suggested or inspired them. Many of them were considerably altered, in subsequent editions; latterly, not always for the better. Some, however, more especially the best, have remained as they were; above all, such as were composed off-hand.

So accustomed was he to versify his thoughts, that many a time, when some home incident, intercourse with friends, or an interesting visit from a stranger, had inspired him, he would write an appropriate hymn, and send it with suitable music to the person who had unconsciously suggested it. Thus our several baptisms and first communions, our return home after absence, our respective birth-days, any departures, births or deaths, in which he might happen to be interested, would furnish subjects for this pleasing method of commemoration. He never set any of his hymns to a strange tune. I do not think he could have done so.

He frequently lithographed them himself, adding a sketch, of his own, of the place where they had been penned, or some other suggestive design in harmony with the subject of which they treated. Many of these fugitive pieces are now in my possession, written either for schools, or without any special object.

As regards the tunes, though he played the violin and flute when he was a boy, and accompanied himself on the organ, he did not possess any very great musical knowledge or skill as a performer. As a proof of this, it may be stated that though the melodies suggested themselves to him so vividly, that on several occasions, for example, he could not sleep till he had noted down an air then in his thoughts, he had some difficulty in rendering them on paper.

As a rule, he was obliged, before completing a tune, to read on a musical instrument the note that he heard distinctly in his mind. For this purpose he generally carried about with him a box containing an octave of steel plates. Thus, in the event of an air occurring to him during his walk, he would adjust the instrument in communication with his ear by means of his stick, holding it in his left hand,—and, touching the keys with the right, set down the notes as soon as he had ascertained them.

The melody once on paper he would play it himself, or get one of my sisters to play it for him, listening to our criticisms, inviting and receiving them (above all, when they were undeniably true) with a certain inexpressible smile of good humour, which those who witnessed it can never forget.

When he was in the vein, the airs, as well as the words, occurred to him together. One day the kettle on the hob gave him the introductory notes of one of the best known of his musical settings. He had frequently said that each air was contained, in his conception of it, in its opening bars. A friend, to whom I related this, mentioned that, happening on one occasion to meet my father on the road, a few years before his death, the latter read him some verses which he had just composed, adding that the melody, which he intended to put to them, had been suggested to him by the sound made by an imperfectly oiled cart-wheel, which had that moment reached his ear.

I give these details, however puerile they may appear to be, under the impression that not only the members of my family, but all to whom the "Songs of Zion" have been old friends, will read them with interest. One association, however, connected with these hymns had a prominent place in my father's most cherished recollections.

It was in 1827, a year the spring of which had involved him in endless anxiety and fatigue; he was so upset, indeed, that his medical adviser insisted on his taking a thorough rest. On the strength of this order, he left Geneva for a village in the northern part of the Jura range, then for Fraubrunnen, near Bern, to avoid fatigue. It must be remembered that at that time he did not speak German.

During his three weeks' absence, he composed a great part of his "Hymn of Peace," several detached pieces of poetry, and a considerable number of his best spiritual songs. Let it be recollected that all these were published afterwards without revise, that to many of them a melody was attached at the time of their composition, that the man who did this was on the invalid shelf,—and the fertility of his life and the power of his thought will in a measure be realised.

In this way, indeed, my father always took his holiday, up to the very end. In proportion as his strength diminished, in proportion as he lost his interest in mere passing events, this special work, serving as it did to elevate his soul, became his supreme delight and his chief recreation. In the concluding year of his life, indeed, it proved the most effectual antidote to the weariness and weakness by which he was visited.

Before 1830, his house was full of juvenile boarders, generally English. Their age, as a rule, varied from eighteen to twenty. The object of those who entrusted them to his care was to secure for them his influence and guidance, as well as to forward them in a knowledge of French. He devoted himself entirely to their interests, and many of them dated their conversion to their residence with him. That good man, Charles de Rodt, whose memory is so precious, decided on the ministry when he was living under his roof.

So it was with John Adams, who left Geneva to devote himself to foreign missions. I have several of his letters in my possession, indicating the feeling with which he, in common with many others, looked back upon those early days. Only to instance Adams, whose life has been published :—the letter of the well-known missionary Lacroix to my father, dated the 23d April 1831, announces his premature death in the following terms : "My brother,—the London missionaries in Bengal have commissioned me to communicate to you the departure of your old pupil and son in the faith, John Adams. He died on the 21st, after a very short illness, brought on chiefly by over-exposure to the burning Indian sun, while he was fulfilling his work as a minister of the gospel. His missionary career was short-lived, but not so will be the traces of his labours, nor do I doubt that the great day of judgment will show that he has not toiled in vain. In every possible quarter,—in the market, at the great places of concourse, by the highway, in villages and hamlets,—you might have found him distributing tracts and speaking the word of life. His zeal for the glory of God and the good of man, his love for his brethren and for all the children of God, his firmness of character, his spotless life, his thoroughly Christian spirit, secured universal esteem. We lament his death as one of the greatest disasters experienced by our mission since its formation in Bengal. May I but secure a place near him," writes this man of God, now also in the presence of his Master, "when it shall please the Lord to call me hence! His grateful remembrance of you, my dear sir, of your anxious care, above all of the blessing you were the means of conveying to his soul, knew no bounds. He often spoke of you, and never without enthusiastic declaration of the love and reverence he experienced towards you; even in his delirium, I heard him speak of M. Malan with peculiar delight."

An illustration this, among many, of my father's lifehold on the young men under his care. He looked upon them as his own children ; and by many of them who will possibly read these pages his memory will be cherished as that of their father in the faith.

But, besides his boarders, his catechumens occupied no small share of his attention. He prepared each of the lessons he gave them, assigning them the chief parts of the day's teaching, marked with Scripture proofs on cards lithographed by himself. He had been from an early age accustomed to teach ; hence his predisposition, throughout his whole life, to devote himself to the young, and to interest himself warmly in their welfare. The very day of the opening of his chapel the institution of schools was devised, where children might receive at once the rudiments of a sound education, and the elements of a religious training. In the midst of the conflicting emotions which that event occasioned, my mother felt strongly the necessity of adding the erection of schools to the original design, and spoke of it to my father as they left the chapel.

He at once assigned a place for the purpose, and the school commenced with seventy or eighty little girls. Great exertions were made to provide a mistress. Remaining in the place where it was first established till 1864, and maintained from month to month, and week to week, by voluntary contributions procured through my mother's exertions, it still continues,—ruled by the same principles on which it had been founded in 1821, and universally regarded as a model establishment of its kind.

Its foundress, when at length her great age precluded her from taking any active part in its work, was gladdened by witnessing a continual accession of new supporters and protectors of its interests. After the chapel was pulled down in 1864, the school was necessarily removed from the apartment where it had·been originally commenced, and has recently been settled in a building erected for the purpose by an old friend of my father's, whose fame is in all the Churches, M. de Laharpe, Professor in the Free School of Theology in Geneva. My father used to visit it from time to time, and never failed to preside at its annual feast.

Some years afterwards he endeavoured to start another for boys, on a similar model; but it did not continue for more than three or four years. About 1828 he turned his attention to an infant school founded by a Dutch lady in his congregation; nor did he confine himself to efforts like these. Scarcely had he set on foot these movements of which we have just spoken, than he endeavoured, in 1829, to form a superior institution for the education of young women. This enterprise he zealously followed up for eighteen months, when the death of the directress, and the loss of some of the most helpful members of his congregation, compelled him to abandon it.

His affection for the young showed itself in his writings, from the very first. Besides the little catechisms, mentioned already, he published in 1824 his " Child's True Friend," to supersede Berquin's work, almost the only one at that time known to children. His object, as he himself describes it, was to furnish them with a kind of literature which might serve to amuse them, while at the same time it set before them something higher than mere human excellence.

This work (translated into English forthwith,—the last edition of it, in four volumes, appearing in 1850)—is a collection of minor pieces, chiefly narrative, setting forth some leading moral principle, or truth of doctrine. They have been found fault with, indeed, as being too dogmatical, yet there are many families in which these books are still welcome friends ; and, if I may quote my own feeling in reference to them, and that of many others, it must be a matter of regret that they should remain unknown.

With such a love of children, as an instinct of his heart, it is not to be wondered at that he should have espoused so zealously the cause of infant baptism. In 1823, at the time when his refusal to withdraw himself voluntarily from the Established Church placed him in a questionable and altogether untenable position towards other communions, with which he nevertheless greatly sympathised, the question of baptism was started in the Church of the Bourg de Four by English influence. Finding no counter argument at first with which to meet their representations in favour of what was to him a new doctrine, my father was won over by its absolute character, and declared himself convinced. Once persuaded, that firmness of his in testifying to what he believed to be true came out in its full force. His advocacy of the new belief was ardent and emphatic. He determined to be baptized afresh.

However, on his arrival at Sécheron, at Mr Drummond's, under whose auspices the ceremony was to take place, he passed in review the various passages of Scripture with which the doctrine is generally supported. Suddenly he was struck with the apostle's language to his converted brethren, "Your children are holy." He immediately left the room, sought retirement, and reopened the whole question in private.

The result of his study was a volume of two hundred pages, published in 1824: "God Ordains that Children in the Church of Christ should be Consecrated to Him by the Seal of Baptism." Recapitulating the primitive arguments in favour of the practice, he added the opinions of some of the fathers, and then examined the passages of Scripture urged by Baptists. The only trace of its authorship which the book reveals, is its energetic maintenance of the theory that as baptism, like circumcision, came direct from God, it could not be said to require any human preparation before it was administered; that the only possible preparation for it must emanate from sovereign grace, and be as accessible to an infant as an adult. Furthermore, baptism with water is but a sign, and the grace it confers a mere summons to salvation. These opinions he vigorously defended in 1835, in a publication entitled, "The Baptized Family."

The first of these works was refused by the bookseller, on the plea that he himself was a Baptist. This may serve to show how high, in those days, party spirit ran on that question.

It will be generally remembered that, in 1824, a few of the junior members of the clergy of the Canton de Vaud began to hold meetings for worship out of regular hours, and thus became subject to official persecution and popular odium. At this crisis, my father did all in his power to encourage his brethren, and render them personal help. His house was open to refugees from amongst them ; to many of their members he became personally attached; and, not satisfied with appealing directly in their behalf to the magistrates of their canton, he declared himself as their champion, in his published " sermon."

This brief treatise, only thirty pages long, transports us instantly to those forgotten days when, in their fervent espousal and advocacy of the faith, " the sectaries," as they were called, endured an open and often ferocious opposition. Inspired by the remembrance of suffering such as befell the brothers Olivier and Juvet (the latter of whom, so said his friends, fell a victim to their intensity) these pages abound with traces of that anguish of soul with which their author contemplated the evidence of a Christian people's downfall, and the harbingers of divine judgment. At the same time, they live with the thrill of anticipated triumph for the faith, and deep-rooted conviction of the reality of the eternal kingdom. The stirring incidents they record, — in their least details full of interest, — combine with the language in which they are written to render them a precious monument of the time they describe.

N

In this same year, when the general discussion of the controversy between my father and the clerical party had in a measure abated, a member of that body, M. Chenevière, Professor of Dogmatic Theology in the Academy of the Establishment, issued his Precis of the theological debates which had gone on for some years in Geneva, causing a translation of it to be inserted in the "Monthly Repository of Theology and General Literature," at that time the English organ of the Unitarian party.

On receiving this publication, in which he himself was made the subject of personal attacks, my father wrote the following letter to the author:—

"I remember, my dear Chenevière (for *dear* I must still call you), that one of the last things you said to me, five or six years ago, was that nothing could interrupt our entire mutual unreserve, or render it possible for us to condemn or abuse each other as enemies. I believe I have adhered to this sentiment, and that no word of mine, whether written or printed, has assailed either your person or character.

"Your last publication, however, has convinced me that your feeling towards me differs widely from mine towards you. As soon as I had read it, I formed a wish either to see or write to you; and, if I have suffered any delay to interpose between my design and its execution, this has simply arisen from a desire to rid myself as much as possible of all such unworthy impulses, as attacks from without are too apt to arouse in us."

Going on to assure him of his own anxiety to continue unimpaired the interchange of private courtesies, he proceeds to say that, as a minister of Christ, he could no longer maintain any relations with him. "I am compelled to draw a distinction between my old friend and the theological teacher. In this last capacity I cannot hold any intercourse with you, nor even acknowledge you. In the first, I turn to you with all my heart, and with the word on my lips, 'If I have spoken or done evil, bear witness of the evil; but if well, why smitest thou me?' That your way of thinking in religious matters should have disposed you to see error in the doctrine I hold as absolutely true, in no way surprises me; that you should have written in contradiction of what you hold to be error, is no more than fair. Thus you would have provoked inquiry and research, and have tended to throw light on that truth which you and I profess to seek after, and to value above all our own views and prejudices.

"But why attack *me*? What connection can you find between my humble individuality and the course I have followed, whatever it has been or may be, and the verities of Christian faith? Why have you thus dragged me forward, and stigmatised me with reproach? No mere injury of *me* can affect *the truth* I preach; and these assaults, however justifiable they may have appeared to you, and may be in themselves, can only draw from him who experiences them the words of the psalmist: 'The Lord hath said, Cursed be David! who shall then say, Wherefore hast thou done this?' (2 Sam. xvi. 10.)

"What most pains me is your attack upon my Master Himself. That regret is deep and abiding. I have said to many, and what I have said is true, 'If I could by the entire sacrifice of that prosperity with which you reproach me, and with which God has blessed me in common with many other heads of similar institutions in Geneva; if, by

resigning this very day the whole of the worldly goods
which I enjoy here, I could bring you to a knowledge of
that truth which divine mercy has revealed to me, how
thankfully would I return to poverty for the attainment
of such an end! Good would it be for me and mine to be
once more deprived of all we possessed, if by our poverty
you might be made spiritually rich. This is no mere idle
sentiment, Chenevière, I earnestly assure you; no mere
gushing outburst of passing feeling. I know it is the
emotion of my heart, and of my wife's as well. Truly we
should bless God for such a dispensation.

"What I actually possess, my dear friend, I have won
by hard work." He then proceeds to detail to him the
ways and means by which his competence had been
attained.

"I have nothing to reply to your written attack by way
of detailed rejoinder. To do so would have been easy to
me, without assailing you personally, a thing I never do
in any case. I could easily have rectified certain errors of
fact and inference set forth in your Precis, by reference
to a work I published last year, immediately after my
official connection with the National Church had ceased,
under the title of 'Testimony to the Gospel by a Minister
of Christ.' I know that, in the general judgment, that
publication would have cleared my personal character of
all the reproaches you have addressed to me; but I have
been most unwilling to appear even to raise my voice
against you.* Many others will do this. I learn that a

---

* This work, although it had been printed, was kept back from publication by my father, at the request of one of the magistrates, for the love of
peace, and in order to avoid raising new disturbances. Being repeatedly

reply has already been published in England, and that its tone is in thorough accordance with the lofty spirit which has dictated it. You will have to be prepared for numerous rebukes, and the general displeasure of many different communions. The nature of your written sentiments is such that, passing by all purely personal matter, it will provoke against you and against the Church in which you are an authorised theological teacher, a unanimity, not indeed of attack, but of rejection on the part of all those who reverence the Bible, and believe in the salvation which is to be found alone in Jesus the Son of God. You have, I learn, inflicted a terrible wound on the Church you would fain defend.

"But there are more important considerations still in reserve. The safety of your own soul, dear Chenevière, is a matter more intensely solemn, and demanding even greater interest and anxiety. Had I but the right to speak to you now, as I have spoken to you in times past, I would tell you of my great desire to see you, to converse with you, to explain to you in detail what your writing proves you to be as yet unacquainted with—our principles and conduct. Not that I have any wish to bring you to think as I do, or to win you to my side, as a partisan; I am but governed by a consideration of the peace and life which would flow into your soul through the knowledge of Jesus as He is, against Whom there may be found in

---

called upon to reply, however, after Chenevière's attack, especially by friends out of Geneva, he determined, not indeed to issue his work publicly, but to communicate it to his friends, as occasion required ; taking care first to make the magistrate acquainted with his reasons for so doing. My mother tells me that this was the only occasion she could recall on which he displayed any hesitation as to the part he ought to take.

your writings something approaching to positive blasphemy.

"What I intensely desire," he adds, "is that He Who has called me by His grace to the knowledge of Himself, would incline your heart to listen to and accept the good tidings of that salvation which is 'from Him, by Him, and for Him.'"

He concludes by assuring him, should anything in his letter have given him pain, of the affection by which it had been dictated.

In January 1826 came on for hearing the case of the minister Bost. It was a great event in Geneva, not only on account of the sensation likely to be produced by a public debate in which the respective rights of the official clergy and the press were to be discussed, but more particularly from the decision that followed the first trial, as well as the final judgment of the supreme court of appeal. Bost was acquitted of calumny against the Venerable Assembly, while he was at the same time condemned for various injurious expressions which he had made use of with reference to them. Everybody understood the drift of this sentence, that from that day forward,—certain forms and proprieties being adhered to,—there was absolute liberty in Geneva for the public discussion of the rights of the old Protestant clergy.

My father, however, was in no way concerned in the affair. The less so, as the lawsuit was prepared at a time when Bost, (as he himself declares in his "Memoires,") was in a position with reference to him which led him to believe that he would not be prepared publicly to espouse his cause. This, however, was not the case. Ignoring all personal considerations, he hastened to join the friends who surrounded the accused, and, in concert with them, he never quitted him till he had seen him safe out of the reach of the mob who had followed him with hootings. He it was who made a sign to the guard to shut the gates on the crowd, whilst Bost and his friends, (himself among them,) escaped by a side gate.

In 1825, the Synod of the Secession Church of Scotland, by a decree of the 1st of September, had enrolled Malan in their body, after anxious and solemn deliberation, and after having been convinced, on the personal testimony of many of their members, as well as on good authority variously collected, that his faith was sound, and that he attached himself to the Presbyterian form of Church government. In February 1826 he received from the same assembly the offer of pecuniary aid. In his reply, declining their liberality, he contented himself with expressing a desire for the continuance of that brotherly union of which he said he felt increasing need, along with an increasing sense of his isolated position with reference to the Church of Geneva.

My reason for mentioning this arises from the rumours incessantly circulated in Geneva by the enemies of the cause to which my father had dedicated himself, explaining his opposition as the result of a salary received from abroad for that purpose. I shall have occasion to recur, (in the record of the year 1843,) to these calumnies,—as gratuitous as they were treacherous.

Though I purpose deferring to another chapter the account of his missionary journeys, I cannot altogether overlook, at this point, what he did that year in England and Scotland. It was then that he found himself the object of that overflowing, though transient enthusiasm, so frequently meted out to foreign guests in England, whose career has been in any way prominent; more particularly to such as have exhibited those qualities of vigour and independence in the discharge of duty, to which that great nation so justly awards the highest honour. My father, however, was little able to adapt himself to the experience of a religious public character in England, or the demands it involved, nor yet to fall in with the frequent lionising accompaniments of English " meetings." So far from having " cleverly availed himself of his position to advance his temporal interests," as was alleged by those who ought to have had more self-respect than to bring such an accusation against him, he rather neglected the advances frequently made to him by men of high standing and position. Not indeed under any motive arising from the simple fact of their rank; he was no radical, but a spiritually-minded and dignified man, to whom any confusion of temporal with eternal interests was eminently distasteful. While, as regards his English friends, he often chilled them by the openness with which he criticised certain ways which they deemed obvious and right.

After having been received in London, and introduced to some friends by a nephew of Robert Haldane, who had stayed with him at Geneva some years before, he preached in the metropolis before going to Scotland, where his presence attracted much observation, and where he made the acquaintance of several eminent men. On his return to London, he led a more private public life, no longer preaching, as he did before, to crowds of eager hearers, though he kept up the numerous relations formed during his previous visit, with members of all the various evangelical denominations. I may add that this journey, the éclat of which, increased by distance, stirred up against him an envious spirit in Geneva, is simply mentioned in his "Church Journal" in these words:—"The four and a half months which I have spent in England have been owned of God by a demonstration of power accompanying the Word."

Shortly after his return he received from the University of Glasgow the degree of "Doctor of Divinity." His diploma, dated the 10th October 1826, and signed by the chancellor and eighteen professors, was sent to him "as a very faithful pastor, an excellent man, commendable in the highest degree for his piety, and the holiness of his life, and especially worthy of the highest theological honours."

Delighted and encouraged by the reception he had experienced abroad, he continued to display, during the years that followed, extraordinary energy and activity.

It was at this time that he established "La Société du Bon Dépôt," and renewed his efforts to induce his friends to unite with him in the endeavour to found a school of evangelical theology in Geneva.

The Society "Du Bon Dépôt" (as it was called) was started in January 1827, in a pastoral assembly of the Church of Testimony, for the purpose of defending and disseminating the faith by religious tracts, by the circulation of the Bible, and by home and foreign missions. This association, of which my father was the very soul and principal agent, acquired considerable importance, which it preserved up to the time when the Evangelical Society of Geneva became the centre of all activity of that kind.

With reference to originating a theological institution, this was a movement in which he necessarily required the assistance of his brethren. He had had the idea of it in his mind from the close of 1825, and it was by his advice, indeed, that one of the nonconforming pastors of Geneva applied himself to the study of ecclesiastical history with a view to this project. In 1827 he again brought the subject under the notice of his brethren, urging the necessity of founding at Geneva a school to be conducted on strict principles, where young students for the ministry might be brought up in sound scriptural, as well as scientific and secular, knowledge. For a moment it seemed as though the thing were really going to be done. Towards the end of the year, however, on his return, after a brief absence, he found that the friends to whom he had communicated his views were already prepared with schemes for forming among themselves an "Institution" in no way coming up to his idea of what was needed. It so happened that just at that time he had had a visit from a young student in theology in the National Academy, who had been compelled, on account of his orthodoxy, to abandon his idea of ordination in the National Church. My father took him to live with him and superintend the education of his sons, undertaking, at the same time, to complete his course of preparation, a boon which was afterwards shared by three other young men, who soon found themselves in the same predicament.

I have before me the MS. of an inauguration address, delivered to these students on the 18th December 1827. It contains no great display of learning; it simply sets forth, in glowing and animated strains, the nature of the

Christian ministry, representing it as a holy trust, not, indeed, committed to delegates direct from Christ Himself, but to mere re-declarers of the inspired testimony of prophets and apostles. They are not required to tell the world of any other message than that which issued directly from God Himself. That message is to be found in the Bible, wherein faith apprehends it under the influence of the Divine Spirit, and requires to be studied, vindicated, and upheld by means of theological research.

I select from this introductory address the following passages which may serve to illustrate that ardent love of truth which was at the foundation of my father's dogmatism, as well as that direct personal communion with God which stamped his faith with absolute independence and certainty.

" . . . . . Truth, as she actually exists, as she has ever been, as she continues to be, as she will be, world without end, — this truth is the witness of the Spirit of God, *who knows and searches into the deep things of God,* and *who cannot lie* in whatever He reveals. There is no uncertainty here, no probabilities, no questionings, no re-cantings of error, no equivocations, no ambiguities, no seducing argument, no empty declamation, nothing incomplete, insufficient, or imperfectly stated, but everywhere from beginning to end light, purity, perfection, a glow of glory and grace. Truth is set forth as ' a strait and narrow *path,*' as clear and deep *waters,* as *refined gold,* as *silver seven times tried in the fire,* as luscious and fragrant *honey.* St Paul speaks of its treasures as 'treasures of wisdom and knowledge.' It is the knowledge of heaven, for it is the word of God."

And further on, in his enumeration of a preacher's duties :—" Consider, gentlemen, how jealous is the faithful servant of the sovereignty of his Lord and Master over his conscience ; he is free, he has been emancipated by the Lord Jesus, though for the love of his Master he is servant of all. He is under the yoke, indeed, but it is the yoke of God and His Spirit, through the Word. He acknowledges no other, he knows no other ; no persuasion, no seduction, no force, no constraint, can reach his conscience ; and while he knows that it is neither in a spirit of insubordination, nor from a desire to create a reputation for himself, or to surround himself with disciples, that he severs himself from ties which had held him in his ignorance, he honours first his Master's word, and submitting himself to it as a trust for which he must give account, he declares loyally and fearlessly, in public and in private, that the kingdom and glory belong to God, and that those who fear Him should bow to Him alone."

Let me quote further a distinction between the orthodox professor and the believer, as laid down in his " Prolegomena" in the same course of reading :—

" The one bases his faith in the divine authority of revelation on his own arguments and deductions ; the other establishes it on what God has made known to him ; the one rests on the truthfulness of God, as on one of the perfections which he has learned to attribute to the Divine Being ; the other, on the truth of God as revealed to his soul by an act of divine power ; the one accepts, through his reason, the witness of God ; the other receives that witness in his heart."

These instructions continued for more than a year. In

March 1829 a thesis appeared on "Original Sin," addressed
to students in theology by the candidates of the Church of
Testimony, and entitled, "Who can bring a clean thing
out of an unclean?" That same year one of these candidates, M. Vivien of Geneva, (now a pastor in the French
Protestant Church at Arras), was ordained by my father,
who was assisted on the occasion by some of the nonconforming Genevese pastors, with others from abroad.
Among the former was M. Bost, who says, with reference
to the occurrence, "that it was one of the very few ordi-
nations in which he had never regretted having taken part."

To return to 1827. On the 20th of May in that year
our home was laid waste by the inundation which M.
Bost describes so graphically in his Memoirs. It was on a
Sunday evening that the event took place. About six
o'clock, the atmosphere being dull and oppressive, black
clouds swept suddenly over the sky, and scarcely had we
fled for shelter from the garden to the house, when a water
spout broke over the Pré l'Evêque with unparalleled vio-
lence. The water rushed into the garden, and flooded the
basement of the house. My father, up to his waist in the
flood, endeavoured, with my elder brothers and some of
the boys of the Sunday school, to rescue the furniture and
numerous articles which the stream was bearing away.
At one moment, rushing into the current, he had great
difficulty in saving a servant girl who had been carried
away while she was trying to render assistance. From
time to time he stopped to ask if we were all safe. The
storm was terrible. The roar of the water, mingled with
the crash of the crumbling garden walls, and the cries of
the neighbours who retreated into our house, escaping by

the roof from their own, which was threatening to give way. The road had become impassable. This lasted for several hours. Meanwhile, night came on, but found us unable to procure a light, or to prepare food for the little ones,—the cellar and the ground floors having been taken entire possession of by the waters. Whilst the family was assembled in the rooms above, one of the children (six years old) asked his father to pray to God to stop the rain. At the request of the little one, he fell on his knees, and as he was praying the rain and the fury of the storm suddenly ceased, whilst at the same moment a voice was heard calling him by name. It was an English friend who came, half swimming, to our rescue from our neighbours, the Wolffs, pushing a basket before him full of provisions, with a supply of candles. The next morning the garden and the basement of the house presented a scene of mournful desolation, the road and plain of the Pré l'Evêque being covered with mud and gravel, while a quantity of fish accumulated round proved that the water spout had, in the first instance, passed over the lake.

But this was not all. An excited crowd had collected to view the havoc which had been created, and assumed from time to time a threatening attitude. One of the lower orders, having forced his way into the house, caught sight of the passage of Scripture over the drawing-room chimney, which my father (according to a frequent habit he had of decorating his apartments after that fashion) had painted there, in large characters, many years before: "We know that if our earthly house of this tabernacle be destroyed, we have a building of God, an house not made with hands, eternal in the heavens."

No sooner had the man seen it, than he called to his comrades and harangued them to the effect that "the miserable hypocrite, instead of exerting himself to save his family, had occupied his time with writing these words." The mob soon prepared to proceed from words to deeds, but an opportune arrival of gens d'armes cleared the premises.

Our friends the Wolffs, whose country-house was hard by, lost no time in offering shelter to my mother and the children, while our dwelling was being repaired. As for my father, so far from being depressed by the misadventure, he named his garden thenceforth the Pré-Béni, a name which he transferred to the new country-house to which we removed three years afterwards, and which adjoined the one we had left. This new abode has been for more than thirty years a home of peace and signal blessing to us and many others. Thus God Himself testified abundantly to the inextinguishable faith of His servant.

Meanwhile my father, who had suffered considerably from the anxiety and fatigues occasioned by the May disaster, felt in need of repose. It was then that he paid the visit to the village of Fraubrunnen, which has been already referred to.

In the summer of 1828 he made another expedition to England and Ireland, visiting Scotland at the same time. It was during this missionary tour that he was seized with an attack of faintness while he was in the pulpit, having preached three times in one day, and on several days in succession. Finishing his sermon with great difficulty, and returning to the friend's house where he was visiting, he became very ill. He was confined to his room for six weeks, but availed himself of his period of recovery to publish, in English, a little book on the assurance of faith. It is entitled, " Theogenes ; or, A Plain and Scriptural Answer to the Solemn Question, Am I, or am I not, a Child of God ?" It passed through several editions. During his absence his place was filled by theological students, whose sermons, however, he read himself before they preached them.

Shortly after his return, a committee, formed for the purpose of erecting a statue to Rousseau, handed him the subscription list. Those at the head of the movement regarded it, not merely as an act of homage to a man whose reputation had reflected renown on his country, but as a sort of reparation to his memory, and, at the same time, as a protest against the opposition which he had experienced in his lifetime from the clergy and magistrates of old Geneva.

My father, however, held Geneva to be no other than the city of the Reformation, the Christian city, the asylum of pure truth. Not only, therefore, was he unable to aid the project, but he felt constrained to regard it as a public denial of that faith, whose recognition in high quarters constituted in his eyes the sole glory of his country. Hence he replied, in November, to the deputation which had been sent to him, in a pamphlet of several pages, entitled, "Rousseau's Statue : Answer of a Citizen of Christian Geneva to an Application made to him to contribute to its Erection," and addressed to the members of the committee formed for that purpose.

With singular eloquence and feeling, he stated his

reasons for refusing his co-operation, under the three heads
of religion, patriotism, and the republic. As a Christian,
he wondered that the jubilee of the blessed Reformation
should find them preparing to erect such a statue; as a
citizen, he recalled to their recollection the fearful revolu-
tionary scenes which had terrified his childhood, and asked
those whom he was addressing if they hoped, by honouring
anew the object of popular incense and adulation at a
crisis of popular delirium, to promote the welfare of a
generation already saturated with scepticism, infidelity,
and licentiousness. Finally, as a member of the republic,
he disputes the right of a mere section to involve an entire
populace in its own individual preferences.

The greater the courage and uprightness of this reply,
the more certain was it to irritate those who had been
taught to regard the scheme as a vindication of the
national honour. "Who knows?" was the language of one
of the brochures called forth by my father's answer, and
declaring that the time for rendering justice to Rousseau
had come, "Who knows whether M. Malan himself is not
giving a proof of genius in laying the foundation of a new
Church?" Then urging in a very pointed manner, "an
absolute separation between the spiritual and temporal,"
it pretends to see, in the earnest protest of which it com-
plains, not only such idle declamations as are suited only
to a conventicle of sectaries, but a return of that old leaven
of clerical despotism, the mere mention of which, it was well
known, sufficed to arouse in Geneva the sensitive susceptibilities of a nascent liberalism.

The effect of this publication on the people was such,
that the magistrate begged my father to abstain for a little

o

time from appearing in public. He replied that it would be impossible for him not to leave his house when the duties of his ministry required it. That very day, however, as it happened, he was seized with lameness, and so kept a prisoner for more than a month. His family and friends looked on the incident as providential, the physician being unable to account for it; while he himself was as capable as ever of writing, or receiving friends.

He turned his forced seclusion to account by reading anew the entire works of Rousseau, and then issued, under the title of "Rousseau and the Religion of our Fathers," a picture of manners in which he depicted vividly the infidelity as thorough as it was artful, which the false sentiments of that author had been the means of diffusing, and of which he saw such abundant fruits around him. This brochure which appeared under the title of "Folly of a Wise Man of the World," was only a republication of a production which he had issued in 1826, in English. He now sent it forth with a few additional pages, in which, under the influence of the self-imposed study, from which he had just risen, and while appealing to the ancient faith of Geneva, he criticises briefly the shallow and dangerous theories of the man, whom it is now the fashion to call "The Philospher of Geneva."

Meanwhile, the statute was executed by Pradier, and was inaugurated with great pomp in "L'Ile des Barques," called thenceforward, "L'Ile Rousseau." My father never set his foot there from that day.

After having published, in the February of that year, a new edition of his "Songs of Zion," containing two hundred hymns, and later, of his "Theogenes," he next issued the tracts, "What God Keeps is Well Kept," "The Heathen at our Doors," and "The Chateau Weather-cock."

In 1829 he issued some new works, besides two sermons on "The Love of our Neighbour," in which he dwells on the sources and practice of true charity, and "The Two Baptisms," delivered on the occasion of the baptism of his twelfth and last child. It was then that he again sided openly with the dissenters, against whom persecution had broken out into new ardour in the Canton de Vaud, where many of them had been doomed to imprisonment and exile.

This he did in his publication entitled, " The Liberty and Fatherland of the Children of God,"* where, in a dramatic style, he claims liberty for the persecuted, and presents a picture of those pious and brotherly assemblies —their substitute for the Fatherland—the Fatherland that had rejected them from its bosom. "War with God"—a tract of a few pages—is an urgent and solemn appeal addressed to the Grand Council of the same canton, in the name of justice and right, and of the liberty of the citizen; above all, of the peril which that Assembly incurred, like the Sanhedrim of old, of being found fighting against God.

Of course, such published utterances could not fail to bring down upon him the odium of the persecuting set, as well as of the populace which they had roused.

It was at this crisis, I think, that, happening to be at Payerne, where he was detained by an accident to his

---

* " Liberty and Fatherland," the motto of the scutcheon of the Canton de Vaud.

horse, an occurrence took place in which he owed his safety, under God, entirely to his Christian presence of mind. It is related, at full length, in his "Quatre-vingt Jours d'un Missionaire," page 445.

The same year saw the issue of two fresh tracts, "The Good Bargain," and "The Hypocrite."

The "Good Bargain" is a dialogue between two peasants on the gift of salvation through the atonement of Jesus Christ, and on those fruits of joy and holiness which are a necessary consequence of a hearty apprehension of it. It evinces, in numerous niceties of language and gesture, if I may so put it, that correctness of observation which, in my father's case, proceeded from a thorough love of, and sympathy with, the people, while, at the same time, it is easy to trace, in the sentiments which he puts in the mouths of his rustics, the compact and logical development of his own system of theology. Thus in "The Elder Son," in "The School of Amont Dale," and in many of his other tracts, we find rather a lucid exposition of evangelical doctrine than a testimony of Christian faith, powerful from its very simplicity—an exposition of truth calculated to affect any who might as yet be strangers experimentally to personal Christianity.

"The Hypocrite" was merely a narrative of one of the numerous incidents which happened to him in his dealings with "pious beggars." Throughout his long life he was continually obliged to reply to certain deceitful assaults on his benevolence by forwarding "The Discomfiture of Master Rusard."

At the close of that year occurred those disturbances in his church, of which mention has already been made. As soon as they were over, my father, surrounded by a numerous family, and free from ecclesiastical quarrels, gave himself up entirely to foreign missionary work, while in Geneva itself he stood forth as perseveringly, as watchfully, as faithfully as ever, a witness for the truth. It is under this twofold aspect that we must now regard him, after we have endeavoured, as succinctly as possible, to summarise that doctrine which, with him, constituted " The Truth."

BOOK II.

PUBLIC LABOURS FROM 1830.

CHAPTER I.

HIS DOGMATISM, AND THE DISTINCTIVE CHARACTER OF HIS TEACHING.

"I know whom I have believed."

How can I err in trusting Thee,
  O Thou in Whom I move and live?
Since Thou hast given Thy life for me,
  What lack I that Thou will not give?

ENOUGH has been said to show that the causes that interrupted my father's ministry (so far as they are to be traced to himself), arose principally from the manner in which he thought it his duty to state his personal opinions in the midst of his small congregation.

Before turning, then, to the tale of his missionary activity, which, from the year 1830, engrossed more and more his time and energies, it would be as well, at this point, to say something on the subject of his doctrinal views. And, in doing this, we are at once attracted to an investigation of the charge of dogmatism, so frequently and so early alleged against him, both by friends and foes. It will be our future task to account, as briefly as possible, for that distinctive doctrine which he was accused of making too prominent in his teaching.

There is one thing in the history of my father's religious thought which is ever striking me with fresh force. I allude to its unchanged and permanent continuance through the progress of years. From 1818 I find, both in the notes of his first sermons and in his correspondence, the same ideas, embodied in the same formulas, clothed in the same phraseology, and illustrated with the same metaphors even, which he employed to the very last. So that if, as we know to have been the case, he experienced a great change in reference to his ecclesiastical principles, this was in no way true as regards his theological tenets, which, so far from modifying, he asserted to the end with increasing conviction and clearness of definition.

Of course, he had not been slow to arrive at the conclusion "that the conversion of the heart to God was a work for which the mere argumentative force of truth, dogmatically declared, was utterly insufficient." But if he found himself thus driven to conclude that an indiscriminate, unregulated declaration of truth was to be avoided, he did not, on that account, vary either the positiveness or clearness of his testimony, nor yet the special form in which it had uniformly been invested. Of course, this involved him in a degree of monotony, not always redeemed, with those to whom his teaching was most familiar, by the solemnity and authority which his singularly lively and heartfelt convictions imparted to his delivery.

It may be admitted at once that he was rather a faithful and courageous witness to the truth, than a theologian, in the strict sense of the term. Not that his contemporaries regarded him thus. One glance at the so-called theological productions of the French world of that day will show this. And indeed if, according to an old saying, prayer, hard work, and earnest study of the Scriptures make a theologian, he has, in good truth, a right to the title, and that in an eminent degree. After distinguishing himself in his youth as a correct and graceful Latin scholar, and a dialectician of no mean capacity, he gave himself up exclusively, from the year 1817, to the daily study of the Scriptures. He had continued to read the New Testament in Greek, and as Hebrew had scarcely been taught at Geneva during the period of his education, he devoted himself to the study of it as soon as he had the leisure. For several years he kept up the custom of reading one or two psalms a day in the original, and was able after a time to quote many of them by heart.

With reference to his study of the Scriptures generally, he prosecuted it chiefly during the early hours of the day, till, by degrees, his morning reading developed into his habitual occupation. I remember the smile with which, one day towards the close of his life, he thought it right to explain to me, when I found him turning over the leaves of a Virgil, how he happened to be making acquaintance once more with a friend of his youth.

As regards the careful toil of his researches, some of his writings have sufficiently demonstrated that he had by no means failed in his efforts after patient scholarship. His correspondence on such matters is occasionally very striking; such a letter, for example as one containing a searching criticism of a work on which his opinion had been asked. There are others, too, (copies of which are in my possession), complete treatises of Biblical dogmatism, as it was understood at the time; and I have often asked myself, as I studied his closely-written pages, full of quotations and discussions of texts, all accurately reasoned out, and not unfrequently punctuated and arranged in paragraphs, whether I was not rather reading a work prepared for publication than letters written hastily and addressed to a private friend, as their style and personal allusions running through them, abundantly prove.

The truth is, that even if my father had not bequeathed to the Church a system of dogma capable of satisfying the requirements of the present time; his testimony, bearing as it ever did on what is the central point of all true Christian dogma, has not the less succeeded, on the other hand, in silencing such negative and erratic views as have elicited its attacks.* Passing by the fact, that he has left her what is better far than a new system of dogma, a truly apostolic example in the proclamation and defence of the Christian

---

* I cannot help expressing my regret that the Rev. E. de Préssensé, in the retrospective view which introduces his remarkable essay on Redemption, should not have pointed more clearly to this fact. As he has named my father as the representative of the system of theology, admitted by the instruments of the revival, it would have been but fair if the gifted author who criticises the narrowness of view which seems to him to be the consequence of that system, had indicated the difference between Malan and his contemporaries. Speaking even of the revival as a whole, if de Préssensé thought it his duty to impugn it as leaning towards "antinomianism," he certainly ought to have stated that, whatever might appear to be the natural result of the doctrines then most conspicuously put forward, the fact remains, that the leading characteristic of that great religious movement was a strictness of morals bordering on austerity.

faith; nor yet recalling in how many hearts there is reason to believe he was the means of writing the everlasting name of the Lord and Saviour Jesus Christ,—in how many souls his clear teaching dissipated the mists of an uncertain faith; what he has done for the Reformed Church in general, by means of his controversies with Rome—what he has given to the Church in his writings and hymns—these alone are grounds sufficient for according him the title of Doctor of Theology, with which, first of all those connected with the great revival, he was honoured by a foreign university.

At the same time, he used invariably to maintain that he was no theologian. "All I know," he would often repeat, "is the sovereign grace of God in Jesus Christ, the trust committed to me, of which I must give account."

Yet, in spite of this modest self-depreciation, it is clear that, even as a theologian, my father exercised a marked influence over other minds, as well by the precision and patience with which he reiterated the doctrines of grace, at that time little thought of, as also by the firmness with which he maintained the divinity of Jesus Christ and the divine authority of the Scriptures. Still, if he was a theologian among his contemporaries, he was supremely a *dogmatic* theologian.

Already, at the commencement of the revival, his opponents among the Genevese clergy had reproached him with exaggerating the importance of what seemed to them little better than theological subtleties. Even then he was publicly attacked, on the ground of being too much given to hair-splitting rationalism;* a fault imputed to him from

* "Un rationaliste trop scrutateur."

a very early period, though under another name, by his own brethren.

As for the attacks of those who had no part in his faith, none deserved the reproach of rationalism less than he; at least, if the word is to be taken to mean that disposition of spirit which will not believe in anything which reason has not grasped, not merely in the recognition of its existence, but the understanding of its essence. To employ reason to defend the expression of faith already arrived at, is not rationalism. Hence everything depends on our ascertaining whether the dogmatic reasoning of Malan did or did not meet the negations which encountered evangelical faith, or whether it did or did not bear upon points which belong exclusively to instinctive heart piety.

To ascertain the exact truth on these points, it will be necessary to form a correct idea of the negative theology with which he had to deal, and of the state of the religious atmosphere round him.

At the present time, unquestionably, thanks to the unmistakable clearness with which the debate was carried on (more especially by Malan himself), unbelief has been driven to a denial of the positive or direct authority of the Bible. Appealing therefore, in support of its negation of religious truth, to distinctions of which Malan, in his youth, had not a conception; it seeks its weapons of attack in the inner facts of the present life of the soul. To follow the adversary successfully into such a region, the champion of the faith finds it needful to analyse these facts attentively. And, as an inevitable result, the only authority which will remain available for his purpose will be that one tribunal, ever supreme in this subjective sphere, the tribunal of conscience, and the absolute character of the moral obligation it imposes.

Looking, then, at the question from this point of view, which, as we regard it, may be stated as that of the actual apologist, it is evident that a mind which, as we have seen, was the case with Malan, discarded in the investigation of religious truth all thought of the human element considered as such, would fail to exercise any very general influence. Moreover, this point of view, the mere propounding of which might possibly scandalise the orthodox believer, had not then been assumed. At that time friends and foes of the revival alike confined themselves to the region of religious supernaturalism. Neither side thought of making those facts the subject of theological study, which belong to the so-called anthropological science. It never occurred to them to suppose that it was the business of the theologian to determine the essential relation subsisting between the divine and human element. Nor was this only the case with such as denied the Incarnation; even men, for whose faith this fact had remained holy and precious, considered it after all as an isolated miracle without an essential and distinguishable cause. Religious doctrines included only, in the general judgment, theological truths properly so-called; such verities as referred to the being and work of God, considered apart from man and the world.

Both sides, therefore, concurred in taking, for the first and only base of religious argument, not so much a just appreciation of the nature of the facts of revelation and salvation which are stated to us in Scripture, as of the words themselves which transmit to us the historical knowledge

of these eternal verities. Thus it was that these words of
Holy Writ were universally designated as being in themselves "the written revelation," so that no one would have
thought of appealing to any other religious authority than
that which they contained. It did not occur to any one
to indicate that first and primitive authority which precedes, and which alone establishes for us, that of the
Bible. On this last point especially, not only did the
Genevese Church remain true to her traditional history,
but for more than a century and a half, during a controversy with Rome, in which texts had been freely bandied
about, the disputants had assumed a position which not
even the Reformers themselves had definitely taken up—
the verbal inspiration and oracular character of the sacred
writings. Every one admitted the divine authority of the
very letter of the Scripture, regarding it as the direct
result of a supernatural action of the Holy Ghost.* It
never occurred to any, even the most determined opponent
of the revival, to relegate the fight to that point. As for
the men of the evangelical party, intent on the thought of
reviving, in the midst of a people who had entirely lost
sight of them, the holy and essential truths of the personal will of God, and of the sovereignty of His grace,
they loudly denied any sort of moral liberty to the human
soul in the spiritual phenomenon of individual faith.
Thus it was that such men had been forcibly brought to
substitute, for the living and personal principle of that
faith, the mere passive acceptance of a divine action sub-

* The first man in Geneva who, at a later period, undertook to reply
publicly to the letter of E. Scherer against the inspiration of Scripture, was
Professor Chenevière, the representative of the most decided opposition to
the religious movement of the revival.

sisting entirely apart from the believing soul. Hence it followed that the action of the Holy Ghost, exclusively and strictly attached to the written word, existed for religious thought independently of the action of personal faith. Another corollary was, that the sacred character of this same action bore specially upon the clergy, the sole expositors of the written word, and also on the general fact of the visible Church, through whose instrumentality alone it has been handed down to the faithful. Nor did it ever occur to any evangelical believer to distinguish between the authority and the inspiration of the Bible, between the objective truth of the facts to which it testifies, and the perfect accuracy to be attributed to the varying mode of expression in which these facts are set forth.

And what abundantly proves our assertion is, that as soon as one courageous champion was heard declaring earnestly for that word which received honour in theory, and profound neglect in practice, those whom he appealed to confined themselves, in reply, to such empty and vague generalities as are apt to move public opinion; or, when they found themselves, after all their rhetoric, pressed into a corner by his clear and cogent reasoning, imported into the discussion the rancour of personality and partisanship, thus disturbing the calmness of debate, and diverting attention from religious to party interests.

At the present moment, undoubtedly, this state of things has ceased to be. And yet the question still remains, whether loud opposition, fraught though it be with the danger of passionate excitement, is not to be preferred after all to that dead silence of indifference which threatens to invade the minds of men.

Be this as it may, when once we regard the question as one of supernaturalism, depending wholly on the verbal and oracular authority of the Bible, it must be acknowledged that Malan's was not one of those minds, meriting the judgment of being too much given to investigation, because he brought once more into light doctrines long passed by, dogmas for many a year despoiled of their authority; on the contrary, it is but right to maintain that he was a man of progress, of active thought, espousing with faithful courage the cause of a recognised but neglected authority; in a word, the champion of the sacred rights of conscience and of religious sincerity.

As for his dogmatism, so far as it displayed itself, not more in the defence than in the confession and communicating of what his faith disclosed,—about this there could be no question. It was impossible to hear him preach, or to read the greater part of his writings, without being struck by the fact, that he did not content himself with rendering simple testimony to the reality of his objective faith, but went on to explain, and even to lay down the intellectual process by which, in his own mind, he apprehended the object of his faith.

This characteristic, however, is in no way surprising, when we take up the position he shared with those whom he addressed. For, as a matter of fact, there was nothing in the intellectual formula which he deemed the issue of his personal thought. But he and his hearers held it to have been directly dictated by God Himself in the inspired Word, — and revealed in its pages. As for the introductory question, bearing upon the way in which Scripture should be received and understood, no one had even raised it. While, with reference to a further point, embracing a still wider scope—the inquiry, how a divine revelation is to be communicated to the human soul, whether by direct experience of divine realities, or by the intervention of the thought of an intelligible presentation of them ?—this most important consideration, which ought to introduce all dogmatism on religious truth, was at that time utterly ignored. Thus my father remained unable to distinguish, in precise terms, between the essential authority of his faith and the relative importance of his doctrine,—the latter representing to him his Christianity and theology;—between the authority of his faith, and dogma; so that dogma, in his judgment, conveyed not merely truth, but *the* truth.

And yet, inasmuch as his faith, as is invariably true of living belief, was experienced by him as " the gift of God " to his soul, he could not but repudiate indignantly the reproach he had already incurred, that he considered it as the result of a simple process of thought. Still, the way in which this assertion was persevered in, proved conclusively that, whatever his personal experience might be, his teaching lent a colour to it. The fact was that, inasmuch as his whole attention was absorbed in the devout contemplation of the salvation of God, the act by which the soul apprehends that salvation seemed to him so simple and so natural, that he did not care to inquire curiously either into its history or elements.* Here, as

* In Malan's eyes, to believe was no act. "To believe does not give any trouble," are his very words. " We must believe without stirring." (See *Quatre-vingt Jours d'un Missionaire*, p. 16.) Such sentiments denote clearly, not a credulous mind, which his never was, but that confiding disposition which appears in the whole tenor of his life. He was called upon, as such natures generally are, to live rather with God and of God than with men and of men.

appears to us, was the defect in his teaching; the point to which he, perhaps, did not realise the necessity of directing sufficient attention. We may go further, and characterise it as the general want in all the revival preaching,—the feature that, for the present generation, leaves it, so far, entirely unsatisfactory. We charge that tendency, not indeed with denying to faith the character of a free, and, as it were, original work of the conscious will of man, but with going further still, by failing to see it, as it really is, a free and voluntary act of the instinctive powers of the heart. It seems as though, by such an exclusive representation of it as the result of an operation directly wrought from above, we are forcibly drawn into the danger of denying to it all essentially moral character. Meanwhile, how is this defect to be explained? Not by alleging, for that would be unjust, indifference to the moral interests of the soul. That there were unhappy men in that great awakening who " turned the grace of God into lasciviousness" is possible; is, unhappily, only too probable. But that so terrible a stigma could be affixed to the revival generally, much more, that it could be charged upon any one of the devoted band whose names figure in its history, will be utterly denied by any who have had the least acquaintance either with them or the time in which they lived.

Such a reproach was, indeed, undeserved. Only, carried away by an energy of zeal which took its rise in sincere faith and charity, those who were the heralds of that awakening applied themselves to what was, at that time, the most pressing want,—the proclamation of the objective reality of a salvation hitherto universally lost sight of.

Thus only, and from no laxity of moral views, they failed to advance all that appertained to the human appropriation of the divine tidings,—equally with the truth itself objectively, a part of the divine message. Thus it was that, in some instances, they ran the risk of offering to those whom they taught a mere half-gospel, while, it must equally be believed, to obviate this danger God raised up, in the midst of the revival, the mighty voice of Vinet.

But to confine ourselves to what immediately concerns the subject of these memoirs. It must be allowed that we have completely accounted for his dogmatism. Engrossed in absolute contemplation of the work of God, considered as an historical fact, he had no leisure for a slow and patient investigation of that work in the centre of the believer's personal life. Himself supremely a man of action, he was neither a thinker nor a psychologist, and mere subjective contemplation, in his judgment but useless dreaming, appeared in his eyes a sin. Admitting that he often divined and anticipated the secrets of the human heart, he never patiently examined its mysteries. He even refused the task as useless and wrong. In his eyes, it seemed nothing short of passing over the consideration of the glorious salvation of God, viewed as an external fact, for the sake of inquiring into the method of laying hold of it, on the part of a creature himself powerless for good ; leaving, in short, the celestial accents of the voice from heaven to listen to the confused mutterings of degraded and sinful humanity.*

* Thus it was that Malan did not even hesitate to affirm that we should offend God if we were to pray to Him for a salvation which He declares

Hence, while he never scrupled to protest against the reproach already quoted, he may very fairly be charged with want of decisiveness in specifying the nature of that faith so prominent in all his teaching. Assuming that it is to be regarded in itself, according to his experience, as a moral act,* it is no less clear that it did not so present itself to his thoughts at its first commencement. Faith, it is urged, was in his eyes the heart's trust. Granted; yet it is at the same time a trust only to be reposed in God after, and merely so far as, we have come to believe in His salvation as an historical fact. It is therefore principally, and at first, heartfelt confidence in a work of God plainly understood, a God revealed to our intelligence,—or at least in an operation of God clearly apprehended in our minds. In his judgment the moral element was indispensable to constitute our faith. Here, indeed, is the distinction between his fervent living piety and that dead orthodoxy, that abstract contemplation, which has never affected any but those who have had thrust upon them its icy declamations. Yet, while he is perpetually recurring to the necessity for faith being thus living and heartfelt, that moral element which he so constantly claims as an essential constituent, does not, according to his view, appear in its earliest origin. That element, if we watch for it, is ready to interpose for sanctifying and spiritualising what was at first

He has already accomplished.—(See *Quatre-vingt Jours d'un Missionaire*, pp. 140, 412, &c.) We may add that this sin, as he viewed it, was not so much a want of confidence in God's moral character as a doubt of the truthfulness of His written word.

* He defines it, the firm and sure confidence of the heart in what God says.—*Ibid.* p. 279.

but a simple deduction of the mind. In a word, he rejected the idea that before we could come to know God, we ought first to have been taught to love Him, believing that we ought to know Him first before we come to love Him.*

The faith he preached is in short that central reality in the human soul, that new life of the affections, which the apostles were for ever setting forth. But in consequence of the decisive part which, according to him, the understanding had to fulfil at its very earliest up-springing, the object of it remains in his teaching, if not in his own mind, rather a doctrine about God than God Himself; rather the name and history of God than that living Being Whose influence is felt in the soul before it has intellectually apprehended His work, before even it has learned to stammer forth His name. Hence possibly his hearers ran the risk of mistaking for saving faith a mere belief in the salvation of God rather than in God the Saviour; reliance, rather, in God's work than the confidence that work inspires in the personal character of Him Whom it reveals as a righteous Father.

* The following expresses his entire thought on this point. The passage occurs in a letter addressed by him, in March 1827, to one who saw in religious faith an exclusively intellectual operation : " Saving faith is an Almighty act by which the Holy Ghost enlightens the mind or touches the heart. Thus it is that the faith which concerns the understanding only is a mere science, or knowledge ; whilst that which apprehends and receives Christ is a living science, received by the mind and the heart, by which is to be understood the willing and acting principle in man. This faith is not, therefore, as you state it, the full evidence of truth as it is known and accepted by the mind or the understanding ; rather is it that same truth perceived by the understanding, and received by the heart, namely, by the affections, or the will, of the soul. There is, therefore, in that faith an operation of the Holy Spirit wrought upon both the powers of human nature, the understanding, and the will, and not one which merely touches the former."

Thanks, however, to the life and fervour of his piety, he was so far from incurring this peril, that he did not even see it to be a legitimate consequence of his teaching. Moreover, we are not now speaking of the believer, but simply of the teacher.

To confine ourselves, therefore, to his doctrine. It is indisputably true that, from the time that faith presented itself to him in the manner indicated, he gathered also that the individual intelligence of every believer necessarily appeared as capable, not only of reflecting clearly in itself, but also of rendering to others a true account of, the faith which constitutes the central life of the believing soul. Thenceforth, nothing was more natural than that my father should ally with his definition of saving faith his entire system of theology. Hence the charges of ultra-Calvinism and generally of scholasticism, which were so often urged against him, even by his best friends; while he, on the other hand, regarded them as so utterly incomprehensible, that his only reply was a still more exact statement of his dogmatic views. He failed to see that what staggered his brethren was not the want of accuracy in his logic, but the place he assigned to it. And yet, it never occurred to any of them to point out this distinction; they were satisfied with their censures, but they never went further and explained their vague criticisms. No one was bold enough to say that the point in dispute was not a religious truth, but a psychological fact. No one put into plain terms the question at the root of the allegation, whether an experience as yet instinctive, and not reflected from the understanding, can be in us an experience really objective, a direct operation of God upon the soul.

Above all, my father held such an acting of instinct to be nothing more than a subjective issue of imagination or personal feeling, in every instance a mere outcome of separate personality.* Hence, in his opinion, the whole work of salvation, whether viewed absolutely or relatively, stood out as wrought before us, and consequently as wrought without us. As regarded our interest in it, its claims upon us, these he held as questions purporting to be the issue, not so much of instinctive experience as of clear intelligence.

From this it will be easy to infer, what we have just asserted, the great importance which he attached to clearness and precision in dogma as the expression of faith, regarding it, as he did, not merely as the human version of that faith, but above all as a divine idea preceding the entrance of faith into the soul, and which faith at its first up-springing is bound clearly to apprehend. We shall understand, too, how it was that his dogmatic teaching, being the expression of his faith, clothed itself in a distinctly syllogistic form; the more so, as his own fashion of thought was logical and acute. Hence, not satisfied simply with stating his faith as a living reality within him, he could not refrain from explaining it as a reliance based upon considerations approving themselves thoroughly to his reflection. Hence, moreover,—assurance of salvation, to be complete, had to rest with him on a clear and conclusive syllogism. In a word, and this was the obnoxious element in his dogmatism, it was only by an effort of charity that

---

* "To *feel* that I am rich, is to deceive myself ; but to *believe* that the king is rich, because he says it, is to be certain of a *fact*, although I do not *feel* it."—*Quatre-vingt Jours*, &c., p. 218.

he credited those with living faith who failed to formularise their creed exactly as he did.

Having thus given a thorough analysis of the characteristics of my father's religious opinions, I must hasten to recall the circumstances in the midst of which they were developed. Not only had he been occupied in secular and religious teaching from a very early period, as well as in pulpit ministration, but the very atmosphere he had imbibed, and in particular the character of his studies, had contributed to favour what was beyond a doubt a leading trait in his disposition.

Not to go back as far as Calvin, which would have been necessary had we wished to have a full insight into the earliest beginnings of the tendency with which we have just been dealing, it will suffice to remind our readers that the catechism in which my father and his contemporaries had been instructed, commences by defining religion as "a science."

So it was an admitted fact in Geneva that the religious life could only exist in those whose minds were illuminated with clear religious knowledge. Hence it was, possibly, that earnest men, when they saw religious life decaying around them, so far from supposing that the eclipse of dogmatic teaching which prevailed had resulted from this decline, attributed to that doctrinal obscurity alone the symptoms which dismayed them.

Thanks to the essentially dogmatic atmosphere which surrounded alike their opponents and themselves, their zeal could hardly fail to express itself dogmatically, and that in direct proportion to the fervour of their faith. This remark applies not merely to the Protestantism of Geneva, but equally to that of Scotland, as well as to the tendencies

of the English "evangelical party" which so decisively influenced the origin of the revival, and especially my father.

It was not, however, from the positive influences alone
to which Malan was exposed, that he derived his dogmatism ; it was also fostered by the reaction he was called
upon to oppose to other influences of a directly opposite
character. At Geneva, as everywhere else, an excessive
intellectual dogmatism had aroused a correspondingly
vehement opposition. Underneath and alongside of the
prevalent official intellectualism there existed in the religious world a counter mysticism, as vague as it was
fanatical. Whilst, among its disciples, men of education
drew towards the lofty aspirations of a St Martin for
example, among the masses the same tendency frequently
expressed itself in superstitious devotion or exaggeration
of the imaginative faculty.

Both these types of religious thought had been encountered by him from an early period. As a young man
he had been a member of a lodge of theosophic and mystic
masons.*

Afterwards, however, the spectacle of the enthusiasm
existing in certain minds in connection with the visit of
Madame de Krüdener to Geneva, contributed, possibly
more than he himself was aware, to throw him into that
attitude of prudent reserve, to which he carefully adhered,
with reference to the earliest manifestations of the revival.

But more yet remains. His studies favoured this intellectual tendency. After his humanity course, followed
as it was by no sound philosophical reading, he proceeded
to theology, only to discover it to be, as conducted in his

* See De Goltz, "Genéve Religieuse," pp. 120, 121.

experience, of dogmatisms the coldest and most pedantic, the dogmatism of a disguised and emasculated Christianity. Impelled, however, by his mental bias to bring everything within the compass of a precise definition, instinctively averse to all confusion of thought, as well as to all formulas which evade and twist, instead of boldly grappling with a question, he soon found himself unable to rest satisfied with the superficial, vague, obscure, and diluted teaching, which the theological professors dealt out. Not only according to his way of looking at things, (so thoroughly French in this respect,) was it sufficient to prove an idea false, if it could not be clearly shaped; but none of his studies had led him to distinguish between truth and reality, between a thought, and the fact of which every thought must necessarily be but an inadequate expression.

Such were the influences which, in conjunction doubtless with the peculiar bent of his intellect, while they did not, of course, result in any positive confusion of the moral and purely intellectual elements of the soul, still made him regard the one as so intimately allied with the other, that the state of the heart might fairly be inferred from the conclusions of the mind. Hence, we may not only understand the syllogistic and definitive character of his teaching, but also arrive at a just interpretation of his position as head of a church. We see how he thought himself permitted, or rather considered it his duty in the interests of ecclesiastical discipline, to form clear and definite judgments on the inner life of those who availed themselves of his ministrations. Regarding conversion, not merely as a reality indispensable to salvation, (as every believer would admit,) but more than that, as an event, the occurrence of which may always be specified with certainty, even to the extent of setting forth its earliest dawning in the renewed soul, he felt himself driven, spite of his sound judgment and thorough large-heartedness, to separate men into two classes, Christians and worldlings, and this not merely, in a general sense, as one stating an abstract fact, but most strictly and uniformly relying for decision, not merely on the fruit of the heart, but of the understanding also.

But let it be stated emphatically, in reference to this last point, that, as he judged others, so he judged himself. In his own case, we find him dating his conversion, not from the earliest impressions of his childhood, nor yet from the religious convictions of his youth, but emphatically from that precise moment, when, under the influence of the study of the Scriptures, he gave a thoughtful and intelligent assent to what he had so long practically though unconsciously held. Not, indeed, that he failed to distinguish between the period when he became orthodox and that of his soul's awakening, but even in admitting this distinction, it was with a view to maintaining that the latter would never have transpired except as the issue of the former.

In general terms, it may be affirmed that his thoughts were more given to the objects, privileges, and life of faith, than to its subjective analysis. His care was to meditate upon and to proclaim to others the celestial fact revealed to his soul; his one absorbing consideration, the fact itself, its greatness, and the assurance and rapture with which his spirit overflowed. It was not a question with him how he received it, still less did he dwell on the accompanying conflict, his thoughts were given up wholly and absolutely to the possession, the assured possession, of the salvation of God. Begotten again to a new life by the sudden manifestation of this wondrous grace, when once by a simple act of will he had laid hold of the promise, instinctively and irrevocably,—he could not suppose for a moment that any soul experiencing a similar manifestation could ever pause or consider. Full of adoring gratitude to the God of all grace, believing implicitly and with his whole heart the gospel of salvation, he had no thoughts to spare for himself, for the nature and justifiableness of the transports he experienced, which were to him the joy of a new life. It was not for him to analyse doubts he had never known, or to investigate, even in a speculative spirit, the precise conception he had formed of that Divine Saviour Whom his soul adored. In a word, he left it to others to indulge in researches for which he had no fancy. His one desire was to proclaim daily, with zeal ever fresh, not so much the character as the work of God, not so much what He is up to the present moment to every believing soul, as what He did once for the elect. And this he did in demonstrating and defending the truth of the gospel, and the results to which it leads, not so much as an historical manifestation of the eternal thoughts of divine love, but principally as being the primary origin and first cause of our salvation. Such was the end he strained at with the authority of a conviction ever growing in power, depth, and heart-felt earnestness.

And he was one of the most impressive preachers of the objective and absolute reality of salvation. Here lay the explanation of his dogmatism; here also, its advantage. Nay more, so far from involving him in any spiritual dangers, it became the actual source of a prominently enthusiastic and active piety. Indeed, with his impulsive, ardent nature, glowing with fervent energy, sober-minded and self-contained though he was, with a heart to which simplicity and sincerity imparted genuine greatness, he combined that trait which characterised Calvin himself,—an inability to understand how the reality of a fact could be allowed without the will and life exhibiting all its legitimate results.

So far as any soul might be held back, either by utter ignorance of what God has done for man, and apart from man, or by a want of clearness and precision with reference to this divine gift; for such a soul there could have been, there can be now, no more useful or powerful preacher than Malan. But beyond this he was not prepared to go. It was not his gift to descend from those great heights of contemplation to an attentive, patient, persevering, and occasionally minute analysis such as is the holy task imposed upon the pastor as the trainer of feeble, unwise, uncertain souls. Awe-struck himself by the eternal glories of the work of God, entranced, enraptured again and again by the mere contemplation of it, his eagle eye seemed never weary of dwelling, with an ever fresh delight, on the centre of all that dazzled his soul. For himself, and for others equally, he knew of but one remedy for every soul sickness, one solution for ever perplexity—the written testimony of God, the recorded work of God, the salvation once wrought by God.* Should he be called upon to deal with

* We may quote, as an instance of the manner in which he addressed such souls, the following extract from one of his later works (" Incidents de

a soul, for the needs or sufferings of which this simple message proved inadequate, he never stopped to search out the cause of the evil in the recesses of the troubled heart, or in any special circumstances of the case; but confining himself exclusively to the historical and objective reality of the work of God, he proceeded forthwith to argue from it all the consequences it involved; his penetration, energy, eloquence, and unsparing logic being called into full operation.

Not that it is to be inferred from this that he ever thought of representing salvation itself as being within the grasp of mere reason. He, like every other believer, knew well that spiritual conviction was direct from God, a fact of experience in which the subjects of it are absolutely passive. It was not as one seeking to establish the truth itself, but as one assuming it, and starting from it, as from an admitted conclusion, to which the soul has been brought by the Holy Spirit through the instrumentality of Scripture, that he exchanged testimony for demonstration, confession for exposition. Never caring even to pause and prove the authority of the Bible, he was satisfied to assume it, and to quote it authoritatively in its literal and simple interpretation. Omitting to take into account all the inconsistencies in which the soul of man is involved by his free will, and not satisfied with protesting against all abuse of his independence of action, he occasionally went so far as to turn a deaf ear to its voice, and deny it point blank.

Voyage," Grains de Sénevé, vol. vii. No. 89), which may serve to show the injustice of the reproach of antinomianism, as applied to his popular teaching: "If you ask why you do not possess that salvation, I answer, it is not God's fault, it is certainly yours. Here is the source; rise up and drink!"

Nor did he hesitate to affirm that God and man were separated by a divergence essential, absolute, insuperable. It was not enough for him to say with the apostle, " All is of God," he would go on to say—what should be said, so carefully, or conscience will be outraged—" and nothing is by man."

Thus it has been endeavoured to enumerate the characteristics of his dogmatism which repelled those who, while they shared his faith, by no means shared his views. Himself a sincere and thoroughly convinced believer, the perfect submission of his faith rendered his teaching clear, convincing, and irresistible by its strength and life, during the whole period of his protracted testimony. Reared, however, in the bosom of a prevalent dogmatism, the victim in his early years of that defective teaching of his opponents which culminates in positive ignorance, and absolute negation, it was not surprising that to a negative dogmatism he was led to oppose what was positive and even aggressive.

Here we would again remind our readers of the fact that he never claimed to be a propounder of religious theories, a theological professor. When he first commenced his ministry, the scientific element in divinity had as little ascendency in his thoughts as the mere question of ecclesiastical polity; and even when it did present itself in due course, it never engrossed his whole attention. His one aim was to testify to the faith which he had so powerfully realised in his own soul by openly avowing it, and, above all, by declaring to his brethren, whom he believed to be in soul-destroying error, the sovereign grace and eternal salvation of a personal living God. For this purpose he adopted the only formula within his reach—what had been, in the society in which he moved, the latest embodiment of the faith he was then experiencing. He found it in " Pictet's Doctrinal Summary," and in the " Confession of Faith of the Reformed Churches of Holland."

It was not at the bidding of this theology, however— so utterly antiquated in the opinion of the Genevese clergy, but to him the expression of an eternal truth,—that he gave forth his testimony. It was in the name of faith he spoke, and not of orthodoxy. If he had recourse to the systems of schoolmen, it was not for light to see how to fight ; it was only for weapons with which to thrust back the negations by which he was surrounded. This is the only point of view from which to take a fair estimate, not only of his dogmatism, but also of the real motives which drove him from the Establishment, and also of his after isolation from his non - conforming brethren in Geneva. To those who accused him of schism with reference to the National Church, he replied that his faith constrained him, at the cost of every other consideration, to declare the eternal Godhead of the Lord Jesus. To such, again, as appealed to him to go hand in hand with his brethren, his answer was, that while he welcomed communion with them as heirs together of the grace of God, he considered himself bound to preserve the speciality of his ministry, which was to proclaim the doctrine of restricted election.*

Meanwhile, it remains for us to consider whether Malan, trained in another school of religious thought, would have

---

* He goes so far as to call himself "the minister of election by grace."— *Quatre-vingt Jours*, &c., p. 147.

been equally well fitted for the work which had been given him to do. If we recall to mind the atmosphere by which he was surrounded, we do not think there can be any hesitation on this point. The sentiment, not to say the sentimentality, of the author of the "Imitation," Fenelon, or Lavater, admirable as an expression of pious thought, and mightily illustrating the manifold grace of God, would have failed utterly—indeed, it actually had failed—in common with every other attempt to deal effectually with the heartless scepticism which, fifty years ago, had overrun Geneva. That—in the present day, when a wide breach has been effected in the fortress of infidelity, when no hindrance offers itself to the promulgation of the doctrine of a free salvation, and of the divinity of our Lord, from the pulpits of our churches, when none would be held to blame for propounding openly the most distinctive truths in the apostolic teaching—that in such a day, zealous men should show themselves anxious to enlarge upon the gradual subjective appropriation of salvation, is not to be wondered at. The more earnest, however, such efforts are, the more will those who make them do justice to the bold and powerful teaching which God employed to win them leisure for their great meditation.

Meanwhile, it will be our wisdom, while we abstain from disparaging Malan's gifts on account of his dogmatism, to seek gratefully to avail ourselves of the inheritance bequeathed to us by that faithful and devoted minister of the gospel: but should we fear, on the other hand, with his categorical formula of living faith in our hands, that in listening to the servant's utterance, we run the risk of becoming his disciples, we shall do well to remember that we have one only Master, even Christ. At all events, let us not be backward to recognise the place which belongs of right to the confessor of the Lord Jesus, whenever, in the present day, we are called upon to dissipate some special error, or to throw light upon some special obscurity in the faith. Let us admit the power with which he calls to, and awakens slumbering souls; with which he presses them— we had almost said *forces* them—" to enter." In these respects his place is clearly marked out as useful, glorious, and great; to refuse it to him would be wrong to the Great Disposer Who raised him up at a special time to serve His Church.

Passing on from his dogmatism, considered solely as the general tendency of his mind, to the particular form which it assumed; in other words, to his definite opinions: it is sufficient to state that they were those of the old Protestant orthodoxy, as embodied in the Confessions of the Reformed Churches, more particularly in those of the Calvinistic Synod of Dordrecht in the seventeenth century;* in short, the strictest type of what is generally known as Calvinistic Scholasticism.

We must observe, however, that it was by independent ways, and through the close personal study of the Word, that he arrived at these doctrinal views; more particularly must it be stated that he was not indebted for them to his intercourse with Mr Robert Haldane. Not only, as we have seen, had he arrived at his fixed opinions before Haldane's visit; but, so far was he from regarding himself as a disciple of that truly apostolical man, that he did not

---

* He refers himself to that Synod as embodying his theological views.— *Quatre-vingt Jours*, &c., pp. 138, 403.

even adopt his views on the subject of baptism. Moreover, though he willingly read the writings, both of the reformed doctors of the "Federalist School" of Holland (H. Witsius in particular), and also of the English divines of the Westminster Assembly, as well as of the Nonconformists generally, with many others of the same kind, he by no means gathered his opinions from their pages, though he studied them with interest as recording his own convictions. Above all, I know that he never read Calvin, whom he resembled in the most characteristic aspects of his religious thought, till long after his convictions had become indelible.*

He has often stated himself that it was Scripture alone that enlightened him. It was not Haldane, but "the finger of Haldane," that governed him with the sentence, "How is it written? how readest thou?" which that good man loved to repeat to his young friends. Haldane was neither divine, scholar, nor theologian; at home in the history of theology, or accustomed to investigate it. He was not even an ecclesiastic. He was a simple believer, but one profoundly versed in the knowledge of the Word. Hence it is of far greater moment, in determining the special influences which operated on my

---

* The following verses he wrote, as far back as 1820, under a portrait of the Reformer which hung in the dining-room :—

> "Si nous voyons en toi ce qu'un docteur doit être,
> Et si nous admirons les dons que tu reçus ;
> Comme nous serviteur, tu n'es pas notré Maître,
> Mais avec toi, Calvin ! nous adorons Jésus."

> "While the great doctor in thy form we see,
> And reverence the gifts thou didst receive ;
> Servant like us, in spirit one with thee,
> Great Calvin, to the Master praise we give."

father, to dwell upon the details of his conversion, than to specify this or that article of creed which might be found clearly set forth in the history of Protestant Dogma. So that it will be well for us now, without entering into minute particulars, to consider, from a subjective point of view, his apprehension of the great fact of salvation, to the entire satisfying of the hunger and thirst of his soul.

What first arrested his attention was the truth, that the initiative in the great work of salvation is to be ascribed to the sovereign will of God ; or, as he expressed it, " the free sovereignty of the grace of God." It was to this supremely that he yielded his earliest homage, going no farther, remaining transfixed with gratitude, and silent with reverence. No sooner had this view penetrated his soul, and flooded it with light, than it governed and absorbed his thoughts. Ever new as a theme for contemplation, ever living as a fact of experience, this truth of a God Who loves, because it pleases Him to love, and not because of anything attractive in the object of His affection, Whose love precedes all attractiveness and produces it ; this truth, be it understood, aroused and governed the glowing activity of his piety. Never, from the moment of his conversion, during his long career, through all the difficulties, toils, and treacherous experiences with which it abounded, not even in the last agony of death, did the shadow of a doubt come across his perpetual sunshine.

All which is easily understood. Let the eye of the soul be once fixed on God, and so be withdrawn from the earth, and it has before it only what can sustain, console, and invigorate. That such was my father's happy experience may with confidence be asserted.

And in making this statement I wish to imply that, even before what he himself called his conversion, faith in the living presence of God, if not in His grace, the fear of a personal and living God, was the ruling sentiment of his being. Here was the rock on which, in obedience to Christ's own words, he erected his faith. It was this holy reverence that kept alive in his soul his mother's pious teachings, despite the temptations of youth, and the freezing generalities of his studies. These teachings had come to him when she had made him read the Gospels at her feet. Thus it happened that he afterwards recognised in free salvation the work of that God and Saviour Whom, as he was heard to say, he had preached when he knew Him not. I would not for a moment suggest that this feeling had, at its first uprising, brought liberty to his soul; all I wish to contend for is, that with him, in a manner more marked than with the majority of others, it may be seen how the fear of the Lord was the beginning of wisdom.

At all events, this clear, definite apprehension, this indelible, personal experience of the free grace of a living God, lay at the bottom of all his after work, whether as preacher, missionary, or religious author.

In meditation on this truth, to him ever new, he armed himself for controversial encounters,[*] while from it he derived those principles which imparted vigour to his morality.[†]

---

[*] The destruction of every heresy and falsehood is to be found in the entire accomplishment of the work of salvation, in the expiation wrought by Christ. Hence it is that Rome denies and rejects it with the greatest animosity.—*Quatre-vingt Jours*, &c., p. 279. Compare also p. 127, and the whole of his method of controversy.

[†] He makes gratitude the exclusive basis of the whole moral life of the believer. Is not the possession of a crown worth some reforms? And when once that crown has been given us, shall we sacrifice it to frivolous trifles, or to low and impure instincts?—*Ibid.* p. 370.

This central experience of his faith is to be detected even in his hymns, where, if he does not teach it, he avows it, and is never tired of celebrating it.

It was this experience of free salvation which presented itself not as the reward of imperfect efforts, but as an act of sovereign and unlooked-for favour to a wandering soul, blind and lost; it was this blessed revelation which led him to rest in Jesus, not as a Helper merely, but as a Saviour. Thus it was that he meditated in adoring gratitude on the omnipotent and essentially divine character of the Atonement. Thus he apprehended, in its supreme importance, the eternal divinity of the Saviour, to the confession of which truth he sacrificed, with all he had, the dreams and ambitions of his youth.

Here also we must judge of his doctrines by the tendency against which he was called upon to protest. In Geneva, as well as in the rest of the Protestant world, men of faith and piety even had gradually withdrawn from what will ever constitute the special and glorious character of the great religious revival of the sixteenth century. Under the influence of a dogmatical reaction, into the history of which we cannot enter here, the justification of the soul had gradually come to be represented, not as having been wholly accomplished by eternal love, but as being, even according to the divine purpose, the result of the faith of the believer, and of his regeneration by faith. Thus, even in the teaching of men of the most exemplary piety, that triumphant assurance which had been the strength of Luther or Calvin had gradually been replaced by the anxious pre-occupations of a humility falsely so called, and by the hesitations of a religious morality which had no really firm basis, and no absolute value. These considerations are well calculated to show us the great importance of his special teaching.

Finally, if we remember that Malan, with all who hold the reformed faith, never for a moment supposed the possibility of the extension beyond the limits of this present life of God's saving work towards man, if we remember too, that, in consequence of his dogmatism, he never deemed it possible for a work of grace to commence in any soul—that soul remaining unconscious of its operation—we shall be in a position to understand how it was that his belief in the divine sovereignty led him to the special dogma which characterised his teaching, in other words, to that reiterated affirmation of restricted election, or of individual predestination, as we find it stated in the writings of the reformed divines of the seventeenth century.

According to his view, this doctrine, as set forth in the Word, was no mere declaration, that when any man comes to a knowledge of salvation, he is warranted, nay, even required, to believe that his salvation is the issue of a pre-existing, fixed purpose of God. Nor was it simply an affirmation that this fact, in virtue of which the man is then elected amongst others, so far from remaining a matter of indifference to him, involves actually a privilege deliberately conferred, and with it a solemn responsibility. He saw in the doctrine of election far more than this. With him it was a formal declaration that when a man received by faith the revelation of salvation in Christ, not only had he touched the threshold of a new life with new responsibilities, but he had also been the subject of a personal decree from God Who had deigned to choose him by a personal election, and that the divine purpose thus apprehended, his salvation is set forth to him as already effected, and as calling only for his future gratitude and praise.

In his judgment the knowledge of the gospel was not only set forth by the apostles as a providential fact, which ought as such to attract our earnest attention ; he held to a positive assertion that the return of a wandering soul to Christ issued inevitably in its salvation, inasmuch as conversion is the work of God Himself, and, from the first, of God alone.   The presence of faith in a believer appeared to him miraculous, and demanding assurance, on the part of the subject of it,—with regard to the proof it supplied of divine operation,—that his salvation was already accomplished, completely, irrevocably, from the very day, in short, when Christ died upon the cross.   Of course, in arguing thus, he referred not to mere historical knowledge of evangelical truth, but to its living apprehension in the heart.   This point, however, once set at rest, he never scrupled to recognise in such a living faith the issue of a special purpose, a personal decree, and a fore-ordained irresistible act of God Himself; and, as far as its subject was concerned, a direct revelation to him of a salvation wrought out and irrevocably determined long before.   So that God cannot be said actually to save a soul at the moment of its return to Him.   He does but announce to it, by the faith He imparts, its place long ago established among the ranks of the saved.   This faith, His gift, is not only the life of that soul; it is its pledge of safety :— the evidence proving, not that it is one of those given each day by the Father to the Son, but that it is one of that limited number, purchased once for all by the Son's eternal sacrifice.

Hence, it follows that the believer is expected to seek out this hidden force of the new life, rather in the revelation which his faith procures for him than in his faith itself; rather in the assurance of salvation than in the daily exercise of an ever fresh act of belief; in short, rather in the liveliness of his gratitude than the activity of his trust. With Malan the new life was the result rather than the extension of salvation. The safety of each soul he held to be absolutely secured from the first, and from without. "Either such a soul is saved," he never hesitated to affirm, " or it never will be." And since, according to his idea, faith would never fail to be accompanied by an illuminated understanding, it naturally followed that it was in the power of each one to ascertain whether he was or was not a child of God, and that, allowing for human fallibility, it was possible to discern even here, with reference to others, not only between one whom God has already called to Himself, and another to whom that call has yet to come,—but even more, between the soul loved and saved from all eternity and the soul which, if it believe not in this present life, is for ever excluded from all hope of salvation.

Such opinions were not likely to remain long unchallenged. Aiming at the honour of God, they appeared fatal to that liberty of the creature, which after all constitutes one of the conspicuous glories of the Creator. An attack upon them was all the more inevitable, because their author, in the intensity of his conviction, sought every opportunity of promulgating them.

During the greater part of the controversy, however, his opponents gave him fair play. In short, with the exception of a very few who went so far as to assert, with reference to a man whose life would have been his best acquittal from the charge, that he was "an unprincipled antinomian," —the attack was directed solely against that side of his teaching, which affirms the absolute freedom and initiative sovereignty of God.*

Here was the point wherein the truth and holiness of his opinions were gathered; here, too, the aspect under which they revealed themselves, with increasing clearness, to his religious faith. Moreover, the objections urged against him in this quarter, could not fail to recall to a man, nourished up as he was in the Word of God, the similar

---

* At the commencement of this chapter, I referred to M. de Pressénsé's criticism on my father's doctrines. I now allude to such accusations as assailed his personal life.

The expression I employed in the text is borne out by many passages in Bost's Memoirs, referring to my father. As this book has been noticed in England, I must be allowed to enter somewhat into detail.

He applies to my father's doctrines the epithet *loose*, (" des doctrines relâchées," vol. i. page 87 of the French edition.) And what shows that he means to attribute that character to the man as well as to his writings, is the fact that he explains the discussions between Malan's congregation and that of the Bourg de Four, as arising out of " vile money questions," (" de honteuses questions d'argent.") As he immediately adds that the pastors of the Bourg de Four did not receive any remuneration for their services, the entire odium of the remark falls upon the opposite side.

It may suffice, by way of reply, to recall what has been stated in the former chapter about the annual sum my father received from his congregation during twenty-five out of the forty-five years of his ministry. It would be easy to add abundant documentary evidence, showing how he toiled himself, that he might be able to help the needy of his flock, never resting until his benevolent purpose was accomplished. But any one who knew him personally, knew him to be conspicuous for his generosity, disinterestedness, and real superiority as regards those money questions which play so wearisome and incessant a part in Bost's Memoirs.

But dismissing this point, and dealing simply with the censure which the experiences of the Apostle Paul, thus leading him to accept this opposition as an absolute sanction of his doctrine.

The only point to which his attention ought to have been directed was, not the mystery of the absolute liberty of the divine will, since that (though beyond the reach of syllogism) is even further beyond the reach of doubt. Truly his opponents should have contented themselves with the peculiar side of that question which belongs to our human experience; in other words, to that kind of responsibility which, not the eternal will, but the historical action of the Supreme Being imposes upon its human object.

In proof that, by those regarding the question of destiny from this point of view, a common understanding might easily have been arrived at, it may be remarked, that Malan never presses his doctrine on this head to its legitimate detailed practical conclusions. That doctrine

book pronounces on my father's doctrines, it scarcely comes well from one who, even in his old age, admits that he is unable to shake off the hesitation and doubts which unsettled his mind in his youth. (i. 245; ii. 63.)

Passing over numerous other passages of direct accusation and indirect inuendos, I notice one sentence which seems to explain many of them. He tells us, (i. 404), "that both in Geneva and abroad they attributed the whole revival to Malan." "In Geneva and abroad," they were undoubtedly very wrong, they should have referred it to God alone. Malan invariably did.

Should any of my readers wish for a fuller review of these volumes, they will meet with one of singular ability in the *Record* newspaper, November 28, 1855, and November 30, 1860.

As to my father's judgment on a work whose author he had so intimately known, I quote an extract from a letter he wrote to a friend, in December 1855: "I have not read Bost's Memoirs. I have received from different persons requests that I would answer sundry assertions which my friend has put forth. But I prefer leaving this and many other things to Him Who knows the truth as regards this series of incidents and writings. I have greater things to do at the end of the week than to rescue from imputation the work I have done in the course of it. To the Master, and to the Master alone, I commit the task of judging it."

remained the natural and necessary expression of the
obedient adoration of his heart, and therefore produced no
other result than humility and thankfulness, the two most
prominent elements in the activity of true piety.

As to the inevitable influence of his teaching, on his judgment and conduct towards others, those who knew him
best will remember the temperate sobriety which characterised his discussions. Not only was he never seen to
manifest a Pharisee's self-righteous pride or a fatalist's
indifference, but it will be in the recollection of many how,
while from the pulpit he appeared to delight in enlarging
on the vileness of the creature, he showed himself privately
ever ready to think and hope the best of all, and to manifest a spirit of universal and most sincere charity. Nor will
such forget how easily his sympathy and esteem were
secured; and, above all, how careful he was not to pass
judgment upon others.

As far as regards the central point in his views, I have
precious recollections of long and intimate conversations,
in which, especially in his closing years, I found myself
often hurrying on before him, expatiating upon the infinite
mercy of God, and the presumption of seeking to fathom
the divine counsels. Sometimes he would add a word.
One day—can I ever forget it?—after having listened to
me in silence (it was on the occasion of a visit I paid him,
shortly after the death of one of my children) he stopped
suddenly as we were walking on; then raising his head,
and fixing his ardent gaze upon me, grasped my hand in
deep emotion, and withdrew, thoughtful and silent.

Of course, such recollections are only significant to
myself. But what will have been universally noted by

those who knew him, was that persevering, patient, and devoted activity, that life marked throughout by charity and courage; marked, too, from first to last, by that passion for the salvation of souls in which, as has been demonstrated by no feeble pen, resided the grandeur and glory of those men of the revival, among whom my father was one of the mightiest and most prominent. And this shows the fallacy of that charge of self-confident fatalism urged with such complacency, from time to time, against those who professed their faith in the election of grace.

I cannot undertake to say whether my father's friends share in my impression. But the spectacle of his living theism, which revealed to him on all hands the direct, actual personal work of God Himself—of his authority, courage, and utter clearness in teaching; of his convictions, so resolutely practical and uncompromising; of his faith, circumscribed indeed, but ever watchful and constant; and lastly, of the special use which he made of the text of the Word—the spectacle of all this, I say, has often made him appear to me like one filled with the peculiar spirit of the prophets and faithful of the Old Testament, rather than that which characterised the disciples of the New. Descended directly from the old Huguenots, the latest son of the Geneva of Refugees and Confessors, his grand form, slowly disappearing from the horizon of the religious world, so levelled and so superficial, has ever appeared to me the type of an essentially theocratic character. With him the kingdom of God, however invisible to sense, was to be realised directly in practical experience; separation from the world was no mere preservation from evil, it was to be illustrated in the acts and habits of common life. The service of God was blended, in his eyes, with his daily history and deeds, his opinions, and special duties; extending itself, moreover, to the minutest detail of ordinary existence. Hence, it came to pass that, isolated as he was from all ecclesiastical ties, he remained, notwithstanding the romantic enthusiasm of his temperament, and the ardour of his imagination, a practical, consistent, energetic believer; thus it was that he escaped, on the one hand, the perils of a frigid intellectualism, as well as of mere visionary abstraction or sentimental pietism, on the other. For this he was kept in that living holiness which has its spring in an abiding realisation of an ever-present living God; that apprehension of the divine will as sovereign and absolute; that confidence in the divine love, the reality of which is in no way dependent on the manner in which our human feeling comes to acknowledge its greatness. To sum up,— that perfect clearness of understanding, that inextinguishable assurance, arrived at only by those who have a believing view of a salvation perfected for them, and despite their utter unworthiness.

Satisfied with having thus dwelt on the central principle —the ruling thought, if I may so term it—in his system of faith, and referring my readers for details of his views to his numerous writings, I shall confine myself, in what remains of this memoir, to exhibiting him as a witness for the truth—a gospel missionary. In this capacity supremely he displayed the resources of that Christian life, the hidden mystery of which defies analysis or exposure, and which exhibited itself in his case, invested with all the lustre and endowments of an attractive and powerful nature.

CHAPTER II.

Sow blessed seed, in hope
Its precious fruit to see—
In God's own good appointed time ;
That is the time for thee !

THE year 1830 was a decisive date in my father's history.
Whilst his private life and that of his family expanded,
while his testimony came by degrees to exercise a definite
influence, and even to hold a fixed place in the public
life of Geneva, he continued to occupy an increasingly
isolated position in that section of the religious world identified with the revival. This circumstance was, however,
largely compensated for by the growing activity which he
displayed both in Geneva as a witness and defender of
gospel truth, and abroad as a preacher and missionary.

In 1829 he bought a piece of ground adjoining his property, and added it to the garden he had occupied up to
that time, in which his chapel stood. Then he exchanged
a small abode on the public road for a much more con-
venient dwelling, in the centre of a large walled enclosure.
There, for thirty-five years, he lived with his numerous
family in a retreat which, situated though it was in the

immediate vicinity of the town, was nevertheless entirely withdrawn from the tumult and excitement of the outer world. Sufficiently extensive to afford us good air, exercise, and even privacy, with flower-borders and orchards adjoining, and fresh and peaceful shades,—this garden of the Pré-Béni, with its chapel and school, was, as it were, to us a sort of world in itself, in which the childhood and youth of the youngest of us were passed; while with it our father's life in Geneva was more exclusively associated. Subsequently, as we began to drop off, and establish ourselves in foreign countries, his position became gradually isolated. At the time of which we are speaking, however, it did but secure to him that entire liberty which he increasingly needed for his various undertakings. There, too, it was that he displayed the greatest vigour and activity.

Surrounded by his children; his once often-failing health now gradually recruited; he received visits more frequently than ever from strangers distinguished for their personal piety, or for the place they occupied in the religious world. Yet he could not but feel painfully conscious of his isolated position with reference to his Genevese brethren. After having withdrawn, unhesitatingly, and even with a certain eagerness, from a clergy which appeared to him to oppose gospel truth, he felt himself constrained, to the end of his life, to stand more or less apart from those whom he regarded as his brethren in the faith.

We have just seen how his position, in reference to those whose work had preceded his in the first revival, may be explained. As for the new movement which has been occasionally styled the second evangelical revival in Geneva, my father had watched it from its birth. Its success was in a great measure due to the decisive spirit in which he had originated it.* Yet these men, honouring as they did, in his person, the decided testimony to evangelical truth, never thought of uniting themselves to him for the work which they inaugurated with so much enthusiasm. It was evident, especially during the earliest years, that they carefully avoided anything which might lead to the opinion that their operations were connected with his.

At first glance, it would seem surprising that this could have been the case. As a matter of fact, the establishment of the Evangelical Society in 1831, with its oratories, and soon afterwards with its school of theology, was but in reality, after all,—with such a wider scope as a committee composed chiefly of laymen and men influenced by their position could avail for,—the realisation of what had been undertaken fifteen years before by the young ministers of the first revival, and more particularly by my father.

Moreover—to refer only to the later movement—none of the men who were at the head of it refused him their esteem and respect. He was even personally connected with the three ecclesiastics whose names had already secured well-merited fame. We have heard him say that Galland and Gaussen had been the friends and models of his youth, As for Merle D'Aubigné, who had just arrived from abroad, he put himself into immediate communication with my father, and continued to be to him, and to his family after him, an invariably kind and faithful friend.

---

* M. Gaussen remarked to my mother at the time, in reply to her expressions of sympathy with reference to the difficulties he was experiencing, " What are they when compared with those which your dear husband has been called upon to encounter! He broke up the path in which we are simply called upon to follow."

Malan, on his part, so far from standing aloof from all that was going on, recognised the first beginnings of the revival, and followed all its vicissitudes with the liveliest interest. He was identified with it in heart and thought by his prayers, and by the many testimonies of his brotherly regard. For him and his, the establishment of the Oratory had been a great event—the expansion of our sphere of daily life, till then painfully contracted—the end of years in which their name alone had placed them outside all social relations in this little country. From its commencement, he sent his children to the new meetings, just as afterwards, on several occasions, he made his sons follow the course of the new school. All these things considered, however, it was but natural that his relations, in the earliest years of the movement, especially with the Evangelical Society, should be limited to simple personal intercourse. When it started, indeed, the congregation of the Oratory was in precisely the same position with regard to the National Church as that assumed by my father before 1824; in other words, while, in the matter of preaching, it was separated, in every other respect it continued with it. So that it felt the importance of carefully avoiding any course that might tend to change the position it desired to maintain into one of open secession.

It is true that in 1835, by celebrating the Lord's Supper, it took the first step towards the establishment of a distinct church. But the men who directed its affairs had no desire, even at that time, to be confounded with the small Church of Testimony, which was held to be in a position of ultra dissent. Moreover, the members of the new church belonged to quite a different class of society

R.

from that which had recruited the ranks of the movers in the first revival.

That work, indeed, had stood in no need whatever of external support. Having from the very outset developed considerable proportions, it soon became the centre of the religious evangelical movement in Geneva, and of a more extended mission abroad. Union with my father, especially, so far from presenting itself to the founders of the Evangelical Society as a step likely to add a new element of power to the influence they already exercised, could appear to them in no other light than as a measure useless in itself, and which would have inevitably compromised them.

The fact is, that neither my father nor the men of the evangelical party dreamt of it. We have seen what his sentiments were on this point, and how he held to the view that it was wrong to destroy that diversity which, in his eyes, was the expression of a divine purpose, for the sake of building up external unity. Besides, in this special case, his convictions with regard to attentive discipline of a flock, and, above all, his scruples on that subject which constituted in his eyes the purity of evangelical dogma, would have of themselves sufficed to prevent his uniting with his brethren of the Evangelical Society, except in the mutual interchange of fraternity and regard :—a union which subsisted between them from the very beginning, increasing year by year.

Afterwards, undoubtedly, in 1849, when the congregation of the Oratory, which, for fourteen years had communicated outside the National Church, showed a desire to unite themselves with the old seceders for the sake of forming jointly an Evangelical Church of Geneva, it might have been reasonably expected that the Église du Témoignage, reduced as it was to a very small number, would be unwilling to hold back from a movement which was uniting all those in Geneva with whom it was in communion. We shall see, when the time comes, why it remained separate.

Let us revert for a moment to the time immediately following the crisis which marked the history of that small congregation in 1830.

When its founder saw his work, as a pastor, suddenly diminished in importance, he redoubled his activity as a preacher and gospel witness at Geneva and abroad. This, with his literary labours, which were never interrupted, constituted from that time the occupation of his life. Let us turn our present attention, therefore, to his work in Geneva, beginning with a description of what he was, for more than thirty years, as a preacher in his own chapel.

It was, as we have already seen, in November 1818 that he began to preside over the small "meetings" which were forming around him, after his exclusion from the national pulpit. From that time, up to November 1863, (that is, for forty-five years,) he never passed a single Sunday (with a few rare exceptions, when he was ill, or on an evangelising tour) without mounting the pulpit, at first three times a-day; while he continued the weekly prayer-meetings, till fatigue and the infirmities of age compelled him to give them up.

In his earlier days, especially before his chapel was built, in 1820, he held four of these meetings a-week.

After 1830 he reduced the number to two, and eventually to one, which he continued till he settled at Vandœuvres in 1859. These prayer-meetings were devoted to familiar expositions of the Scriptures.

It would be difficult to form an idea of his activity as a preacher. I have before me his MS. notes of all his sermons from 1818 to 1821, from which it appears that that which he delivered on the occasion of the dedication of his chapel was his one hundred and eighty-seventh. In this, we may almost say that he resembled such men as Whitfield and Wesley in England, or Gossner and Lindl, his contemporaries, in Catholic Germany. Not only during his missionary journeys was he called upon to preach several days in succession, and several times a-day, but in Geneva even, he had, in addition to the afternoon sermon in which he addressed himself to a mixed congregation, a more elementary and more methodised exposition in the form of a catechism.* This service, though particularly intended for the young, was none the less regularly attended by numerous adults. At its close, (it was held at ten) a " pastoral assembly " met—comprising, generally, members of the Church, gathered for his exhortations, or mutual edification.† Then, too, he had an evening ser-

---

* I find, for instance, in his French mission in 1836, he preached fifty times before he reached Perpignan, from the 12th April to the 31st of May, while in his mission to the same county in 1841 he preached one hundred and fifty-four times from the 3d of February to the 30th May. (See *Quatre-vingt Jours d'un Missionaire*, p. 338.) Let me observe here that he seldom gave the same sermon twice (I only find one 'or two instances of his doing so), and it will be seen what pains he must have taken in his daily preparation.

† The deacons' meetings, when the business of the Church was discussed in his presence, were held during the week.

vice which he held during the first years of his ministry
in the asylum already referred to. On the first Sunday of
each month he celebrated the communion, generally after
the morning service. In addition to this, for a long
period, several of the surrounding families having expressed a wish to participate in his family worship, he met
them every morning in summer in his chapel at eight
o'clock, and in the winter in his schoolroom.

It would not be the truth to infer from this vast activity,
that he was comparatively careless in preparing his discourses. At first he never entered the pulpit without
having previously written the whole of his discourse.
Soon after 1821 he found he had not time for this, so he
contented himself with noting down the heads, writing
only the most important passages. Later still, when he
was led to pure extempore preaching, he never failed to
prepare for it by a long period of meditation and prayer.
However great his facility of utterance might be, however
small the number of his hearers, his preaching ever
appeared to him the most important act of his life. I
frequently find in his notes of travel, at the moment when
he is called upon to preach, a few words, occasionally a
prayer, a lifting of the soul to God, which betray the
depth of his feelings with regard to this duty. He
prepared even the few words he addressed to us, night and
morning, in family worship. As for his public preaching,
the feelings I have referred to never weakened in intensity,
not even during those years when Sunday after Sunday
he addressed but a very small congregation, composed
invariably of the same persons.

Did he appear in the pulpit as the minister and witness

of Jesus Christ, it was because he began by thoroughly realising that he actually was such : and to the very end of his life no one would have ventured to intrude into his study during the hours immediately preceding his pulpit ministrations. To this, too, must be attributed his invariable custom of never taking a meal till after his last service, when he joined, for the first time, the family circle.

His very appearance in the pulpit was, in itself, remarkable. The calm and serene dignity of his demeanour, the animation of his expression, the placid and benevolent seriousness of his striking figure,—everything in short about him, arrested and riveted the attention. As soon as he opened his lips his hearers felt swayed, in spite of themselves, by such a voice as enchains an audience, not so much by the depth of its volume as by its clear sympathetic tones. Even before he spoke the very sight of his noble head, with its early and abundant snow-white hair, never failed to attract attention, when, after slowly passing up the chapel, he mounted with thoughtful and measured tread the pulpit steps.

After silent meditation, sometimes tolerably long, he commenced the service by his invariable invocation— "Que notre aide soit au nom de Dieu, le Père, le Fils, et le Sainte Esprit. Amen!"* After reading the commandments and the beautiful confession of sins in use in

---

* "Our help is in the name of the Lord, the Father, the Son, and the Holy Ghost. Amen." Malan had from the first substituted this formula for the one in ordinary use in our churches, "Our help is in the name of God Who created heaven and earth!" This substitution was, according to his idea, a kind of profession of that faith in the doctrine of the Trinity for which he considered he had been called upon to suffer.

our churches, he gave out one of his hymns, beginning to
sing it generally himself, with a voice easily audible above
the roll of the organ, and the strains of the congregation.
Then followed a brief extempore prayer, and a portion of
Scripture, before he announced his text and began his
sermon.*

His manner and delivery were natural, grave, profoundly earnest, and often enkindling and awe-inspiring :
he was never affected or pompous. Exhibiting, in his
whole mode of utterance, the perfect reality of his character, he avoided stereotyped phraseology, and never indulged in that sing-song, artificial tone of declamation,
enough of itself to alienate the sympathies of the most
favourably disposed congregation. To quote a favourite
expression of the sainted Vinet, "he spoke, he did not
preach." His exposition was always brief, rapid, and clear.
Confining himself, as a rule, to indicating the idea which,
as he used to say, preceded in his mind the proposition
which formed the subject of his discourse, he would
designate in a third point the consequences which the
acceptance of that proposition involved. These three
points thus laid down, he expanded them one after
another with greater elaborateness than variety, which
failed, however, to weary his hearers, because he never
gave way to repetitions in the same discourse. His
addresses received attention, if not by an invariable succession of new ideas, at least by his perfect intelligibility
as well as by the uniform clearness and precision with

* This form of worship has just been adopted in the Church of Geneva ;
the only difference, at that time, consisted in the reading of a portion of
Scripture by the preacher himself.

which his thoughts travelled to the mark indicated from
the first. As a rule, it was not till after his three points
had been discussed that he appealed directly to his hearers.
Giving free scope to a powerful conviction, he became
from that moment urgent, glorious, and vehement. Then
it was especially that the orator betrayed himself—more
than that, the popular orator—never, in his judgment, to
be confounded with a careless, irreverent, or vulgar
preacher. The sermon ended, there followed a prayer,
taken for many years from the old liturgy of our churches.
He then gave out a hymn, and, when the singing was over,
dismissed the congregation.* Such was the form of public worship in the " Eglise du Témoignage." Though
after 1830 the number of regular worshippers had
diminished, the congregation continued to comprise,
especially during the summer, a large number of strangers.
The sanctuary was pervaded by a refreshing atmosphere of
silent adoration. Everything contributed to this ;—the
position in the midst of a quiet garden, the habit of
silence which my father had from the very first carefully
impressed upon his congregation,† the style of the hymns
sung there, and the manner in which they were sung,

---

* As a rule, it was the beautiful doxology, "Agneau de Dieu, par Tes
langueurs," ("Lamb of God, by Thy sufferings,") composed by himself in
1819 or 1820, which the congregation sung standing without the organ.
That doxology was afterwards adopted by the National Churches of French
Switzerland, who retained the beautiful air which he composed for it, but
without its slow and solemn rhythm.

† Thus he interdicted all talking, even in the lowest possible tones, in the
house of God. More than once a conversation, or whispering, or any want
of decorum in his hearers, drew from him either a significant look or a
sudden pause in his sermon—sometimes even a direct admonition from the
pulpit. If any one went to sleep he did not hesitate, in the most natural
manner, to request a neighbour to arouse him.

contrasting so forcibly with those in use in the National
Churches—above all, the profound seriousness and unremitting earnestness which breathed through the preacher's
words—everything combined to produce the spectacle of a
congregation, sometimes of a very mixed character, leaving
the worship of God Sunday after Sunday with no trace of
eagerness, the result of fatigue impatiently endured, no
hubbub of a thousand voices, in reaction from the monoto-
nous tones of a minister, but, on the contrary, in that
thoughtful silence indicative of the universal desire to
retain in its integrity the deep impression that had been
produced.

Thus it was that, through a long succession of years,
the Church of Testimony saw many happy days, while it
remained, to the very end, the scene of sacred emotions
and much spiritual blessing. As an example, apart from
my own recollections, I will give my readers an account of
a communion Sunday at "Pré-Béni." It is derived from
a recently published narrative by Dr A. Ostertag, of the
Missionary Institute of Bâle, of a visit he paid my father,
for a few days, in 1836.*

As I shall have occasion shortly to recur to this description (as striking from its evident truthfulness as from the
courteous sympathy which it breathes), I will content myself at present with a short extract—

· "It was on the 4th of September that Malan gave us a
truly exalted sermon on the kingdom of Christ; and, on
the afternoon of the same day, an even more striking discourse, full of rare unction, on the words, 'Rejoice, that

---

* It appeared in the number, for March 1867, of the "Bibelblätter" of
the Evangelical Mission Magazine of Bâle.

your names are written in heaven.' But my richest experience was reserved for this same Sunday, which was that of the monthly communion.

"Intending to participate in the rite, I entered the chapel (its windows gleaming through the trees of the garden) with a heart profoundly drawn towards God, the mighty and living God. The congregation was singularly numerous. I was motioned, in common with an English clergyman, who happened to be visiting the place, to take my place on a reserved seat.

"The preacher commenced by wishing us all 'the grace of our Lord Jesus Christ, the love of God, and the fellowship of the Holy Ghost.' After a short and earnest prayer he read the 15th of St John; then, in a few words of most spiritual exposition, he pointed out to us what the Saviour said of the love which His disciples should cherish towards Himself. This opening portion of the worship closed with a fervent prayer, breathing confession, trust, and thanksgiving. Then, after reading the words of the institution of the Supper from 1 Cor. xi., he gave a brief explanation of the Sacrament, based upon the Calvinistic view, which approaches closely to the Lutheran.

"Then taking the bread in his hand, he broke it, invoking the name of God; he next approached the English clergyman and myself, and spoke to us of blessed and holy communion with Christ, of fidelity in the pastoral work, and of brotherly love; after which he gave us the bread, then the cup,—partaking with us. The recollection of that moment will never leave me, so full was it of heavenly light and life.

"He now invited the elders and deacons to approach

the communion table, and distributed the bread and wine to them, exhorting them to love of Christ, and faithful discharge of their trust.

" It was not till after this that the deacons proceeded to carry the sacred elements from seat to seat. A solemn silence reigned through the assembly, broken only, from time to time, by words of hearty exhortation from his lips. The distribution over, the solemn celebration finished with prayer and a hymn, after a few words pointing out that the blessing of the Supper extends to the eternal life of the soul."

It was not, however, in the presence, and under the restraints, of his chapel congregation that my father was able to pour out his fullest power of speech. Though gifted with extraordinary powers of successful extempore utterance, he was only thoroughly at home with a mass of eager and intent hearers. Then, especially, his thoughts (always intelligible and perspicuous) clothed themselves with impromptu illustrations, the appropriateness of which left an indelible impression on the mind. Endowed, in a high degree, with that sympathetic fibre which enables the speaker to read the hearts of the listeners, he possessed no less that quickness which foresees objections, anticipating or refuting them as they presented themselves to the hearer he sought to persuade.

It will be inferred from this that he soon betook himself to the work of addressing the masses, and that his own experience of divine life would only strengthen a necessity which arose out of his character and special gifts. Thus in 1820, when on a pedestrian tour in Switzerland, in the course of which he preached in all the towns through

which he passed, I see that at Correndelin he preached
in the public square. His ardent faith made him seize
eagerly on every opportunity of witnessing to the gospel.
Not content with doing this daily, in private conversations
which he was an adept at promoting, he knew perhaps
better than any—at all events he was among the foremost
of those, in the midst of whom he lived—to put aside,
when necessity arose, the traditional custom which re-
stricts the delivery of divine truth to special times and
places.   Disposed as he was, by the very reverence of his
character, to impress, invariably, the highest solemnity on
the particular worship he directed, the all-important
element, with him, resided not in imposing ceremonial
accessories, but in the grandeur of the message he had to
deliver.   This explains how, at the time when he was
interdicted from entering the pulpit of the National
Church, a magistrate having suggested the possibility of
the government prohibiting him from erecting a chapel, he
did not scruple to say that, in that case, " he would hire a
boat and preach on the lake."

This reply, mentioned by De Goltz, reminds me of an
occurrence of which I was an eyewitness in 1828 or 1829,
which took place on one of our lake steamboats.   Having
received the captain's consent, my father, with a few
people round him, mounted a pile of cables in the forepart
of the vessel, New Testament in hand, and invited those
present to gather round and hear the good Word of God.
I see him now erect above the listening crowd around him.
I seem to hear his penetrating voice borne upon the fresh
breeze of the spring morning, our beautiful shores stretch-

ing out before us. What is more, I well remember a
gentleman standing next to me (who had betrayed signs of
very natural impatience at first at so unusual a scene)
came up to my father after he had finished speaking, and
grasping his hand with much fervour, addressed those
present himself, declaring that his heart had apprehended
the gospel for the first time, and that, from that day, he
would avow himself its disciple. We shall have occasion,
by and by, to recall more than one of these incidents,
illustrative of the joyous earnestness of the first years of
the revival. Afterwards, a declared opposition imposed
its ceremonious proprieties. To the involuntary expression (so to speak) of personal enthusiasm has succeeded
an avowed antagonism which entrusts to a faction its antecedents, and the flag it has erected. This last characteristic was always foreign to my father's missionary zeal.

With reference to that zeal, we cannot do better than
insert here an extract from M. de Goltz, in which he refers
to my father and F. Noeff. "They possessed," he says,
"mighty faith and ability, were thoroughly men of prayer,
and displayed a boldness in bearing witness to the truth
which brought down a signal blessing on their labours.
Their individual influence was great; they carried, wherever
they went, the witness of Jesus Christ. They never missed
an opportunity afforded by a walk or by an accidental
meeting. They never heard a hostile word, they never
took a journey, without finding or making an opportunity
of speaking of their Saviour. Ever in His presence, they
could not help feeling a holy interest in the souls which
God threw in their way; nor did they mix with other

men without availing themselves of every occasion for this
work of soul-gathering.*

"They had a passion for the conversion of souls," says
M. Guizot, in speaking of the instruments of the revival
generally.† "God ever in communication with man, with
every man," he adds, "present to the actual life of each,
and hereafter deciding his future destiny, the incalculable
worth of every soul before God, and the paramount importance of the future which awaits it :—these are the convictions, the declarations comprised in that passion for the
salvation of souls which filled the life of our Lord Jesus
Christ Himself."

These words exactly describe the sentiments which lay
at the bottom of my father's missionary zeal.

At the same time, it would be a mistake to imagine that
he was entirely unmoved when he saw himself the object
of envious looks, whisperings, or jeering smiles from a prejudiced people; or that he was not pained by the gross
insults of the lower orders. In his own home, of course,
in the Garden of the Pré-Béni (given to him by God as
an asylum to hold his treasures), among those who came
to him for light and teaching,—in his pulpit again,
where he only looked upon himself as a minister of Jesus
Christ,—he knew neither embarrassment nor hesitation.
Yet we ought not to infer the absence of sensitive emotion
from his composure of manner, imparted by the upright
simplicity of his faith, and his courageous devotion to the
service of Him Whom he loved to call "his good Master."

---

* De Goltz, Gen. Relig., p. 226.

† "Reflections on the Actual State of the Christian Religion, 1st series.
Meditation on the Christian Revival in France."

In his first tract (Germain le Bûcheron), written in 1819, he says, " I have often found it difficult to start a religious conversation with strangers." How frequently have I seen him, myself, bow down his head with an expression of keenest pain under public insults which followed him through so many years, almost every time he quitted the garden enclosure! How often did he conceal from me, as though it were a wound refusing to be healed, the secret anguish he experienced at ever finding himself disowned, despised, misunderstood, by those whom he longed to convince of the love he bore them, and for whose spiritual enlightenment he ceased not to pour out his soul before God!"

All these feelings vanished, however, when he was called upon to give his testimony to the gospel of salvation. Then he was Cæsar Malan no longer; he was the minister, the servant of a faith to which we all bow, the herald of Him Who alone is to be honoured. Eternity, thenceforward, with eternal interests, eternal life and eternal death, silenced at once all personal feelings and considerations.

At the very outset of his career as a preacher of the gospel, he replied to a friend who expressed surprise at the firmness with which he had laid aside all his literary occupations, " My life is too short for that." * Nor is there anything in this sentiment to astonish those who have followed him through his daily career. There was, as it were, a pressure in it; we feel that he hastened to work while it was day, and that, in his judgment, the only work which seemed worthy to engage his energies and his leisure was labour in the vineyard of the Father of the

* Schickedantz.

family,—the advancement of the kingdom of Christ in the heart.

This was the feeling that made him one of the bravest and most persevering witnesses of the gospel. Doubtless, what at first required from him an effort of will became, by degrees, a second nature.

In the intimacies of private life he knew well how to lay aside the gravity of his public character. For my own part I never met any one whose conversation was more constantly varied, more intelligent, readier, or more animated, at suitable times, with a frank good humour, and a gaiety of the best kind. But from the moment any appeal reached him unexpectedly, as a minister of the gospel, whenever he found himself face to face with any one whom he had no expectation of seeing again at his leisure, he felt himself carried away by the thought thus uttered by an apostle of old, " Woe is me if I preach not the gospel ! "

Setting aside, from that moment, every other consideration, he went straight to the mark : he addressed to the soul before him some one of those questions by which he knew so well how to break over all barriers, and seemed to penetrate with living force into the very spirit of his inquirers. Such questions from any other lips would have appeared most singular ; but they were submitted to, without protest, from him, in consequence of the impression produced by the serious and at the same time affectionate anxiety, and perfect kindliness with which he proposed them.

Not only, as he said himself, was he thoroughly convinced " that a single conversation is often more efficacious than many sermons," but he took much interest also in distributing religious tracts, and lost no opportunity of doing so.*

Nor was it merely abroad that my father acted the missionary. At Geneva his daily walks, even to the very end, were availed of for this kind of dealing with individual souls, of which it might be said, among us at least, that he alone knew the secret, and for similar instances of which we should have to betake ourselves to the religious world in England or America.

Many examples of this work may be found recorded by himself, either in his various tracts, or in the accounts he published on his return from some of these missionary tours.† I could not undertake to repeat here what he has himself related, but I may be permitted, before passing on to an account of his evangelising expeditions, to mention a circumstance which came under my own observation about the year 1840, in a pedestrian trip which I made with him, in company with a young Englishman who was staying with us at the time.

My father wished to revisit with us the picturesque gorges, north of the Jura, which he had explored in his youth, and remembered with enthusiasm ever since. Taking the boat from Geneva to Lausanne, we went on foot to Yverdon, no opportunity being missed by him of proclaiming the gospel. On the lake of Neufchatel I remember well

* "Quatre-vingt Jours," &c., p. 390, and elsewhere.

† See for example the chapter headed Bible Anecdotes, in his "Gospel Sowings," (1830); the preface of his "Grains de Senévé;" tracts, such as "Germain le Bucheron," "la Valaisanne," "L'épi glané sur une grande route," "Ce que Dieu garde est bien gardé," "La Route perdue," &c., &c. See also several pages in his "True Child's Friend," and in "Twenty Swiss Pictures:" some episodes in "Can I join the Church of Rome?" and especially his descriptions of his missions, to be referred to by and by.

S

sketching him seated in the bow of the boat, with a young man at his side, to whom he was speaking about his soul. His New Testament was in his hand, while a mountaineer, leaning against the gunwale, let his pipe go out as he listened to him.

A few days after, we climbed, one glorious evening, the road ascending from Bienne, and following the torrent of the Suze. Reaching the inn at Sonceboz, my father, as he unhooked his knapsack, said to the landlady that he intended having evening prayers with us after supper, and that if she and her household liked to come they would be welcome. "We don't require that sort of thing here," she replied, apparently very much pressed with business, adding one or two expressions of impatience. Thereupon my father forthwith resumed knapsack and staff, saying to me, as he did so, "Do you feel up to another hour's walking?" little heeding the amazement of our would be-hostess, who was anxious to detain us. "Come, boys, I cannot pass the night under a roof where there is no desire for prayer, and no fear of God."

A few minutes afterwards, as we were following the road leading from Sonceboz through pine woods to the defile of Pierre-Pertuis, we came up to some waggons laden with planks, which were going in our direction. My father called to me, and pointing out a tall young man who was driving the first of them, gave me a tract, asking me to hand it to him from him. The driver thanked me very politely, and I rejoined my travelling companion, who had stopped for a moment to admire a particular part of the landscape. In a few moments, however, the man to whom I had given the tract, and who had set to work to

read it aloud to his mates, came up to me, and asked me
to request my father to explain to them a few things in it
which they could not understand. My father joined the
men, and we left them coming on slowly after us, and
keeping alongside of the waggons. Shortly afterwards,
when they had rejoined us, I overheard him, as he
stretched out his hand to the man who had read the
tract, inviting him and his companions to our evening
worship at Tavannes. They promised to come, and
kept their word. "Was it not the Lord who drew us
away from Sonceboz?" he asked me, when we were by
ourselves.

The next morning we started at the dawn of day.
After having walked for about two hours, we went to a
village inn to have some coffee. Whilst we were waiting
for it, my father noticed that the young woman in attendance stopped from time to time to put her apron to her
eyes. "You seem to be in trouble?" he asked. "Alas, sir,
only a few days ago I lost my poor husband, and of course
I am very unhappy." Making room for her beside him
on the form, "Come here, my poor woman," he said, "let
me speak to you of the comforting promises of the gospel."
He had not got far when his companion interrupted him
by asking if she might go and fetch her friend Jeanette.
"She will be delighted to hear you," she explained, "she
too speaks to me very often of these good things." She
soon returned with a young peasant, and we left my father
alone with them.

A moment afterwards, he beckoned to us through the
window to go with him to visit Jeanette's father, who
was lying ill, close by. We were conducted to a little

wooden house, and into a large room, at the end of which, near the window, lay a white-haired old man. "Father," said she, "I have brought you a minister of the gospel." "God be praised," said the invalid, as my father seated himself at his side; soon discovering in him signs of genuine and touching piety. In the conversation which followed, he asked him how he had arrived at a knowledge of his Saviour. "On this bed," he replied, "where I have lain for many years; and through reading a book written by a Mr Malan of Geneva. Ah! had I not been aged and infirm, I should long ago have gone there to see him. Look here, sir, you cannot think how earnestly I have entreated the Lord that I might see him before I died. For a long time I thought He would grant my desire, but I'm afraid I shall have to give it up." I stole a glance at my father, who was sitting silently looking at his hands. "What is the name of the book you refer to?" he suddenly inquired as he raised his head. "Stay," was the reply, "here it is, it's always by me;" and he drew from under his pillow a well-worn copy of one of the earliest editions of my father's hymns, and handed it to my father. "Do you sing any of these then?" asked my father, as he turned over the leaves. "Oh, Jeanette knows some of them; she often sings them to me, and I derive pleasure and profit whenever I hear them," adding, as though speaking to himself, "If I could only see the dear gentleman who wrote those beautiful hymns; he must be a good Christian."

"Listen, brother," said my father; "these young gentlemen and I have just come from Geneva." "You have come from Geneva? then perhaps you have seen M.

Malan?" "Certainly I have; we all know him well; and
I can assure you, that if he were here he would remind
you that he has only been a feeble and imperfect instrument of good to you; and he would speak to you, above
all, not of himself, a poor sinner as you are, but of the
eternal grace and perfection of our blessed Lord." The
conversation lasted a few moments longer; my father
prayed; then, when we had sung together one of the
hymns which Jeanette knew, he prepared to leave, telling
her that he was to preach the next day, Sunday, at Moûtiers.
When he had got to the door, however, he stopped, and
returning once more to the bed where the old man was
lying with folded hands, said to him, with emotion, "My
father, God Himself to Whom you will so soon depart,
has granted your prayer. I am Malan of Geneva; your
brother in the faith of our blessed Saviour."

The poor old man, fixing his streaming eyes upon him
in a long and ardent gaze, and slowly raising his trembling
hands, exclaimed, "Bless me, bless me before I die! You,
whom I have so long prayed God to send to me, bless
me now that I have the joy of seeing you!" Falling on
his knees at the bedside, my father replied, in tones which
betrayed his deep feeling, "You ought rather to bless me,
for you are old enough to be my father. But all blessing
comes from God alone; let us once more ask it of Him
together." And, folding in his arms the lowly brother
whom he felt he should never see again till they met in
the better country, he invoked upon him "the peace which
Jesus gives," and we left the hamlet.

The next morning he preached at Moûtiers, and in the
afternoon at the village of Grandval. To the former place

came Jeanette, with her friend, and quite a crowd from their village, a distance of more than three leagues, to hear the foreign minister.

My story may have seemed a little long, but I trust I shall be forgiven for having described in its details, (preserving as far as possible the very words of the conversation,) a scene which made so deep an impression upon me in my youthful days.

An incident which occurred the day after the sermon at Moûtiers may serve to illustrate the easy and affectionate manner with which my father was in the habit of addressing the first person whom he might chance to meet. As he stood behind me watching while I was sketching some rocks at the opening of an abrupt gorge, a tall old man passed us on his way. I said to my father,—why, I cannot tell,—" I feel as if that man was a pious Christian." " Nothing easier than to find out," he replied; and quickly turning to the stranger, said smilingly, " Will you take my hand, sir, if I offer it ?" " Eh, sir," said the old man, removing his hat, " you do me a great honour." " And what if it were in the name of the Lord Jesus that I offer it ?" " Then give me both your hands, my beloved brother," he exclaimed. A long conversation followed between them, and we saw him frequently afterwards in a neighbouring village, and found that he was well known through all the country side for his gentle and active piety.

Let me give here one or two additional illustrative incidents extracted from his correspondence, which teems, especially during his missionary journeys, with passages well worthy of being preserved on record.

" In a town in the north of France," he writes to a

friend, in 1849, "a shoeblack of a certain age, to whom I had applied one rainy, muddy day, said, in an undertone, as he looked at my boots, 'Faith, and they want it too!' 'Not so much as our souls need the blood of Christ,' I rejoined, solemnly. The shoeblack started, 'I beg your pardon, sir,' he said. On receiving his answer, he recommenced his task, saying to himself, 'I never heard of that before!' He heard it then at all events, clearly; and appeared to listen eagerly."

A letter to my mother, dated Heidelberg, 9th Sept. 1849, contains the following :—

"The country is overrun with Prussian soldiery, and two captains and an Israelite have been my fellow-travellers the whole day. They talked a great deal, all the way along, of their campaign of Baden, and they noticed here and there the battle-fields, redoubts, burnt dwellings, &c. I held my tongue. At length, after about three hours of it, when they had warmed up a little in their description, I said to the Israelite, 'Tell them from me that in heaven there will be no more war.' He did so; upon which one of the captains remarked to me, 'Yes, yes; but if there were Baden men there, there would be no peace.' 'There, there will be neither Baden nor Prussian,' was the reply, 'but children of peace—the saved.'

"A deep silence succeeded the military storm. Then I said to the Jew, 'Tell them the Lord Jesus calls Himself the Prince of Peace.' Again he complied, very seriously; whereupon the captain next to me turned round and said, in an undertone, 'If we were lovers of order, there would be no more war.' 'Rather,' said I, 'if we were Christians. But it is not so : we kill one another, though we are men, and of the same blood!' He sighed, and pressed my hand. Thenceforth the conversation was quieter, and when we parted, we wished one another a pleasant journey."

These ways of proceeding were the perfectly natural result, in my father's case, of heart impulse. Moreover, however much surprise he might produce at first by broaching at once the most sacred topics connected with the hidden life of the soul, I do not think any one ever resented his conduct as an offence. As far as he was concerned, the motive which prompted him was a constant, earnest desire to be the means of bringing souls to the knowledge of Jesus Christ. This was an aim he never lost sight of. How often, as we paused in our solitary walks on one of the eminences which gird our town, and suffered our gaze to wander over the villages and hamlets visible on every side; how often have I heard him arrest the expression of the admiration, with which the sight of our beautiful country never failed to inspire him, exclaiming, "If we might only hope that each of those villages and dwellings contained if it were but one who knew and loved the Lord Jesus!"

And then I was led to ask myself how a nature like his could endure the thought that the people over whom his heart yearned so lovingly were so effectually deprived of the blessing of salvation; till I remembered that his soul was in constant submission to that silent obedience of faith which taught him to abjure either the thought or desire of penetrating into what he held to be a mystery known only to God. I recalled, too, that child-like trust which led him to believe that the glory of God would appear as fully one day in what is at present concealed, as it does now in what is revealed.

With reference to what I have just recorded, the reader will understand that to attempt a thorough description of the missionary activity of my father's life would involve a record of each day's history, from the time that that absorbing passion just referred to, took possession of his soul. Reserving, then, allusion, as occasion may arise, to various evangelising expeditions, I shall confine myself at present to a mention of his principal tours with this object.

Up to the year 1830 he scarcely ever preached abroad,—except in England, in 1822, 1826, and 1828.

When he went there in 1822 he had no idea of preaching in public. He was, as it were, forced to do so, in spite of himself. A clergyman with whom he had dined introduced him, without previous warning, into a room where a numerous company was assembled, saying to him, "These persons are assembled here for the purpose of hearing you." My father did the best he could. Soon afterwards he managed to preach easily in English.

It was to the connections which he formed thus early with the religious community in England, more especially with the evangelical party, and dissenters and Presbyterians of Scotland, that we must attribute the special direction which, from a remote period, his religious habits assumed. For example, it was there that he acquired those strict views which he maintained all his life, on the sanctity of the Lord's day; and by which he was distinguished even from the other adherents of the revival of Geneva. It was there, too, that he acquired that freedom from conventional trammels which accompanies zeal for the propagation of the faith among English believers. To the same quarter he referred the habit of publicly distributing tracts, of holding meetings in other places besides churches, and, generally, that independence with reference to prescribed forms, which characterises the evangelical party in free England. There, too, he made acquaintance with the writings of the Anglican theologians of the seventeenth century, which were popular at the time among those with whom he was brought into special contact, and which continued to be amongst his favourite reading.

The visit to Great Britain, in which he came most prominently forward, was that which he paid in 1826, and to which I have already had occasion to refer. As regards his missionary work there, I find the following in the preface of a little work published by one of his hearers, and containing notes of some of his sermons delivered in Scotland.*

After premising that it would be impossible to find simpler and more powerful setting forth of the confidence which the believer is called upon to exercise in what God declares, the author, quoting an expression from an old English theologian, goes on to say that Malan's merit as a preacher consisted in bringing believers to accumulate two heaps—one of their merits, the other of their sins; and, to leave them both, to take refuge in Christ Himself. He has no hesitation in affirming that "the manner in which Malan presented evangelical truth, recalled to his hearers the days of Luther and Rutherford."

My mother has mentioned to me one more incident in

* "Recollections of the Rev. C. Malan, D.D., of Geneva, being notes of sermons preached by him in Edinburgh, in May and June 1826." James Nisbet, 1827.

connection with the impression which he produced, in his public speaking at that time, on men capable of forming a judgment. He had just been preaching to an attentive congregation when he was stopped, on leaving the pulpit, by an old man, entirely unknown to him. "I bless God," said the stranger, "that I have this day heard Romaine and Whitfield." On my father asking who it was that addressed him, "My name," answered the stranger, "is Rowland Hill!"

He continued in England for some months of the summer of 1833 and 1834. On that occasion he visited Ireland, where he stayed with his friend Lord Roden. It was in that country that he was happily instrumental through one of those lucid expressions inspired by his faith in the sovereign grace of God, in giving light to the soul of a Methodist lady whose mind had been affected by the dread of eternal condemnation.

In 1839 he again visited London and Edinburgh, passing through Holland, where he had already been, on his return in 1834.

I append a few details of his journey in 1839, which I have gathered from the letters he wrote at the time to one of my sisters in Scotland. I may mention it was at the time of the revival in Kelso:—

"*Sept.* 1839.—After having preached an hour and a quarter at Dundee, I had to speak for the greater part of an hour to nearly two thousand persons, silent and impressed. It seemed to me as though the Word of the Lord were descending upon their souls like rain on the mown grass. What joy my God has given me this evening! My mission has been blessed! I have been welcomed everywhere as a messenger of peace! I preached five times at Kelso. The last time the same scene occurred which I had experienced at Dundee. After the blessing every one sat down again, and remained,—their eyes fixed on the pulpit. We understood that they wanted more spiritual nourishment, and I spoke again, at some length. It was very solemn."

A few days later, from Edinburgh, "My good Master has strengthened me here. I have been enabled to preach twice to large, attentive, and thoughtful congregations. Days of strength, power, and blessing."

Later still, on board ship at sea, "I return to Pré-Béni full of gratitude. Our gracious heavenly Father has singularly blessed my journey. My soul glorifies Him, and I recall, with peculiar joy, the days I have spent in England and Scotland."

His last expedition,—and not an unimportant one,—to Great Britain was in 1843; on the occasion of the Secession of the Free Church of Scotland.

Meanwhile he had for a long time directed his attention to the continent. In England he associated, almost exclusively, with the religious world. What he longed for, however, above everything, was the privilege of carrying the Word of God where it was entirely unknown. It was this desire that urged him to undertake, in 1836, his first evangelistic tour in France. He returned to that country in the spring of 1841. In 1842 he bent his steps towards Belgium and Holland. In 1845 he visted the churches of Holland again, and after returning to France in 1849, in 1852, and in 1853, and visiting Elberfeld in 1856, he achieved his last missionary journey, that same year, to the Vaudois Valleys in Piedmont. Already his advancing years disqualified him from any longer undertaking alone the fatigues of a missionary expedition, and in this visit of his to the Churches he had so long desired to see, and which he regarded as the ancient home of his sires, he was compelled to have one of my sisters with him.

It may be asked how it was that his zeal never sent him in the direction of Savoy. The fact is that he had endeavoured, at an early period, to penetrate it with gospel light, but, as is well known, the Jesuits were paramount there in those days. Indeed, at that time, my brothers and I were always especially careful to take with us a Greek Testament when we crossed the frontiers, for fear of being involved in any difficulty by the discovery of a French New Testament in our knapsacks. Let me mention an incident which occurred when I was a child, and which will serve to show to what extent our fears were justified.

One of my father's boarders, about 1820, had given a Bible to a Savoyard of Chablais, who was able to read. It would seem that he had even employed him to introduce a few into the province. The circumstance having come to the knowledge of the authorities, the unfortunate man was dragged from his home by carabineers, and conveyed to the galleys at Gênes. It was in mid-winter, and his daughter, who, with her two little brothers, had run after the sledge-truck on which their father lay bound, being repulsed by the soldiers, begged her way towards Geneva. She died, however, of cold and wretchedness, before she reached it, and the younger of the two boys, having lost all trace of his brother, was taken home by a gardener, who had seen him before at my father's. Many years afterwards, when he was still in this man's service, he saw, on the road near the town, a traveller clothed in rags and covered with dust. The stranger, halting before the young man, asked him to direct him to the house of this very gardener. He took him there at once, and ascertained that the unfortunate wanderer was his father. The latter part of his punishment had been remitted, but he was almost reduced to idiocy by the sufferings he had had to undergo.

This fact alone will suffice to show how difficult it was to introduce the gospel among a bigoted population, very few of whom, moreover, knew how to read. Notwithstanding this, however, my father happened one day to hear a Savoyard curé, with whom he had been conversing on their journey, complain of two pests which corrupted the youth of their village, one was emigration to Paris, and the other a certain M. Malan of Geneva, who spread the Bible and little heretical books in every direction.

From before 1830, however, my father was compelled to keep out of Savoy altogether. Stopped by the gendarmerie at Chamounix, where he had been summoned by the illness of one of his boarders, and transported as a criminal to the head-quarters of the province, he owed his liberty solely to his firmness and presence of mind. He has recounted the circumstance himself in pages of the greatest interest, adding details which always encouraged him to hope that God had permitted the arrest for the promotion of the spiritual good of the officer who had been charged with it.[*]

During his missionary voyages, he not only preached in

----

[*] See "Quatre-vingt Jours," &c., p. 281.

all the pulpits open to him, whatever the denomination to
which they belonged, but he also applied his special attention to endless details of work in individual cases. Though
in many places his efforts led to the formation of a tract
society or the inauguration of fresh schemes of evangelisation, still his special work lay with separate souls. He
was far more the instrument of conversion to individuals
than of foundation to Churches. The ideal ever before
him was, as he said,[*] that of "missionaries travelling alone,
skilled to accost those whom they met, and to offer to
them, with the courteous greeting of genuine charity, small
religious tracts, or even the sacred volume itself; thus
leaving with them preachers to accompany them through
their daily occupations, and appeal to them at home." This
ideal no one perhaps approached so nearly as himself.

Some of his journeys were originated solely by himself;
though the greater part of the time, he was delegated or
invited by various Churches and religious societies. Invariably, however, especially after 1830, we see him availing himself eagerly of every opportunity of escape from
the confined atmosphere which surrounded him in Geneva,
that he might seek out populations thirsting for the living
Word; opened hearts; and numerous and awakened con-
gations.

While he was away from home, and his place in his chapel
supplied by his brethren at Geneva, his letters to our
mother enabled us to follow his career week by week. His
return, announced beforehand and impatiently expected,
was a fête-day for his family. He took out of his travel-

---

[*] " Quatre-vingt Jours," &c., p. 300. See also the Preface of the
" Grains de Sénevé."

ling-bag small presents for the youngest of us, which excited
their wonder—sea shells, foreign playthings, a few children's books not to be had at Geneva—while his arrival
seemed to infuse new life into the house. As for himself,
he came back to us happy, refreshed, encouraged; bringing
with him manuscripts ready for printing, or hurried notes
which he revised, or a concise account of the mission for
his Church, or a more detailed report for those who had
sent him.

During the time immediately subsequent to his return,
he was surrounded and cheered by the remembrances conveyed in numerous letters from those he had visited in the
course of his travels. It is in reading these letters, perhaps
even more than in hearing his account, that a precise idea
of the effect of his ministry is to be arrived at. In England
and Holland, where he was specially called upon to address
those of a certain amount of educational proficiency, these
recollections of his labours subsisted perhaps longer in the
minds of his hearers, taking the form, however, in the
majority of instances, of an intellectual interest in his
doctrine. In Belgium and France, where he came more
directly in contact with the masses, the impression he
produced was more general; displaying itself more widely,
but appearing to have been more fugitive. The Belgian
Churches inspired him with the most affectionate recollections,—the closest, I may say; while his visit to the Vaudois
Valleys (where he had been sent at the cost of some
American friends) was not only the last, but was probably
the richest of his happy experiences in his evangelistic
work. "Nowhere, in all my mission spheres," he said to his
young friend the Pastor Coucourde, who repeated his words,

to me;—"have I met with a more favourable field for my work than among those worthy inhabitants of the valleys."

If the accounts he published of some of his journeys give a very striking idea of his method of evangelising, they do not at the same time furnish us with a history of his labours. In order to follow him step by step in his work, it would be necessary to take up each of his expeditions in succession, by means of letters and documents which still remain, while his missions on the Continent alone would furnish material for a volume. Instead of a long list of dates and names of places, my readers would doubtless prefer to find in these pages, after an account presented by my father himself to his Church, some more enlarged details of his mission in the south of France, in 1836.

At the commencement of that year, he had felt a strong desire to carry the Word to countries asking for it, or deprived of it. He set out, commended to the Lord by the prayers of his Church, which he left under the pastoral supervision of candidates in theology at the Oratory, and some of the pastors of the "Eglise du Bourg de Four." But we will proceed to the further narrative in his own words.*

"There had long been a felt need in France for some minister of God to come and preach the gospel. I was invited to respond to this appeal; and, after having received funds sufficient to set forth, and depending upon the Lord

---

* The MS. book from which the following account is derived, is not in his own handwriting; it consists of notes of the history of his expedition, which he delivered in his chapel, taken while he was speaking. 26th June 1836.

T

for the rest, I can say now, as the apostles said when asked by their Master on their return from their mission, whether they lacked anything—'Nothing, Lord.'"

Detailing a conversation with a Roman Catholic in the public conveyance from Geneva to Dôle, he says, "The great error under which I once laboured was, that on certain occasions we ought to engage in controversy. When a wolf carries away a lamb from my flock, I ought by no means to use force to rescue his prey from his teeth. In doing so, I should injure at once wolf, lamb, and myself. I must endeavour to persuaded him to relinquish his booty of his own accord and follow me whither I will. It is easier, no doubt, to speak of points of difference, than of the centre of union. But we act as we are able. As for my travelling companion from here to Dôle, this was the course I took with him. I simply said, 'I should like to speak to you about your soul, but I don't know how to begin.' 'Well, sir, proceed,' he replied with promptitude. I continued, or rather we continued, to converse, and on parting, I had the happiness of hearing him thank God for sending me to speak to him of that salvation which comes wholly from Him, and he begged me to send him a Bible. As a rule," my father goes on to say, "I have found that if you enter upon a conversation of this character, with kindness and courtesy, you will always be listened to. Moreover, that is the only way to succeed. Apropos of this, I should like to tell you what happened to me one day when I was on the top of the diligence between Paris and Marseilles. Sitting beside me were five young merchants, whom I heard for a moment chatting in a lively strain about a thousand things. Suddenly I turned and said to them, 'You Frenchmen appear to me like paper-kites without string.' 'First of all, sir,' said one of them in reply, "you will be so good as to prove that we are paper-kites, and then you will tell us how we come to be without string.' It was not difficult for me to prove, with the Gospel in my hand, that man is but the sport of vanity, and that if he is not held in by the strong cord of the Spirit of God, he is inevitably carried away by the unruly wind of covetousness and passion. They listened to me as I asked them if it were not their case; and, four of them leaving us at Sèvres, I had an earnest and prolonged conversation with the fifth.

"I have always found that, whether with Romanists or Protestants, the best way to commence such a conversation is to bring them, at once, face to face with the doctrine of election by grace." *

Arrived at Paris, he remained there a week to be present at the annual meeting of the different religious societies. "The most striking thing I remember," he says, "and which penetrated my heart from the Lord, was that, as He has not decided the question of Church government in His Word, we ought not to attach too much importance to the differences which divide us on this point. I thank God that I went to Paris, if it were only to learn this."

He visited the Pastor Vivien at Versailles, and rejoiced greatly in the zeal and activity of his old friend; preached several times in Paris, and took part in the Temple Chapel

---

* See "Quatre-vingt Jours," &c., p. 147, for a similar statement on the same subject at the close of his mission to Belgium in 1842.

in the ordination of a candidate, whose course he had directed at Geneva some years before.

Not being able to decide, in the midst of the bustle of Paris, as to the aim to be given to his mission, he went to St Cloud to spend a day in the park. There he resolved to set out next day for the south.

At Angoulême a young Parisian, amiable and of well-bred manners, took his place in the conveyance, and accosted him at once with the question, "Come from Paris, sir? of course you've seen the Huguenots?" "No, I did not; but I have their treasure here," drawing a New Testament from his pocket, and presenting it to him. "Ah," said the young man, "good enough for children that—mere fables." "How about your soul then?" "My soul! I haven't one; when you die, you die altogether," and he proceeded to expound the system of materialism. "I could scarcely keep from showing him the folly of his arguments by others in reply; but I thought it better to let the Word speak for itself, and read him several passages. He got annoyed; I saw then that they pricked his conscience, and I went on; he worked himself up into a great rage, however, and sate silently biting his lips. In this condition he remained for about half an hour, and then exclaimed, suddenly, 'I should like to have such a book as that, for I begin to think that its contents are true, and that I have been under a delusion.'" My father gave him his New Testament, and met him afterwards at Bordeaux, where he constantly attended his ministry, and showed, in a thousand ways, that he had received a deep impression. "When I saw this fruit of the Word of God," he adds, "I rejoiced that I had not spoken of myself, or employed my own arguments."

His stay at Bordeaux was laborious. He had written from Paris to an old friend, M. de Laharpe, in that city, saying that he would go south on condition that he had work to do, and that he should be enabled to hold, at least, two meetings a-day. His correspondent welcomed him by saying, "I received your note ; you will hold your first meeting in an hour." "That is what I call a true hospitable greeting to a minister of God," my father adds. It was at Bordeaux, at one of the meetings, that a young Romanist, a native of Bretagne, was brought to a knowledge of the gospel,—a workman in the city, and who, after a course of suitable study, became a faithful pastor. His history, for its own sake, would deserve to be recorded.

My father preached also in the churches of the Establishment, and before very numerous gatherings. But it was when he left Bordeaux that his mission, properly speaking, began. He quitted the city in company with the pastor Henriquet, one of his old friends, and Mr Laharpe, a candidate for the ministry, the son of the friend who had received him on his arrival.

After various occurrences, too long to relate, the three travellers arrived at Libourne. There, at the table d'hôte, they met a man who said openly, " For my part my religion is gastronomy." "I must confess," said my father to his hearers, in reference to this remark, " that I have often had great difficulty in starting a religious conversation at a 'table d'hôte.' Here, however, it was started for me, so I merely turned and said to the speaker, 'that a wiser than he or I had declared that the belly and its meats were made to be destroyed.'" From that time the conversation proceeded with animation, and my father ended with distributing tracts to those present. At Bergerac also, at the "table d'hôte," he interrupted a sharp discussion on the comparative merits of Spaniards and Frenchmen, by saying, in a loud, clear tone, "that in the eyes of the Supreme Judge no one nation is better than another," and "that he alone is really '*better*' who has been renewed by the Spirit of God." Then availing himself of the sensation he had produced in the company, he put a tract in each of their plates and left the room.

After visiting St Foy, they arrived in lands immortalised in the recollection of every Protestant, for the persecutions endured there by the confessors of a pure gospel. Here M. Henriquet, whose church was in the neighbourhood, had to part with his friends. "Some of the fishermen, who comprise the population of that country,—simple-minded and honest men,—came to convey us in one of their large boats. The sailing was delightful; and, as we were quietly towed along by the oxen, we sang with loud voices the praises of the Lord. On approaching La Nougarède we found the bank crowded with groups waiting for us. The church was close at hand. I preached there for many consecutive hours to three or four hundred people, who listened with unwearied eagerness to the message of the gospel."

As they were leaving, a physician of Bergerac, who had heard my father at Bordeaux, entered into a conversation

in the diligence with M. Laharpe. On their arrival at
Bergerac early in the day, the two travellers found that the
diligence did not leave till very late in the evening. My
father therefore proposed to M. Laharpe that he should ask
the physician, with whom he had been conversing, whether
they couldn't have a meeting? One was held forthwith,
and lasted from seven to nine. About midnight, just as
they were starting, they found there were no vacant places.
As there seemed no prospect of the hotel being opened, a
gentleman in the town received the two missionaries into
his house. At their departure, the next day, he assured
them that he had cause to bless God for their stay.

At Castillonnez they took a walk in the town while the
horse was being baited. " How many servants of God,"
said M. Laharpe, suddenly, " have passed under the arch-
ways of these gates to go to martyrdom!" " How I
should love to preach the Word of God to this people,"
replied his companion. Then, observing some children
who were leaving school, he called one of them to him,
and, asking him if he knew how to read, gave him a tract.
" Soon," he goes on to say, " all the school was round me ;
so that I took one on my knees, had another at my side,
and gave a tract to every one who could read ; and thus
the truth of the gospel was disseminated through the entire
place."

At Clairac my father held a meeting every day, and
preached twice on Sunday. On Monday, after visiting the
pastor, he distributed tracts, addressed the workmen on the
road separately, and, in the evening, presided again over a
meeting.

Malan and his young friend preached at Montauban, where the latter stopped. At La Garde my father's address created a lively impression in the minds of some who were present, as well as of the pastor himself. Near there, he had the gratification of thanking one of the gentlemen of the neighbourhood, who had been mentioned to him as being the person who, at the commencement of the building of his chapel, had sent him thirty louis d'or, with an anonymous letter containing the following sentence: "It is written, Extend thy curtains; but it is also written, Strengthen thy pavilions! I have received this sum, and I send it to you."

At Toulouse he met M. Chabrand, that delightful character, who, the more he is known the more he is beloved; with those servants of God, so zealous and so devoted in their work, the MM. Courtois. "I begged them," he adds, "not to be sparing in their supply of work, as I had not come to visit museums and curiosities, but to preach the Word of God."

So he preached frequently in that town; among other places, at the Military Hospital. "The place where I had to speak," he says, "was sufficiently large, and the soldiers who occupied it had, the greater portion of them, risen from their beds, and came in leaning upon one another. There were some bedsteads which had been stripped in the room. 'Come, my friends,' I said to them, 'we must draw the table near the beds that you may be able to sit down.' Otherwise, they would certainly have fainted. I then preached to them, but in language suitable to soldiers. I said to them, among other things, 'You are probably told that there are small and great sins, but this is not the case. Suppose that in time of war you had been posted as a sentinel;' in saying this, I looked steadfastly at an old grenadier with gray moustaches; 'with instructions not to let a single cockade of the enemy pass your beat. While you are stationed there, a little child comes up to you, wearing this cockade, and says to you, "Let me pass, sentry." "No one passes here would be your answer." "But I want to go and see my mother." "No one passes here," you would again reply; and the child would be off. Well, it is exactly the same with reference to these sins sometimes called little.'"

The next Sunday, the soldiers closed their doors on their chaplain; "Go and preach your stuff elsewhere," they cried, "and send us the gentleman who spoke to us the other day." The incident created a stir: it was even referred to Paris, and the final result was a free admission for Protestants into the hospital.

From Toulouse, after visiting the Churches of Ariége, he arrived at Calmont. "The people of this place," he says, "were so desirous to hear the gospel, that every time the bell rang, they came in a body to church. When our dear and honoured brother Olivier came there, he arrived very late in the evening; but as he had to set out again the next morning, the pastor had the bell rung immediately; and though the population had gone to bed, they all got up, and the meeting was held.

"At Mirepoix where we had to stop, we walked into the town—the pastor of Calmont and I—and as we passed by a cutler's shop, I said to the man, 'Ah! I see you make use of coals, as the fire is fiercer, but do you know of the fire that is never quenched.' 'How?' he asked, 'a fire which is never quenched?' and he left his forge and listened very seriously while I spoke to him of his soul."

As they were returning and crossing the market-place, they saw in the distance a species of clerk who was reading aloud. My father passed on, but his companion cried out to him in English, "Doctor, here's a man who says that God's truth is better than man's." The fact was, that this clerk had intended to make a sort of public demonstration against the Protestant preachers. "I retraced my steps," says my father, "and asked the reader to let me see the book he had in his hand. It was a Breviary. Then opening it after the Magnificat, I read these words, 'And this is His commandment, that we should believe on the name of His Son Jesus Christ, and love one another as He gave us commandment.'* 'What glorious words you have got in this book,' I said to those around me. Thirty or forty persons had collected together, and for twenty minutes I preached to them. I took care to keep my friend the clerk at my side, and said to him in a low voice from time to time, 'See that you are not fighting against God.' He replied each time—'Don't be afraid. Yes, indeed sir, it's very good.' When I had finished, I let him go." My father went back to Toulouse, passing La Bastide on his way. There a letter from the pastor of Calmont summoned him to Perpignan, where he stayed ten days.

"I had occasion to remark there," he says, "as in other countries of France, how far the minds of the people are

---

* 1 John iii. 23.

becoming impatient of the yoke. They are not only full of ardour, but also invariably ready to throw off every species of rule. Hence care is needed not to mistake the enthusiasm, which they occasionally display, for an impression produced by the Word. Above all, it must never be forgotten that the doctrines of grace, which, more than any other, tend to set men free, if they are imperfectly understood by these people, will serve to support them in the tendencies to which I have referred.

At Perpignan, the mayor and prefect received the foreign preacher very well. He delivered daily addresses there; frequently to six hundred or seven hundred people; in the large room of a building erected for the immediate occupation of the Catholic bishop. "I told them," he remarks, "that I was neither Catholic nor Protestant, but a Bible Christian, and that if any of them had any scruple as to the copies of the sacred books I used, they might come forward and say so, or, if they preferred it, pay me a visit any day. They asked us for Bibles, and, at the close of each address, came forward to thank us for having come among them."

At Rivesaltes,—an almost Spanish town, famous for the fanaticism of its population, where he had been invited by some one who had heard him at Perpignan,—he spoke in the large room of a school which had just been established by a few friends of progress. "The stir produced among the population," he says, "was like that in the valley of dry bones (Ezek. xxxvii.) Ten or twelve people renounced Popery, and several ladies formed a committee for the diffusion of the Scriptures. People told me that if I stayed a few days longer they would abjure Romanism. I thought it was just the moment for me to withdraw, leaving the Spirit of God to work in their hearts; for what good end would have been answered by arousing in the place nothing short of a religious revolution. I left there, however, full of gratitude to God, longing for a gospel missionary to return to them, provided only it were one of matured experience, and not a young man."

At Montpellier, he met his old friend, and companion of his studies, the pastor Lissignol, whose letters had encouraged him during his work at Perpignan. He preached there, as at Nismes and Montélimart. "At Lyons," he says, "I had the gratification of meeting my dear and honoured brother, Adolphe Monod, who received me with the most cordial affection, and begged me to address his flock on three occasions. What strikes one in this man of God is the deep humility which has been vouchsafed to him." Then after relating how, in the conveyance by which he returned to Geneva, he had had a religious conversation with a fellow-traveller from which he hoped for good results, he concluded his narrative, by calling upon his congregation to intercede for France, where "the harvest was plenteous but the labourers few."

By way of giving completeness to the above, I will add a few passages from a private journal which he wrote each day, during his stay at Perpignan. In the midst of various notes on letters from home, &c., we are enabled to discover, in all their vividness, his most intimate thoughts on the subject of his mission—

" 3d *June.*—Held my first meeting: about three hundred persons of all ranks present: officers of the garrison, advocates, &c. At the commencement I said that I had come in the hope of being useful to my hearers, that they would, therefore, have to listen with attention. The introduction of my discourse was to the effect that, in spite of all the opinions which divide and perplex the thinking world, there were two facts which no error nor attack had been able to overrun—the one, that man is a sinner; the other, that Jesus has been crucified, and is risen again: that these two verities comprised all that man was in himself, and all that the grace of God had done for him."

Saturday 4th.—He meets soldiers who appear interested in what he says to them, and wishful to hear him further. He is told that his preaching has produced a sensation, and he receives many visits from leading persons in the town. " I notice that every one looks at me with curiosity when I go out. Be it so. Let the Lord only spread His net: and, if the fish enter from *curiosity,* they will do what Zacchæus did." Then he adds, " I feel more than ever that I am nothing in myself, I seem to be nothing. . . . I am sometimes disposed to reason with the people, and, following the inclination of N——, to prove first the authenticity of the Bible, &c., but I have been withheld from doing so by an impulse from within. I will preach Jesus, and His Name will vindicate its power over the individual conscience. Under all circumstances it is better, the sword of the Spirit being our weapon, to deal a few blows into human souls, than to stop to inquire into the way in which this two-edged blade has been tempered." In the evening, at 9.30, there was a meeting of seven hundred persons. " I shall have to prepare my discourse very carefully for to-morrow, that it may be abundantly enriched from the Word of God. Oh Jesus, Jesus, my Master, have compassion on Thy servant's ignorance, and help him with Thy Spirit and Thy Word! Amen, Lord!"

" *Monday 6th.*—Further conversation with the soldiers. I listened for a few moments to a young girl who played the piano, before the lady of the house. Then, on being asked, I played and sung a hymn, which gave rise to a very singular conversation in which a gentleman took part, and which the servants listened to on the stairs. It was followed by several others with the same persons."

8th.—After his return from "that day of peace and blessing" at Rivesaltes: "this morning, a resident in Perpignan, who met us in the town, said to me, 'Courage, you are doing good. People are thinking and speaking of what you are saying. If you do not see the results, they are none the less sure to come. Go forward!' O Lord, Thou who art the beginning and the strength of the life of Thy people, have compassion upon me!" In the evening: " This morning I was exhausted, but it did not last, and the joy of my heart increases in proportion with the work."

" *10th.*—As I was leaving the N.'s I met in the courtyard the Spanish nobleman whom I have mentioned before. I talked with him for more than an hour on the efficacy of Christ's death. At the end of our conversation he embraced me warmly. A mason had just been erecting a scaffolding in front of the door by which I left the house; as I crossed to the other side M. N—— said to me: 'May God bless your journey. Perhaps we shall meet above; and'—pointing upward with his hand—'He will lead us to His heavenly abode.' I thought that which intervened between my soul and his—so devoted to his Roman faith, was but the scaffolding of his observances."

13th.—Leaving Perpignan, he writes: "How I ought to magnify the Lord! He has brought me here—He has sustained me in health and strength — He has suffered me to preach several times a day—He has enabled me to speak to many souls, and to write, besides, four tracts which, by His grace, will serve to recall what I have said to the memory of some, and will be the means of communicating to others the message of salvation."* Such is the history of his mission to the south of France in 1836.

It is not our intention to follow him through his other missionary tours; the details we have just given will serve to convey a true idea of them. Indeed, he has published an account of some of them. In 1842, for example, he issued his " Quatre-vingt Jours d'un Missionaire ; or, A Simple Narrative of the Various Toils of one of the Labourers in

---

* The day after his arrival at Perpignan he wrote the tract, "The Best and Surest Way," which was sent by him to his friends at Toulouse, and immediately printed. On the 10th he began " La Route Perdue." Finishing that, he composed, on the 12th, an address to the congregations he had visited ; and returning home, after having taken leave of his hearers, he prepared, in connection with an expression he had overheard on the way, the tract, " None are Born Christians." He wrote at the same time also " The Primitive Christians."

the Great Harvest;" being notes of a preaching tour that year in Belgium and Holland. In 1843 appeared "A Visit to Scotland;" in 1845, "A Fisher of Living Men," the narrative of a second trip to Holland; in 1850, "A Week in the Mountains;" in 1856, "Travelling Experiences;" and lastly, in the same year, after his return from the Vaudois Valleys, "In Season and out of Season."

In all these publications, in addition to his personal way of presenting the gospel, and the special importance he attaches to setting forth the doctrine of sovereign grace, his pages abound with a variety of striking thoughts, and display a simple and fervent piety; and also, as years advance, abundant proofs of the matured strength which a long habit of living with God and for God gives to a simple and devout heart.

I shall content myself with quoting here a few of these passages. For example, the following may serve to illustrate his sentiments, as well in reference to the results which he anticipated from his mission, as also in regard to those which he had already witnessed.

"At the commencement of my ministry I often attributed to the Holy Spirit's operation, impressions produced only by persuasive human language. More than once have I had to note of that time, that I was building with hay and stubble. For many years, however, I have learnt that not every religious emotion comes from above. I know that the Holy Spirit alone gives life. I try to discern His whisper within, and to follow Him as I repeat His teachings. I pray God to send down His Spirit on those I address before they receive the Word. I am careful, moreover, to commend to His grace such souls as tell me of good received. But I leave everything to the Lord. I prefer rather to wait for the result than to anticipate it."*

Further on, on quitting Belgium: "Oh, gracious God, how easy has been the path Thou hast marked out for me in this beautiful country! Thou hast brought me here to speak of Jesus. Thou hast strengthened me by the Spirit of peace and grace; and, to crown all Thine acts of loving-kindness, Thou hast kept me perpetually in the comforting and cheering society of those who love Thee, and who have declared to me their love in the faith."†

Further on still, speaking of his visit to Holland, where he had just preached twenty-nine times in twenty-seven days: "It was a time of peace, of heavenly joy, of cheering, brotherly love. Received by all as an old friend, as a beloved brother, and as the messenger of Jesus; hearts and houses opened to welcome me."‡

Dismissing for the present his account of his visit to Scotland in 1843, which only bears upon his intercourse with the Free Church in that country, I will insert here a few extracts from his "Fisher of Men." In this book, especially written, as we have seen, after a fresh mission to Holland in 1845, are to be found his characteristic traits and those felicitous expressions which he invariably had at his command.

Thus, at Bâle he stopped a quarrel at its commencement, by whispering in the ear of a peasant, "Fear God and forgive. God give you His peace." Afterwards the peasant came up to him, and began an earnest conversation with him. On another occasion, at the time of the Sonderbund campaign, he asked a Swiss of the liberal party, who used

---

* "Quatre-vingt Jours," &c., p. 269.   † Ibid., p. 371.   ‡ Ibid., p. 385.

U

violent language in speaking of the Jesuits, "Whether a truncheon or stone-throwing would avail to drive away darkness?" A remark also followed up, in its turn, by a prolonged conversation.

In the railway from Amsterdam to Arnheim, we see him "sitting in his corner of the carriage, quite silent, and watching for a moment when he might if possible introduce some serious topic." He was not long in finding his opportunity. On another occasion, to a traveller describing the "religious impression produced upon his mind when he entered certain churches," Malan replied, "Then if you were blind, your piety would suffer." Again, he asked a joiner who was enlarging upon his desire to render himself worthy of the grace of God, "whether any amount of polishing would transform a piece of common wood into mahogany?" I wish I could have quoted his conversation with a student, on true and false philosophy, and with the Jesuit on proselytism, a perfect model of guarded and courteous irony. I might have referred to various incidents, giving clearest evidence of his benevolent feeling towards the poor, the weak, the wandering, the unfortunate, and children. I will confine myself here, however, to relating an unlooked-for interview which he had with a pious stranger. "I feel," he said, "that the cordial affections which are in Christ belong in effect to a separate existence, are a divine power from which we have to descend before we can take up earthly cares: just as, after having breathed the invigorating air of the high Alps, and contemplated the majestic summits, we have to force ourselves back to the plain, to trudge on once more along the dusty roads, and through the midst of the towns and their surrounding death." We recognise in this language the man who, whilst he had been so often called upon to meet with brethren, lived with them so little. These words of his,—the expression of a feeling deep and lively,—may furnish to a thoughtful mind the key to many traits which tended to separate my father from his brethren, and to withdraw him from ordinary life.

What I should like, however, to quote more freely, is his little publication entitled, "A Week in the Mountains," in which he describes a story in the Bernese Oberland, in the summer of 1849, which contains numerous pages as remarkable for the grace and the freshness of their style as for the genuine feeling they so abundantly betray.

In 1856, after his visit to the Vaudois Valleys, he published, as we have seen, his little book, called "In Season and out of Season;" where we find, among other things, the advice which his long experience dictated, to young ecclesiastics. He was then nearly seventy; it was his last foreign mission.

In looking over all these volumes it is impossible to help being struck, again and again, by that absolute assurance of the personal love of God which forms the foundation and centre of his entire spiritual life. This it was that stirred up and sustained his activity. Thence he derived his entire self-possession when he was confronted by the smiles of the indifferent or unbelieving. Here was the source of that strength which he was enabled to maintain, in the midst of his isolation; of that joy and peace which breathed through his lightest words; as well as of that simple ease, with which he addressed each and all. This is the sentiment, moreover, to which must be traced that piety, the object of which is the Lord Jesus,

Whom he calls his Saviour, his Master, his Brother, and to Whom his whole heart is manifestly devoted. Here, and here only, is the basis on which he rests his assured triumphant life of future glory—here too, that consciousness of the love of God for him, with which he feeds the springs of his benevolent and charitable heart. To sum up all in one word, this confidence is so conspicuous in his life, that it is impossible to follow his career without seeing that it realises the scriptural picture of the just man living by his faith.

If such, however, be the impression produced by descriptions such as these, with reference to the spiritual life which animated the subject of them, there remains yet one, entirely distinct, connected with the expression which as a preacher he gave to it. At the first glance we cannot but be struck, on the one hand, by that elevation invariably produced in the soul of the believer by personal and actual communion with God Himself, constantly present in that soul's experience, and, on the other, by the touching simplicity and infantine freshness of his personal and devoted love for the Saviour, the more remarkable in a man distinguished for the manly vigour and independence of his character. As for the impression produced by his method of teaching, shown in these incidents, it is much more decided.

On this point, it is impossible to refrain from the inquiry, as we lay down his treatises, whether, after all, the gospel is altogether comprised in the invariable syllogism they set forth; whether that strictly logical form, that instinctive search after clearness in thought, and intellectual truth, really exhausts the whole of the divine response to that heart-hunger and thirst which the gospel pre-eminently meets. We ask involuntarily whether the fact that this analysis of the divine scheme is so complete, would not of itself empower us to think that what we read there can only be one side of that salvation of God which, like all that is infinite and divine, can never be thoroughly apprehended except by faith of heart. Recurring, in justification of this remark, to what has already been said about my father's dogmatism, I content myself with expressing a regret in this place, that these writings of his are not more generally known.

Having taken this general survey of his missionary activity abroad, from the year 1830, 1 now invite my readers to retrace their steps, for the purpose of noticing his labours during that same period in Geneva itself.

CHAPTER III.

Till the day dawn,
And the Day Star arise,—
Church of the Living God,
Pursue thy upward road ;
Look not behind nor stray
From the well-trodden way.
Be not ashamed to bear
Thy cross on earth, nor fear
Reproach and poverty,
For Him Who died for thee.

Section 1.—Controversial Protestantism (up to 1836.)

THE year 1830, so decisive an epoch in the history of modern society, was similarly marked in Geneva, especially by the development of that evangelical revival of the French Protestant world, which took its rise in that city. The agitation for freedom which passed at that time over the whole of Europe, made itself felt in the limited sphere where those events unfolded themselves with which we are now occupied. It was afterwards that the liberal movement, which the revival had inaugurated, began to exercise an increased influence on the public mind, in connection with Protestantism. At the same time, this movement changed its character. To the fervour of individual faith was added with augmenting force a claim for the rights of Churches in reference to their external existence.

Meanwhile, if this is generally true of the part taken by the instruments of the revival in Geneva, it does not apply to my father. He continued to dedicate his thoughts with ever-increasing earnestness to the life and faith of the individual believer. While labouring at the progressive development of Churches, he never took a direct part in what may be called the polemical aspect of the question. Moreover, we notice invariably how little he appears on the scene when topics of this kind, which, before 1830, had involved him in so much obloquy in the little world of the first revival, began especially after 1835, mainly through the powerful influence of Vinet, to obtrude themselves, not only upon the attention of believers, but also on all intelligent minds and friends of progress. Without holding himself entirely aloof from so decisive an agitation of the public mind, he nevertheless abstained altogether from enrolling himself among those who appeared to attach to it an essential importance. More solemnly engrossed, as he ever was, with the eternal interest of souls exclusively, he devoted himself supremely to labouring in that direction, wherever it might be, which presented openings bearing upon those interests.

Thus, for example, he followed with sympathising attention the agitation which developed itself, with daily increasing clearness, in the bosom of the National Church. The return to it of a new life appeared to him nothing short of an answer to his constant and fervent prayers. Moreover, it might have been said that he felt himself personally called upon to protest whenever he saw any error publicly appearing, which seemed to him to embarrass the progress of that movement.

Meanwhile, however strongly he appreciated the marked impression produced in the official faculty of theology by the teaching of his old friend Diodati, however much he rejoiced to note how that teaching by slow degrees served to give a new direction to the minds of the junior clergy, however manifestly he afterwards participated in the re-awakening of the Protestant sentiment which had mani-fested itself in Geneva from the year 1835, he nevertheless abstained from taking up the pen except when he considered himself called upon directly to do so by circumstances themselves. On this point, he never thought that the simple fact, that he entertained a lively conviction, gave him of itself a right to speak out. Here, as in everything, he left it with God alone to take the initiative, and waited for God to show him the way. When once such indications had been undoubtedly granted him, he considered that, had he kept silence, he would not only have been wanting in a most sacred duty, but also that he would have been negli-gent in that direction whither the deepest feelings of his heart carried him.

In short, up to the very last he loved, with an unfeigned love, his country and the Church of his fathers. There was that in him, in this sentiment, which reminds one of the feeling of honour that binds a soldier to his post, and com-pels him to raise the alarm at the enemy's approach. He loved to compare himself to a sentry, whose sole duty and glory consists in earnest and faithful watching: to a sol-dier whose charge depends only on the will of the com-mander who has placed him where he is, and who alone has the right to recall him. "I am but the mere depository of my testimony," he used to say. "It would be simpler and easier for me to hold my tongue; but then how should I give account to my Master of the ministry He has committed to my keeping?"

Throughout the years to which our attention is now to be drawn, his testimony bore in two special directions. At first, as in 1831 and in 1835, he was stirred up by the party demonstrations among the ranks of the senior clergy of the National Church, whether directed against the doctrines or the very existence of "Methodism." At the commencement of 1838, certain writings which involved him personally, induced him to descend, for some years, into the arena of the Roman controversy.

In January 1831 Professor Chenevière issued his "Essay" on "The Theological System of the Trinity;" in which, restricting himself to the recognition of Jesus Christ as a divine being, he made a vigorous attack on the Athanasian faith, in the name of the history of the Primitive Church, of reason and of Scripture.*

This publication, in which, for the first time, as it would seem, the majority of the "Compagnie," gave definite expression to their views, appeared of sufficient importance to the members of the Evangelical Society, to determine them on founding their "school of theology."

As for my father, he could not ignore an attack which, while it, undoubtedly, did not concern him personally (like the Precis from the same pen seven years before), was nevertheless directed, and that conspicuously, against the doctrine for which he had already suffered. So, but a

---

* See De Goltz, "Genève Relig.," p. 377.

few days after the appearance of M. Chenevière's publication, he issued a reply addressed "to those families in Geneva, who are sincerely seeking after, or who possess and love, the truth as it is Jesus." He characterises the work which had just been issued as "a detestable production of the spirit of darkness;" and, while reminding his readers that "controversy is not piety, and that wranglings and disputes never proved the truth which the Word of God contains for him who studies it in faith," he appeals, in their presence, "to the simple testimony of that Word."

Shortly afterwards there appeared, as a second edition of the Protest, a volume of two hundred pages, entitled, "Jesus Christ is the Eternal God, Manifest in the Flesh; A First Reply to the Writings of Professor Chenevière against the God of the Christian. By C. Malan, Minister of our Great God and Saviour Jesus Christ." This work reached its second edition immediately. An introduction, on the danger of looking for a new meaning in the Word of God, closed with these words, "Be old-fashioned in your principles, in your views, and in your sentiments. You never can be so as much as the Word or Spirit that reveals it. Attend to, and read what God declares. Enough for you if, with a heart surrendered to the Christ of Whom all the Scriptures testify, you wait for the Holy Spirit to reveal to your eyes the glory of Him Who only is come from the Father." He then proceeds to draw the attention of his readers to the importance,—decisive, so far as the interests of the soul are concerned,—of a right acquaintance with the nature of the Lord Jesus. His Bible in his hand, he examines one by one the four declarations—that Jesus Christ is self-existent—that He possesses sovereign power—that adoration is due only to God, and that it is rendered to Jesus Christ—that glory belongs only to the Eternal, and that Jesus Christ has it. A few notes are added on passages referring to the divinity of the Lord Jesus, and of the Holy Spirit.

It would be useless to seek in this volume an investigation of the divinity of the Lord Jesus, founded on a specific idea of what divinity involves, in respect of its approaches to a divergence from what we are accustomed to specify as humanity. It contains simply a lucid, and invariably animated exposition of the numerous passages of Scripture which have been quoted in all times, in favour of the cardinal doctrine stated above. While in this exposition is to be found merely that special theology according to which the whole Bible in every one of its parts, and even in its very form, remains not only the testimony of the divine operations for salvation, but also the rule of the impression with which our faith in these facts should be clothed; while, as a natural consequence, it contains no historical estimate of the testimony of the sacred writers; while the passages quoted are all brought forward on the same footing;—it is at the same time evident that the writer is dealing with no mere process of thought, but with the very centre and source of his own religious life. In the introductory address, still bound up with the book, this feeling is very evident. "See to it," says the witness for living faith in Jesus Christ, "in what way Christ is revealed to you. To this end, open, read, search, study that Bible which teaches nothing but the truth. Either Jesus Christ is the eternal God; in which case worship Him as such, and repudiate with abhorrence all blas-

phemies directed against Him; or He is only a created
being, and you have no right to serve Him, or to partake
of the sacrament of His Supper. For in a word, to sum up
all discussion on the subject, and to give the result of the
most diligent inquiry that it is possible to make, either
the Saviour of the Church is the Creator, the eternal God,
or He is not; and this alternative involves two faiths, two
religions; as different, each from the other, as the Creator
is from His creatures."* Whatever be the opinion entertained as to the value of this reasoning, it would be
impossible to deny the importance of so eloquent and so
explicit an avowal in favour of the ancient faith, thus
presented as a confession supremely of the Saviour of the
soul;—a confession destined never to die out, but to be
accepted in the world, for all time, so long as souls shall
exist conscious of their need of salvation.

It is difficult, at the present moment, to form an
adequate estimate of the sensation which this publication
produced in Geneva at the time of its first appearance.
That city resembled then a large family. More particularly,
nothing which transpired in the sphere of its religious life
remained a matter of indifference to any of its inhabitants.
" Public attention was so deeply aroused that the printing

---

* A remark upon the language invariably employed by my father, with
reference to our Lord, will not be deemed unimportant. Neither he nor his
orthodox brethren ever made use of the apostolical expression, " the
Christ," to this hour employed only by a very small section of the evangelical party. In speaking of the Saviour they always called Him " *Christ.*"
A natural custom, inasmuch as they were confronted by an express denial
of the divinity of the Lord Jesus. For the former of these designations,
indicating the office rather than the Person, tends to raise our contemplation from His own Person to Him Who conferred that office. This is no
longer the case when the term *Christ* is employed; inasmuch as that is an
essentially individual designation, in fact, a proper name.

office, from which the reply was issued, was surrounded by a crowd of people, who carried off the sheets, still damp from the press, and read them in the street," as an eye-witness assured me.

The year 1835 brought round, for the third time, the celebration of the centenary of the jubilee of the Reformation. The majority of the people regarded the ceremony as nothing more than a great national fete, intended to recall the first rise of their political liberties. As for the clergy of the National Church, their aim was to avail themselves of the opportunity to recover an influence threatened alike by the measures which the government were adopting with the view of abridging their preroga-tives, by the increasingly alarming advances of an aggressive catholicism, as well as by the rapid spread of orthodoxy and religious activity, the starting of which they felt they had too thoroughly abandoned to the dissenters.

Their first step was unfortunate. They chose that moment for publishing a new translation of the Holy Scriptures, prepared after much care, and many years of labour, by the members of the "Compagnie." This was that "Bible of Geneva," the language of which is un-doubtedly very superior to the occasionally unintelligible versions of Osterwald, and more especially of Martin, but which, even in the Church of Geneva, is about to be set aside for a new one. It is notorious that that publication brought about a decisive rupture between the Britannic and Foreign Biblical Society and the Biblical Society of the Church of Geneva at that time.

My father could not hold himself aloof from a festival which associated itself with his deepest feelings as a believer and a citizen. And, even had he desired to maintain silence, the opponents of the revival would never have permitted it. Filled, indeed, with a sense of triumphant security, inspired by the reappearance of the Protestant sentiments of the population, they imagined that the moment had come for asserting publicly, and almost officially, their opposition to that "Methodism," which they persisted in regarding as nothing more than an ephemeral and half-conquered innovation. At the very beginning of the year, accordingly, there appeared an announcement to the effect that a prize of one thousand florins would be awarded to the best essay on the under-mentioned subjects; the prize to be confined to Genevese clergymen, and the MSS. to be sent to Professor Chenevière.

1. What are the causes which have led to the introduction of Methodism into Geneva?

2. What are the evils and perils it brings to the State, the National Church, and the well-being of separate households?

3. The best methods of attacking and driving it away.

The essays to be handed in to the care of Professor Chenevière.

In replying to this announcement my father issued in February, under the title of "The Trial of Methodism submitted to Competent Judges,"* a pamphlet of eighty pages, perhaps the most striking of his numerous special publications.

"The subject is difficult," he says, in his Preface, " not

---

* "By Cæsar Malan, Doctor of Theology, minister," declared to be deposed of the Church of Geneva, and regent, " ejected of the college of that city," with the motto, " It is time for Thee, Lord, to work."

in itself, our passions have rendered it so. For it invariably happens in all that pertains to religious questions, that, when opposing principles meet, Truth, whose voice is not of this world, appears to speak in too low a tone, while passions raise their cries to help her."

Such is the misfortune which attends discussions least of all meriting it,—discussions on faith. It is true, that if they were conducted by the people, and that, if the people themselves were not led by others, they would, undoubtedly, be calmer, and, above all, less protracted. Of this Geneva has had more proofs than one. Asperity, occasionally malice, and even irony and satire have wielded the pen which justice at least, to say nothing of charity, ought alone to have employed; and religion has wept over the advantage which it was thus pretended to afford her. I desire to shun these evils in the important investigation on which I am about to enter. The subject is grave; on the one hand, it involves the glory of the gospel, on the other, the welfare of Geneva; two considerations dear, each of them, to my heart.

Then in a style of great occasional rapidity, and thrilling with emotion, he analyses one by one the three subjects of the programme.

In replying to the first, he appeals, at the outset, to the evidence of facts, as showing that the Methodism of Geneva is nothing but the doctrine of the blessed Reformation — the religion and faith of our forefathers — the religion of the Bible, summed up under these three principal heads:—The Most Holy Trinity, Original Sin, and Salvation by Grace, accompanied in the heart by the love of the Lord Jesus. "Only," he adds, "if in 1535 those who loved the Bible were esteemed in Geneva;—in 1835 the fête of the jubilee of that glorious and mighty event is inaugurated by utterances directed against those friends of the Lord Jesus, and by the issue of a programme in which it it is suggested as a subject of debate, how they may be driven from Geneva." He then shows that this Genevese Methodism, a vigorous offshoot of. the religion of our fathers, or rather of the sacred truth of the Bible which they professed, was called forth by the heresies of the last century, and appeared when the tree of the Reformation was threatened with death.

In his answer to the second question, (in which he refers to two of his previously issued publications : " Are Momiers injurious or necessary to the welfare of a State ?" 1823 ; and " Genevese Methodism," in 1831, a reply to an attack by the Journal of Geneva of that time), he unfolds the principles of these " Methodists." They belong to the Universal Church ; they follow the Bible. As for their morals, they exhibit individually a humble, pacific, just, charitable, temperate, pious, religious spirit. In proof of all this, he appeals to facts patent to his opponents, which he presses home with clear and direct appeals, through which may be traced the indignation which an honest man experiences at the spectacle of prejudice and injustice.

As to the means of banishing Methodism, after enumerating forces which had been already tried in vain,—contempt, hatred, opposition, and the secular arm,—he finishes by naming the only one likely to prove effectual. " Take away the Bible," he exclaims, " and Methodism disappears. Without that, you may abandon all hope of success. Methodism is Christianity ; be assured of that : and Christianity is the Bible; and the Bible is the Word of God; and God is over all. Fear Him."

" I have replied," he says in conclusion, " but without competing for the prize. I neither judge nor condemn. Alas, who would judge unhappy souls! I would rather humble myself before God for the grace that has rescued me from such ignorance and unbelief. I, too, for many years neglected the Holy Bible. I, too, despised and contradicted the doctrines of grace. I was then a candidate for the ministry. I was afterwards a minister, and I preached error. I, too, denounced the meetings of the brethren, and at that time wished they would cease, while I carefully kept my friends away from them. God has had compassion upon me. He has opened my eyes, and shown me my sin. He has granted me repentance. He has converted me to the Lord Jesus. The riches of His mercy are ever the same. He can rouse a slumbering heart, and give understanding to those who lack it. He has done all this for *my* soul. Oh that in His loving-kindness he may do it for *others*, and that it may soon be said in Geneva, ' Those who once persecuted the faithful now preach the faith which lately they destroyed.' "

At the same time that he issued this pamphlet, he announced, as " The Unanswerable Reply of John Calvin himself, and of his Brethren, the Pastors of the Church of Geneva, to Professor Chenevière's book against Divine Election," a reprint of " The Congregation of Calvin." A copy of this little work, for a long time nearly forgotten, had been sent to him in 1820, with a few jesting words, by a bookseller in the town, and had proved to him for a long time, as he says himself, " a constant and precious study."

x

With reference to the programme on " the Extirpation of Methodism," it does not appear that the prize of one thousand florins was adjudged.

Meanwhile, every preparation was being made for the fête which was to take place in August. After having assumed the defence of the cause of evangelical revival, my father wished to make known to the public what the festival ought to be.

In one of those popular dialogues which he knew so well how to write, entitled, " The True Jubilee," he shows the impropriety of celebrating the festival of that Reformation, founded, in common with all Protestantism and Christianity, on the truth that Jesus Christ is God manifest in the flesh, if the solemnity is to be regarded as merely a national commemoration of the dawn of a new era of social and political liberty. Reminding his readers that the Reformed population of the Canton de Vaud, of Scotland, of Holland, and other parts, had declared that they would have nothing to do with those in Geneva, as far as the jubilee was concerned, so long as their only idea of celebrating it was in effect, as he says, to raise a subscription for curtains and painted windows for their cathedral, he repeats to his fellow citizens that text which " neither people, nor priests, nor ministers, nor philosophers, nor learned men will ever be able to destroy, ' If any man have not the spirit of Christ, he is none of His.' "

Thus, then, no less as a Genevese Protestant than as an orthodox believer, he found it impossible to unite with the promoters of the fête. " Originally," he said, " Popery, by means of the Reformation, was expelled from the State ; now it is recovering its ground among us. Moreover, the

Reformation founded the Church of Geneva on the sacred truths of original sin, the divinity of Jesus Christ, and the justification of the sinner by faith in the blood of Jesus; now, this very essence of the Reformation is generally denied both by ministers and people. Finally, the Reformation established in Geneva a firm and holy discipline, insuring respect, at least externally, to the authority of the commandments of God; now there is nothing of the kind. I am persuaded," he exclaims, "that the troubles which have visited Geneva, for the last century—her revolutions, her enslavement, and the return of Popery to her midst— have sprung out of her unfaithfulness, her unbelief, the rebellion of her people against the Lord Jesus Christ; and I have no doubt whatever, that a festival celebrated without repentance and humiliation will prove to the nation a new snare, in which she will be yet more and more involved."

As for himself, he will "join in celebrating the jubilee, with all such in the State as love the Lord Jesus Christ in sincerity, by prayers to God for the poor Genevese." "While the people were in the highest pitch of their excitement," says de Goltz, "the three dissenting congregations occupied themselves in praying fervently to God for the conversion of their fellow citizens. In Malan's chapel especially, they sang 'the four hymns for the third jubilee of the Reformation in Geneva,' which their pastor had just published."

The anticipation which closed the earnest and thoughtful pages from which we have just quoted, could not but be realised. The celebration of the Reformation Jubilee of 1835, in Geneva, was unquestionably attended by most

lamentable consequences.* Not to speak of the religious
life of the Protestant population, we are compelled to date
from this period that destruction, in the very home of the
Reformation and the great Reformer, of the wholesome
reverence with which they had hitherto been invested.
Calvin, in the popular judgment, was regarded no longer
as a kind of prophet and providential legislator,—a
representative of a roused conscience and of the heart's
return to repentance and a holy God. He came to be
looked upon only as one of the many "great men" of
Geneva. Robbed of their evangelical aspect by a clergy
which had expelled from its dogmatic traditions everything savouring of this special character, the recollections
of the Reformation ceased to be associated in the public
mind, with an all but miraculous interposition, by which
the hand of God revealed itself in the national history.
They became the bare remembrances of a national revolution in the political and social life of the country. Nor was
it possible thus to blot out the record of the work of God in
history, without effacing by degrees its presence from
individual life. Thus it came to pass that, from that
period especially, unbelief—and that too in the most fatal
of all its phases, indifference—began to show itself among
the Protestant masses of Geneva. A natural result was
that absolute contempt of all authority, which has characterised from that time, and through so many years, the
civil life of the population.

But if the forebodings of good men were thus mourn-
fully realised, their prayers were undoubtedly heard. To-

* See de Goltz; "Genéve Religieuse," p. 426.

gether with this perilous indifference, appeared another phase of it, of a totally opposite character.

The very year which was to witness the extinction of Methodism proved, on the contrary, in the revival of that faith and life to which the stigma of this name was attached, the commencement of a period in which it depended only on itself to stamp its impress on the public life of the country. From 1835,—the period of the issue of the "Trial of Methodism,"—the attacks upon it, more or less official, ceased. The evangelical movement, recognised by the majority in its true character, was admitted by degrees, in public opinion, to the privileged position of a common right. This arose from various causes. In the first place, the revival of old Protestant animosities, produced in the people by the celebration of the jubilee after the fashion conceived of by the national clergy, induced the more serious portion to betake themselves afresh to the consideration of religious questions. Such persons soon discovered that all that the clergy had thus accomplished was the rekindling of the religious passions of a by-gone age. Nor could they fail to observe that all this official agitation had tended to no practical results beyond the secret formation of the "Protestant Union." Apart, however, from sundry partial efforts at reintroducing some of the religious customs of old Geneva into family life, this Union was, at bottom, nothing more nor less than a secret society intended, under the pretext of defending Protestantism, to isolate the Catholics from the population of which they formed a part. Reflecting men, who saw in Protestantism something more than a mere remembrance of national glories and a hatred of priests—men who had come to see in it the very liberty of the soul, and free access to the word of the gospel for themselves and their families—such men soon discovered that it was not by methods like these that it was possible to dissipate the perils that threatened them, whether from superstition or unbelief. Instructed by the dismay caused them through ultramontane fanaticism, they went on to repudiate fanaticism of every kind; and, by degrees, understood that their only possible weapon of defence was a clear, earnest, and, above all, definite faith.

This became apparent when my father (to return to the subject of these memoirs) found himself called upon, as we shall soon see, to take in hand the defence of evangelical truth. Moreover, the men, to whom we have just referred, gave their attention; and the people, generally forgetting the gibes and insults which they had so recently lavished on the "Momier," adopted him from that time as the champion of the slighted rights of the old Protestantism of Geneva.

From this time also, he came to be invested with a certain amount of consideration among the population generally. This reversion of opinion came too late, indeed, to effect any change in the position he had occupied through so many years; and it is to be questioned whether, secluded as he was from the society in which he lived, he even perceived the gradual change in the popular feeling towards him. To others, however, the reaction was very evident. It happened at the same time with a distinct revival in a considerable portion of the population, if not of religious life, at least of sincere attention to the religious interests of the country. Continuing firm in their attachment to the Church, the very name of which recalled in itself the old associations of Protestantism, they soon learned to separate the sacred cause of that Church from what was, after all, nothing more than the cause of her clergy. This speedily became apparent when, on the occasion of a change which supervened in the political administration, it was decided to deprive the clergy of the exclusive direction of ecclesiastical interests.

Scarcely had this occurred, however, than it was followed by a marked change in the life of the National Church. The prohibition of the preaching of the gospel being withdrawn, it soon revived on all sides, while liberty of worship, hitherto existing only in the habits and manners of the people, found its way into the statute book.

From that time, too, my father was no longer summoned to repel attacks directed against him, more or less openly, by the national clergy. The few publications of this kind which he continued to issue became mixed up with writings of a generally controversial nature, or, at all events, are impressed with the special and occasionally personal character of the circumstances which give rise to them.*

---

* We may quote here, in illustration of the above remarks, the following publications: In 1845, "Sectaries Discharging Pastoral Functions," "A Unitarian Pastor of Geneva," and "Christians, Beware of Arianism," directed against a production of the pastor Othamare. In 1846, "The Essential Lacking," on the occasion of conferences held at the time by "orthodox" pastors of the National Church ; and, in 1847, "Protest of an Old French Refugee against the Sophisms of a Socinian Work," called forth by a book, entitled, "Doctrine of Sacrifices, in their relation to Christ."

For the rest, not to mention a volume of sermons published in 1833,* he had also issued, in March 1835, his "Mistake of Christians, with regard to Assurance of Salvation," and a little narrative work, entitled, "Manasseh;" in May appeared the first edition of his "Speaking Vignettes," got up in little stanzas for children; in December, "The Baptized Family," already referred to; and, lastly, a metrical version of the Psalms, on which it is necessary to say a few words. †

It will be remembered, probably, that in 1824 he had issued, under the title of "A mere Essay," a first instalment of this work, containing the first fifty psalms with the music. The universal success of his hymns, however, prevented attention being directed to this new issue. The one hundred and fifty psalms, published in 1835, attracted even less notice. In short, after having aimed at rendering the thoughts of the Psalms in strictly evangelical language, he decided, in the end, on following the advice of some friends, who, out of respect for the literal authority of the Scriptures, urged him to confine himself strictly to the very words of the Old Testament. What inclines us to believe that, had he adhered to his original scheme, his versions would have been more popular, is the fact that several of those which he wrote in 1824 became generally known, and are sung up to the present moment. He

---

* "Six Sermons delivered in the Chapel of Witness," also published separately under the titles, "The Love of the Spirit;" "The Unbeliever Perishing through his own Fault alone;" "Sanctification Inseparable from Salvation;" "Good Seed Sown in Good Ground;" "The True Treasure;" "The Supper of the Lord is Truth and Life."

† "Songs of Israel; or, The Psalms, Hymns, and Canticles of the Bible, versified and set to music."

reverted himself to his primary idea in the selection he made of some of the psalms for the latest editions of the Songs of Zion, as also, wherever he attempted fresh versions of some of them, employing always New Testament language.

Section 2.—Malan testifying to the truth in his own house, and to strangers who visited him.

Before noticing the labours to which my father devoted himself from 1837, in the matter of the Roman controversy, it would be desirable to pause in what might prove to be but a mere nominal list of publications, for the sake of glancing at his private ministry, if I may so describe it, in his own household.

These, indeed, were the years of his vigour and maturity. The attacks of the Genevese clergy had ceased. The fierce and brutal opposition of the lower orders had begun to subside; the recollection of the trying disputes with the extreme dissenters before 1829 had worn away. He was in the prime of life, and a missionary career, for which he felt himself peculiarly adapted, opened widely before him.* At Geneva, while he followed an independent course, and held aloof, in this respect, from his brethren, his life was energetic and fully occupied. His house was visited by numerous strangers,† his children were nearly all at home

---

* In the spring of 1836 he made his first great missionary expedition to the south of France.

† There might be seen Darby, Tholuck (who stayed some time at Pré-Béni), Kirk, or Cheever of New York, with men like Count Zaremba, the Polish missionary, or Scélatz, the Hungarian. In connection with the last named, I remember that one day the conversation at table was to be conducted in Latin, as the only language common to all.

at this time, his whole existence was bright, prosperous, and full of force.

I cannot refrain from inserting here the notice from the pen of Dr Ostertag, to which I have already adverted. While it records the testimony of a well-known and highly-esteemed man, it is, moreover, the witness of one who was wholly apart from the prejudices and partialities of Geneva; more than this, of one who, as we shall see, would have differed from my father on those very points to which he attached the greatest importance. Presenting, as it does, various traits of the personal and family life of the subject of this memoir, this circumstance alone would warrant me in submitting it to my readers. I only regret that a translation, necessarily abridged, must fail in reproducing the glowing tone and graceful style which mark the original. It may be as well to add that I have omitted (only, however, when they occur in eulogistic expressions) a few superlatives, for which the German is better adapted than the French.

He commences his description by telling us that when he arrived at Geneva, (he was then a candidate in theology), " his first proceeding was to visit Malan," and that he found in him " a man of God who had already exercised a conspicuous influence over his own inner life."

" His house was outside the town, in a pretty large garden, at the bottom of which might be seen the chapel—a simple but suitable building. When I came inside the enclosure, I was told that the evening service was then going on. After listening under the windows till it was over, I saw the venerable man come out in company with a stranger from Scotland. He greeted me in the most affectionate manner with that grace and dignity which characterised him.

"The first impression produced in my mind by seeing Malan was that of a noble and imposing personage. His figure was a little above the average height ; his frame compact and vigorous ; while his attitude had about it a semi-military air not the less simple and natural. There was nothing in him studied or affected. His broad shoulders supported a magnificent head ; his forehead was expanded and lofty, suggesting the idea of power ; his eyes sparkled with wit and fire, while at the same time his affectionate expression captivated you on the spot, and held you in chains. His finely carved mouth betrayed an iron will and a thorough benevolence, while it indicated at the same time that special gracefulness which stamps the orator. His luxuriant hair, already white (he was then about fifty years old), flowed down to his shoulders. For the rest, his black dress, straight collar, and white cravat, at once marked the clergyman.

"After greeting me as an old acquaintance, he conducted me to a room which opened into the garden, where he introduced me to his wife and to some of his daughters. She, with her distinguished, yet simple air, recalled to me the picture of a mother of a family in a German household.

"'And what brings you here ?' he asked, as soon as we were seated. When I had told him that I had come to pay a visit to Geneva, he interrupted me by asking, 'Where are you lodging ?' 'Come,' he added, 'when I had named the hotel, 'have your things brought here, and make yourself comfortable under my roof.' I was afraid of being in the way, partly because Malan was not equally admired by all those whom I purposed visiting; but even more, because, in my youth and inexperience, I dreaded his superior powers, and that sort of evangelical fanaticism with which he endeavoured invariably to bring others over to the exaggerated rigour of his Calvinism. Guessing my thoughts apparently from my silence, he said, ' Don't be afraid to come; you are perfectly free with us; go and settle your affairs, and be back to tea.' This decided me, and many a time since have I thanked God for my decision."

When Ostertag came in the evening to stay with his host, he found there, amongst others, the Rev. —— Bennett, well known for his voyage round the world with his friend Tyermann, to visit the different stations of evangelical missions. "To me," he says, "the evening was full of interest and instruction. It may be generally remarked that Malan's hospitable roof was a rendezvous for people from every country, and that never a week passed without strangers of every kind being gathered beneath it. To these he devoted himself with an entire oblivion of self; and as he was not only a man fitted for society, but one also who knew how to bring out of his treasures things new and old, the conversation at once became, if not thoroughly serious, at least invariably instructive. When he invited his visitors to tea, as he often did, he took his place in the centre of the large table, his guests being arranged on either side, or opposite to him, and his numerous family to the right or left, in such a way as that he might take in all at a glance. A look sufficed to keep his children in order, or to admonish them of any carelessness or omission. The style of the repast was a mixture of Genevese and English customs.

" There were no brighter seasons in his domestic life than the periods of family worship—these were precious hours of blessing and revival. It is needless to say that all who were in the house were present, guests and servants included. One of the children brought a round table,* which was drawn forward, with the family Bible and a book of Malan's hymns upon it, and placed before the chair to be occupied by the head of the family. His eldest daughter took her place at the piano, whilst the rest of us were arranged in a circle with our Bibles in our hands.

" He commenced with a very short prayer, which he offered sitting. Then he gave out a hymn, which those present sung, generally from memory. He next read, with great solemnity, a chapter of the Bible, putting such expression into the words as was often an exposition in itself. Then he spoke for about a quarter of an hour on what he had read, generally with special unction, and always taking care to apply it to the individual needs of those he was addressing. Last came the prayer, when all knelt; it was full of the praise of God, and of thanksgiving for the great work of salvation. He was in the habit, moreover, in his concluding prayer, of commending to the Lord, great and small, individuals and communities, the Church of Christ, her internal quickening, and her extension through the world. His native country, Switzerland and Geneva,

---

* I possess that round table still. My father made it himself, for my mother, as an offering on her wedding-day, with several other specimens of his workmanship. In those days (as my mother has often told me) his position was very straitened, while he was not the man to offer a present of which he could not have defrayed the expense out of his own resources. Throughout his whole life my father scrupulously avoided debt. Both he and my mother knew how to content themselves with little.

the city he so dearly loved, his little church, with its especial needs, the members of his household, whether as regarded their interests or their pleasures, with the circumstances of their daily life. He made special reference also to his guests, following the calling of each, the state of his soul, his projects and personal position. All these requests were laid before the Father of mercies in the name of the Lord Jesus, with such confidence and intimacy of communion, that in rising from a prayer like that one felt refreshed and strengthened.

"I now understood the source of that sweet temper, always the same, that freshness of mind which distinguished this noble father of the household. I could account for that cordial attachment and mutual kindliness which reigned among his children; I discovered the secret of that cheerfulness and radiance which produced so favourable an impression on every guest privileged to visit there.

"I soon discovered, too, that the spirit of prayer pervaded the whole family life. I could see that, whenever any of his children or of the members of his family happened to be anxious or troubled by anything whatever, this true head of the household either urged him affectionately to seek God in prayer, assuring him that he himself would do so for him at the same time, or else took him aside and prayed with him, after a few words of earnest private converse."

What Ostertag says on this point recalls to my mind powerfully reminiscences of childhood, too early effaced by the events of after years. My father was most thoroughly a man of prayer. He was often supplicating for himself; and, as for his intercourse with others, he was in the habit,

as far as possible, of leaving no one with whom he felt himself in communion without praying with him. Never did
he set out from home ; never did he see any of us, or even
a friend, set out ; without assembling all the household, to
commend to the Supreme Head those who, however they
might be separated from one another, were still one under
His eye. So, too, the first thing he did on his return from
a journey, after he had embraced us all round, was to return
thanks to God for the protection he had vouchsafed to him
and us, and for His mercy in reuniting us. Never did he
sit down to table, were it only to take a basin of broth,
without first bending his head a few moments to return
thanks, whether he were in his room, or among his family,
or at a table d'hôte surrounded by strangers. It was in
this necessity which lay upon him to ask God's help in
everything, that he illustrated his view of the principle,
"all things of God," his dogmatic expression of which has
pained so many people. "We must go to God at once,"
he used to say to us, "and not wait till we have exhausted
all other means. Before deciding on, or undertaking anything, whatever it be, we should never forget to ask counsel
of the Lord."

After remarking that the Sunday services failed to make
the impression upon him that he expected, either because
the chapel was so thinly attended, or because he recognised
in my father's words evident allusions to conversations they
had had together, Ostertag goes on to say, "I can nevertheless testify, with joy and gratitude, that his ministrations were always animated by a spirit of true charity, and
that they never produced in my mind an unfavourable
impression against that excellent man. I found in them

invariably such unction, solemnity, and warmth of heart, that I never went empty away.

"In his house, the Sunday was observed with all the rigour of Scotch Protestantism. To me this was a source of trouble and discomfort. Everybody knows that, on this point, the Lutheran Church, in its teaching and tendency, differs from the Reformed Church of Scotland. Beyond all doubt, one cannot help detecting in the Scotch fashion a return to those fables and weak rudiments of the world from which Christ has redeemed us (a return which may not be regarded as a matter of indifference). And yet this zeal seemed worthy of all praise, when we compare it with the habitual profanation of the Sabbath in our towns and villages, as much among Protestants as among Romanists. One fact remains, that God has blessed the seventh day, that He set it apart for all mankind (long before the Levitical law, long time even before there was a people of God), that men may relinquish labour for rest, disturbance for repose, distraction for reflection; in a word, the world for Himself. But to return to Malan.

"One Sunday I heard his voice from the garden into which my window looked, calling to me, and asking, 'What are you about just now?' 'I am writing some letters,' I replied through the window. 'Come into the garden then,' was his reply, 'we have important things to talk about.' I lost no time in complying with his request; and we were no sooner seated on a bench than he said, 'Do you know that you are breaking God's commandment by doing work on the Sabbath?' 'By doing work on the Sabbath?' I replied in amazement. 'Do you know the fourth commandment?' (the third, according to the Lutherans).

'Certainly," I answered; 'but how have I broken it?'
'Thou shalt do no manner of work on the Sabbath-day,'
he rejoined, in solemn tones; repeating, while he laid emphasis on the words, 'no manner of work. 'To write
letters is to do work, is it not? Is this work connected
with God, to Whom the day belongs? Have you no spare
time for this during the week? Have you nothing to-day
to put in order with your God, with reference to the past?
Nothing to say to Him? Nothing to ask of Him for the
days which are before you? My friend, you keep back
from God the honour which belongs to Him, and you wrong
your own soul.'

"I felt the force of his words, though I made no reply;
while, at the same time, many counter arguments occurred
to me. 'Undoubtedly you will have many objections to
make to what I say,' he continued; 'but listen to me
nothwithstanding. No true Christian has, as yet, ventured to declare that the sixth commandment, "Thou
shalt do no murder," is obsolete, and has ceased to be
a rule for Christian practice. On the contrary, in the
economy of the new covenant, this commandment is so
enforced as to be made to extend even to uncharitable
words, even to thoughts of ill-will. It is the same with
the seventh and eighth, with all the commandments of
the two tables. Should, then, the fourth be held to be
abolished? Ought we not rather to allow of this commandment what is true of the others, that it, too, is even
more strenuously enforced under the new dispensation.
My friend, turn over this sentence in your mind, honestly,
seriously, 'Thou shalt do no manner of work.'

"I was about to reply, when he interrupted me with,

Y

' Hear me out. There is my house ! There we keep the fourth commandment in an earnest way. My youngest children realise the obligation of desisting from the six days' work, and of living on the Sabbath-day only for God and their Saviour. Now notice the result of that obedience among us. God has blessed the seventh day, and that blessing is renewed to the present moment in all its power. God has blessed my house. You may trace that blessing in our domestic happiness, in the peace which reigns among us. You may see it in my children. Yes, my friend, we must be in earnest in dealing with the commandments of God. Then He, for His part, will be found true to the fulfilment of His promises.' "

After replying that, notwithstanding the serious and convincing arguments he had listened to, he still was unable to admit that the Christian Sunday was the Jewish Sabbath, Ostertag tells us that he assured my father that he preferred his rigour to the opposite tendency, and that, at all events, he would cheerfully bind himself, so long as he remained under his roof, to order his own conduct by the rules of the house.

"Malan," he adds, "was not satisfied. He interrupted me constantly, and endeavoured with much persuasiveness, and often with marvellous skill of sophistry, to overturn my arguments.* Obliged, however, to be satisfied

---

* I imagine that this word *sophistry* does not bear in the German the unfavourable sense that is attached to it in our language. I believe it applies there to a man who reasons falsely, and does not necessarily convey, as it does with us, the idea of a dishonest man—that is, of one who seeks to take advantage of, and to trip up his opponent. I would add, moreover, with reference to my father's Sabbatarian views, that allowance must be made for the impression produced on a young stranger by the way in which they were presented. As a matter of fact, the Sunday in the Pré-Béni was

with the promise I had made to him, he concluded by saying that he trusted that 'during that time I should be converted.' That hope was not realised, certainly, in the sense in which he expressed it; and yet, in that matter also, I carried away with me from his house a great and lasting blessing. Since then I have sought, with God's help, not only to cherish more earnest views as to the thorough sanctification of the Lord's day, but also, in course of time, to seek, as far as I could, to introduce the blessing into my own house."

Ostertag saw, at this time, an example of what he calls, in my father, "an Old Testament tendency," in the manner in which he, in common with all Reformed Churches, interpreted the commandment against images, on the authority of which he repudiated every species of representation of the Deity, as well as the crucifix, as an object of worship.*

Meanwhile Ostertag went to Lausanne, on the occasion

very far from being a Jewish Sabbath. For my own part, while I entirely agree with Dr Ostertag on this point, I can only recall with regret, on many grounds, that these Sabbaths of my youth are passed.

* It was not altogether as an image that my father objected to the crucifix, which, as every one knows, is adopted by the Lutherans. He himself placed in the hands of his younger children illustrated Bibles, from which he only banished representations of the eternal Father and of the devil. He rejected the crucifix chiefly as being a false resemblance. See his tract, "Why am I a Protestant?" p. 20.

In a letter to one of his children, in 1850, I find the following :—"For my part I do not like to see representations of the Lord Jesus. He appeared to John, and the apostle 'fell at His feet.' He is never represented as He is, not even as He was ; for He is God, and God cannot be represented. Let His marvellous meekness and kindness be ever more and more demonstrated to our souls ; but let it be through the Holy Spirit, in the heart, and not by our own imagination, and the work of man's hand." This shows us that my father never supposed, for a moment, that the Holy Spirit could ever avail Himself of the faculty of imagination.

of the religious anniversaries, and my father joined him there, later on.

" On the 4th of August a large company of us returned to Geneva, in the steamboat which, thanks to the glorious weather, was full of strangers of every kind." While Ostertag, in conversation with his friends, enjoyed the liberty which succeeds all mental strain, he perceived, he tells us, " that Malan had just seated himself by the side of a foreign lady, and had, in the most courteous manner, exchanged a few words with her. The conversation became increasingly animated. In her features there appeared, by turns, the expression of surprise or the smile of contempt. Her face reddened and paled alternately. Evidently she was a prey to the conflict of most opposite sentiments. Frequently might she have been seen speaking and gesticulating in great excitement ; it might have been conjectured that she was seeking to defend herself against unjust attacks. Then she set herself to listen attentively, silently, with her eyes bent down. By degrees these intervals of silence became more frequent. At length she gave up speaking entirely. Malan, on the other hand, appeared to grow increasingly serious and earnest, and more and more confident of success. Tears were soon seen coursing one another down her cheeks, while she applied her handkerchief to her eyes.

" For a long time," writes Ostertag, " I watched this scene from a distance, with the liveliest interest ; for it was plain that Malan was seeking to bring that soul to Christ. Had I not already heard him spoken of as one, not only filled with the most ardent zeal to gain hearts over to the kingdom of God, but as one possessing, moreover, an extraordinary aptitude for winning souls? Many and many a glorious instance could I recall, going far back, of what God had thus wrought by his means. I had heard how, during his walks, in the diligence, at hotels, and among people of every class, he had been enabled at times to fix in the heart, by a single word, an arrow incapable of being extricated. And now, for the first time, I saw him at this work. Whilst the rest of us were scattered about doing nothing — looking about us, and chatting on subjects more or less trifling—he was preaching the gospel with indefatigable zeal and ardent love.

" About half an hour afterwards, as I was standing by a young German of my acquaintance, Malan passed close to me, and whispered in my ear, 'Another soul gained over to the Lord.' A quarter of an hour afterwards, while I was still in the same place, and just as a young theologian from the north of Germany joined us, he passed me again, touched me on the shoulder, and said, in a low voice, 'Preach the gospel—sound the trumpet.' Through the whole of my journey after that—indeed, through all my after life—that sentence has resounded in my ears, and never did I faithfully obey it and repent of doing so."

He then mentions how he received a proposal that was made to him to become a tutor in a distinguished English family. " According to my custom," he says, " I reserved my decision till I had consulted my family, and got at the opinion of experienced men. Moreover, as soon as I had written home, I went to find Malan.

" After quietly listening to my tidings, he asked me what decision I had come to myself? 'To accept the invitation,' I replied, 'if my family approve.' He shook his head, and began to set forth with vehemence and increasing warmth the inconveniences of such a position; pressing me, at the same time, with an appeal to my conscience, to remember that I was called to preach the Word of God—to proclaim the gospel, and not to become the guardian of a young man of family. 'Go to France,'* he exclaimed, 'to America, to Africa, anywhere you please, provided you preach Jesus. Win souls to the Lord, that is your work. Go, and sound the gospel trumpet!' A little disconcerted at this dispersion of my pleasant dreams, I endeavoured to show him the advantages of the offer I had received. 'Delusion! delusion!' he replied; mercilessly upsetting all my objections."

He next goes on to tell us how in the afternoon of that day he felt himself demolished again, as some of the little ones spoke to him on the same subject; and that too, quite naturally, to the same effect as their father had done; only with the decisiveness and exaggeration of their age.

A few days afterwards, on his return from an excursion in the neighbourhood of Geneva, he decided on taking a professorial chair in the mission house at Bâle. He tells us how my father, to whom he hastened immediately to communicate his intelligence, tried his utmost to dissuade him, while he attacked the Missionary Institute to a degree all but amounting to bitterness, on account of the errors which he thought he had discovered in their religious government.† "I confess that this attack pained

* He had just returned himself from his first missionary journey there.

† Ostertag mentions the charges of Arminianism and Socinianism. As for the first, I remember myself hearing my revered father urge it against

me, for I thought it unjust. I soon recollected, however, that nothing found favour in his eyes,—admirable as he was in every other respect,—that appeared to be in the slightest degree opposed to his favourite doctrine of predestination. So I left the matter there; expressing a firm belief that God would guide me in days to come, as He had done up to that moment."

He then goes on to relate in detail the conversation in which my father sought to win him over to this special doctrine. As we have already had occasion to notice Malan's dogmatism, I shall content myself with a few quotations, and one or two observations of my own.

To commence with the latter. Ostertag frequently asserts that this doctrine was held by every member of the family; and that, " with iron obstinacy." His examples, however, would but serve to prove a most natural circumstance, namely, that we succumbed as children to the only dogmatic influence to which we were exposed, I may venture to say, in my father's public teaching. I mention his public teaching intentionally, for he had too much tact to make his theological dogma the special subject of his private conversations with his children. I think I may safely say that the decided influence he exercised over us was not due to any special opinion which he taught, but rather to his living faith and true piety.

We may now observe how Ostertag sums up his own impressions on this head. "It cannot be denied that on

---

Bâle; especially just at that time. I imagine, however, that the second is due to a misconception. According to my father, Arminianism was the error of a multitude of true and dear Christians, while a Socinian he holds to have no right whatever to the title of Christian.

the one hand the grandeur and the imposing logic of this doctrine is calculated to make a deep impression on any one, while, on the other hand, Scripture, in a certain sense, supports it."

He tells us next how my father commenced a discussion of the subject with him by the abrupt question, "Are you one of the elect?"—how he pressed him not to rest his assurance of salvation on that sandy foundation, for ever shifting and changing, which he denominated our own feelings and sentiments, or, generally speaking, on anything in ourselves. "No," he added, "we must found that assurance on a firm indestructible rock, without us; in a word, on the declaration of God. Faith is to believe what God declares."

"I shall never cease to be grateful to dear Malan for this conversation," he continues, recalling further, how my father was for ever urging him on this subject of particular election, and the death of Christ for the elect only. On that point Ostertag would have had plenty to say, but "whenever Malan grew animated in a discussion, he gave his companion no chance of speaking. No sooner did he hear the commencement of an objection than he would cut it short at times with some such an exclamation as I heard from him at the time. 'Oh those German heads!' or else by saying, 'I understand what you are going to say.' On the occasion referred to, after unfolding his views with much fervour and eloquence, he finished with the triumphant exclamation, 'You see the dialectics of Geneva!'"

A few days afterwards, a fresh discussion was started by my father on final perseverance. Ostertag maintained that the believer might fall from grace, quoting, in support of

his argument, the well-known texts of Scripture. My
father, after explaining the passages from his point of view,
added ;—suddenly exchanging scriptural exegesis for dialectics :—"Answer this question, 'Is it we who preserve
our salvation, or is it our salvation that preserves us ?' I
simply replied that we were certainly unable to take care
of it, but that we might nevertheless lose it through our
own fault. Malan rose with the air of one about to deal a
decisive blow. 'Come into my room,' he said. There,
opening a large Bible, he showed me numerous passages,
on the authority of which he sought with amazing force to
prove his view, and ended by asking, 'Are you convinced
now ? Are you willing to give God the glory?'* 'I
should not be telling the truth,' I replied, 'if I said I was
convinced.'" "Let us pray," said my father; and, rising
from his chair, he knelt down and asked God, in fervent
prayer, not that He would vouchsafe general enlightenment
to him who knelt beside him, but that he would convince
him on this one point. "I do not think," says Ostertag,
"that any prayer ever gave me so much pain. Exhausted
with fatigue, with tears in my eyes, tears which he interpreted very differently from the truth, I left his study and
sought to be alone."

* Here we see the essence of my father's thought, and the only interpretation of a persistency which otherwise would have been painful to recall.
Moreover, had not the scene which Ostertag describes been recorded at the
moment, and on this ground had a claim to insertion here, and had I not
known that I was writing for readers capable of appreciating the sacred
rights of religious opinion, so fully recognised by my father when he established this special dogma on such high ground, I should not have referred
to the occurrence. Such readers will be well pleased, on other accounts, to
have had an opportunity of studying a scene, so full of interest from the
way in which it illustrates the characters of the two excellent men who
figure in it.

As we read this, we recall what another very distinguished man wrote, after a conversation with my father in 1841 (the Rev. F. W. Robertson): "I love old Malan from the bottom of my soul, but I hate arguing with him, even though the discussion remained that of Christian brethren."*

Shortly afterwards, Ostertag, who had retired for the purpose of looking into a German work on Calvinistic theology, which my excellent mother had handed him, at my father's suggestion doubtless, heard his voice calling to him. "He invited me into his study, against the wall of which there was a chamber-organ. Placing a music-book on the desk, containing a beautiful hymn tune, with the text in French, he asked me to play it. I complied at once, while, with a superb tenor voice, in clear, full tones, he sang the three verses of the hymn. Both words and music were quite new to me. It was a hymn on the communion of saints, the sweetness of brotherly love, and the blessed hope that a day will come when all the children of God will come into the unity of a perfect knowledge in Christ, and will unite in praising the Lamb. I was delighted, and asked him as I finished if he would let me copy the words and music. 'That copy is for you,' he replied, with a pleased expression in his bright face, the result of a heartfelt kindness which has produced the desired gratification. 'It is my good-bye to you,' he added, and I saw then that the sheet had a sort of dedication to me. Not a very important incident this, yet it gives us a near view of the admirable life of love which characterised that excellent man."

* "F. W. Robertson's Life and Letters." London : Smith, Elder, and Co. P. 65.

After having narrated to us, in the style already quoted, the communion on the last Sunday he spent under our roof, Ostertag finishes his description of that day by remarking that "the salutary sacredness which marked it throughout was present even at the evening meal, when the English minister was present, who had assisted at the celebration. During tea a box was handed round, with passages of Scripture.* Each read the text he had drawn, and the head of the family took occasion to say a few words of exhortation or application, as the case might be. Before we separated the English minister offered a prayer of singular power and unction.

"It was with tears in my eyes that I took leave of that excellent family, having to start the next morning at five o'clock.

"As for Malan himself, he took me by the arm and led me into the garden; there he displayed the fulness of his affectionate spirit. In a few clear words he brought in review the days we had spent together, and added excellent advice with reference to my contemplated journey to France, with kindliest messages for an entire list of friends

---

* The contents of the Sunday box were applied to different charitable purposes. For a long time they were given to my mother's school. For some years the collection was devoted to the redemption of young girls enslaved at Cairo, a work to which one of our English friends at that time—an English lady—was devoting herself. One of these slaves, after having been instructed in the Christian faith, received at her baptism our family name. Afterwards, my father sent the proceeds to the evangelising work in Belgium. As for the texts of Scripture, one of us usually wrote them on the Sunday afternoon. At the present time, some pious families having adopted this custom for the Sunday evenings, such texts may be had, printed for the purpose. My father instituted it with the view of fixing the conversation, at a table so numerously surrounded as ours, on subjects in harmony with the religious character which he wished to keep up to the very close of the day of rest.

and acquaintances. It was then nearly midnight, and I wished to say good-bye. ' No, no,' he replied, ' to-morrow I shall see you to the coach-office.'

"The next morning he was at my door at four o'clock. ' Is your luggage ready ?' was his first question, after giving me a hearty good morning. He assisted a servant to carry it down, and accompanied it himself to the garden gate. Not till he had done this did he come to escort me. The town was still wrapped in silence, not a sound was to be heard in the streets through which we passed. On the edge of the horizon, a streak of sky, faintly lit up, heralded the approaching dawn. ' What will it be,' said Malan, ' when the day of Christ appears, and He shall suddenly return to awaken every sleeper in the twinkling of an eye ?'

" Conversing thus, we reached the place from which my journey was to commence. Coach and horses were ready. Malan embraced me, invoking upon me the blessing of God. The next moment the diligence was bowling on its way.

" I have never seen him since. He has gone to his rest, but his memory remains—a blessing that can never be effaced—with me and many others."

May he who wrote these touching lines receive a blessing himself, for the reminiscences they have called up in Malan's family ! As I transcribe them, I seem myself to behold and to listen anew to him whose pure and exalted image they so vividly recall !*

* Further recollections of visits to my father from men of note may be met with in " Notices of the State of Religion in Geneva and Belgium," by Dr Heugh of Glasgow, 1844 ; and in the work of Dr Cheever of New York, " Wanderings of a Pilgrim under the Shadow of Mont Blanc," published in 1845. Full of interest as these two volumes are—the former especially

*Section 3.—Roman Controversy from 1837, and literary
activity to the close of his life.*

It was in the year 1837 that my father appeared publicly on the stage as the avowed opponent of the pretensions of Romanism.* Up to that time he had always
purposely avoided a controversy which, in his judgment,
could only lead to the stirring up of passions. Convinced,
as he loved to assert, " that darkness never retreats before
the blows of the cudgel," he was satisfied with testifying
—whatever the error with which he had to contend—both
in the presence of Catholicism and of Protestant unbelief,
to that divine and living Christianity which remained with
him a celestial and eternal fact, and which consequently
was anterior, and essentially superior, to what deserved
only the name of Catholicism or Protestantism. Thus we
found him, in 1820, declining to exact from sundry Catholics a formal abjuration of their errors as soon as he discovered them to be true Christians. These principles he
urged in 1823 in his " Protestant truly Catholic," while he
did not scruple to avow them openly before his Catholic
hearers in Perpignan in 1826.

I discover them, moreover, in the letters in which he
exhorts priests who applied to him, with the view of embracing Protestantism, " to become not the mere proselytes

being rich in detailed information with regard to the religious world of that
time—they do but add to what has just been quoted, the testimony of the
personal feelings of their authors, who were both of them among the number of my father's friends.

 * He refused, in common with English evangelicals, the title of " Catholic" to the Roman Church. " Nothing is less catholic or universal than the
Latin Sect—the schism which Rome has made with the orthodox Church
throughout the world."—*The Future of Romanism in Geneva*, p. 4.

of a man or a party, but the disciples of the Saviour Himself."

Nor did he meditate entering the arena of direct controversy till he found himself personally challenged. And even then his controversy consisted supremely in the application to such special points at issue as presented themselves in those grand principles of his faith in the sovereignty of God.

At first the representatives of Catholicism had taken, with reference to the revival, a position tending directly to compromise its partisans in the eyes of the old official Protestantism of Geneva. Publications such as the "True History of the Mômiers," or articles of the same kind in the ultramontane journals of the period;—while they held up the evangelicals as the sole representatives of the traditional orthodoxy of Christianity, and the victims at the same time of most unrighteous measures on the part of the national Protestant clergy;—could not but result in making the old Genevese hate a party which they thus beheld defended by the most inexorable foes of their liberties.

On the other hand, those whose defence was thus espoused by the Catholics were the first to discover the gulf which separated evangelical liberty from that principle of authority which their new allies upheld. They had no sympathy with men whose zeal, in their judgment, was the mere issue of calculation and a party manœuvre. These sentiments were all the more avowed and natural as just as that period, (immediately before 1835), Catholicism had assumed in Geneva, under the energetic direction of the Curé Vuarin, a position as hostile as possible to everything held dear, as much by the friends of liberty in

Geneva as by those of the pure gospel. As for my father
—to confine our attention to him—he did not scruple,
out of that very frankness with which he professed his
faith, to encounter the priests with an opposition which, as
may be remembered, all but endangered his personal liberty.

Of course, side by side with the fanatic ultramon-
tanes, there was, especially at that time, a large number of liberal Catholics, and even of priests, who, up
to a certain point, showed themselves friendly to evangelical doctrine. It is notorious with what intensity
this movement of faith and liberty displayed itself definitely in the Catholic Church of South Germany. My
father soon found himself in communication with kindred
spirits even beyond the German frontiers. He refers
often, in his missionary narratives, to his interviews with
priests, in whom the spirit of evangelical Christianity
revealed itself, through, and in spite of, the ecclesiastical
traditions of the Latins.*

* Many of these facts will be found related in the extracts I have already
given from his missionary journal of 1836, at Perpignan, as well as in the
missionary narratives he printed. He relates some also in his, " Shall I
be Able to Enter ?" in his Vendelin, p. 114 ; in his publication, entitled,
" Is the Religion of my Fathers the Religion of the Fathers?" I append
the following extract from a letter addressed to him in 1837 by a French
priest, as giving a very fair idea of the position assumed by the priests above
referred to, towards the evangelical revival : " I have read with great
interest your ' Evangelical Sowings,' and your sermons preached in the
Chapel of Witness. I rejoice to hear you speak of our Lord Jesus Christ
so differently from many Protestants, whose works have come within my
reach. They are thorough Socinians. To them the Saviour is no more
than a man, though they do not openly avow this. Moreover, the impiety
which, since the time of Louis XV., has waged so bitter a war against
Christianity, has never had to encounter their opposition. May you reach
the goal to which Providence is conducting the Methodists, though they
may not perceive it ! May you complete "our work of restoration, and
bring into the bosom of the Catholic Church the Christians who are following you ! "

He no sooner found himself, however, face to face
with men of this stamp, than they had either to throw
up whatever he demonstrated to be a contradiction
of the faith which they professed with him, or else to
submit to his open charge of inconsistency. More than
once he had the satisfaction of seeing some one of them
adopt the former course; but, when this was not so, he
was prepared to put himself in their place, and estimate
the full force of the considerations which held them back.*
At all events, he never advocated what is generally termed
a change of religion. With him the important point was
to impress upon all he met, whoever they might be, what
he had experienced in his own soul as the glorious salvation of the sovereign grace of God.

He was convinced that when once that light penetrated
within, it dispelled the clouds of a credulous and slavish
superstition, as well as the deadly chill of a reasoning and
negative unbelief.

"I am far from condemning either books or conversations appertaining to what is properly called controversy."
Thus he writes himself, in 1850, to a friend who was at the
head of a missionary work among the Catholics. "But I
consider them as being very secondary, and as being
designed not for conversion, but for instruction. I believe
that, as regard souls who are still ignorant of the truth of
salvation, whether Romanists or so-called Protestants, we
shall be more useful to them, the more simply we show
them the fulness of the sacrifice of the Son of God. Con-

---

* An unbelieving young Romanist once said to him, " Must I change my
religion, then?" "Sir," he replied, "it is necessary, first of all, that you
should have one to change."—*Quatre-vingt Jours*, &c., p. 312.

troversy may come after that, just as you would prepare a tree after felling it; but, in order to have it laid low, we must first seize the axe of grace. Its edge is powerful." It may be said of him that he did not so much ask his partners in discussion whence they came, as whither they were going.

Meanwhile, if my father supposed that he could thus demonstrate the weakness of Roman Catholicism by resting on a simple faith in salvation by grace, there were Catholic priests who saw, in the doctrine of the divinity of Christ, of which he was rightly styled the champion in Geneva, a truth which ought, unquestionably, to have won him over to the Roman Church. Towards the close of 1837 an Abbé de Baudry, formerly a professor of theology in the seminaries of Lyons and Paris, published a work, in which he declared that the essential principles of Protestantism were subversive of all real authority.* Thence he appealed for confirmation of his doctrine to the history of the introduction of the Reformation into Geneva itself. A few days after the appearance of this pamphlet, my father published a brief reply, entitled, "The Divine Rights of Protestantism."

After distinguishing between evangelical Protestantism, and the Arianism or Socinianism, which had usurped its name in Geneva, he passes rapidly in review the history of that protest which is, from the nature of the case, the essential character of the position of the Church of God outside, and opposed to the world; shows what antiquity

---

* "A Defence of the Sacred Rights of the Episcopate, and of the Holy See," &c. This brochure was not specially levelled against Protestantism, which it only referred to casually. It had been called forth by a discussion among the priests themselves, and concerned the Church of Rome alone.

is, the promise of God,—what is "apostolicity," the doctrine of a free salvation. Such is that eternal Protestantism, which is the religion of the Bible, and the faith of the children of God.

Public opinion, among the Protestants of Geneva, received with acclaim so firm and courteous a vindication of the right divine of its traditional beliefs. As for M. de Baudry, he had recourse to party personalities. In a few pages, in which he adopted an unctuous tone of excessive mildness, he took care to insinuate that my father's opposition to his views was, at bottom, merely an expression of his ill-will against his old enemies, the clergy of Geneva. Such a course, however, as my father took care to show in his reply, could only bring him nearer to that Church "which Rome has had reason to fear, and which she may fear yet more hereafter."* "No, sir," he writes, I do not think that the holy Church of God consists only of those whom you style Methodists, since I believe that every soul that worships the Lord Jesus, in sincerity, is a member of that Church which the Saviour has purchased. I consider the Church of God in Geneva as composed of all those who, whether dissenters, semi-dissenters, or state-church men, believe in the eternal Godhead of the Son, and in free salvation." Then, having replied, by an appeal to facts themselves, to the insinuations and accusations of his adversary, "Greater things," he says, in conclusion, "require our meditations and our watching. The invisible world is too near for us to employ our time in quarrels and disputes. Our contemporaries, moreover,

---

* "Réclamations Nécessaires, presented to the Abbé de Baudry, in reply to his former observations."

are far from requiring us to form parties among them. The world, alas, is too divided already; so I withdraw from the discussion altogether."

But in this he was mistaken. The abbé, seizing upon my father's declaration with reference to the divinity of Jesus Christ, published a few days afterwards a small pamphlet, entitled "Dr Malan, Protestant minister of Geneva, led by the force of his own opinion to embrace the Catholic religion."

Of course my father was bound to explain, and he was not backward in doing so. Setting to work with that ardour and assiduity of which he had already given such ample proofs, he issued, in less than a month after the publication of the last pamphlet, a volume of two hundred and fifty pages, entitled, " Can I Enter the Romish Church so long as I Believe the Whole of the Bible ?" a question submitted to the conscience of every Christian reader, with a motto taken from the 119th Psalm, "Thou art my portion, O Lord, I have said that I would keep Thy words."* This work, which has been often reprinted, deserves a passing notice here.† What strikes us, at first glance, is the basis of its arguments, which is purely and simply the Bible itself, as presented to the conscience of every Christian reader. So that it is not so much a volume of *Protestant*, as a treatise of *Christian*, controversy. The faith of the Christian, in its expression most simple and most general,

---

* He advertised it in the papers immediately after de Baudry's announcement of his book, with these words :—" In the press, and to be published a fortnight hence."

† M. de Baudry merely replied in a tract of a few pages, called "Final Observations," in which, "in presence of the evidently prejudiced mind of his opponent, he declares his wish to be silent from that time."

forms the ground-work of the entire argument. As for Protestantism, in the special sense of the word, there is no reference to it ; except in so far as the individual conscience of the believer in the grace of the gospel, finds in it the expression of his faith. This faith itself is defined there as that of a man who, because he believes in Jesus Christ, and worships Him, knows that he is justified by faith, has peace with God, possesses *now* life everlasting, and is sealed by the Spirit till the day of redemption.* It is that faith which rests alone on the declarations of the gospel, and which, speaking for himself, he says, "has been for more than twenty years his precious unfailing portion." And now he finds himself driven to the inquiry, whether really, as the question is submitted to him, that faith has been a delusion ; whether he has misunderstood the Bible after all ; whether the Roman creed is actually more in harmony with the infallible utterances of Holy Writ.

With this end he examines the Romish faith under three general heads,—revelation, government, and possession of salvation ; in other words, he examines it in respect of what it affirms of Holy Scripture, of the Church on earth, and of the peace of God and holiness of heart.

On each of these three points, after submitting to the reader, first, the Roman dogma, next, the difference of opinion which the Church presents in its fathers, councils, and popes, he asks whether his own faith, as being based upon the Bible, should not remain the subject of his preference.

Thus he passes in review, first, the authority of Scripture

* "Can I Enter ?" &c., p. 11.

(the Apocrypha, Tradition, the Vulgate, and the Bible in the Vulgar tongue); secondly, the question of unity, antiquity, permanence, catholicity, the hierarchy, and the services of the Church; thirdly, possession of a free salvation, assurance, final perseverance, penance, and purgatory, — all which is submitted to the reader in a glowing, animated style, and with great diversity of handling. After treating the first and second points as a simple exposition of doctrine, he adopts, on arriving at the heading of worship, a narrative and occasionally dramatic style. He relates his personal recollections of his conversations or journeys. Thus "the pilgrimage" is merely a description of a visit he had made in his youth to Einsiedeln; while the deeply interesting episode of the old curé in the chapter on purgatory, is a description of what happened under his personal observation.

Owing to the diversity of its style, the more we read of the book, the more pleasure we experience. Founded on a believer's faith in the Word of God, written with a graceful simplicity, and interspersed with interesting stories; hastily compiled as it was, it reveals none the less, in its numerous pages, evidence of conscientious research and extensive scholarship. Moreover, it was widely circulated, and frequently quoted, and remained not only a monument of my father's industry, but also, in one particular respect, a lucid and complete manual which it was very easy to consult. After several reprints of it had been issued, my father, in a preface to the fourth edition (Brussels, 1854), stated, that He Who makes use of the smallest instrumentalities to accomplish the designs of His grace, had blessed the scriptural truth which the work contained.

Not content with reprinting some extracts from the work in 1840 and in 1843, he frequently took up his pen as new controversies arose. For example, in March 1839 he was the first to accept the challenge which a certain Abbé Espanet had flung out to the Protestant clergy. The Abbé was a Lent preacher in Geneva, whose violent language especially excited the reformed population, inasmuch as it was uttered at the time when Father Ravignan and the Abbé Combalot were holding out Protestant virtues as a pattern to Parisian Catholics.* In 1843, he wrote an answer to a Catholic of Versoix. In 1845, he replied to the attack of the Abbé Angelin, in his publication, "Sectarians and the Primitive Faith." In 1846, he was induced to publish "A Friendly Reply from an Old Soldier of the Gospel," to a paper signed "A Veteran and Good Catholic." In 1851, he addressed his "Réclamations Publiques" to the Abbé Mermilliod; and replied, in 1852, to the "Catholic Annals of Geneva." Lastly, in 1853, he published a fresh edition of his tract, "What Men Call our Prejudices against Popery, is our Heart Belief in the Bible."

It was only most unwillingly, however, that he participated in this paper war, which, as he himself said, too easily diverted the soul from better and eternal things. At the same time, he no less felt "that, if patience and courtesy required him to allow free speech to his adversaries, so long as they confined themselves to personalities, he could not concede the licence when their attacks were directed against the truth of God." †

---

* "The Priest and the Minister ; or, The Reformation as it is: Letter from the Rev. Dr Malan to Two Priests."

† "Our Doctrinal Anarchy," p. 4.

His constant aim, too, was to handle every question in the light of faith in the authority of the Gospel. This was the ground he had already assumed in his work, "Can I Enter?" and again, in his "Questions of a Genevese," in 1844, as well as in his "Manual of a True Protestant," 1845.

The three "Questions of a Genevése, on the Particular Doctrines of the Church of Rome," consist of a re-issue (with a few notes and explanations) of his edition of three English works of reformed controversy, compiled in the seventeenth century. They treat of Protestant rejection of the mass, of Mariolatry (translated from Willet, Synopsis Papismi, 1600), and of the reading of the Bible in the vulgar tongue.

"His object," he says, "is to provoke a sincere discussion, much needed in Geneva." "Its people love the truth," while he seemed to "detect an awakening of attention to these subjects in the Romish parishes of the cantons of Geneva." The following is his explanation of the little success the preaching of the gospel meets with among certain Romanists :—"A species of idealism, a religion of imagination and poetry, or of brilliant, but too indefinite and too confused, conception, engages and arouses the feelings. . . . . A sensuous devotion may captivate souls that hanker after mere emotions. It offers them ready food, and a religion, so to speak, ready made, accommodating itself easily to the exigencies of a contemplative mind, and of an ardent and impassioned heart." *

Far from wishing to copy the Church of Rome by saying that, out of Protestantism, there is no salvation, he declares "that everywhere, where Christ is proclaimed,

* "First Question," p. 113.

salvation is to be had;" and that, " if the Romanist looks with faith to the one sacrifice of the Saviour, by that he abjures papacy, and experiences the benefit of the promise made of God to faith." *

At the close of the third question; " reminding his readers that the writings of actual controversialists, such as Wiseman and Mœhler, are but the repetitions of errors encountered in those very writings of old time to which he is now referring, he addresses his Protestant fellow-citizens especially, with the view of submitting to their attention, in a few glowing words, the true meaning of their old Reformation symbol, ' Post tenebras lux.' "

As for the "Manual of a True Protestant," it is a little catechism of popular controversy, based on the authority of Scripture texts, and designed especially for evangelists and colporteurs. It was translated into English, soon reached a second edition in French, and is in use still.

Engaged in controversy, my father displayed, not merely the believer in the gospel, but the true Protestant and Genevese patriot. No one loved his country more than he did; no one realised more than he, the tie that bound every true Genevese Protestant to the ancient confessors and defenders of the faith.†

---

* " First Question," p. 118.

† " I love my country. I have ever honoured and loved its paternal government. I seek its peace: of this, I and mine have given proofs." (*Réclamations de l'Auteur de la Fête-Dieu, à MM. les Rédacteurs du Fédéral*, published by my father, in connection with an article in that journal, June 13, 1843.) In speaking thus, he alluded doubtless to the way in which, at the commencement of the year, at the time of the riots in February, he had sent one of his sons, whom youth might well have absolved rom such service, to the succour of the government.

"Already, and more than once," he says in the passage, a portion of which is quoted in the note, "I have had to oppose myself, in our dear Geneva, to the scorn, the attacks, the encroachments of Romanism. I am confident that I have done this with as much moderation as truth requires, as well as with the energy which it demands. I have respected persons, while I denounced error or heresy. I am a Genevese, and, as such, I think that same Bible, which has made and ennobled my native city, ought to rule among us, above every superstition and doctrine of men. Geneva must perish if she rejects the Bible. I am a Protestant, and, as such, I think that Romanism, even in its most modified form, is as far removed from evangelical faith as the merits of man from the grace of God. I am, above all, a Christian, and, as such, I think that the eternal salvation of my fellow-countrymen is not to be found in Popery, because it is only in Jesus Christ, God blessed for ever :—Who has perfected a salvation for His Church, through faith in His blood, without the aid of human merit. For this reason, as a Genevese who fears God, I am bound, with all my might, to uphold, in our native land, the authority of the Bible, the purity of our holy faith, and the dignity of the true cross of Christ. Many will blame me, some will be offended, others will despise me ; but who ever defended truth, whether in religion, politics, or science, without encountering opposition ? And what is there to be wondered at, if he, who maintains the cause of the gospel, is set at nought by the world ?"

Nowhere do these sentiments of a Christian patriot shine out more brightly than in two publications issued by him

in 1842, " Rome and Geneva, or, The Impossible;" and " The
Future of Romanism in Geneva." The last (a pamphlet of
fifty pages) deserves particular notice. After having
recalled in it the vital principle of the Reformation itself;
after having shown the real action of this principle in certain of the conversions to Protestantism of which it was
the instrument; he argues thence that Romanism, which is
Trinitarian in its character, will never recede except as the
Bible advances, nor yield its ground except to this principle
of grace, " Man cannot earn salvation." Then addressing
himself directly to the Protestant families of the Republic
of Geneva, " as one shuddering at the bare idea of a Catholic
Geneva," he exhibits Rome " as a famished vulture, hastening to trample the reformed city under its talons;" and
exhorts them " to repel that indifference and infidelity
which alone could hand them over to its powers." " As in
1835, faith in Jesus and in salvation by grace liberated
Geneva from the snares and fetters of Rome," he cries,
"let Geneva, once more regenerated and blessed from on
high, say with confidence to her Roman parishes, ' I am
Christian : will you join me ?'"

It is evident from what point of view my father regarded
the question. Representing the ancient Genevese of the sixteenth century—or, to speak more exactly, the last representative in modern Geneva of those French emigrants who
had succeeded, after many attempts, in rekindling and maintaining in that city the life and decision of a new faith—he
had already ceased to belong to that generation whose
frivolous shallowness had been so incessantly appealed to
by his earnest convictions. Hence it was that, during the
whole of his life, he felt that he was regarded as an alien in

that Geneva, concerning which it may be said that those
who pray for her fear even now that, except in the event of
some special divine interposition, she will relapse once
more into that easy but deadly superstition from which,
three hundred years ago, the Word of God, as imported by
a few French emigrants, availed to rescue her.

And this was one of the reasons why his faith and
efforts failed to be appreciated by the majority of his
fellow-countrymen. Endued with a warm heart—his creed,
an intense reality; his conscience, an irresistible power—
he was at the same time a man of the past, a witness of
bygone days. Hence he lived a baffled and despised life, in
the presence of that superficialness and hollow dilettanteism
which seems to characterise increasingly every day the
times in which we live, more especially in a town which
may be scarcely said to exist as it was, save in the old
memories of some of its sons. Thus his testimony from
the very first met with more acceptance with Romanists,
among whom, thanks to the discipline of their Church, the
shallowness to which we have referred had made less way,
or among the Protestant population of the Vaud and of
Neufchatel, who had remained in a measure unaffected by
the influences to which Geneva had so long succumbed.

The fact is, that in Geneva itself his Church comprised
very few Genevese; while, from the outset, his ministry
found special acceptance with foreigners and Romanists.
His earliest tracts have already demonstrated this.* Proud
of the past history of their city, confident in the renown
brought them by the memory of their antecedents, the

* The greater part of his first tracts are narratives of conversations with
Romanists.

Genevese of that day ceased to experience that hunger and thirst which alone prepare for the successful preaching of the gospel of the grace of God. Since that time, undoubtedly, weary years of suffering and spoliation seem to have succeeded in awakening once more in that same population feelings with which they had so long dispensed.

At all events it must be allowed that, after 1830, my father was called upon to address himself especially to Romanists. His mission, out of Geneva, was directed chiefly towards France and Belgium, and in Geneva itself the most acceptable among the literary productions of his latter years, are almost all composed with reference to Romanists. This may be said especially of "The True Cross," in 1837,* of "Vendelin," in 1844, and of his numerous tracts which he collected together in 1853, in the sixth volume of his "Grains de Sénevé," as well as of others of the same kind.† Such were his labours

---

* Ten or twelve years ago, one who devoted himself at Turin to the evangelisation of Italy, assured me, that of all the means which he and his friends had employed in their work, they knew of none which had been attended with such striking results as the dissemination of the two tracts, "The True Cross," and "La Valaisanne." "We cannot print enough of them," he said.

† We append the titles of such of his writings as have not been noticed hitherto. In 1844, "I have left Rome and her Altars : an Account of a Conversion ;" in 1845, "A Romish Priest become a Disciple of the Bible ; or, A Few Facts and Conversations, relative to the Abjuration of Romanism, made on the 5th January, 1845, in the Church of Testimony, at Geneva ;" in 1846, three brochures, entitled, "The Watchman and the Sentry, a Dialogue between a Native Protestant and a Foreign Romanist"; in 1847, "A Morning at Lauterbrunnen," "L'Essentiel, Messieurs, l'Essentiel!" and "Is the Religion of my Fathers that of the Fathers ? a Letter to the Abbé Beaujard ;" in 1852, "One Little Word ;" in 1853, several minor tracts, "Catholics, you are not Invited to Change your Religion, but to become Christians, an Authentic Anecdote ;" "The Two Pieces of Wood,

among Roman Catholics. He appears not so much in the light of a controversialist, as of a missionary of the grace of God.

It still remains for us, however, before we close our history of his literary labours from the year 1830, to mention rapidly such efforts as have not yet been noticed.

It was not merely by the zeal with which he protested in Geneva against everything which tended to obscure those truths which lie at the foundation of historical Protestantism, that he was for ever displaying the feelings of an earnest and devoted heart. With him these emotions were not only the expression of that patriotic pride which so often displays itself with all the greater self-complacency, from the very fact that those who abandon themselves to it would blush to display such vanity under any other form. He was truly and deeply attached, not merely to that which constituted, in his judgment, the greatness and glory of his nation, but to the nation itself; that is, to the welfare and safety of his fellow-citizens. His patriotism was but one of the expressions of that deep devoted love with which

---

or, Faith and Superstition, an Historical Tale ; " " Do the Words, 'Ave Maria, Gratia Plena,' comprise, 1. The Immaculate Conception, 2. The Title of the Mother of God, 3. The Assumption, 4. The Royalty, and 5. The Worship of the Blessed Mother of the Saviour ?—a Dialogue between Two Sincere Men, the one a Romanist, the other a Protestant ; " " Our Lady of Geneva—Is Hers to be the Temple of Jerusalem, or of Gerizim ? " " The 'Galimatias' of Geneva and the False Prophet, a Reply to Attacks in which these Terms had been Employed to Designate His Teaching and Himself ; " " The Mass does not Recognise Jesus Christ as God, as Priest and Everlasting King ; " " Who Goes and Who Stays? " Many of these were written before 1853, but I do not find them anywhere except in the volume of " Grains de Sénevé," which appeared in that year. Lastly, in 1856, " The Three Visits," &c. &c.

he felt himself continually inspired towards his fellow-creatures. Nor do we see him waiting, so to speak, for such critical occasions as serve to bring into prominence any one skilled enough to make himself the organ of the sentiments of such as agree with him. His aim in addressing himself to those among whom he lived was, above all things, to avoid attaching to himself any new influence or authority, but to minister to them, supremely to their souls. Thus the most fugitive opportunities were seized by him for uttering words of Christian sympathy and appeal.

Let me adduce an instance of what I have just stated, from my own observation. In September 1838, on the afternoon of the Fast Day, which was on a Sunday, a small boat, with eight persons on board, foundered in the lake, under an unexpected squall. The passengers consisted of a merry party of friends—young men and young women, belonging to families of the middle class. My father hastened to one of their houses, the head of which was a member of his flock. He shortly published a tract headed, " Genevese, be Warned !" in which, addressing himself to his " dear fellow-countrymen," he spoke to them sympathisingly as a Christian, and a minister of the gospel. It is well known how speedily an effect is produced among a people so intelligent and susceptible as the Genevese. On this occasion, the impression was profound. According to his usual custom, he followed to the cemetery the body of the young man whose parents he knew. After he had offered up a prayer, and addressed a few words to the weeping family, he was implored by the father of another of the victims, who was standing by his son's grave, un-ministered to by any pastor, to come to him there.* I was present at the time, and I well remember the simple and touching scene when, after a brief, pathetic address, and a prayer into which my father flung his whole heart's utterance, we passed through the serried ranks of the crowd,— more than one voice being heard to thank him, and many hands stretched out to grasp his in silence.†

Yet it was not merely the deep feeling of a kindly spirit; it was the earnestness of his faith as well, that led him to issue those occasional publications. To the very end of his life, he never ceased to regard himself as the witness for the truth in Geneva; and, as such, he deemed it his duty to declare openly, as often as occasion offered, what he regarded as truth. Thus we find him in 1846 taking up his pen to refute some recently published assertions on the subject of the resignation of the Vaudois pastors.

In the following year, he wrote on the occasion of the election of a new consistory summoned by the National Church; after having assumed, at the commencement of the year, with reference to the question of a separation between Church and State, a position (as we shall soon see) at variance with that of his dissenting brethren.‡ Finally, in 1850, he was the first of those connected with

---

* It is the custom in Geneva for the ministers of the National Church to conduct the funeral service at the house of the departed, and not to attend the procession to the grave.

† Many years afterwards, on the occasion of the sudden death of a young man in our neighbourhood, my father published a few lines headed, " Dear fellow-parishioners, let us watch, for we know not at what hour our Lord may come for us."

‡ " What kind of a consistory will be chosen? will it be thoroughly Protestant, or will it not be selected from the Arian, if not the Unitarian, party? "

the religious awakening who protested, at the same time with his old opponent, Professor Chenevière, against Professor Scherer's views on the inspiration of Scripture.*

In 1836 there appeared a little book called "New Stories and New Hymns." As for the pamphlet "On Religious Scepticism," which he published anonymously that same year, it merely established one point, which is, that its author had never experienced that fatal paralysis of faith. He looks upon doubts as mere obscurities of the intellect; his heart never wavered in its trust.

The most important of his publications yet to be noticed are his hymns for schools, which are not only circulated, at the present day, among all French-speaking Protestants, but the melodies attached to them have found their way abroad, and even penetrated into Romish schools.

The first edition appeared in 1837, under the title, "Sixty Hymns and Spiritual Songs." "Yours is an amiable and happy age," he says in the preface addressed to the young, "and a gracious God Who has given you your voices as He has given its song to the bird, bids you use them in His praise. And so I have taken care to provide you with no frivolous numbers. I dedicate this book to you with the sincerest and most tender affection, and to Jesus, Who calls Himself the Good Shepherd, I commend you as the lambs of the flock He feeds."

---

* "The authority of the Bible is revealed only by the Holy Spirit ;" and, shortly afterwards, "The whole Bible is the very Word of God." It is of the former of these that De Goltz says (Genève Relig., p. 567), "Malan goes to the very bottom of the question with tact and fairness. Indeed, although he does not expressly state it in so many words, the distinction between divine authority and inspiration lies at the bottom of his whole argument."

It would be superfluous to praise them in this place, as they are more generally known than even the Songs of Zion. The hymns in the first part are more especially intended for worship. The second contains sacred poems of various kinds, such as "Dawn," "Evening," "Spring," "The Primrose," "The Swallow," "The Lark," "The Walk," "Autumn," "Winter," and many others that, with their bright and pleasant melodies, will not soon be forgotten by those who have heard them sung. After having enlarged this small collection in successive editions, he issued the last (and fourth) in 1853. It contains one hundred and twenty-seven poems. The writing of these "Sixty Songs" was one of those incidents which gave evidence of the working power of which he was capable. My mother had asked him for some hymns for her school. There were, up to that time, only a few already written by him at various times, and which existed merely in manuscript copies. My father, without making any promise, set to work, and, as was his custom whenever he was absorbed in some engrossing undertaking, barred his study-door against all comers. After an entire seclusion, interrupted only by family worship, and his ministerial duties, he came down into the dining-room, where he had not shown himself the whole time, and, laying on the table the MS. of sixty hymns and sacred songs, with airs for each, said to my mother, " Here, dear Jenny, is what our gracious God has enabled me to do during these six weeks."

Unfortunately, some of the best of them were soon got hold of for other compilations, and their language so altered, that those who knew them, in their original form, would scarcely have recognised them. Some of them are

2 A

to be met with, even now, in numerous school-books, more
or less transformed, and very frequently attributed to
other authors.*

He continued to publish almost every year one or more
new works. I have quoted several which have a special
character; their titles will be found in the lists of his
writings. I confine myself here to mentioning the following :—

In 1845, he issued two descriptions of pious deathbeds:
"The Christian does not Die," and "Tears and Consola-
tions." The last describes the death of the little daughter
of one of my sisters, and the two indicate the train of
feeling into which the illness of one of my brothers had
led him.

"The Four Voices of God," (Creation, Conscience, Law,
and the Gospel), published in 1847, displays in its opening
pages a singular solemnity of style and sentiment. That
benevolent sympathy for children and for sufferers, so
distinguishable in his earliest writings, appears, from time
to time, with the special charm with which a kindly disposition invests the old, in the tract, "He hath Done all
Things Well !" (in 1847), and especially in another, "God
has Saved us Once for All—it is Enough," (1856).

"Julia's Progress," "Mark and Janot," (1847), "Lis-
beth and Jean-Marie-Joseph, "(1848), "How Glorious is
the Gospel," and "Camille showed his Faith by his
Works," (in 1856), are, like the majority of his publica-

---

* On the first page of the fourth edition, we read, "The author requests
his brethren to consider the injury they would do him by transferring these
hymns to their own compilations. He therefore begs that they will not do
so any more."

tions, descriptions of facts which he had himself witnessed. The charming dialogue, "Mark and Janot," was written "after nature," and sent by my father to two misdoers, who derived so much benefit from it, that their parents felt it their duty to express a sense of their obligation to its author. As for "Camille," it was a narrative of an incident which occurred more than thirty years ago. I knew Camille myself personally.

"When Do You Lie?" "Every Religion is Good if we only Follow it," (in 1847), and "The Catechism and the Gospel," (in 1852), are scenes stamped on the religious life of Geneva; the two last, in particular, characterising that life of the lower classes with which he was so entirely familiar.

As will appear, if we run our eyes over the lists of his writings, he published a dozen tracts after 1861, and the greater part of them he composed for America, where he had recently met with eager and attentive readers. Among his latest writings there is one which, possibly owing to the circumstance that it was issued anonymously, produced an indisputable impression in the religious world of France. I allude to a brochure which appeared in 1851 with the heading, "Are You Happy—thoroughly Happy? Sincere Advice from Certain Friends." The subject had been suggested to him by the Chevalier Eynard, whom he frequently met at that time. It was very eulogistically noticed in several journals; indeed its seventy-five pages well deserved all the notice they received. Different, in more respects than one, in style and thought, from all that my father had previously written; graceful and attractive in language; it was well calculated to produce a serious impression on educated men, whom the bustle of the world, and the influence of an active and honourable life, withheld from giving heed to the promises of the gospel. Then, too, the whole is written from a point of view entirely superior to mere ecclesiastical differences. Catholic and Protestant may read it alike without encountering anything bearing, in the remotest degree, on the traditional form of their respective creeds.

Such was my father's public life from 1830. Evangelising journeys, with domestic incidents, formed the only interruption to his regular pulpit ministry. His religious work among strangers who came to his house, and his literary activity we have endeavoured to set forth. It only remains for us to add what bears upon his attitude (during his latter years) towards different Free Churches, as well as the National Church of his country. This I shall endeavour to do in a few words, after having first recalled my personal reminiscences of his private life.

BOOK III.

MALAN'S PRIVATE AND DOMESTIC LIFE—HIS CLOSING
RELATIONS TO THE CHURCH—THE EVENING OF
HIS LIFE, AND HIS DEATH.

CHAPTER I.

MALAN IN THE BOSOM OF HIS FAMILY.

"There in sweet strains of kindred music blending,
   All the home voices meet at day's decline ;
One are those tones as from one heart ascending—
   There is my home : "——

Thus far, in describing my father's public work, I have
had to deal simply with facts in the knowledge of all, and
doctrines which any one may judge.

At the same time, it has been my duty to temper any
approval with discretion, and to remember that these
facts in his life, public though they were, could only
be regarded by me from one point of view. While, as
for doctrines, I cannot but be conscious that formulas of
his, which I scarcely felt *I* could use, were in him but the

expressions of a faith, to the largeness and simplicity of which I have never ceased to aspire.

In presence, however, of the attempt to record the personal life of one of the best of parents, such reserve ceases to be necessary. The task, as easy as it is grateful, inspires me with but one sentiment of emotion, naturally aroused on the review of a past which has gradually lost its brightness under the influence of the changes of time. Could I at any time be led to hesitate in the task I have undertaken, it would be from a consideration whether sundry details, which filial affection loves to recall, would, in the nature of things, prove interesting to the generality of my readers. This much, however, I may venture to say—and say it to all—that it pleased God to give me, in my father, one whose excellence grew upon me the more closely we were brought into contact. Experiencing this most fully during his life, I have realised it even more during the past year, which has been devoted to the perusal of his most confidential letters, and the survey of the fugitive notes of his youth. Truly, I feel justified in declaring openly my sense of an inestimable blessing, for which I have never ceased to give thanks to God. Throughout all these innumerable papers I have failed to encounter a word or thought—I will not say, which filial affection would have urged me to destroy,—but even which I would hesitate to communicate to any whom it might concern. If they reveal the characteristics of our common humanity with its infirmities and imperfections, they show none of those passing blots from which it would seem almost impossible that the records of so long a life should be free. Not a single sentiment have I discovered, nor a single word, which my feelings as a son would have prompted me to forget. Nor have I found reason for the least regret that I have been thus led to penetrate my father's inmost life and most hidden thoughts. Here, even more than in his public life, he has stood out before me such as I ever knew him when he was upon earth, in the familiar intercourse of the domestic circle. He appears not merely as among the saintly few who dwell from day to day in the very presence of God, but as one to whom it would have been a painful effort to live otherwise.

An extract from a confidential letter, written by him to one of my sisters in 1850, will serve as an illustration :—

" There is nothing *little* for a soul to which all things are dignified by the presence and government of God. How often is the actual help of the Holy Spirit more abundantly evident in a trivial incident, than in a great deed. The wick of a lamp, ever so little charred, will smoke; and our Saviour bids us have ours well trimmed as well as well furnished with oil. But it is not by haste, nor by heedlessness, still less by impatience, that the wick is cleaned and trimmed."

" Even though we lost all the grand and beautiful remembrances that our father has bequeathed to us," said one of my brothers to me once, at the close of a conversation on some points in which we had been led to abandon the traditions of our childhood, " there is one treasure which we have all received from him, which alone would suffice to render his memory a holy and a sacred thing in our eyes. It is that truth which he has impressed upon our souls, that God is not an *idea*, but a *living reality ;* not a Being more or less separated from the details of our daily life, but the living omnipresent One, the actual witness of our very thoughts, to Whom every day and every instant of the day we are all accountable. And," added he, "our father has not been satisfied with telling us this, he has done much more and much better. He has convinced us of it by the practical illustration of his own daily life. He has indeed walked before us, always and to the very end, 'as serving Him Who is invisible.'" The truth of this remark I am in a better position perhaps than any to appreciate. Not only was my father the last man in the world to sustain an assumed character; not only would this have been impossible to a nature so impulsive as his; but having honoured me with a complete intimacy from a very early age, he thus exhibited himself to me with complete unreserve. Meanwhile, during all the years that I lived under his care, as well as during the after period in which not a week passed without my meeting him more than once, I never observed in him anything but what contributed to confirm the assertion here made. Never did I see in him a gesture, or hear from him a syllable, which, looking at it from his point of view, I could regard as likely to yield him subsequent regret. Not that I would have it inferred that his manner was cold and constrained; or that he was wanting in that ease and freedom which alone can secure the society of even the best of fathers from being occasionally irksome to a son; precisely the reverse. To the very end of his life, little children, so quick by instinct to discover any tendency to restrain their liberty, might have been seen pressing eagerly round him, regarding him as "their true friend." As for young men, I can only say that I never felt so thoroughly at my ease as when I was with him. Though I regarded him as the very personification of conscience, I felt none the less that he was always desirous to put himself in my place. He did not appear to me as one of those who, not satisfied with their own conscientiousness, aim at forcing upon their children their personal scruples. He was for ever urging me to recognise the personal voice within me, the voice of God (as I myself had learned) speaking to my soul. I saw that, with his kindness and discrimination, he sympathised with me entirely in all that was not wrong; while, at the same time, I felt so certain of his judgment and absolute discretion, that if I chanced, through the buoyancy of youthful feelings, to transgress in the least degree the limits of justice or charity, I knew that he to whom I spoke was as incapable of sparing me weakly as of reproving me harshly. I never hesitated to disclose to him my whole mind, even when I differed from him. Indeed, he would have soon detected the least symptom of dissimulation, while he himself was the first to set me the example of that entire independence of thought which recognises conscience only as its absolute sovereign. Yet if, with all this freedom and frankness, I forgot for a moment my duty towards him or others, I was arrested at once, not indeed by a spoken word (for he would have shrunk from seeing me blush at his rebuke), but by that authoritative deportment and expression, which he held it his right at any time to assume, even in moments of most confidential intercourse. Whatever might be the topic of our conversation, I was sure of being understood, if not of being approved. It is universally allowed, that the most irritating of all discussions are those which are indefinitely prolonged because the disputants fail to ascertain the measure in which they are agreed. With a man of his intelligence and benevolence, I had no fear of this.

Over recollections of a father of whom I am justified in speaking in terms such as these, it is easier far to linger than to glance. Without attempting, however, to present him in these pages as he was to me in daily life, I shall confine myself to recalling my personal reminiscences of him, commencing from my earliest childhood.

Among the first is the circumstance of hearing him converse in Latin with my eldest brother. It was his wish to spare his son the distress occasioned to most children by the study of that language, as witnessed by himself in his position of master in the college. For this purpose he determined, from the first, to address him only in Latin. Afterwards, when he was old enough to learn to read, my father prepared a book containing vignettes drawn and coloured by himself, having underneath little stories in that language. As a result of this method, Latin is, to this day, my brother's "mother tongue." * I only mention this as an example of the zeal and assiduity my father displayed in the prosecution of any design on which he had resolved. Generally speaking, indeed, he concerned

---

* I find the following in a letter from Mr Bruen, dated from Geneva, in 1817, quoted in Dr Mason's Memoirs, p. 460 :—"What do you think of my sitting down at table at Malan's house, in Geneva, with his little son, six years old, who not only knew the name of everything he wanted *in Latin*, but could sustain a conversation in that language. It may amuse you to hear, that when Dr Mason and myself had engaged to dine with his father, he was told, as something extraordinary, that two Americans were to be there. His first exclamation, on seeing us, was, '*Americani? non sunt cum plumis!*' He had no other idea of Americans than what he had derived from prints, and therefore very naturally expected to see us in the feathers and fantastic garb of Indians."

himself with the education of each of us. My first lessons of any importance—my first analyses—are linked with his memory. Every evening at a certain hour, about the year 1829, I saw my elder brothers and sisters go into his study with their paper books. In course of time I was permitted to be present. Alternate lessons in logic and rhetoric formed the staple of the studies.* At a later period one of my brothers and myself read with him some Latin authors and the elements of geometry. Aided by his varied experience, he gave us, further, our first ideas of natural philosophy. To accomplish this he constructed electric machines, one of them of large dimensions, with the various appendages then in use. Sometimes, on fine nights, he would adjust his large telescope, to show us the satellites of Jupiter, or the mountains of the moon; at others, collecting us round his microscope, he made us handle, as it were, the proofs of the infinite goodness and power of the Creator. He never failed to correct us every time that we used a faulty grammatical expression. Whenever a dispute arose upon a point of language, or of history, for instance, he did not suffer the thing to remain unsettled. " We must never put back till to-morrow the settlement of any doubt," was what he said. When the dictionary or grammar had decided the point at issue, he would exclaim, in a tone of satisfaction, "There is one error less!"

My most vivid recollections, however, of that time gather round certain seasons, in which he used to call us into his room to tell us stories. It was on Sunday evenings after

---

* It will be evident at once, how thoroughly this course of instruction serves, of itself, to illustrate the turn of his mind.

he had had his tea. We used to find him seated in an easy-chair in front of the fire. My brothers and sisters settled themselves right and left of him, while my place—I was very small at the time—was usually at his feet, on a thick rug which decorated the hearth. There, as I watched the flame flickering on the logs of wood, while the fire died slowly down, and the shadows danced on the Dutch tiles of which the sides of the fire-place was composed, I heard him tell us the story of the Watch-Chain, Raoul, or Theobald the Iron-Hearted, with several other original tales, which appeared subsequently in his " Véritable ami des enfans," with "Didier le Vagabond," "Jean des Raquettes, and " The German Tinder Dealer." Before publishing them he wished to test their effect upon us, and so, by the following Sunday, we had to set down what we had heard— while the hints he gave me one day, after I had tried my hand at writing a page, I remember, and find useful still. He was, indeed, much more than a careful and exact grammarian. He never failed, though it was only by a word, and that most kindly spoken, to indicate any defect of thought or character, so frequently betrayed by inaccuracy of language or style. Let it be added, however, that while he thus laid the utmost stress on clearness and precision of thought, he was anything but a pedant. What he had in view, in his teaching, was not so much the idea that struck himself, as how to enable his pupil to apprehend it. Hence these lessons were eagerly looked forward to by us ; and, as for me, the day when I had to exchange his teaching for a tutor's, remains among the saddest of my earliest boyhood.

At a very early period he began to teach us drawing ;

and ever afterwards, when, (among the first in Geneva to do so,) he applied to A. Calame to instruct us, he scarcely ever omitted to come into the room where the lesson was being given, if it was only for a few moments, either to exchange a few words with "the dear master," or to go from one to another with a word of encouragement, or uniformly kind criticism.*

With reference to his sons, in particular,—he it was who gave us an early taste for handicraft. When the weather was bad, and we were at liberty, he opened his workshop. It was a large room, containing a lathe for his own use, and a smaller one for us, a forge with a locksmith's belongings, a carpenter's bench, and a large assortment of tools of every kind, many of which had been manufactured by himself. Here he instructed us in the art of distinguishing the various kinds of wood, and estimating their value, as well as of making and using tools ; or summoned us to help him in some particular task.

He united, to great muscular strength, singular certainty and skilful lightness in the use of his hands. Partial to manly exercises, he was the first to teach me riding and fencing.

* I remember well the day he sent me, about 1830, to ask Calame, at that time very little known, if he could come and give lessons at our house. I found the artist by the bedside of his aged mother. He came the next day, and I have still the oak branch which he painted before me in sepia, and which he handed to me with the remark, "Here is my first copy." Calame never forgot what he loved to call my father's kindness ; he often referred to it with me, as well as to the words of faith and piety he heard him utter. Meanwhile my father, for his part, never wavered in his sincere attachment to one whom he regarded, not only as a gifted artist, but also as a true and humble believer. At Mentone, Calame, at the point of death, expressed his desire to see my father once more, and one of his last regrets was caused by his being informed that Malan had anticipated him,— as it happened only by a few days,—in his entrance into everlasting rest.

Not that he was our only instructor. He had not sufficient leisure for the purpose. But he ascertained for himself, before handing us over to masters, in what quarter our special tastes lay. What he especially desired was, that whatever we undertook, we should do well; and he omitted nothing in furnishing us with the means. He set up for my eldest brother a bookbinder's workshop, completely furnished. Afterwards, on noticing the interest with which another of us employed himself with a child's printing press, he made him a small one of iron, with all the proper accompaniments. The printer, who was then about twelve, was soon informed that, as his printed matter was circulating among the public, he ought to take out the requisite license. It was for this printing press of the Pré-Béni that my father wrote his "speaking vignettes."

In spite of the unfailing and varied character of his activity, I cannot help remembering that, much as he enjoyed the country, he never occupied himself with horticulture. It was a *sine quâ non* with him that the fruits of his exertions should be rapid and reliable. What could not be calculated upon with certainty failed to attract his mind, as it might have attracted others.

Fond as he was of giving away, he would have nothing lost. While out for a walk, I have seen him stop to pick up a nail, a pin, or some other trifling thing; remarking, as he did so, that he would one day find a use for it. It is true, he possessed the talent of turning everything to account. On this point, he used often to quote to us, when we were children, the example of the hero of our age, Robinson Crusoe. One day, I remember, he brought me a

knife, the handle of which he had made out of an old bone
bleached by the sun, while he had forged the blade out of
a piece of steel which I had seen him pick up in the road
some days before.

Devoted to method and order, he left their impress on
every household arrangement. In connection with this, he
congratulated himself on the year he had spent as a young
man in a bank at Marseilles. He required the members
of his family to be punctual, whether at family prayers or at
meals, the signal for which was given, precisely at the
hour, by a bell hung outside the house. Each of us had a
set of tablets, in which he would show us how to enter
hour by hour, at the beginning of each new season, whatever we had to do each day of the week. He was very
urgent in requiring his boys to rise early, and very careful·
to see that we had a short time for recreation after every
meal. In summer our first lesson was at six o'clock.
He was generally up at four himself; and, during the fine
summer days, we often saw him as we met for prayers and
breakfast, returning from his morning walk.

If his activity was constant, it was by no means restless.
No one ever found him in a hurry or confusion, just as, on
the other hand, he was neither a dreamer nor a chatterer.
His recreation was manual labour.

It would be difficult to mention all the various things
he could do. Sometimes I saw him with a graver's tool in
his hand, a glazier's diamond, or a tinsmith's irons. Then,
again, he would be devoted to making ink or sealing wax,
or some other preparation. On other occasions, when he
had a few spare hours, he would paint, or compose music, or
(as was the case especially during the years I most vividly

recall), he would busy himself with lithography, or in his workshop. There, putting on a workman's waistcoat and apron, he applied himself vigorously to whatever he had to do. Always thorough in his undertakings, he might often be heard singing a hymn while he was at work, or whistling the air of it; and when he succeeded in what he was about, he generally came to my mother or me to make us partners of his satisfaction. It may be added that he had a habit of succeeding; and that through the house, and through the houses of his friends, he was looked upon as able to repair anything. I have seen him accomplish, in this respect, perfect marvels of ingenuity and skill.

But to return to my earliest recollections. On Thursday afternoons, when the weather was fine, we used generally to go out for a walk with him, all together. Getting into the country as quickly as possible, we halted on the bank of a stream, or under a cluster of trees, or in some other solitary nook; there,—the little ones being tired with running about,—he would gather us round him, and enlarge upon the habits of various field animals, or tell us the names of the flowers we might happen to bring him. He showed us in everything the wisdom and goodness of God, Whose presence was ever filling his soul. It was on one of these occasions that, observing me striking a little branch in a hedge with my stick, he asked me to bring it to him; and when we stopped to rest he began, with his pen-knife in his hand, to give me my first ideas of the construction of one of those leaves, the wonderful development of which I had been thoughtlessly arresting.

Sometimes, in the summer, he took us rambles of some days' duration through the surrounding country. I was

six years old when I saw him set out with my elder brother to visit the Salines de Bex. The following year I was
one of the party, and that time he took us to the valley
of the Lac de Joux, in the Jura, and the iron-works of
Vallorbes. Afterwards, from time to time, it was my good
fortune to accompany him on various walking expeditions.
Equipped with a light coat and knapsack, he strode on at
a famous rate, and, in spite of my youth, I had enough to
do to keep up with him. I have given elsewhere an account
furnished from my recollection of one of these trips. They
were occasions on which he showed himself the most delightful of touring companions, took part in all the delights
of my age, and identified himself with all my enthusiasm.

In our earlier years, however, it was in the winter time
that he associated himself most forcibly with our young
life. With it came the long evenings, which we spent
with our mother round the drawing-room table. There,
every one was occupied. Whilst my sisters were busy
with needlework, I drew or read aloud. Often we had
music. One of my brothers would accompany my sister
on the flute—she playing the piano—and we generally
finished by singing together one of my father's or Bost's
hymns. To the little ones, meanwhile, winter was
supremely the time of "lantern" evenings, and the glories
of New Year's day.

The optical lantern (we were forbidden to say *magic*)
was a phantasmagoria of considerable size, still in my possession, and a source of great delight to my children. Its
slides were all painted by my father himself. He had
wished, in his first journey to England, to learn the art of
painting on glass, but as an exorbitant price was demanded

2 B

for communicating the secret, he set to work to find it out for himself, and soon succeeded. He then proceeded to paint natural history subjects, cheerful family scenes, &c., but especially moral stories, as also a series of our Lord's parables.

I may be permitted to describe here one of those pictures. As I exhibit them to my own children, they carry me back to the time when, myself a child, at the given signal, a blast from an ox-horn sounding from the top of the stair-case, we hurried, a delighted audience, into the darkened room where my father, standing before his lantern, awaited our presence in front of the great screen.

As an illustration, " The story of poor Diego." The first scene presented the negro, as black as jet. Standing before his hut, shadowed by a palm-tree, he smokes his pipe; while he watches his wife rocking their infant in a tortoise-shell cradle. Next, he is to be seen going to his field, with his hoe and rake upon his shoulder, passing a hedge on his way, the resemblance of which to those in our country I find a little too exact, but which I fully appreciated at six years old. In the third scene, the drama commences. The first thing that strikes us is the appearance of two Portuguese. Not to libel the Portuguese of the present day, they appear with the feathered head-gear and dress of the sixteenth century. One of them, with his sabre, points out Diego to his companion, who is armed with a musket, while the poor negro, whom the latter has just seized by the arm, stretches out the hand that is still at liberty, in the direction of his hut. But the "robbers of men" (as the Bible calls them, so our father invariably added) are merciless; and their canoe is next seen quitting the bank, and carrying off the groaning victim to the slave-ship, anchored a little lower down in the road-stead. This slide disappears from our view, and the next transports us to the plantation of the Antilles. A white man is seen ' elabouring an unhappy black, who had been forced by the scorching sun to suspend for a moment his heavy drudgery ; doubtless to dream of his wife and his poor little one. Then comes the last scene. Diego is stretched on a wretched pallet, in a pent-house, stretching out his hand towards heaven, just as he is about to die in his wretched-ness. " But, my children," said our father, as he heard us little ones trying in vain to keep back our tears, " don't think that our loving heavenly Father has forgotten Diego. He knew what He was doing, in allowing the poor negro to be torn from his far-off African home. Diego met, at the Antilles, a missionary—a true Christian. He spoke to him of that glorious Saviour Who had suffered for black men as well as white. Hence you see him on his bed of death giving thanks to God who had thus caused the message of 'good news' to reach him ; and beseeching him to convey the same tidings to his wife in the land of the blacks ; a request with which the missionary promises com-pliance." It will be seen that my father, while he thus inspired his children with utter horror of the robbers of men, was not at the same time altogether an abolitionist, as the term is understood in our day.

But all these lantern scenes would merit description. One of my brothers, to whom I was showing them not very long ago, put them aside after glancing at them. " Stay !" he exclaimed, " I seem to hear him yet, telling us the story of the Samaritan, or the good Shepherd, or the debtors, or especially of the servant standing, his lamp in his hand, listening, with his hand stretched towards the door, to discover whether the footsteps he heard were those of his tarrying master; while through the window might be seen the moon going down and the sunrise crimsoning the horizon." Amongst them, also, were amusing slides; for example, a school-boy, his cheeks red with cold, his cap on his ears, appears shouting, "Take care!" at the bottom of a slide on which his sledge has already overturned a companion in the snow; or again, the hunt after the cat that had stolen the roast-beef and was being pursued by the old cook, armed with a spit; the man-cook brandishing his cleaver, the master of the house re-adjusting his spectacles, and an old neighbour joining in with a hand-screen. As I recall my vivid remembrances of these evenings, I cannot forget the wish expressed by my father, that some intelligent colporteurs could be sent out, whose sole business it should be to collect the villagers together on winter evenings to witness similar exhibitions. Of course, it would be requisite that such men should be distinguished by that thorough reality of character which made the transition as easy as possible, and free of all outrage to the feelings of the spectator, from sacred to secular subjects. For myself, I try to recall his very words, when I am relating to my children the story of Diego, or of James the chimney-sweep; or when, with the pictures in my hand, so full of liveliness and expression, which my father painted, I repeat the parable of the talents, or of the prodigal son.

But the great event of the winter to us was the New Year feast. It was then especially that my father poured out the fulness of his loving heart. By dint of great pains

and personal sacrifices, he contrived the means to enrich us
all; and the ever varying way in which he planned the
celebration of the evening of the 31st of December, or New
Year's Eve, the part he took in it himself, the joy he
experienced in our joy, and the few hearty spiritual words
which he addressed to us the last thing before we knelt
down together with our mother and him to render thanks
to our gracious God and heavenly Father,—these are
things that remain indelibly engraved on the memory of
us all.

The next morning after breakfast (when we received the
presents exhibited to us the evening before), we repaired to
the chapel.   In his New Year sermons he displayed all the
earnestness of his faith, and all the force of his eloquence.
Never was he so impressive as when, led thus to place himself and his hearers face to face with the solemnities of
eternity, he made us realise in a measure the vanity of
our days, and the nearness of that departure which was to
be to him, as each year brought it nearer, a blessed entrance
into the heavenly city.

After service, we repaired to the home of his parents (my
mother's had died before 1828). He himself walked first,
with my mother on his arm, and his children behind.
He did not omit, in passing, to give little New Year's gifts
to the custom-house officer, or the soldier at the city-gate,
accompanied by words of kindly Christian greeting; while
more than one passer-by stopped to salute him, and to
watch his numerous family going by.

The reader will be astonished, perhaps, to find nothing
as yet indicative of the discipline a father is invariably
called upon to exercise over his children. As a rule he

avoided reproving and scolding. He had, as it were, a
deep respect for the individual liberty even of his youngest
children; and what he aimed at, from the very first, was
to furnish their hearts and understandings with sound
principles, which he had a peculiar aptitude for presenting
to us under a striking form. "A truth well expressed and
well understood," he used to say, "is like a nail well
planted—it is small, but it is iron and solid—many things
may be hung upon it." His rules for conduct bore rather
upon the *will* than the *actions*, and appealed to the conscience in preference to the memory. "If you would know,
my children, what you ought to do," he used often to say
to us, "if you would know whether you have acted rightly,
ask if the Lord Jesus, at your age, and in your place,
did do, or would have done, the same. Never go where
He cannot follow you. Shun, in your companionship, your
amusements, your pursuits, your readings, everything on
which you cannot heartily implore the divine blessing."
Most undoubtedly, when I was a boy, I never knew my
father hesitate either to prohibit or sanction, as occasion
required. Even then, however, he endeavoured to explain
to me, in a manner adapted to my youth, the reasons and
principles by which he was guided. In after years he
contented himself with reminding me of them.

As for discipline, in the strict sense of the term, or,
in other words, punishment,—I can only say that his
memory is identified to us with nothing but perfect kindness.

He only punished very rarely, and always most reluctantly. There was but one fault to which he held himself
bound to be merciless, and that was the least departure

from truthfulness. He was for ever assuring us that a
lie was of the devil, that liars should not tarry in his
house, that that was the only *crime* of which our time of
life was capable, and that exaggeration and detraction
were as avenues conducting to it. Our father never struck
us, in a hasty moment; as need scarcely be asserted. As
for corporal punishment, he by no means adopted those
views which the false egoism of Romanism has made
fashionable. The only consideration with him was his
duty, as a father, to the exclusion of abstruse considerations of this or that theory about the abstract dignity of
human nature. Yet, at the same time, as a matter of fact,
I don't think he ever used the rod, except once or twice,
in the case of his younger sons; and this reminiscence
only recalls to them his quiet solemn grief, which caused
them their greatest sufferings; while his feelings, on the
other hand, were never allowed to interfere with his submission to what he regarded as the order God Himself
(Prov. xxiii. 13, 14; Heb. xii. 7, 10,) has given to parents
in the interests of their children. As for back-biting, he
viewed with displeasure every kind of idle discussion of a
neighbour. He well knew that a proper name was so
called, because it was the proper or private possession of
him who owned it, and that no one has any right to take
liberties with it. At table, where he delighted to hear us
talk, he watched the conversation, and directed it always
himself, with perfect tact, to cheerful or instructive subjects;
introducing, as occasion offered, serious and heartfelt words.
Nor did he ever forget to render thanks with all of us,
standing up with his hat in his hand, before each meal.

Such are my early recollections of my father. They

close in 1835, when I left for the first time my paternal home, and the garden within whose quiet enclosure my whole previous life had been passed.

I was then fourteen years old, and my father took me to Würtemberg to learn German. We stopped at Schaffhausen, where he preached; and there I saw him for the first time receive from the clergy of an official church, testimonies of attachment and respect. At Stuttgardt, where he visited those who twelve years before had sent him the first proofs of sympathy he had received from abroad, he was given the address of Albert Knapp, with whom I was to remain some time. Arrived at the little town where he lived, my father ascertained that the castle, visible from the iron window, was inhabited by that very princess who in 1819 had attended with her daughters the meetings at the Pré l'Evéque. Sending in his card, he was welcomed with the utmost cordiality and respect by that noble Christian lady; and the kindness his son experienced afterwards, for his sake, at her hands, remain among the most cherished remembrances of his early youth. On his return, my father was requested to preach in the Reformed Church of Stuttgardt. The commencement of his sermon produced a marked impression; but a Lutheran congregation could not fail to be irritated when he closed with his personal views on the election of grace. The result was that, in spite of the generally expressed desire to hear him again, no further offer of the pulpit was made. He had left the place, however, when it became known in the town that a decision on the point had been arrived at.

In August 1837 he saw, for the first and last time, and only for one week, his entire family reassembled round his table. At our last meal each of us received five francs from him, with which to purchase some remembrance of that family gathering. At my side, as I write, I see the paper weight I purchased at the time; but what I see even more clearly is the look of radiant pleasure with which, on that last day, our dear father arranged the twelve pieces of silver on the table.

It was not without great difficulty that one of my brothers had been enabled to join us. This brings me to speak of the only occasion for mourning which my father ever experienced in his family circle. Moreover, the death to which I refer, with the long years of pain and anxiety which preceded it, forms a marked epoch in our domestic history. It closes, with the majority of us, the sunshiny days of our childhood. It was the first time the shadow of death had crossed my father's path,—up to that period so clothed with life and brightness.

My brother Jocelyn (who was called after his godfather, Lord Roden, one of my father's oldest and best friends), began, when he was seven years old, and probably in consequence of a severe fall which he had at that time, to betray the first symptoms of a terrible nervous disease. As the attacks only occurred in the night, one of his brothers, with the sanction of the medical attendant, succeeded in concealing their gravity from his parents for about two years. Gradually, however, the disease assumed such a form that it became absolutely necessary to tell them the truth, and we soon began to lose all hope of a cure being effected. My dear mother speedily adopted this sorrowful view, but my father thought otherwise. Such an opinion seemed to him a want of faith; and whilst he encountered the malady with the energy and perseverance of his character, he constantly reminded us of God's promise to hear prayer. He did not know at the time that the years that lay before him were to be sent, not to furnish a new triumph to believing assurance, but to teach him the long and painful lesson of sacrifice and silent submission.

After three years' study abroad, I had to return home. I found my father greatly changed. His expression was wearied and anxious. Before deciding on allotting a room in the garden for my poor brother and the watcher, who soon remained permanently with him, he had had him in a little room which opened into his own. My father and I were at that time the sole occupants of the top story of the house.

Let me mention one of the most vividly remembered scenes of that distressing time. One night, aroused by a cry from my sick brother, I sprang out of bed and left my room. A ray of light fell across the floor of the corridor, through the half-opened door of the room where he was lying. Entering, I saw my father in his dressing-gown, his candle at his side, on his knees by the bed on which my poor brother was writhing in the last struggles of one of his attacks. With head bent, and gaze fixed on the convulsed features of his unhappy child, he appeared to be uttering, in a low voice, a prayer of anguish, and through the flowing locks of his now white hair I saw the silent tears that his rending heart sent forth, trickling down his emaciated face. I retreated without his seeing me. From that time, it was not without awe that I watched, as from a distance, the struggle to which his powerful nature was a prey. I saw him wrestling with the angel God had sent to meet him in his way. I felt that, as with the patriarch of old, so with him; the struggle was to be in solitude, the conflict in the dark; and that if he was to come forth victorious, it would be at the cost of wounds and scars. When the day arrived on which (after years of torture so inconceivable that, towards the last, none but my mother and myself were permitted access to the sick-room) the hour of deliverance sounded, it left him stricken into silence.

As for the poor invalid,—while each day the thought of his terrible pain settled down upon us like a deepening cloud,—while those who saw him (including even the doctors themselves) were overpowered at the spectacle of his indescribable sufferings,—he himself, though at first he seemed as if he could not accept his lot, began suddenly to display a sweetness and resignation so angelic as to strike the very strangers who came to visit him, and to be edified by witnessing his submission.

I have at my side a few pages written by my mother at the instigation of M. Gaussen, and recording what she had seen during her poor boy's weary years of suffering. I cannot quote them entirely, but I may be permitted to insert a few extracts. Apart from the interest attaching to the incidents they record, they will serve to give an idea of the experience my parents were called upon to undergo, as well as to reveal, in a measure, the character of her whose gentle, lowly piety, together with her devotion and courage in every extremity, have ever been at the source of my father's domestic peace and happiness.

After a few detailed accounts of terrible episodes in that

long illness, and various incidents noticed at different times, she writes thus (I give the passage curtailed), a few days after Jocelyn's death :—

" While his life wore away in terrible anguish, I saw him grow in holiness and submission to God. Daily, with three or four exceptions, I passed four or five hours at his bedside, in the most precious and sacred communion. While I witnessed his anguish, I was also the depositary of his feelings; and I traced in them, clearly reflected, the blessed victorious work of the Holy Spirit of God.

" One day, when he was worse than usual, I read to him several times the consolatory descriptions and promises of the 21st and 22d chapters of the Revelation. When I had finished, he said to me, with the sweetest expression, ' How thankful I shall be to be there !' Whether, owing to the circumstance that his distressing malady had too greatly exhausted him to admit of his following an argument, or because a silent awe held me back from intruding on the celestial teaching which he was receiving, under my very eyes, from the Holy Spirit of God, I explained the Word to him very sparingly. Listening rather myself for what God would teach him, I contented myself with offering, from time to time, any explanation he might apply for. But I prayed with him; nor did I ever do so without his countenance assuming afterwards a celestial peace and happiness, of which, indeed, he testified in the most touching manner.

" One striking feature in his character was his holy fear of God, and reverence for His will. One day I was repeating a verse from the Psalms (Ps. xl. 17), ' As for me I am poor and needy, but the Lord careth for me : thou art my helper and deliverer; O Lord, make no long tarrying.' He said, 'Mamma, I love that verse; all but the last bit. It looks like a murmur against God. He never "tarries" in my case.' Alas! how far my own heart was removed from this submission, as I marked the long delay in succouring my darling.

"While I watched him lying day after day and week after week on his bed of suffering, cut off from all that brightens life, he would say to me, from time to time, 'Dear mother, how the time flies on; how short it is!' and then he would add, 'How good God is to me! He graciously dwells with me in my heart. I feel Him ever at hand, dear mother, and I seem as if I could speak to Him just as I am speaking to you.'

"On his countenance, the faithful index of his soul, I never saw a shadow of trouble or distress except on account of sin; as, for instance, when he prayed to be resigned under his sufferings, or had become acquainted with some fault committed around him.

"One day, during his last week on earth, when he could scarcely speak without great difficulty, he said to me, 'Ah, mother, how I long to be patient and submissive to my God;' and on my assuring him that he was, and that he might give thanks for this, he replied, 'Yes, mother, I can; for it is not I that am submissive, but His power working in me.'

"Ten or twelve days before his departure, he said to me, with deep feeling, 'Ah, mother, you do not know what I have seen!' 'What have you seen, darling?' 'Oh, I have seen and heard things I cannot describe; they were so glorious! Oh I have been so happy! Dear mother, words could not utter what I have witnessed. I could not, I must not, tell you. Oh what glory! and it lasted so long!' I saw at once that the Good Shepherd,—to strengthen him, and give him courage for the endurance of his sufferings which were increasing daily,—had revealed to him, by the Holy Spirit, during the watches of the night (it was in the early morning), the glories on which he was so soon to enter.

"His natural character had been singularly upright, but inclined to pride, and sometimes to unkindness to his inferiors; but the grace of Christ made him the humblest of little children. During the last seventeen months of his illness, in which I watched him all the day, I never saw him, but on two or three occasions, in the least degree, exacting. Meanwhile, he never murmured; I never heard a complaint from him, even in his paroxysms of suffering; or even a simple groan. He always begged my pardon for cries unconsciously uttered during his attacks. He never spoke of his sufferings, except to bless the Lord for having sent them to him, and thus led him to know and serve Him.

"Once he said to me, 'I do not envy my brothers and sisters, I assure you; they are still in the midst of the world, with its temptations and vanities: while I am taken away from it by my Saviour's power. Ah, I am happier than they all.'

"The passages of Scripture, which sustained him most abundantly, were, 'I have chosen Thee in the furnace of affliction;' 'He learned obedience by the things which he suffered;' 'Out of much tribulation we enter the kingdom of God.' When I repeated to him the words of the

Lord Jesus, ' Father, not my will, but Thine be done ;' he added, ' Amen !'

"One last grace, which beautified this Christian spirit, was extreme humility. Once, when I emphatically commended him, he said to me, with striking solemnity, ' Mother, don't flatter me !' I never thought of doing so. Alas, I could never convey an idea of his expression ;* the sweet sound of his voice ; and the ineffable celestial peace which marked the least of his actions, and hallowed all his wishes ! His holy, blessed memory will follow me all my life.

" Once, when in an outburst of affection I lavished on him the tenderest epithets, such as ' my darling,' ' my delight,' ' my comfort and joy,' he said, ' Dear mother, you tempt me ; don't say all that to me.' ' I may call you my darling, then, mayn't I ?' His sweet smile said ' yes.' "

In January 1846, after nine years' suffering, the most terrible symptoms of his disease increased in intensity. On the 26th of that month, I spent almost the whole night at his bedside with my father. We had scarcely left him, on his becoming to all appearance a little more composed, when the message came that he had passed away to his everlasting rest.

The following year, after witnessing in a bloody revolution the end of the Geneva of my earliest recollections, I went abroad again. From that time, for many years, I was only at home on a visit. A few words, therefore, with re-

---

* My brother Jocelyn had a singularly beautiful expression. My father referred to it when, in the poem entitled, "A Father at the Grave of his Boy," he wrote that verse—

"How sweet it was to see
Thy soul look through thine eyes !"

ference to my father's attitude towards me in my early manhood, will be appropriate at this point.

No one felt more than he did that the isolation into which he had been brought, together with his family, in Geneva, was calculated to increase the embarrassments which every youth must expect to encounter at the commencement of his career. Hence he effectually guarded himself, by explicit and numerous rules, from interposing any further difficulty in our way, shut out as we already were from the world in which we lived as much by the principles and customs of his household as by the stigma which attached to our name.

Ever ready to listen to us and advise with us when we referred to him, he never took the initiative. It was not by orders, it was by a simple setting forth of principles and of faith, above all, by the unremitting influence of his whole life, that he most powerfully ruled us. It is true that, on the one hand, the discipline of his house was absolute; while, on the other, his influence was such that it would have been impossible for any one to have felt themselves perfectly independent under his eye. But nothing of this resulted from an avowed purpose or premeditated calculation. Above all, there was nothing to remind one, even remotely, of that direct personal authority which, once irrevocably asserted, leaves a son no choice, except between hypocrisy and revolt.

To touch only on my own case: I shall content myself with observing here that, until I came to mature years, my father's will was in my eyes the very personification of the will of God Himself. At the same time, I hasten to add that, so far from seeking to inspire me with this view, he would have been staggered had he become aware of the earnestness with which I adopted it.

Having lost his father in 1840, and received, in 1844, news of the death of his brother (who had lived most of his life abroad), he closed his mother's eyes at Vandœuvres in 1848. That year commences the evening of his life. Not only was he left alone from that time, as regards all who had surrounded his childhood, but never was he so painfully conscious of his isolation in Geneva.

Indeed, it was then that he felt himself compelled to abandon the idea of reunion with his seceding brethren. I will arrest the record of my personal recollections (to which I shall have an opportunity of recurring when I reach that part of my subject), for the purpose of supplying a few details in connection with his last intercourse, in public life, with Free Churches abroad and in Geneva itself, as well as with the National Church of his country. As I was away from home the greater part of the time to which I am now referring, I shall be careful to indicate the sources from which my information has been derived.

Section 2.—*His Final Relations with the Churches.*

If there be one thing supremely worthy to attract the believer's thought, it is the way in which faith invariably succeeds, despite the errors and weaknesses of earth, in maintaining its eternal right in the hearts of all those in whom its empire has been thoroughly established. The spectacle of every really Christian life should lead us to appreciate the victorious development of the spiritual man,—the man born from above. And it is only in propor-

2 c

tion as such is the case with us that we can regard ourselves as having arrived at a proper estimate of such a life.

This thought, frequently present to me in the course of my narrative, comes up with new force now that I have to describe the position which my father uniformly assumed in reference to all that affected the form and outward discipline of the churches.

It has been already observed that in his case the manifestation of the faith of the heart presented, from the very first, two aspects. It revealed itself especially in the form of doctrine. It was in opposing the setting forth of a positive dogma, or of negative dogmatism which it was sought to impose on his preaching, that he testified, at the first, his faith in the free salvation of God, and in the Saviour of his soul. It was this same faith, moreover, in the reality of the celestial gift, and consequently in the privileges and duties resulting from it to true believers, which led him subsequently to unite with his brethren in a separate Church, when the ecclesiastical institution to which he belonged, had prohibited him from freely expressing his views. Thus his separation from the Establishment was, in his eyes, an essentially *religious* act—was, in fact, so far as he was concerned, the simple indispensable testimony of the faith of his heart.

Side by side with this, however, new elements afterwards appeared. A singularly pertinacious opposition soon compelled him to affirm, with increasing precision, the special form which he gave to his protest, and over and over again to vindicate its soundness. Of course, in doing this he was liable to the danger of forgetting for his own part,—

while he concealed this from his hearers,—the supreme importance of that heavenly faith which alone gave to his dogmatical and ecclesiastical position its religious character. He was in peril of assigning, whether to dogma considered as such, or to matters external in ecclesiastical economy, that place which belongs only to living faith, to that reality of the heavenly life which will alone remain after the imperfect manifestation with which we, in this world, have invested it, either in our creeds or forms, shall have disappeared for ever.

To this danger my father would certainly have succumbed, had he been like other men—I mean, had he not been one essentially different from and superior to others, a true Christian.

On the other hand, if nothing in his life had betrayed the presence of this danger, if nothing had occurred to testify to weakness and inexperience, he would not have been like other believers—in other words, he would have been no longer one of those subject to error—called by us not so much saints, as Christians.

It was that living faith—that eternal imperishable principle—implanted by the sovereign power of the Holy Ghost; that everlasting life, so thoroughly established within him—that secured him alike from narrowness of spirit, no better than lifeless dogmatism, and from sterility of soul which would have left him a fruitless sectarian. To prove the first of these two points it will suffice to appeal to the devoted energetic charity of his whole life; while as for the second, the facts to which we are now to call attention will amply establish it.

The reader will remember the position my father as-

sumed before 1830, with reference to the pretensions
which, because they admitted the divine institution of the
visible Church, made it necessary to find the model of that
Church, not so much in the virtues of the apostles, as in
their writings; and this, with the avowed object of realising, in a visible form, the mystic union of true believers.
It will not have been forgotten with what precision and
clearness he had already expressed the right possessed by
each Church of believers to affirm openly its special and
distinctive individuality. What he had to undergo in this
matter, so far from modifying, served only to strengthen
convictions which in him were, after all, nothing but the
natural result of innate superiority of thought and breadth
of sentiments.

In short, in my father's judgment, the Church, as the
visible Church, had but one absolute character with which
everything in it was required to consist—namely, that of
an assembly of believers, (Matt. xvi. 16–18.) Every other
characteristic which might chance to invest it, he regarded
simply as an accessory; as an earthly and fugitive thing; to
which it would consequently be wrong to attach more
than a relative importance. From this, it will appear that
the ecclesiastical institution, in its historical form, had no
importance in his eyes, except in so far as he saw in it
the manifestation of that life produced in believers by God
Himself, through the instrumentality of their faith in His
Word. On the other hand, in thus considering the
Church in the world solely from this absolute, ideal,
eternal point of view, he confounded its origin entirely
with that of the spiritual life of the faithful, of which
it was in his eyes merely a manifestation. At the same

time (and this brings us to the point which, as we have already seen, specially characterised his religious thought), inasmuch as he never recognised faith apart from the intelligible expression of it by the individual believer, the only feature to which he attached any decisive importance in his judgment of any Church, was the doctrine it believed, professed, and taught.

Everything else was in his eyes entirely human; freely submitted to private judgment; the importance of which must vanish before the question of the presence or absence of pure evangelical doctrine. Even those phases of the historical life of Churches which appear, from time to time, to exercise a direct influence on the development of their religious life, even their interior organisation or their attitude towards the civil power, were unimportant in his eyes, except in so far as he saw involved the eternal interests of the ideal, invisible, mystical Church constituted within them, under the headship of the divine Saviour, by faithful souls. Considered in themselves, these circumstances might serve to originate, in our Christian experience, decisions more or less precise, but no matter of faith was involved in them, nothing which might claim to have been dictated by a superior and infallible authority.

Such, in brief, was the conviction at the bottom of the opinions he expressed on ecclesiastical matters; while it also determined his position with regard to the different Churches. 'In this he was distinguished from the earlier seceders before 1830, and this it was that he continued to set forth from that time with increasing perspicuity in his writings, and, more especially, in his conduct.

And first, in his writings. It will be understood, after

what has just been said, how it was that he published so
sparingly on the subject of the visible Church, its constitution, and historical rights. I find little more than a
speech on this subject, in 1845, in a meeting assembled
at Lausanne, to maintain the essential independence of the
Church, with regard to the civil power. Even then he
justifies the part he took in the demonstration, solely on
his abstract idea of the mystic Church. What he aims at
upholding supremely is the spiritual liberty of the true
believer, whose faith he defines by what he deems the
only scriptural doctrine, the doctrine of free salvation,
resulting directly from the initiatory action of the sovereignty of God in Jesus Christ. As for whatever, in the
body ecclesiastical, has no immediate reference to this religious reality, or to its possession and profession; as for
the historical rights of the Church, considered by themselves, he does not even pause to advert to them.

These principles which had already withheld him, before 1830, from sacrificing to mere external unity what he
regarded as faithfulness to his message, we subsequently
discover in the position he assumed towards various
foreign Churches, as well as in Geneva itself; and that, as
much with reference to the old National Church of his
country, as to the evangelical communion of which he
witnessed the origin in 1849.

And it showed itself especially after his visit to Scotland in 1843. While confining himself strictly to testifying his sympathy with the true and faithful, without
distinction of sect, he disappointed the hopes of those of
his friends who had calculated on seeing him take part
openly with the Free Church, the rise of which had

produced so great a sensation. I append a few extracts from a pamphlet he felt called upon to publish on the occasion.*

After setting forth (in a preface addressed to the friend who had asked him to write the tract in question), the gratitude with which the brethren in Geneva had been filled on hearing of what the Lord had just done for His Church in Scotland, and their admiration at seeing so many ministers of the Saviour resolving unanimously to part with so much of what the world values, rather than permit the invasion of what they esteemed the rights of the Lord Jesus,—after adding that, as far as he was concerned, it had been his wish to convey to the Free Church, first by letter and then in person, a testimony of sympathy and respect from his little congregation,— he returns thanks to God that a great number of true servants of Christ had, nevertheless, held it to be their duty to remain in the Establishment, and so maintain in it both the preaching of the truth and those institutions which are in harmony with the gospel, and the glory of Jesus Christ.

At that very time, " while he sympathised with a Church which refused to submit to the control of the decisions which the civil power felt called upon to make in matters of spiritual economy," he foresaw that the disruption, " distressing though it appeared in the eyes of the National Church, was destined to be, in the hands of God, a means of rekindling the zeal of many, and of spreading abroad the Word of Life in quarters where it had not hitherto been preached."

* " A Visit to Scotland in 1843."

At the same time he reminds his friend " that excitement, together with political or material interests, might very possibly have influenced more than one mind, and have even been at the bottom, in more than one instance, of the ready cession of temporalities." Referring to " the days when the Lord Jesus alone, and without visible gain, would present nothing but the cross to His faithful ones," he adjures his brethren of the Free Church " to keep strict watch over the purity of their doctrine."

" My visit to your country," he says, in conclusion, " short though it has been, has been full of solace to my own soul. I have enjoyed the society of many ministers of Christ belonging to both Established and Free Churches. I have actually discovered that there is no division in Christ, and that it is the same Spirit Who is the Teacher and Comforter of all the servants of the same Saviour. If here and there I have witnessed passing exhibitions of a tendency to judge, I have nevertheless observed uniformly the triumph of charity over mere personal satisfaction, and the rights of Christ taking precedence over those of any Church or any special discipline."

He then describes the imposing scene, of which he had been an eye-witness, at Glasgow, where he had been invited to be present at the two first sessions of the General Assembly of the Free Church.

In the subsequent pages he gives an analysis of his sermons delivered at the time in different churches.*

" My desire," he says, in giving an account of his first

---

* At Aberdeen, in the Free Church ; at Edinburgh, in Dr Candlish's pulpit ; at the " Tabernacle " of J. Haldane, and elsewhere. He preached also in French, in St Luke's Church.

sermon, preached in a Free Church, " was not so much
to speak of the power which our Lord possesses, as King
of His Church, but of the right which he has to the faith
and obedience of us all." Recalling the days of the Swiss
revival, " Numbers," he says, " were animated at that
time by carnal motives. While raising the cry, ' Liberty !
Separation ! A Free Church !' they knew nothing either of
that conversion which can alone really emancipate, or of
that still small voice of the Spirit which is the teaching of
the Lord ; and hence they were soon offended. Trust not
then in human wisdom or strength ; do not be so bigoted
as to suppose that, because such and such ministers of
Christ do not go along with us, they are not serving Him.
Be not hasty to judge or to condemn. It is your charity
which will establish before God the proof of your sincerity,
and of the purity of your motives."

" It may happen (it happens frequently), that we deceive
ourselves as to our intentions ; and, while our hearts are
unrenewed, confess the gospel, or utter words of truth and
soberness in mere compliance with the demands of our
reason. But, to follow the example of Christ, to cling to
His side in the presence of the world, carrying His cross
and His reproach, — here, Christian brethren, is a thing
in which there can be no deception. Obedience brings us
into contact with what alone is real ; and our submission
is the evidence of the truth of our devotion."

In another sermon I find these words : " If mysticism, if
a certain religious sentimentality, is the error to which
Christians are exposed in Germany, is it not true that
pride of understanding and an attempt to seek to fathom
God and His mysteries, threaten those in Scotland ?"

These extracts suffice to show the ground which my father occupied, and how little that veteran confessor allowed himself to be affected in his testimony to eternal salvation by the surrounding excitement of the movement.

Decision and absolute clearness on the doctrine of con-. version, as well as of the necessity of a new life in the soul; breadth and toleration with reference to those transient forms which the outward action of that life might chance to assume—such were his characteristics; whilst, at the same time, he furnished abundant evidence of an ever accessible heart, of an ever lively and ardent enthusiasm with regard to whatever event seemed a harbinger of better days for the diffusion of the heavenly message, and for the eternal interests of the spiritual kingdom of Jesus Christ.

But if this catholicity of spirit admitted of his thus stretching out his hand as a Christian to all his brethren, wherever he might meet them, it had its irremoveable limits in what he termed the personal and special ministry ♦ entrusted to him, as he believed, in his capacity as an officer in the Church, and a preacher.

Already, before 1830, we saw that it was not merely the ecclesiastical narrowness of the separatists, with whom he had had to deal, that had prevented him from associating his labours with theirs. This decision of his was equally due to the importance he attached to what constituted, in his eyes, "purity of doctrine."

It was this last motive which chiefly prevented him, in 1849, from joining himself and his church with the Free Church, set up at that time in Geneva, by the fusion of the two nonconforming bodies, the Oratory and the Pelisserie (originally the Church of the Bourg de Four).

My father had much to endure on that occasion. Not only had he been compelled to endure the unjust accusations his conduct called forth; not only did he hear men whom he thoroughly honoured and loved, attributing his decision to a proud and bigoted spirit; but, to speak only with reference to himself, it cost him much to abandon a union which had been the dream of his whole life. Nor did he do it except from a feeling of duty. I myself was abroad at the time, and my father having written to ask me what I thought about the matter, I set before him all the reasons which led me strongly to desire that he should reunite, as a minister in the Church, with his brethren in Geneva. When I found that his mind was by no means made up in the same direction, I gathered at once that he had made a most painful sacrifice at the bidding of conscientious scruples. Afterwards, when I had had an opportunity of speaking to him on the subject, I not only found that I had judged him rightly; but I was brought to see, moreover, why it had pleased God to lead him thus to act. As for him, though suffering daily from the isolation which, from that time more than ever, characterised his position in the limited religious world of Geneva, he never appeared to me to harbour, even for a single moment, a thought of regret at the decision to which he had come.

I append a letter which he wrote on that occasion to one of my elder sisters. I give it almost entire, as it will save me from going any further into detail on this episode in his life.

" You ask me for the motives which have hitherto prevented me from adhering to the plan of the new Church, and I know no other than the fear I have lest, by joining this fusion, I should seem to sanction what I consider error. Here is my entire judgment in the matter.

" It has been customary to distinguish, in the truths of the gospel, between those indispensable to salvation, and therefore described as essential, and those which scarcely appear to have a direct bearing upon it, and which are therefore called secondary. But, among these, I think that a minister of the gospel, charged with guarding the deposit, and even with teaching the observance of 'the least commandments,' (Tim. vi. 20; Matt. v. 10), cannot draw an absolute line, and say, of such or such a point, that it ought to be waived, seeing that this point is precisely one which, some time or other, he may have to contend for with the utmost vigour. Therefore, if I feel my heart overflowing with toleration for those of my brethren, Baptists or Chiliasts,* or whatever else they may be, and if I can join in prayer and holy communion with them, this by no means involves acquiescence in their errors. Such being my conviction, I can easily contract a *union* with different Churches of believers, and so maintain with them hearty and active relations through mutual faith in the Saviour, and mutual love. But a *fusion* I could not form; in other words, a *confusion*, if I saw in them the errors I have pointed out, or some other doctrine which might appear to me to be opposed to the divine truth and

---

* These two tendencies were numerously represented among the elements which composed the new Church.

government. I should be afraid, in thus fusing the ministry of the unadulterated word with error, on the one
hand, of being faithless to my trust as a minister; on the
other, of furnishing a support, a seeming sanction, to that
error.

"Certainly if, in the arrangement just carried out, I
could have detected simple jealousy for the truth, I would
have hastened to subscribe to it. I, who, as you know
and have seen, for more than twenty-five years, have never
had in view any other ecclesiasical scheme than the union
of the different communions in one vast Presbyterian
Church, in which, the flocks remaining distinct, should
keep their individual liberty, their special idiosyncrasies,
especially in the matter of Church government."

After stating how advantageous this fusion would have
been to him in his sphere of action, and even as regarded
his social position in the religious world of Geneva,
"What of all that," he exclaims, "when compared with
the fidelity I owe to what I deem my duty as a minister
of Christ; what of temporal advantages, and the approval
of my brethren, when purchased at the cost of my peace
of conscience as a servant in the presence of his master;
what appertains to me is too precarious to be, for a
moment, considered, and, in fact, I never even thought of
it. No motive have I had, known to myself at least,
springing either from wounded self-love, or *despised dignity.*
Such a feeling I never entertained. No, my dear child, I
have been actuated simply in the way I have explained,
and if God were to show me that I have been mistaken in
that (a thing which I cannot imagine), He would give me
a different view of my duty from that which I have desired

to cherish. I am His servant, and I wish to do only what the Lord commands.

"You can enter into all my sufferings, of every kind; from without and from within. My flock has almost entirely deserted me, and, from all sides, I experience censure and reproach. But what can I do to arrest these evils, since I cannot swerve in anything from what I believe to be the right of God."

Five years after that letter was written, in 1854, he made a spontaneous overture to be admitted into the Evangelical Church, preserving, at the same time, his character of minister, and of special pastor over those who still followed him. But that idea of a confederation of free elements, in which each was to preserve its own individuality, an idea which he had always entertained, and which he delighted to express by the words, "*fusion, confusion, union, communion,*" was no better understood then than it had been in 1849. The strong desire was entertained to constitute a body, in the presence of the National Church, which was to be influential by the unity of its career and the numbers of its adherents. With this object in view, it was clearly inexpedient to take in one so independent in character as my father, while regret could scarcely be felt at the absence of the few people who still adhered to him.

It will be evident from all this that the isolated position which he occupied as regards the other Churches of the revival, was not the result of what had been a mere personal feeling with him, but had been dictated by his conscientious view of a precise duty. This is further evident from the manner in which, in 1855, he defined publicly the position occupied by his little Church with reference to the National Church of Geneva, as well as from the nature of his action towards the latter communion at the time of which we are now speaking.

On the occasion of a declaration which emanated from the Grand Council in 1855, "that the only reason which dissenting Churches had for their existence was their mere negative opposition to the National Church," he took up the subject in a tract, entitled " The Church of Testimony in its relations, as regards doctrine and discipline, with the ancient Church of Geneva."

Having briefly referred to the origin of his church, he lays it down that the sole reason for its existence is founded in the preaching of the orthodox doctrine of the Reformed Churches, and the maintenance of their ancient discipline. So far from being, in consequence, opposed to the true National Church of Geneva, it aspired the rather, in its limited sphere, solely to revive the old doctrines and old life of that Church. He then concludes his exposition of the doctrine and discipline of his Church, by saying, "that if they were actually dissenters, they were not separatists."

But it was not merely by the abstract declaration of his ecclesiastical principles that he manifested towards the National Establishment such a breadth and superiority of view, as to draw down upon him, from many of his brethren, the charge of ecclesiastical indifference. It is all the more important to point out the facts, to which I am now referring, since he has been perpetually accused by the national party itself, of having been actuated only by a feeling of animosity towards the Church from which he had seceeded, and of having done all in his power to injure it abroad. There is evidently some misconception here. It is not for me to inquire how far the National Church could be calumniated abroad. What I affirm is, that my father never did so, unless, indeed, by the loyal and open opposition which he manifested, (whenever he was called upon to do so), towards those negative tendencies which had obtained among the clergy of that Church, and in the name of which they had compelled him to detach his labours from theirs. And now for the facts referred to.

It is well known how far the subject of a separation between the Church and State had succeeded, about 1842, in occupying the attention of all parties. In the Canton de Vaud, Vinet had extensively agitated it, and even in Geneva it had been the theme of public discussions, on the occasion of the elections for the Constituent Assembly in 1842, as well as in the very bosom of the Assembly itself.* When the question of the choice of deputies came up, that point had figured in the very front of the programme of the different candidates.

As my father knew that many of his brethren would stand aloof, he asked me what I thought of doing; especially with reference to the question of the Church. I replied, that whatever might be the opinion required as to the theological doctrines professed in the National Church, that institution did not the less appear to me, at that crisis, a providential barrier against the rising tide of ultra-montanism, and that from that point of view it seemed to me to be incumbent on every friend of the

* See also De Goltz, "Genève Religieuse," p. 340, *et seq.*

country, and of liberty to maintain it. My father told me that such was his judgment in the matter, and we went together to drop our votes into the ballot-box.

I remember that, as we were returning, we met one of the first representatives of the evangelical party in Geneva, who, so far from sympathising with our views, expressed himself as greatly surprised at the course we had taken, assuring us that we were probably the only dissenters who had voted in the same way.

The state of things inaugurated in 1842 having been subverted in 1846, the same question came up again in 1847 in a more urgent manner. Indeed, everything combined to awaken the gravest fears for the National Church, and to strengthen the conviction that the point then to be mooted was no mere modification of the relation hitherto subsisting between it and the civil power, but involved its very existence. It was on this occasion that, in the teeth of the aspirations of an evangelical section which appeared to hail, in the overthrow of the National Church, the advent of a new era, my father issued a three-paged tract, entitled, " Remove not the ancient landmarks which thy fathers have placed," (Prov. xxii. 28.) Commencing by quoting the beautiful and resolute address which the " company of pastors " had just issued to the grand council, setting forth " that they could not die who had with them the power which God bestows," he refers to his " Declaration of Fidelity to the Church of Geneva," published twenty-six years before. " In separating at that time from an unfaithful communion," he says, " neither he nor his brethren dreamt of opposing that ancient Protestant Church of Geneva, which God Himself had planted among them as a barrier

2 D

against the encroachments of Romanism." Giving full
scope to the ardour of his patriotic sentiments, and his
feelings as "an old Protestant," he conjures up before him,
phantom-like, the idea of the final destruction of that
ancient bulwark of liberty and evangelical truth, known as
Genevese Protestantism. "Separate Church and State,"
he cries, "if the State is weary of the Union. Give her
back her symbols and standards if she has been rifled of
them. Restore to its proud place of honour in her midst
the teaching of the Word, if she has been reft of her
dignity! Do this, and all,—yes, all true Protestants—I
mean, all Christians—will rejoice; but have a care not to
remove the ancient landmarks, and, under a show of liberalism, to take away from Geneva what alone has rendered
her liberal, if indeed we are to understand by this word
what the Bible calls true liberty,—given and maintained by
truth, the gospel, and the Christian faith." He goes on to
entreat his fellow-citizens, "instead of meditating the destruction of the Church of Geneva, to strengthen it, on the
contrary, by reminding it of all that it was, and all it
ought once again to become."

This little tract made a considerable impression at the
time. Not only did it find an echo among a people whose
patriotism is so easily stirred up, by appealing to the
memory of their past, but it helped to remove more than
one prejudice against its author. The majority of his
contemporaries, in fact, having ceased for many years to
hold any communication with him, though seeing him
daily, had accustomed themselves to judge him by hear-
say, and had mistaken his dogmatic opposition for what
would have been mere party hostility and sectarian rancour.

For myself, I lay all the more stress on this exhibition of what I may best call his ecclesiastical and religious patriotism, inasmuch as it appeared just after he had experienced a fresh proof of the implacable hatred entertained towards him in that very Church whose ancient and glorious memories he so glowingly recalls. That animosity had, indeed, gone so far as to assume the appearance of personal aversion, and to make its way under the disguise of indirect anonymous denunciations.

Let me refer here to a letter, addressed by one of the influential members of the National Church of Geneva to one of the first pastors of Holland, immediately after my father's missionary tour in that country, in 1842, during which, as will be remembered, he was everywhere received with respect. That letter, which was circulated through the Dutch Churches, aroused deep indignation. It was sent at once to my father, who had hitherto regarded its author (one of his old school-fellows), as a man on whose personal sentiments he could safely rely. He gave him the letter himself, imploring him, in the name of truth, and of their old relations to each other, to spare him the necessity of a reply. His "friend," however, met all his entreaties with absolute silence. I remember well his return from the interview. Pale, and deeply moved, he said to my mother, as he entered the house, "I have lost an old friend to-day." It was not till then that he wrote to the ecclesiastic in Holland his reply to the dishonourable epistle he had received through his hands. Both letters were forthwith published in Holland.* "We

* Papers relative to Dr Malan's last visit to Holland. Amsterdam: Hoogkamer & Co., 1843.

abstain from all comments at this point," so we read in a preface to the reader, "leaving the publication of the truth in the hands of our great God and Saviour, Jesus Christ, the King Eternal, Who knows how to avenge all iniquity, and to punish falsehood and calumny, whatever be the name or title of their authors."

It is needless to add that these libellous personalities, were it only for their virulence, were powerless to injure any but the man who had been capable of uttering them.

As for the manner in which my father resented the outrage, I will content myself with saying that I found after his death, at the bottom of a cupboard, a packet enclosing a few copies of the publication, the title of which is given in the note, which had been sent him for distribution. It remained in the state in which he had received it twenty years before, and I read then for the first time the letter of his "friend" in Geneva. He did not content himself, however, with estimating such attacks at their proper value. While they pained him deeply every time they occurred, they never left in him the slightest trace of bitterness, either against the persons, or parties themselves. We have just had a proof of this; what I am now going to relate will furnish evidence still more striking.

It was in 1853, after his last visit to Scotland, one of the principal preachers of the Free Church in Edinburgh having refused to allow him to preach in his chapel because he would not pledge himself to abstain from preaching in Established churches, several other Free Church ministers came forward at once and offered him their pulpits, so that he realised his wish of being able to exercise his ministry in both communions. In a very numerous gathering of the National Church, when he was asked to say a few words on the state of religion on the continent, he delivered an address, a few extracts from which I will insert in this place.

After reminding his hearers that their Church, the National Church of Scotland, though originally a daughter of the Church of Geneva, had declined to send a deputation to their jubilee, in consequence of the position assumed by the latter towards the evangelical revival, he assured them that he was delighted to seize the opportunity of declaring publicly to the faithful in Scotland—to those Christians who had given him such a brotherly welcome, at a time when, thirty years ago, he was being persecuted by the clergy of the Church of Geneva, and compelled to separate himself from that Church—that it had pleased God to bring thither again the preaching of the pure gospel which, said he, "is now making itself heard with more power and clearness than had marked the discourses for which he had been suspended." He invited them, moreover, to rejoice with him at what God Himself had wrought in drawing out their sympathies to that ancient Church which their fathers had revered, and, above all, in encompassing it with their prayers, that it might be upheld in its onward career.

This explicit address, supported by numerous facts, produced a great sensation in Scotland. A desire was expressed in many quarters that the wishes my father had thus publicly uttered might soon be realised, and friendly relations re-established between the national Churches of

Scotland and Geneva. The sudden feeling, however, was
arrested as soon as started, by letters written from Geneva,
and published in the organ of the Free Church in Edinburgh—letters which tended to destroy the impression
produced by the testimony just given.

The cause was still there. When on a visit to Edinburgh
three years afterwards, I happened to hear the facts I have
just mentioned. I went immediately to the Moderator of
the General Assembly, who, after having heard what I had
to say, encouraged me to resume the good work which my
father had commenced. The Moderator of the Company
of Pastors in Geneva, Pastor Duby, having furnished me,
at my request, with some specific details as to the evangelical preaching in the Church over which he presided, I
handed over the papers, accompanied by a statement in my
handwriting, to a relative, Sheriff Arkley, lay deputy to
the General Assembly. A letter addressed by him to the
President of the Committee, intrusted with the communications with Foreign Churches, was read, in May 1857, in
the Assembly itself. Thereupon that body charged the
Committee to write to the National Church of Geneva in
the spirit of the conclusions adopted by Mr Arkley, which
were based again on the public testimony given by my
father in 1853. The next year these letters were sent to
the President of the Consistory of Geneva, and from that
time there was no further obstacle to the existence of
friendly relations between the two Churches. Thus, my
father had the satisfaction of witnessing the triumph of
his efforts, which he had commenced with such thorough
Christian heartiness. Facts like these are ample testimony

to the emptiness of the accusations referred to above, and for that reason they are quoted here.*

It was not for him to decide whether he should re-enter the Church of Geneva, not, indeed, as a pastor, which he never contemplated, and which his principles, with reference to Church discipline, would have absolutely prohibited, but to exercise his ministry as a preacher of the gospel. I allude here not merely to the protests which he never ceased to make against the inhibition with which the established clergy had visited him, but to the circumstances which occurred at the close of his life in 1859 and 1861, and with which I will conclude my account of his ecclesiastical relations.

The period was 1859. For a long time the friends my father had acquired among the national clergy of Geneva had arrived at the conclusion that there was no further obstacle in the way of his realising a wish he had always cherished of preaching once more, as minister of the gospel, in those pulpits which had only been closed to him by the "Réglement" of May 1817, which "Réglement," as a matter of fact, after becoming practically obsolete, had been repudiated by the Church itself on the occasion of the Jubilee in 1835.† Whilst some desired to see this brought about, simply from regard for an old man who was regarded with general esteem; whilst others thought that it was

---

* My Scotch readers may possibly be interested in knowing that the preceding narrative having been sent by me a year ago to my lamented brother-in-law, Sheriff Arkley, met with his full approval.

† Publicly, if not officially, and in an answer given by the President of the Solemnity, speaking in his official character, to a query put to him on the subject by deputations from several churches.

time that his capacity of minister of the gospel, which no one out of Geneva had ever dreamt of challenging, and which, even in Geneva itself, was universally accorded to him in personal intercourse, should be recognised in an official and public manner, it was their wish that after it had been stated how the exercise of the ministerial office had been unjustly denied him by the ruling section of the Church at a particular period, the history of Geneva might be able to furnish evidence, through subsequent transactions, that that act of injustice had been repudiated.

The men who cherished these sentiments were the true and sincere friends of our National Church, and I was requested to communicate to my father the wish they entertained. I see him now, at the moment when I convinced him that a serious possibility was involved in the question. The old man's eye flashed with sudden light, soon dimmed by the presence of deep emotion. After looking at me for an instant in silence, " Is it possible !" exclaimed the venerable servant of the old Church of Geneva, the Church of confessors and refugees, the Church of Calvin—" Is it possible that I may preach again in St Peter's * before I go into the presence of my God ?"

At the same time, everything depended on the Consistory ; and consequently, as is always the case where deliberative assemblies are concerned, especially when such assemblies have as yet no abundant tradition of precedents behind them, everything depended on the way in which the Consistory was to be secured in the matter.†

---

* The Cathedral Church of Geneva.

† "Owing to a recent change, to which we have already alluded, the highest administration of the Protestant Church had been transferred a

Meanwhile, a preacher of the National Church, whom my father, then in the country, went to hear from time to time, requested him to occupy his pulpit. Having understood him to say that he was ready to comply, the preacher entered upon certain proceedings with the Consistory in May 1859, which he deemed requisite before feeling himself at liberty to place his pulpit at my father's disposal. The Consistory, on a precognition which they demanded from the Company of Pastors, resolved to set aside the prayer addressed to them, on the ground that it was necessary first that my father should withdraw the letter in which he had declared himself, in 1823, to be no longer desirous to remain in the National Church. Thereupon the author of the prayer forebore to insist upon it; and my father, seeing that no further reference was being made to the matter, by degrees regarded it as at an end.

It was only two years afterwards, in 1861, in reply to a letter in which the same pastor referred to what has just been stated, he wrote a reply, an extract of which I proceed to furnish :—

"VANDŒUVRES, *19th August*, 1861.

"DEAR AND HONOURED BROTHER,— . . . To refer simply to the demand that I should withdraw my letter to the Council of State (14th August 1823), before the Consistory could even entertain the idea of re-admitting me into the national pulpit in our Canton ; I cannot tell you how much that clause distresses me, since it declares, what I was far from supposing, that the National Church of our country, at least among those who govern it, holds the same opinions

few years previously, from the 'Vénérable Compagnie' of the pastors, to a 'Consistory,' consisting principally of laymen."

which it held more than forty years ago, when it drove from its pulpits the orthodox ministers of Geneva.

" . . . For me to withdraw now my declaration of the 14th of August 1823, it would be necessary first for the Consistory to give me to understand that it, for its part, withdraws what caused me to retire from the National Church of Geneva.

"My protest will fall to the ground of itself as soon as the cause which elicited it shall cease to exist. . . . May it please God to bring this about! . . . I wait for it with the most fervent desire, . . . rejecting even the thought that I, a minister of the Lord Jesus, could have withdrawn from a Church faithful to the Son of God." The letter closes by permission to his correspondent to publish it if he chooses.

A note in his handwriting, dated 15th of May 1859, shows even more clearly the precise character of his wishes. The same friend, having told him that he ought to address a personal and direct request to the Consistory: "I have replied," he writes, "that I by no means seek admission into the National Church of Geneva, but permission only to exercise my ministry in the State of Geneva; in other words, to preach the gospel, without opposition, in any pulpit which may be offered to me."

We should much prefer seeing in all this nothing more than a misunderstanding. My father had in view simply the sole rights of the evangelical ministry, rights which the Church of Geneva had never hesitated to recognise as pertaining to any ecclesiastic who, without being within its jurisdiction, was accepted as such by any of the Protestant Churches. The Consistory, on the other hand, failing to mark the distinction between the vindication of their rights, and of the rights which appertained exclusively to the ministers of the National Church,—concerned itself only with the latter. The fault, however, seems not to have been chargeable to the Consistory itself, which perhaps could only take into consideration the question of the readmission of my father into the ranks of the national clergy.

However that may be, it is plain that the reply of the Consistory to the demand addressed to it could only be regarded by my father as a veiled refusal, and that he could not meet it otherwise than he did. In fact, his letter to the Council of State, of which the Consistory demanded the previous withdrawal, had been the consequence and not the cause of the interdiction from ministering which had been issued several years before. More than this, that interdict had been based solely on my father's refusal to submit to the " Réglement " of May 1817, which had for so many years ceased to be quotable as having the force of law in the Church of Geneva, so that the Consistory could not possibly have had it in view. The only thing on which it could rely, therefore, was that unfortunate decision by which the " Venerable Assembly," exceeding, as we have seen, the powers of a Protestant tribunal, had gone so far as to perpetuate, by means of a simple administrative arrest, an act of sacerdotal supremacy, in declaring, without discussion, and in the most absolute way, that " Malan was deprived of his holy orders."

In the presence of this fact, it is evident that the Consistory could not at least, without committing the same fault that we have laid to the charge of the " Venerable

Company," annul officially this illusory and illegal decree of deposition from the sacred ministry by one of restoration, which would have been open to the same exception. From the moment its attention was drawn to this first decree, it had no alternative except to invite my father, at his own positive request, to accept a second ordination at the hands of the "Company of Pastors." Evidently, to such a step as this he never gave a thought. It would therefore, we believe, have been much better to have regarded this decree as having been in excess of the legal powers of the ecclesiastical administration to which it had succeeded, and to have utterly ignored it.

From that time, in view of the fact that the interdiction which had been pronounced against my father was virtually annulled by the withdrawal of the "Règlement" which had occasioned it, evidently the only reply to make to his friend was that there was no conceivable reason why a pastor of the Church of Geneva should not admit Dr Malan into his pulpit as a minister of the holy gospel.

The Consistory was all the more favourably situated with reference to the question from the circumstance that it not only had before it the official acts connected with the readmission of the minister Bost into the National Church, in which the questions at issue were clearly discussed, but also that it was regarded universally as having inaugurated, in the history of that Church, a new era of life and liberty.

It cannot but be regretted that, under these circumstances, no pastor of the National Church ventured to invite my father's services. Such a step would have virtually annihilated a "suspensio a divinis," the grounds of which ha.. no longer weight with any one. We think such a course would have tended to the glory of God, and that such a man would have deserved well of his Church.

If, however, it had been deemed desirable to carry the matter before the ecclesiastical authorities, it would have been necessary that one perfectly versed in the facts, and with no personal interests in the discussion, should have taken the matter in hand. Everything inclines to the belief that, if a proposal, based upon the considerations now alleged, had been laid before the Consistory in proper form, that body would have seized the opportunity of closing a long open wound. It would thus have accomplished in our judgment a great act of justice, and, in the interest of the history of the Church, whose progress it directed, a Church which still wears the venerated name of the ancient Church of our fathers, it is certainly to be regretted that this was not the case.

CHAPTER III.

" Abide with me when night is nigh,
For without Thee I cannot die ! "

THE foregoing chapter has already introduced us into this last stage of my father's life, of which it now remains for me to recall the beautiful and affecting remembrance. The close of his career was, in fact, protracted, and, in some respects, painful. To the brilliancy and activity of his youth succeeded early those years of which the wise man says, " that there is no pleasure in them ;" years in which, in an isolation continually more and more marked, he had also to experience, occasionally, straitened circumstances, and continual and prolonged bodily sufferings.

As we have already seen, he had omitted no effort to give his numerous family as careful and complete an education as possible. Himself, keenly conscious of the species of solitude to which they were reduced, he set to work to remedy it by every means in his power; whether by fostering the development of what seemed to him their talents and tastes, or by according them, within the domestic limits, whatever pleasure and relaxation comported with his principles and his means.

But, in all this, he only followed the dictates of his fatherly heart. Hence, when he had completed the education of his large family, and, at his advanced age, could no longer take boarders, he found himself reduced to a position which would never have been suspected by those who judged of his circumstances only by what they had seen him do for his children.

At the same time there appeared in him, at a very early period, symptoms of a disease which, if it does not at once reach the vital parts, affects no less the centre of the bodily strength, and even the mental energy. In his case, meanwhile, the disease assumed a special character. Whilst, generally, the physical weakness, which is one of its most distressing features, not only shakes the soundest temperaments, but calls out, even in the kindliest and happiest characters, discontent, murmuring, and rebellion,—this was never the case with him. For a long time we were unacquainted with his sufferings, and, when we came to understand them, we were amazed to see how far, in spite of them, and of the nervous unrest which resulted from his complaint, his force of will and entire self-forgetfulness triumphed. Here, however, were virtues which he had practised all his life. I remember when I was a young man discovering, accidentally, that he was obliged to look closely to his expenditure, and that he allowed me then to speak to him about it. After a brief discussion, he recommended me to take no more notice of the matter, and, above all, not to mention it to my mother: "These

are things," he said, " with which I had rather not
trouble your dear mother, she must not know anything
about them. As for me, my dear boy, I have felt for a long
time that the silver and the gold belong to my God and
heavenly Father, and that He will never suffer us to want
what is needful."

But while his faith remained so strong that, instead of
seeking to disturb those around him, he continued constant
to his old practice of concerning himself especially with
making every exertion for them, his suffering was none the
less evident to all of us. The visits of strangers, who were
perpetually coming to see and hear him, and even of
his best friends, instead of proving a source of recreation
and interest, as they once did, had begun to weary him.
The cramps in his stomach, from which he had always
suffered, were now combined with headache, which deprived him of rest, and soon loud buzzings in his ears
very often took away his sleep.

Under these circumstances it was not strange to find him
sometimes smarting too sensibly, perhaps, under a sense of
his isolated position in Geneva. Not that his intercourse
with his brethren of the evangelical party was ever devoid
of mutual respect, or that he was not asked from time to
time to speak in their places of worship, but only on exceptional and very rare occasions. If the old man—worn out
with the sufferings of age, and the deceptions by which
ardent and confiding natures will ever be weighed down—
exaggerated a little, perhaps, the extent of his annoyances,
it is not the less true, for all that, that he experienced
mortification in his old age so intense and profound as
could be fully described to God alone, by him who was

called upon to endure them. Nor were they altogether without adequate cause. He heard men whose efforts had long ago been anticipated by himself, who had even at the time hailed him with acclamation, who had only walked in the path cleared up for them by his courage and devotion,—boast publicly, amid the applause of their friends, that "they had been the first to wave in Geneva the banner of orthodoxy." Thus he not only found himself withdrawn from the efforts of his youth, but he saw others enter into his labour, and parade it as theirs under his very eyes, while they impressed upon it a character totally alien to his sympathies. He received from officious sources copies of such of his own works as had appeared anonymously, which were sent to him as models to follow, and as a criticism on those which he had issued with his name attached. At the gatherings, to which his brotherly spirit was for ever taking him, he heard his own hymns sung to strange, and often ill-chosen airs, altered, too, occasionally, by unskilful hands. He saw himself, if not put aside, at least left aside, by men whose opening career he had followed, if not guided, with interest. In a word, his great soul had to submit in silence, year after year, to the sacrifice of personal feeling, as well as to that general desertion by which it pleases God that the evening of His beloved ones should be accompanied after their day of action and energy is over, and by means of which, in His wisdom and love, He is wont to ripen for glory those strong and generous spirits whom He had at one time appointed to be head over their brethren.

And this gracious purpose He commenced, by revealing it to His servant. Lamenting with my father one day that

the path he had to traverse was so arduous, he replied,
"Yes, it is painful; but then it is God Who has bid me
walk in it, and He has excellent reasons for doing so.
When I was young and strong, I was a hammer of iron,
which His mighty hand made use of to break up the
stones. Now it is still His work; it is still His fatherly
hand which, after having handled me for use on others,
is forging me for myself."

Thus it was that his faith in God kept him from being
irritated or beaten down. Thus, as we have seen, in connection with his literary activity, his latter years were, in
this respect, his most productive. As for his private life,
it was cheered by the news he received of his numerous
absent children, and by an active correspondence with
Foreign Churches and the leaders of the evangelical movement; while through all his dejection might be seen, side
by side with the remains of an ever manly energy, the
constancy of a faith which became each day more simple
and touching.

His thoughts dwelt also, the older he grew, on the
memories of his childhood. "Alas," he wrote, in 1843, to
his mother's eldest sister, who was living abroad, "Clavelière is almost in ruins. The linden-tree and the great fir-
tree have both been cut down. They have knocked down
the clock wing, and changed the old porch. The fashion
of this world passeth away; God seeks to turn our thoughts
to that which passeth not away."

We have seen the effects of my brother Jocelyn's death
upon him, in 1846; and how, in 1848, he had to close the
eyes of his gentle and pious mother, "after having had the
privilege of remaining incessantly with her,"—so I read in

some notes of which she is the subject,—"during the five months that she was confined to her bed."

"Everything goes on here," he writes to my mother, "like the glacier which looks as if it never changed its place, though it glides on every day with an irresistible motion. My good mother is so very pale and cold." After saying how the old lady had prayed "God bless thee," accompanying the exclamation with some one of the endearing terms with which she had been accustomed to address him in his childhood, he adds, "Alas, she'll soon be unable to utter even that below; but what endless things her soul will utter in heaven, where our glorified Jocelyn already is!"

"I have lost her," he writes in another place, "who was, for sixty years, my earliest and my constant friend and benefactress."

It was at this time especially that he began to appear depressed and dejected—his elasticity gone. "I find myself much as I was in 1819," we read in his Church journal for 1849, at the time when he saw the remainder of his little congregation showing symptoms of an intention to desert him and join the new Evangelical Church. From that time, he began to feel himself no longer happy at Pré-Béni. On the removal of the fortifications, the town had been extended. The gardens which had surrounded his dwelling changed rapidly into noisy suburbs, and high houses looked down on all sides over a spot which till then had been a shadowed and secluded solitude. After having married two of my sisters to foreign husbands, on the same day, he found the house too big for him and my mother, and the garden too deserted. Moreover, his writings were no longer eagerly caught up ; new voices were heard instead of his. With all the deference paid to his name, it was with difficulty that he could get his articles inserted in the different religious journals which were being rapidly started on all sides. Meanwhile, he could not understand how the discussion of this or that passing topic of the day was regarded as more important than his grave and lucid expositions of scriptural doctrines. The truth is, that a new movement, and one with which he was only remotely connected, had begun gradually to obscure, among the adherents of the evangelical cause, those eternal interests of salvation and that personal love of the Saviour which had been at the bottom of the courage and perseverance he had displayed in his youth, and which had continued to characterise his best years ; while a special prominence was awarded in many minds to the distracting consideration of the rights of Churches, and of the liberties of a religious world in which he felt himself out of place, and the several factions of which invariably wearied him.

This is evident from his correspondence at that time. His letters are almost always called forth by some necessity arising to vindicate the position of independence he had assumed with regard to the ecclesiastical parties, whether in Geneva or abroad. The impression produced on reading them is of a mixed character. While they evince an elevation of thought and catholicity of spirit, developed with ever-increasing clearness, it is impossible to feel indifferent at the proof they give of the degree to which his isolation had weighed him down.

"I have ever received at my own table, as at the table of the Lord, all the disciples of Jesus Christ," he writes to a friend who had deserted him because he had entertained a professor of the Established Church of Scotland. "Whatever might be the form of the Church to which they belonged, I have ever shown them respect and affection. Dissenter though I am myself, I am far from supposing that my friends are confined to dissenters. No, no! the Lord Jesus has not forsaken His sheep because the pasture in which they feed is under the protection of the great ones of the earth."

At Geneva, where he suffered daily, he never hesitated to cross-examine himself over and over again as to whether by any possibility he could follow a different line. This appears in the numerous letters which passed between him and the pastors of the evangelical Church at that time. We see there, side by side with an entire intercommunion of faith and piety, the evidence of two opinions clearly defined. On the one side predominate the interests and the unity of the visible Church; on the other, purity of doctrine, and the hopelessness of attempting to confine the free action of the Holy Spirit to fixed institutions. The correspondence, from this point of view, is full of interest. Whilst the thorough uprightness of the men to whom it introduces us prevented them from having any reserve with one another, their sentiments of mutual deference and fervent charity invariably reunited them, in a stronger bond, at each point of separation. I refer especially to the letters between my father and Merle D'Aubigné, in which the tenderness of an old friendship blended with the traits arising out of the character and piety of the two men.

" It is good," he says, in a letter to one of his children

to whom he had been in the habit of speaking his mind very freely, after a passing reference to his regret at finding himself estranged abroad from many old friends,—" it is good, it is necessary, that heaven should reveal itself to us as a reality, utterly different from this poor world, even from the so-called Christian world. The heart draws closer to the Friend who remains the same for ever—even the Lord Jesus. So faithful, so sincere, so real!"

Gradually he withdrew altogether from the scene. After 1848 he used to pass the summer in a little country house which he had inherited from his mother at Vandœuvres. Eventually, in 1855, he resolved, by his son's advice, to take up his abode there entirely. This he did in 1857, after having exhibited once more in the sale of Pré-Béni and in the thousand matters of detail which such a change involved—the decision, energy, and activity of his best years. It was no light thing, indeed, at seventy years of age, to leave the neighbourhood of the town where he had always lived, and the house in which thirty-five years of domestic life had been passed, and to carry out such repairs and building arrangements as were necessary for an entirely new establishment in a retired village, with no further change in prospect; to have his library conveyed there; to set up his workshop and lithographical machinery; above all, to change his study,—to desert the old one filled with endless memories, and which had been for so long a time the sanctuary of his joys and sorrows in the presence of his God.

His plans determined on, however, he did not hesitate; indeed, so far was he from regretting his decision, that we even wondered at the readiness with which he adapted

himself to the change. We soon found him becoming
daily more enamoured of his retreat. Moreover, he was
the first to recognise with gratitude to God that that decision which had been to him so painful originally, had
nevertheless, by determining his position, led to a provi-
sion for his old age amply sufficient for his moderate wants
and simple and orderly habits.

The traveller landing at Geneva by a lake steamer, on
one of those warm, bright summer evenings which lend to
our climate the glow of an Italian sunset,—after gazing
wonderingly at the crimsoned ridges of the glaciers of
Mont Blanc, will notice, as his eye forsakes the paling
mountain, a hill which skirts the shore by the margin of
which he is being rapidly borne. Many villas cluster on
its beautiful ridges, gleaming among the dark green masses
of park and thicket foliage. Its name is " Cologny," the
name, too, of the village which crowns it on the west,
within twenty minutes' walk of Geneva.

Setting out from the city and arriving there, he will
leave behind him the dusty roads of the suburbs, and
even the distant views of the bridges and quays. Extending his walk a little further he will reach the summit of the hill, where he will be compelled to pause. The
sublimest of prospects unveils before him its sudden
splendours. Face to face with him are the eternal Alps,
surrounding with their sky-piercing pinnacles the snowy
form of their majestic monarch, and encircled by an outer
range, alternately bare and wooded. At his feet he sees,
not here, as on the other side of the city, the blue and
motionless surface of the Léman, but a long wide plain,

spreading under his gaze, with its towns, cottages, and
woods,—and melting by degrees into the nearest declivities
of the Voirons, of Môle and of Salève ; while the eye
follows its last windings into the heart of the populous
valleys which lose themselves between the above-named
mountains.   Here and there, on all sides, country houses
of the citizens,—some of them veritable chateaux,—face,
with their groves and lawns, the tranquil and majestic
landscape.   Near him at his feet glitters, among the trees
which conceal its base, the summit of a modest steeple,
with peasants' cottages grouped around.   It is the
church and village of Vandœuvres, one of the loveliest
retreats a sage could covet, wherein to forget the turmoil
of busy towns ; or a Christian, wearied with the tumult of
life, to prepare himself for those eternal mansions which
the distant view of the lofty Alps, more vividly even than
the ocean itself, seems fitted to suggest to the soul.

At the extremity of the village, out of sight and hearing
of its houses, stands the modest dwelling where my father
spent the seven last years of his life.   You scarcely enter
it when you see right in front, through the glazed door,
Mont Blanc himself, the centre of the landscape the
details of which we have endeavoured to describe.   Close
at hand a long terrace, supported by a low wall, stretches
in front of the house, extending beyond it on either
side.   Lower down is a flower garden with a vine-clad
arbour, and, lower still, a small orchard bordered with oaks,
and shaded here and there by a few fruit trees.   At one
end of the terrace a wooden summer-house offers its
shelter from the north wind.   Brought here from the
Pré-Béni, it bears on its front the passage of Scripture

which my father inscribed upon it in 1823: "Then they that feared the Lord spake often one to another: and the Lord hearkened, and heard," (Mal. iii. 16.) Seated there, we see before us, on the other side of the garden, an old house almost entirely covered with a wild vine. It still contains some habitable rooms in which my father used to put up those of his family who came to stay with him from time to time.

Such is the retreat to which my parents withdrew in 1857, with one of my sisters who never left them, and who still lives there with my mother.

At the time of the sale of the Pré-Béni, my father took care to reserve the usufruct of his chapel, as well as possession of its materials. His object in this was to prevent, after his death, a building so long consecrated to the preaching of the gospel, being handed over to secular uses.

So, while living at Vandœuvres, he continued to minister at the chapel. Giving up the week meetings, however, he confined himself to the Sunday services; generally walking over for the purpose. He contrived a little room in the summer-house where he had commenced his meetings in 1819, in which he rested a few moments before entering the pulpit, and where he received, after the sermon, any who might wish to speak to him.

Who shall conjecture his thoughts in that place where he had commenced his courageous testimony, and where he came forty years afterwards, a white-haired old man, not to contemplate the triumph of his own labours, but to bow down before the same Lord and Master Who had so wonderfully accomplished the work under his own eyes.

In those concluding years his preaching changed wonderfully. There were days when he seemed to have summoned back the fire, the clearness, the eloquence of his youth. His congregation, too, which had been so reduced after 1849, increased very perceptibly. For himself, his pulpit ministrations alone gave importance to a life which was becoming feebler every day. Sometimes, on a doubt arising, as to whether he would be strong enough for the next Sunday's service, he would appear to hesitate, yet, when the day came, he would set out on foot for the city, often through rain and snow. It was not till afterwards that he had recourse to a conveyance, and, at first, only for his return. Not only throughout his whole life did he avoid, as far as possible, occasioning Sunday labour to any, but he seemed positively on that day to regain something of his former vigour.

That vigour, however, was only called forth in him, in connection with eternal interests. As we have already seen, he never attached much importance to the strifes of parties, and the excitement of what is called the religious world. Now, more than ever, the invisible kingdom, the work of God in human hearts, the return of wandering souls to a holy and merciful Father, Whom the Saviour reveals, and to Whom He conducts,—became each day increasingly his constant and soul-absorbing concern.

When he asked me for news from Geneva, it was in this direction that his inquiry pointed. It was his delight to hear of the gospel being preached with life and warmth, whatever might be the Church where it was delivered, and whose-soever the lips that delivered it. As for the ever-changing affairs of men, and the ever-deceiving promises of parties, he ignored, and, what is more, he wished to ignore them. He felt it a relief to be, as he used to say, "removed from all that." Almost lost sight of by those who had come after him, he was, to the general public, merely an old man, whose irreproachable life and habitual benevolence commanded universal respect. Educated men, while they saluted him with marked respect, were in evident terror, "lest he should question them about their souls." The people, however, who were not so over-sensitive were instinctively drawn towards him. His departure from Eaux Vives was a positive grief to many families in that populous parish, and at Vaudœuvres he soon found himself invested with the confidence and respect of all the villagers.

There, too, he found, in the good pastor of the place, a man as courteous as he was large-hearted. He made a point of attending his church whenever his own service was in the afternoon, as it usually was in winter. While, on their part, M. Theremin and his family never ceased to evince towards my mother and him the most thoughtful and devoted attention, which tended greatly to diminish the solitude of their life, and the remembrance of which they will always gratefully cherish.

From time to time a return of strength arrested for a moment the weakness and infirmity of age. Thus, during the first years of his stay at Vandœuvres, he was greatly occupied with the publication of several of his tracts in America. A gentleman, till then unknown to him, having read some of them, wished to see English versions of them distributed through the United States. Correspondence with him, his warmth of heart, and his zeal for the interests of the gospel, were among the sweetest mercies with which it pleased God to brighten the last years of my father's life.

Another great delight was the festival of the Evangelical Alliance, which took place at Geneva, in August 1861. Nothing could more thoroughly harmonise with what had been all his life long the one earnest desire of his soul, than the idea on which that Alliance had been established. We may recall his words in 1818. "Whatever be his confession or denomination, the man who believes with all his heart in the merits of the Lord Jesus is my brother, and as soon as I recognise him as such I will make him feel it to the utmost of my power." It is well known that the leaders of the Genevese branch of the Alliance thought that they ought to replace, by a dogmatic formula, clearly expressed, the simple declaration of faith and piety which had served till then as the rallying standard of the Association; my father, though he did not start the idea, certainly supported it. Indeed, he had long cherished a wish that the Alliance would adopt what he called "a more open and living confession," while, at the same time, he deplored the fact that his brethren of the National Church kept aloof from it.* From his point of view,

---

* I find the following opinion on the subject of Confessions of Faith in a letter he wrote, in 1862, to a friend of his :— "For my part, I always looked upon Confessions of Faith, in Christ's Church, not as obligatory formulas and rules for thought, belief, or profession ; but as (what they really are) solemn manifestations of conviction ; sign-posts, as it were, on the high-roads ; placed to show the way where paths diverge. Did the sign-post ever constitute the road itself ? . . . . . The science of sciences must also declare what it is, not in order to make itself what it already is, but in order to manifest itself openly." "It certainly does not

indeed, he could only see, in such a formula, a sign of
fidelity and frankness in the confession of the faith itself.
Letters, which he wrote to a friend at that time, show the
indignation he felt at the protest which emanated from
twenty-two of the National clergy, against this declaration
of orthodoxy. One would have said that the cry of
"Negation" had been heard again after a long silence,
denounced once so openly by his powerful voice.

It was not without emotion, and gratitude to God, as
evinced by these same letters, that he found himself on
that occasion, after an interval of more than forty years,
one of a multitude of godly men, present from all parts, at
this great solemnity, in the church of St Peter, which, to
all Genevese Protestants, is the sanctuary and palladium of
their country. He had not crossed its threshold since the
day when, in August 1818, he had preached that sermon
which had resulted in his inhibition. Now it was no
longer to strive, or to protest, but to render thanks, that
he was present there. His joy, too, was unalloyed at the
thought of what God had done in Geneva since that day,
so many years ago, when He had chosen him "to raise
from the dust the fallen standard of the gospel of truth.

Apart from the sufferings and infirmities entailed upon
him by his great age, it may be remarked that his life at
Vandœuvres was a period of repose, and retrospect, and of
sweet and peaceable meditation. He received visits—not,
as at Pré-Béni, from a number of strangers who came to

imply that the minister of God ought to be made a slave to a prescribed
form, but teaches this first, that it behoves him not to presume, as if he
were infallible ; or, secondly, that he is called upon to examine for himself
how far such a Confession of Faith expresses the Holy Spirit's actual
teaching."

see the man whose fame had reached their ears, but from those exclusively whom affection or genuine spiritual concern induced to seek him out in his retirement. Numerous enough in the summer, they were often productive to him of sweet and sometimes sacred pleasure.

It was not only strangers, however, who came to see him. A gentleman who, though much younger than himself, had been one of his oldest friends, and who spent, like him, the last years of his life in the country near Vandœuvres—Col. H. Tronchin—never ceased, to the very last, to cheer and enliven his solitude. " How often," writes my sister, who lived with my father and mother, " has that excellent man thought nothing of the distance which separates his house from this, while his own health was shattered, and even sometimes the worse of the two,— to bring a word of cheering encouragement and affection to his old friend. The character of their minds, the frankness and the firmness of their faith, agreed so well. Our door was never closed to him, nor did the two believers ever meet on the threshold of the eternal world without my father feeling rejoiced and re-animated by the interview."*

It was my privilege to see him constantly during these years; and often have I been elevated, strengthened, aroused, by his clear, positive, simple, earnest teaching. Never was he more thoroughly my guide, my comforter, my friend, and the father I mourn! The days when, as he used to say, he *felt* I should come, he would go a little way back with me for a walk. Sometimes, towards the end, I had to urge him to take his stick.

* Col. Tronchin died a year after my father.

Scarcely, however, had we started than he raised his head, his step recovered its elasticity, and his conversation recalled his brightest days, alternately familiar and lively, or grave, earnest, and affecting. Then, as always, there was no mention of proper names, as that would have been but idle gossip. We talked of family news. He never forgot to inquire after my little ones, whom he had baptized, and whom he tenderly loved; as well as their mother, whom he delighted to call his "beloved daughter."

Occasionally, during that period, in the summer months, he would visit me early at Geneva. Seating himself at our table, his presence alone was a treat to our elder children, who are now described by their juniors as "those who knew their grandfather." He entered into all the details of my earliest joys and sorrows as a father; and his image is inseparably associated with the remembrances of the commencement of my domestic life.

On the 25th of April 1861, my parents celebrated the fiftieth anniversary of their marriage. Some of their children were able to collect for the occasion from foreign parts. A simple repast, with a few choice dishes and flowers sent by old friends of the family, and a piece of plate, the offering of a few members of his reduced congregation, was prepared for the festival, at which were present a few of his children and grandchildren. My father began by returning thanks to Him Who had led him safely so far, then he addressed a few graceful words to our mother—courteous and appropriate. Amongst the many congratulatory letters, there were several which it would have been a pleasure to preserve. One of them contained some verses from the minister Bungener, by whose sentiments my father was deeply affected. I give the poem, which was entitled *Les Trois Couronnes.*

" The first was on the brow
Long years had covered o'er with tresses white,
Ere at a joyous feast the glad sun's light
    Silvered its locks of snow.

" The second served t'adorn
Father and mother with its rim of gold ;
The blessed fruit of half a century told
Of wedded love, were gathered at their feet,
Children and grandchildren, their hearts to greet,
    Upon their marriage morn.

" The third, unseen, awaiteth him on high,
Where at the solemn hour—to man unknown—
The Lord shall faithful labours own,
    And crown his long-wrought service in the sky.

" And sons and loving ones cried, ' Wait awhile !
    Lord, yet a little while, in mercy stay ;
Ere yet his boyhood had begun to smile
    He caught the gleam of Thine eternal day !
Leave him in love and hope to linger yet,
    Quench not the shining light, its lustre spare ;
And, Jesu, when on earth his sun has set,
    Be his the crown of righteousness to wear ! ' " *

---

* Translated from the original of M. Bungener.

The translator would take this opportunity of adding a version of one of Malan's hymns—omitted from that portion of the book for which it was originally intended. The original was composed by the author at a time when he was called, in a measure, to suffer for the truth's sake, and was often sung by him, voice and heart in full tune with the words.

He wrote it in 1821, after a pedestrian tour in Switzerland, and a visit to Constance. The sight of that city—once so prosperous, now, as it were, visited with the displeasure of the Most High—struck him deeply. While he lived among the traditions of the blessed Reformation, the names of John Huss, of Jerome of Prague, and of the English Wickliffe, were specially dear to him.

His first care was to visit the State in which the persecuting council had

We were just preparing to return home,—our father and mother being exhausted with the day's excitement. He indeed had already retired to his room, when an unwonted

---

assembled. Thence he turned to the martyr's prison, and saw the "cage" in which he had been incarcerated. A piece of this he brought back with him, and hung it over his mantle-piece among other similar relics.

HYMN OF JOHN HUSS IN PRISON.

Jesu, Son of God most High,
　　See me in this dungeon drear ;
For Thy glorious name I lie
　　Fetter bound, a captive, here.
Vengeance this of foes of Thine,
Dooming me till death to pine :
Yet, O Saviour King, for Thee
Sweet is suffering to me !

In my life was never cause,
　　Thus, for meed of savage ire ;
For the rigour of their laws,
　　For their baptism of fire ;
Love of Thee was all my sin—
All they sought without, within ;
Yet, O Saviour King, for Thee
Sweet is suffering to me !

When I told them from Thy word,
　　How Thy cross atonement made—
How Thy "precious blood," outpoured,
　　All redemption's price hath paid—
Curses hailed my loving warning,
Hurled by men Thy message scorning ;
Yet, O Saviour King, for Thee
Sweet is worst reproach to me !

When I spoke of all Thy grace,
　　Of salvation perfected,
Of a pardon for the race—
　　They but heaped upon my head,
(Scowling, with contempt irate,)
Insult fierce and withering hate ;
Yet, O Saviour King, to me
Sweet is all, endured for Thee !

2 F

light, and the first notes of a choir of male voices brought him to the window. Some students in theology, with a few friends, had come from the city to greet with a torch-light serenade the man whose very name they had learned to reverence. Such a termination of the day crowned it worthily. After addressing them in a few heartfelt words, my father retired, full of wonder and gratitude at the general sympathy which he had encountered on this memorable anniversary.*

It is of those first years of my father's retirement at Vandœuvres that M. J. A. Bost gave such a true account, from which I may be permitted to make a few extracts :†—

"What a peaceful charm !—what blessing !—what sweet and precious remembrances I have of afternoons and even-

---

Thus this body, faint and frail—
    Far removed from gleam of day—
Pangs of cruel thirst assail,
    Pangs of hunger waste away ;
And the gyves and clanking chain
Drag me down to deeper pain ;
Yet, O Saviour King, for Thee
Bright the dungeon is to me !

Now I wait their crowning deed ;
    Soon their vengeance will be o'er ;
Death, the captive exile speed,
    Swiftly to a painless shore !
Upward borne on wings of flame,
For the honour of Thy name !
O Lord Jesu, Saviour King,
    Whispers oft my heart to me—
Can Thy service suffering bring ?
    Is it death to die for Thee ?

* It is worthy of remark that my father was not the oldest surviving member of his family at that time. His mother's eldest sister was then living at Florence, where she shortly afterwards died, having all but completed her 100th year.

† "Cæsar Malan: Impressions, Notes, and Souvenirs." 1865. P. 59.

ings spent at his house. On the terrace, in the garden, in the drawing-room, in his work-room, everywhere, he was the same; simple and unpretending, his manner affectionate and brotherly, his conversation lively and diversified; though he never forgot that he was the ambassador of Christ, and was constantly discovering means of introducing the solemn subjects which filled his thoughts. I was soon in his room, and seated by the organ on which he had composed and played all his hymns ; the mantlepiece before me, the ornaments of which recalled so many episodes in his missionary life ; inscriptions on all sides ; texts from the Bible ; drawings, portraits, beads, and other relics,—the fruits of his influence over the souls he had been the means of enlightening ; all kinds of souvenirs of his family, his journeys, his friends, his youth, his children in the faith, the deliverances God had wrought out for him. That room was a museum, a library, a workshop ; he ought to have written its history. He sometimes thought of doing so. But it was a sanctuary, too."

Again : " Round the tea-table, what inexhaustible animation—what usefulness—the old man displayed ! If there were children present, how he exerted himself in their behalf—disinterring the memories of his youth that he might find something to interest them. Then when, after family worship, we took our leave, he would give his friends a parting word, and we separated in the sincerity and delight of brotherly love."

My father was much occupied with his hymns at that time. This was his last work, with the exception of his daily study of the Scriptures—a study to which he devoted himself to the last. He revised those he had in his portfolio, and composed fresh ones, never deceiving himself as to the inequality that existed among them ; and enjoyed reading portions of them to his friends, asking, " Do you think that worth printing ?"   " He brought more love than self-love to his task, and challenged friendly criticism spontaneously, making notes at the time," we read in Bost's notice,—he being, I believe, one of the "friends" referred to. As I have already mentioned, my father left behind him more than a thousand hymns, a great number of which he had carefully revised. This was his favourite employment, and he regarded it as a legacy to his brethren. His correspondence at this time closes with precious testimonies of that life of faith and personal piety which became increasingly his absorbing care. I give an instance from a letter which he wrote, in May 1861, to an aged friend drawing near his death :—

" I often anticipate that solemn hour which is to witness the close of my earthly life, and I ask whether my peace and hope are steadfast, and whether I can enter fearlessly the realities of eternity. It is then that I realise the worth, the power, the calm sovereignty of the promises of God. ' He that hath the Son hath life:' and I realise that doctrine of grace that I have Christ indeed, because I firmly believe that He is living in His Father's presence in heaven, and that in Him and by Him have been wrought out and fully accomplished the redemption and eternal salvation of those whom the Father has given Him. Here,—emphatically here,—is the repose of my soul, and the ground of my expectation. Here alone I find my assurance of being in heaven, in that heaven which I see so near me, wherein I behold only the Eternal, the glorified saints, the elect angels, and where I could never have entered had it not pleased the Father to choose me in Christ, and to give me true life in Him, and to prepare me for His presence."

From time to time some unexpected joy befell him. Among the greatest was a visit in 1853 from his old friend Paul Henry of Berlin, whom he had never met since 1815, when they parted at Schaffhausen, and who died in the following year.

I may be permitted also to refer in this place to another visit which my father was far from expecting. One day, in the autumn of 1862, on my asking him, as I entered his room, what had transpired since our last meeting, he told me laughingly of the dismay of an inexperienced young servant whom my mother had just engaged. The girl, amazed at seeing a carriage stop at our little garden gate, and a noble lady issue from it with her attendants, had run to my father's room announcing the stranger by some inconceivable name. Going downstairs he found himself in the presence of the Queen of Holland, who had spared a few hours, in passing through Geneva, to pay him a visit at Vandœuvres. I did not know till then that he had ever been presented to her. I asked him if he had been careful, at all events, in addressing her, to observe the prescribed forms. Recovering his seriousness in a moment, he replied, " Ah, my dear boy, I know nothing about that, positively; all I know is, that I addressed her as a minister of God. I had no time to think of any but eternal things. The one important consideration is the gospel and the Saviour. We spoke of the salvation of the soul; of that vast eternity to which we are hastening."

" Your father's words are engraven in my recollection, and

I often recall them with gratitude," writes the illustrious lady, who was so willing to mark her interest in the venerable servant of God by visiting him in his humble retreat. The Lord remember this cup of cold water given to one of His children!

And my father needed refreshment and encouragement by the way. His strength decayed rapidly. Each time I saw him I found him more infirm, and, at first, more silent. For a long time certainly it was a gradual and almost insensible change, but I noted with concern its too evident progress. His image comes back to me at that time, as described by my sister, to whom I have already alluded.

" Like Abraham, sitting at the door of his tent and contemplating, in protracted and sublime meditation, the divine promises, so did this second Abraham,—this calm, peaceful old man,—sit in his chair, and hold silent communion with his God. How often we found him,—with clasped hands and uplifted eyes,—apparently plunged into the invisible world: his expression calm, gentle, and serious. The sacred volume was before him. · He never left off reading it till the approach of death veiled his eyes. For hours he meditated on it; studied it; searched into it again and again. His Bible; covered with notes and his writing; is, as it were, a monument of his declining years.

" One of the last religious services, at which he presided in his chapel, was the ordination of M. Lenoir to the sacred ministry, in June 1863. Three or four pastors had gathered round the pulpit. Learning from one of his deacons that a minister from abroad, with whom he had

kept up an affectionate correspondence, was present, he
sent to ask him to come up, and greeting him tenderly, as
a father might a son, rapidly exchanged with him a few
earnest words, and then placed him in the midst of the
ordaining pastors. The sermon and prayers had no other
preparation than the long experience and fervent piety of
the preacher, but the congregation remained under a sense
of the real presence of the Spirit of God, and their intercessions will ever follow him for whom they were offered."*

A few days before the ordination (June 19th), I find the
following in my father's journal: "Dear Gaussen is with
the Lord! What ineffable bliss for his soul!"

And my father craved no more for himself. He had
done with the world. Already he had witnessed the departure of many of his fellow-labourers and the friends of
his youth—Empeytaz, Rochat, Olivier, Galland, and numerous others. We felt, too, as if we saw him gradually
withdrawing from us. One might have accused him of
apathy, had not his tenderness to us, and his faith in God,
remained as deep as ever. It was evident that, if he did
thus alienate himself from the world, it was because his
soul was rapidly approaching that heavenly country, where
eternal glory and bliss were never more joyously, more
victoriously, anticipated.

On the 11th of October he had a baptism in his chapel;
on the 8th of November he mounted the pulpit for the last
time.

He had long been silently battling with his disease. He
found it increasingly necessary for him to drive to his Sunday service, which he was compelled occasionally to entrust

---

* J. A. Bost. Ibid.

to others. At the end of November, I learnt that he was in bed; but as I was ill myself, he sent to forbid my going out to see him. Hearing, however, the next day that he was in great pain, I went to him. The same evening I returned with a surgeon. After a few days, in which he was a little better, he had to take to his bed again, and permitted me at once to call in Dr Duval, a physician whose skilful services in my own family I had learnt to appreciate, and who, up to the very end, displayed a zeal and devotion to my dear father which powerfully contributed to soothe our distress, and to alleviate the sufferings of the invalid.

It was not long before the doctor told me plainly that the case was beyond cure. My father, was now confined to his bed by paralysis in the extremities, though his sufferings had somewhat abated. Conscious as he was, however, of the gravity of his attack, I knew him too well to hesitate as to whether he should learn the whole truth. Reserving it for myself to tell my mother, I begged the doctor to take the first opportunity of letting him know everything.

The next day, when Dr Duval had left him, he called my mother and myself into his room. Addressing her, he said, " Well, my dear Jenny, it seems that I am nailed to this bed." Then, asking me with a look how far he might go, " The dear young man," he said, speaking of Dr Duval, " was quite distressed; he was afraid of paining me. I soon put him at his ease. I told him that all was well; that I understood what he had to tell me; that I was given over by human skill, and then we spoke of heavenly things." Dwelling no longer on the thought of his death, he recurred frequently to his sensations at noticing the natural hesitation which the doctor, who might easily have seemed young to him, had manifested in the discharge of his solemn duty.

It was only to spare us, however, that he was thus silent; for, from that moment, he was another man. While he had never regarded his sufferings as being merely temporary in their character,—the anxiety they occasioned, and the helplessness to which he found himself suddenly, and for the first time, reduced, had combined to make him restless and depressed. Though he never uttered a word of fretfulness or murmuring, still it was evident that it was only by an effort that he could maintain his patience. But from the moment that he was told that he would never "quit the bed on which he was gone up," * a peace and an absolute calm took possession at once of his whole being; and, when the pain was not too great, his expression, if words were wanting, never ceased to utter the most tender love to all who approached him.

Such was his state during the last four months of his life; especially during the two last, which literally were nothing short of a terrible and prolonged agony.

With many others of our family who had come from various parts, I established myself in his house. He could not bear long visits—it was even evident that he did not like us to sit by his bed. One day, on catching the look of intense sympathy that the sight of his sufferings called up in me, he said, "Do not stay, dear, this is not the place for you." Sitting in the next room we could see him through the half-open door, propped up with pillows, his hands cramped with pain, his eyes lowered, whilst his

* 2 Kings i. 4.

moving lips showed that he was breathing out a low-voiced prayer.

These were his worst days, however; he had better ones, and then he would have his Bible open on his bed at some part of the gospel, in which he read at intervals. One day, when one of my sisters had entered after his doctor had just left, " What honour!" he exclaimed, what joy!" laying his hand on the sacred Volume. "God has given me grace, enabling me once more to preach the glad tidings of the gospel from my deathbed!"

By degrees the news of his sufferings became widely spread. On all sides, at Geneva and abroad, as we afterwards learnt, his brethren assembled to pray for him. This was the case in all the dissenting chapels in Geneva. In his own church, where meetings had been held for two years, under the presidency of some pious men, every Friday evening, they did not cease to intercede for him. In one of these meetings, which was particularly affecting, says one who was present, there was a presentiment (afterwards realised) that it would be the last.* It was presided over by the Pastor Barde, who, after mentioning that at the time when that chapel was built, he had been among the opponents of the "Methodists," invited those present to join him in pleading with the Lord for its founder, then in his last struggle.

Towards the close of his illness he was seldom able to see any one. One of his friends, on leaving his room, said in my hearing, as though he were talking to himself, " He had, as it were, a halo of glory around him!" I was not surprised to hear him say so. Indeed, if my father's was a

* J. A. Bost's Notices, p. 64.

silent deathbed, it was truly glorious. He spoke little; sometimes he never uttered a word the whole day. But he did more. His whole soul absorbed within itself,—he endured, without a murmur, without even a groan, sufferings, the mere sight of which deeply affected the servants, and even the medical attendants. Night and morning he apologised to his attendant for the pain he had given him. The servant, an old artillery man, who never quitted his room for a single instant, felt in his own soul the grandeur of that simple, silent, calm submission. "Our master," he said to me, "is no soldier running up to the guns, he walks into them."

"Those six months," I wrote, shortly after his death, to Merle D'Aubigné, "and especially the two last—months of torture borne without a murmur, with silent adoration, with (allow me the expression) a grace and tenderness, touching and sustained, I cannot describe in writing."

In fact, his deathbed seemed to those who witnessed it the most surprising of all his achievements. Said the doctor to me one day on leaving him, "I have just beheld what I have often heard of, but what I never saw before. Now I have seen it, as I see this stick I carry in my hand." "And what have you seen?" I asked. "*Faith, faith,*" he answered; "not the faith of a theologian, but of a Christian! I have seen it with my eyes."

Ten or twelve times was I summoned to pray by his deathbed. "That's the thing to do me good," he said to me once, when the prayer was over. "How fearfully you are suffering, my dear father!" I exclaimed. Raising his hand with an effort, and looking at me with his long and speaking gaze, he replied, "I do not suffer a moment too

much. I say not that God allows it! No, no!" he added
earnestly, " but God ordains it ;" and, the next moment,
" It is *that* that gives one real consolation !"

Who would not long after such a faith in the eternal
decrees of God which can thus endue the weak soul of
man with a hero's strength, in the anguish, humiliation,
and down-crushing of the bed of death !

On another occasion, shortly after, I spoke to him of the
heavenly glory, of entrance into the dwelling of the Lord,
of the sight of Jesus, of his beloved Master. Fixing on
me a deep, calm look, conveying an expression of semi-
surprise, " Why, God," he exclaimed, " Heaven, glory,
the Saviour — these are realities — realities ! Why
employ them to work ourselves into an excitement?
They are realities," he repeated. " It is *this* that passeth
away : " showing me his emaciated, and all but paralysed,
hands.

One day I asked him, after having again prayed with
him, if he felt any distress of mind, any doubt, any obscurity in his heart. Raising his eyes, and casting a glance
around him, " No," he said ;" I am not alone !" and repeated twice, " No, there are no clouds over my sky !"
When I said again to him that " even our Saviour, in His
agony, had felt the need of the presence of His friends,"
and implored him to let me know if a season of trouble
visited him, he promised he would : and would seek the
ministry of my prayers. He never did so.

In general, his faculties remained unimpaired to the
last. To one who visited him he could say, " The Lord
is with me,—as I have ever known Him ; " adding the
next moment, with his sweet and tranquil smile, " I have

always accepted the entire gospel without disputing either its commandments, its mysteries, or its promises. The Lord is faithful.*

A few days before his death he asked my eldest brother, who, with me, was standing by him, to repeat the 23d Psalm. As he never spoke anything but Latin with my father, he began it in that tongue ; but he asked him to give it in Hebrew, reciting it after him with folded hands, in a low voice. He thought, too, of all of us. He gave me directions as to what to do after his death ; he bequeathed this or that article to one or another; but he did not dwell on these matters. Having once arranged them, he never again referred to the subject.

The nearer he approached to his end, the more silent he became. If we no longer came to hear him speak, we could not grow weary of watching the saintly heroism which the great Christian knew how to put forth in his death.

M. Tronchin himself was deeply impressed by the spectacle. One day, when we were talking together of the manner in which my father was bearing the sufferings it had pleased God to lay upon him, and when I expressed my surprise that, after a life like his, he was called to such an end, he replied that it was in the very character of his career that he found the explanation of his protracted agony. "How often have I heard even his friends say, when I have been dilating admiringly on your father's work, 'Malan serves God with energy, with courage, and perseverance, because the service which God requires of him is an activity that agrees with his tastes and talents,

* Notices by J. A. Bost, page 66.

but pause before you fix your judgment—wait till you see him summoned from an active, to a passive, service.' God is doing that now," he added, "under our very eyes, at this moment; and in our eyes, too, His servant is found faithful."

A matter which still occupied my father's thoughts was his chapel. His wish had been that it should continue dedicated, after his death, to the ministry of the gospel. At the very beginning of his illness, he asked me to relate over again to him certain steps which had been taken some years before to transfer it into the hands of his brethren of the Evangelical Church. Those to whom I had applied in the matter wished it for themselves, but they could not come to terms with the society to which the site had been sold. Moreover, its position, in consequence of new embankments which had thrown it into a hollow, made it impossible to think of setting up there any but a temporary worship.

Under these circumstances, my father, in view of his end, charged me to have it taken down, lest, if it were left standing, it might come to be appropriated to secular purposes. As I was detained at Vandœuvres, one of his deacons, a man who had given his whole life to the service of Malan's church, and who had stood by my father through nearly his entire ministry, was ready to undertake the mournful task.

Scarcely, however, had he commenced to do so, when he ascertained that the building which, at the beginning, was very lightly constructed, was in so dilapidated a condition that it would have been dangerous to allow it to remain.

It was even necessary to take special care lest its demolition should involve some accident.*

So ended the Chapel of Testimony, in which two generations had received spiritual nourishment, and the recalling of which evokes, even at this hour, in Geneva, tender and sacred memories in many a pious heart. All that now remains of it is the title, " Chemin de la Chapelle," given to the road which skirts its site. Allied with my father's personal work, it was fitting that they should end together.†

But to return to our beloved one. We had never ceased to entreat the Lord to diminish his sufferings, and to put an end to the anguish of our dear mother, who saw him slowly departing without power to utter a single farewell. These prayers were now to be heard. My father descended, step by step, into the dark valley; but, as the tranquillity of his features showed, his lonely pathway was lighted with radiance from on high. A peace superior to the sufferings and dissolution of the bodily frame—the peace and assurance of a believing soul —that assurance which he had spent his life in proclaiming to his brethren—surrounded him now. Nor did it ever leave him, but proved his one support. He could

* Geneva being still in 1820 a fortified town, the military administration could not allow the chapel to be built of stone, on account of its proximity to the fortifications.

† The proceeds of the sale of the materials of the seats, and of the organ, amounting, after expenses deducted, to 1900 francs, was placed by me to the account of the Girls' School founded by my mother, as we have already seen, on the very day of the consecration of the chapel. At the desire of Madame Wolff Hanloch, the organ which had been given by her family in 1820 was sold in the interest of the same charity. It was bought for the vestry of the church in Coppet, in which, as it happened, my father, when a student, preached for the first time.

not always hear our voices, but his assured and peaceful look showed us that he still enjoyed an unclouded mind.

In his last sleep on the eve of his death (it was a Saturday) he smiled constantly, while he folded his hands. On the Sunday morning, the 8th of May, my eldest sister, coming into his room with me, greeted him with the words, "Father, this is the day when the Lord Jesus will come to receive you unto Himself." I saw him smile that gracious, winning smile, ere he fell asleep to awake no more. At 1.30 on that day, while we were all gathered round his bed, waiting for his last sigh, his breathing, which, since the morning, had been quiet and regular, ceased by degrees. He had departed without a struggle.

As the paleness of death swept solemnly over his features (which, through the whole morning, had been singularly bright, and, one might almost say, grown young again), his face flushed up with a sudden gleam of delighted surprise. The servant, who was standing in front of me at the foot of his bed, broke the stillness by exclaiming, "Oh how glorious—how glorious! Look, sir, look!" I did not catch his expression at that particular moment, but I heard one of my sisters reply to the appeal, "Yes, our father's spirit was introduced at that instant into the presence of celestial glory."

When his death became known at Geneva, there was a general mourning among his friends.

On Tuesday, at two P.M., a large concourse of sympathisers came from far and near to pay him their last tribute of respect. The Pastor Theremin conducted the funeral service at the house. The bereaved family were represented by the only one of his sons who was still

there; another having been summoned home at a time when it was not anticipated that his end was so near. Fifteen ministers—National and Independent, Anglican and Lutheran—gathered round the grave. The son of Malan, who was present, gave a brief address, and offered a prayer, amid the reverent attention of the bystanders. A clergyman present invited the people to join him in singing the following verses of one of Malan's most popular hymns, commencing, "Du Rocher de Jacob," No. 199 of the "Chants de Sion :"—

> " C'est pour l'eternité que le Seigneur nous aime,
>   Sa grâce en notre cœur jamais ne cessera.
>   Alléluia ! Alléluia !
>   Car il est notre espoir, notre bonheur suprême !
>
> " Notre sépulcre aussi connaîtra sa victoire ;
>   Sa voix au dernier jour nous ressuscitera ;
>   Alléluia ! Alléluia !
>   Pour nous, Ses rachetés, la mort se change en gloire." *

The hymn over, the throng silently dispersed.

Malan rests in the cemetery of Vandœuvres, by the side of his beloved mother whom he had laid there himself in

---

* The Translator offers the following English version :—

> " Ever doth His love enfold us,
>   Ever will His grace uphold us,
>   Alleluia !
>   This our hope and happiness,
>   This our perfect blessedness,
>   Alleluia !
>
> " Death, discrowned, can ne'er appal us,
>   From the grave He will recall us,
>   Alleluia !
>   Death to His Redeemed is life,
>   Glory crowns their toil and strife,
>   Alleluia !"

2 G

1848, under a cypress which he loved to look at as he sat on a seat in his garden, which commanded a distant view of it, and which had consequently become his favourite haunt. My mother has made it hers. Thence she sees the granite block which marks his grave, and which stands out in snowy contrast against the cemetery trees; while above soars Mont Blanc and that amphitheatre of mountains which he, whose absence she mourns, loved to contemplate.

It is her desire that a resting-place may be reserved for her beside that tomb on which, under the vivid impress of the deathbed scene, she has caused to be engraved, in memory of the past life of him who has gone from her side, and in prospect of the blessedness into which he has entered, the following words :—

CÉSAR MALAN,

Dr en Th.

7 Juillet 1787.

8 May 1864.

———

" Bienheureux sont les morts qui dorénavant meurent au Seigneur! Oui pour certain, dit l'Esprit, ils se reposent de leurs travaux, et leurs œuvres les suivent."—Apoc. xiv. 13. *

I feel, more especially after writing the last few pages which have awakened the most affecting of all my recol-

———

* CÆSAR MALAN,

Doctor in Theology.

7 July 1787.

8 May 1864.

———

" Blessed are the dead which die in the Lord. Even so, saith the Spirit, for they rest from their labours, and their works do follow them."—Rev. xiv. 13.

lections, that, in laying down my pen, I am quitting anew the society of one who was to me more than the great and strong-souled man, so simple in his faith, his piety, his uprightness, as known to all ;—even the friend of all earthly friends the truest, and of fathers the most devoted.

Dr Malan's name will remain blessed in the Church of God. He will never be forgotten among those who have learned to rank high above all other interests "the progress of the spiritual kingdom," which consists pre-eminently in individual regeneration, in personal conversion. Assuming that his immediate sphere of action was very limited, his influence has made itself felt beyond the limits of the French Churches.

Yet no mere expression of my feelings or convictions added to the facts I have submitted to my readers, would serve to bring him more vividly before them. I should certainly never have accomplished the task committed to me, —I should have been out of tune with the central thought of the life I have laboured to depict,—if these pages tended to the glory of man.

On the other hand, we should fail in ascribing due honour to God, were we to refuse to recognise, in the man from whom we are now about to separate, that greatest of the living works of the Most High, a Christian worthy the name, and a true confessor of the gospel ; a man who, after having put his hand to the plough, never looked back ; a servant heartily faithful to the uttermost, to all that he knew of his Master's will.

And in taking a last look at such a life, we can but recall the words in which the King Himself has declared His purpose to reward His devoted ones. " Well done, good and faithful servant: thou hast been faithful in a few things: I will make thee ruler over many things. Enter thou into the joy of thy Lord."

For my own part, as I turn away from his hallowed resting-place, I seem to realise more vividly than ever that one thing alone holds its ground. Standing firm amid the ever accumulating ruins swept on by the torrent of the ages, we see the heart constancy of the man who, after having been led to lay hold on the living God in humble faith, has been enabled to persevere unto the end, in constant service, up to the full measure of his light.

And I wait in hope for a happy day, when I shall see him again whom I have so long reverenced and loved.

FINIS.

SANSON AND CO., PRINTERS EDINBURGH.